Charles-Jean-François Hénault

A new chronological abridgement of the history of France

Charles-Jean-François Hénault

A new chronological abridgement of the history of France

ISBN/EAN: 9783337270353

Printed in Europe, USA, Canada, Australia, Japan

Cover: Foto ©ninafisch / pixelio.de

More available books at **www.hansebooks.com**

A NEW
CHRONOLOGICAL
ABRIDGMENT
OF THE
HISTORY
OF
FRANCE,

CONTAINING

The Publick Transactions of that kingdom, from Clovis to Lewis XIV. their wars, battles, sieges, &c. their laws, manners, customs, &c.

Written in FRENCH by

M. HENAULT,

PRESIDENT of the Court of Inquests and Requests in the Parliament of Paris;

AND

Translated into ENGLISH, with additional Notes, relative chiefly to the History of England,

By Mr. NUGENT,

From the FIFTH EDITION, corrected and improved by the Author.

VOL. I.

Content, if hence th' unlearn'd their wants may view,
The learn'd reflect on what before they knew.
                    Pope's Essay on Criticism.

LONDON,
Printed for J. NOURSE, opposite *Katherine-Street* in the *Strand,*
Bookseller in Ordinary to his MAJESTY.
MDCCLXII.

AUTHOR's PREFACE.

FROM the title of this work the reader would hardly expect any thing more than a recital of dates and facts; and yet it certainly had a more extensive plan, though confined at first to private use. I was desirous of being thoroughly acquainted with the French laws and manners, and whatever constitutes the essence and marrow of our history; but, on the one hand, the want of abilities for so great an undertaking, and, on the other, a strong desire of drawing up something for my own improvement, were the cause of my adhering to the simple scheme of a chronological abridgment. I took the liberty to disclose my mind to M. Daguesseau the chancellor, and he approved of the design. In pursuance hereof, the dates of years,

years, and the succession of ages, have been diligently observed, at the same time that a variety of remarks, the result of private conferences, and of forty years application, have been interspersed through the work. My secret I kept in *petto* a long time, and only imparted it to a few friends, whenever there was occasion to inform them of some particular fact, or to clear up any difficulties concerning the public law.

Such was the rise and progress of the present work: my friends, judging it would be of some utility to the public, advised me to print it; and I must confess, that they met with no difficulty in persuading me.

Yet, when I came to follow their advice, seeing the eyes of the public upon me, I was struck with awe; so that I dared not to discover the whole scheme at once, but thought it more prudent to commence with an essay, which should comprehend only what was most necessary to be known in regard to the French history. Having been so fortunate as to meet with encouragement, the author was gradually emboldened to part with a

con-

PREFACE. vii

confiderable fhare of his ftock, till this work was moulded into its prefent form, by means of different editions, of which the prefent fhall be the laft.

Hence this performance has been fucceffively enlarged above two thirds, fince it made its firft appearance in 1744: but the reader will eafily perceive, that thefe additions make no alteration either in the form or fubftance of the work, but are all fubfervient to the fame defign. If fuch augmentations be neceffary, the public will readily excufe the multiplicity of editions; fince, in an undertaking of fo extenfive a nature, there will always be a neceffity for rectifying errors, for illuftrating particular facts, and for fupplying omiffions of confequence: in a word, the utility is a fufficient plea for the additions; efpecially when care has been taken to publifh a fupplement.

But, in regard to the conferences which occafioned this work, may I be permitted to mention a word or two on that fubject in general. The advantages arifing from fuch converfations are fo very confiderable,

A 4   that

that the Author cannot help exhorting all magistrates not to neglect them. By discourses of this kind they will cherish a taste for learning, and a desire of real knowledge; as they enrich their minds with mutual discoveries. And let no one imagine, that they are designed for young people only: the more we are advanced in knowledge, the more we shall improve by these learned discussions. We need only to observe the great men of the last century; those oracles of the law, the Talons, the Bignons, the Harlays, and the Lamoignons: by such colloquial meetings they relaxed their minds, and recovered new vigour, after they had been almost exhausted by the great fatigues of their office; in short they found those meetings equally conducive to the advancement of morality and learning.

From such conferences, where men of real abilities presided, and where the most important questions of the common law were frequently debated, the author freely owns to have derived the principles, on which this chronological abridgment is founded. The reader

reader accordingly will be sure to meet with whatever essentially relates to the different subjects, that have been handled in the course of this history. For instance, what concerns the fiefs, the peerage, the regal succession, the regency, the Salic law, appanages, crown lands, public offices, whether judicial, military, or fiscal, reunions, renunciations, the regale, infranchisements, corporations, ennoblements, the principles of French liberty, elections, councils, the concordate, the power of the crown in ecclesiastic concerns, the famous league, laws, ordinances, regulations, usages, the police, establishments, foundations, &c. all these are treated of in a summary manner, which supposeth however some little knowledge of the subject: for an expression, which perhaps shall escape the eye of a less diligent reader, or of a person but indifferently acquainted with the history of France, will have a very good effect on such as have made it their particular study. Some reflexions are occasionally interspersed, whenever they appeared conducive to the solution of difficulties. I have likewife endeavoured to point out the characters of many persons of eminence, whether princes or private men, to the end that the public may be the better able to form a judgment of their conduct, and of their influence in state affairs. In short, the reader will here find the substance of the French history, varied with a recital of foreign transactions, whenever these happen to be any way relative to the affairs of France, or deserving of our attention. Care has been also taken not to omit the most striking passages of the present reign; but, as they did not properly belong to my subject, I embraced such opportunities as were most favourable for introducing them.

The index has been considerably enlarged: it was not sufficient to put a figure after each word; the several subjects have been also specified, in order to assist the inquirer. This has been a most laborious task; but without it, the book would hardly be of any use.

THE TRANSLATOR's PREFACE.

THE following work has very little in common with the generality of chronological abridgments, most of which contain scarce any thing further than the dates of births, marriages, battles, and deaths, intended chiefly to exercise the memory of children. The president Henault has engaged in a more extensive plan. While his work must be of service to those who inquire for the dates and succession of ordinary events, it points out, at the same time, the foundation and progress of the French monarchy, the different revolutions in their form of government, the fundamental maxims of the state, the real source of the French public law, the origin of their customs, the rise and progress of the crown offices, the institution of the different

ferent courts of justice, the succession of the chief magistrates, with the names of the ministers, captains, and literati, who have flourished in that country.

Such is the president *Henault*'s plan; as will appear to those who shall peruse this work with attention. They will perceive, that the inquiries of the historian have been directed by the magistrate and the statesman. They will be particularly struck with the remarks with which this history is embellished. To point out their beauties would lead us far beyond the limits of a preface; they are diffused through the whole performance, and constitute its peculiar excellency. But those on the establishment of the French in *Gaul*, on minorities, on the origin of nobility and ennoblements, on the administration of justice, on the sale of public offices, on the alienation of crown lands, on duels, tournaments, crusades, &c. are like stars of the first magnitude, that cannot escape even a vulgar observer.

True it is, there are many hidden beauties in this excellent author, which require a nicer eye to discover. He frequently seems to sow

the

the seed as it were of an intire treatise, and lets his reader enjoy the pleasure of unfolding it. There is scarce a sheet, or even a page, but contains some passage which deserves a particular commentary. In short, he is allowed to convey as much instruction in the compass of a few lines, as others in extensive dissertations.

Hence it is obvious, that this is a work of a very different nature from other performances of the same denomination. I must further observe, that it contains several eclaircissements which are not to be found even in the most copious histories. For instance, we no where meet with so clear an account of the famous treaty of Bretigny, in regard to which he greatly differs from M. Rapin. He is likewise singular in his opinion concerning Catharine de Medicis, whom all other historians suppose to have been regent of France; and he clearly shews, that this is the first instance of a minority without a regency, and of a minor king appointing his own ministers.

But it is impossible to help admiring his well-drawn characters of several of the French kings,

kings, and other persons of eminence. That of the cardinal de Retz, for instance, is a master-piece in its kind, and would do honour to the most celebrated historian. With regard to the historical detail, it becomes more enlarged in proportion as the author approaches nearer to his own time. For the narrative of past transactions is always more interesting, and of greater use in life, when the examples it exhibits are adapted to our present customs and manners. Hence our author has been more diffuse in the reigns of Lewis XIII. and XIV. than in any other part of his history.

As to the form of this work, it is intirely new, being neither a meer history, nor a meer chronology, but a judicious mixture of both. Our learned president, says [*] *a very good imitator of his manner of writing, has favoured* the public with a compendium, almost as interesting and instructive as a large body of history, and accommodated the result of several years study to the lowest capa-

---

[*] Macquer, in the preface to his Chronological abridgement of the history of Rome.

city, without the least affectation or shew of art: he avoids long details, yet omits nothing material; he draws similar characters, yet gives their peculiar features; he exhausts the subject, while he appears to skim over the surface; in short, he gives us a complete landskip, where, at a single glance, you may distinguish an infinite variety of objects.

This kind of writing, for which we are indebted to our celebrated author, has been admired by the ablest critics of the present age, who have honoured its inventor with the highest encomiums. His Prussian majesty (whose judgment in the polite arts, as well as in that of war, will always be revered by this nation) observes*, that this work may be considered as the substance of every thing remarkable and worthy of notice in the French history; that the judicious author has the art of embellishing the dry study of chronology; and that whoever is once master of this performance, may be said to be perfectly acquainted with the French history. *Another good judge,*

* Preface to the Memoirs of the house of Brandenburg.

with

with whose authority I shall conclude, says [*], we are indebted to M. Henault for the shortest and best history of France; and perhaps for the only manner in which the history of all great kingdoms ought hereafter to be written. For the multiplicity of facts and details is swelled to such an enormous size, that we must soon be contented with reading only extracts and dictionaries.

One thing more to be observed is, that the notes to this work have been all added by the translator. The intent of these was to explain obscurities, to supply omissions, or even to rectify some little mistakes in the original. These however are not numerous, and chiefly relate to the history of England, where, if the author's usual accuracy should sometimes happen to fail him, the public, I hope, will excuse my endeavour to set him right.

[*] *Siecle de Louis XIV*, in the catalogue of writers.

A Chronological Abridgment

OF THE

HISTORY of FRANCE.

THE FIRST RACE.

IT is customary to place Pharamond, Clodion, Merovæus, and his son Childeric, at the head of the kings of the first race; but we are so little acquainted with the transactions of their reigns, that I intend to begin this chronological series with Clovis, who may be considered as the real founder of the monarchy.

CLOVIS.

481. 2. 3. 4. 5.

CLOVIS, the son of Childeric, and grandson of Merovæus, king of the Franks, established the dominion of this nation in Gaul, where they had been settled ever since the year 287. This settlement was confirmed to them in 358 by the emperor Julian, and was absolutely fixed under Clodion towards the year 438, after the expedition, by which this prince obtained possession of Cambray, and of the neighbouring country as far as the Somme.

During the first five years there happened nothing remarkable.

486. 87. &c.

The battle of Soissons, obtained over Syagrius the Roman general, whom Clovis ordered to be beheaded.

Cotemporary PRINCES.

Pope.
Felix III.   492.
Emperor of the East.
Zeno.   491.
King of Italy.
Odoacer.   493.
Kings of the Goths settled in Spain towards the end of 414.
Euric.   484.
Alaric II.   507.

CLOVIS.

The seat of the monarchy fixed at Soissons.

491. 92.
The conquest of the city of Tongres.

493. &c.
Clovis marries Clotilda, the daughter of Chilperic, king of the Burgundians.

The conquest of the provinces situated between the Somme, the Seine, and the Aisne: the inhabitants of the city of Rheims submit to Clovis, by the interposition of S. Remigius. The kingdom of the Goths in Italy under Theodoric, the conqueror of Odoacer.

496.
The battle of Tolbiac, in the neighbourhood of Cologne, gained over the Alemans. Clovis is converted to Christianity, and baptized, in consequence of a vow he had made, if he should prove victorious. He was the only catholic king at that time, either in the eastern or western empire. This monarch extends his conquests beyond the Waal and the Rhine.

497. &c.
The Armorici, who had shaken off the Roman yoke, submit to Clovis; and their example is followed by the Romans who guarded the banks of the Loire.

Britany in the earliest ages bore the name of Armorica, which was common to all that tract of country situated between the mouths of the Seine and the Loire. But when the Bretons, a people of Celtic original, were obliged to abandon the isle of Albion (England), and to take refuge in a part of Armorica towards the year 458, they gradually communicated their name both to the inhabitants, and to the country itself.

500.

Cotemporary PRINCES.

Pope.
Symmachus. 514.
Emperor of the East.
Anastasius I. 518.
King of Italy.
Theodoric. 526.
King of the Goths in Spain.
Alaric. 507.

CLOVIS.

500. &c.

Clovis concludes two treaties of offensive alliance this year against Gundebald, king of Burgundy; the first with Theodoric, king of the Ostrogoths, who had married his sister Audefleda. Theodoric's interest in the convention between him and Clovis, for dividing their conquests, was to preserve to himself that part of Burgundy, which gave him a passage into Italy. The second treaty was with Godegiselus, Gundebald's brother, who was dissatisfied with his share of Burgundy. Gundebald is defeated by Clovis; but the two kings having soon after concluded a peace, Godegiselus is sacrificed to this accommodation, being killed in an engagement at the gates of Vienne. Theodoric was the only one that profited by this war.

A famous conference at Lyons between the Catholics and Arians.

506.

The council of Agde in the fourth canon forbids all persons, whether clergy or laity, to practise the art of predicting future events by looking into the Bible. This abuse was introduced by the superstition of the people, and afterwards gained ground by the ignorance of the bishops; since there were prayers at that time read in churches for this very purpose. This appears evident from Pithou's collection of canons, containing some formulæ under the title of *The Lot of the Apostles*, which M. Pithou the elder found at the end of the canons of the apostles, in the abbey of Marmoustier.

507.

The battle of Vouglé in the neighbourhood of Poitiers, gained over Alaric, who was killed by Clovis.

Cotemporary PRINCES.

Popes.
Felix III.   492.
Gelasius I.   496.
Anastasius II. 498

Emperors of the East.
Zeno.   491.
Anastasius I. 518.

Kings of Italy.
Odoacer.   493.
Theodoric.   526.

King of the Goths in Spain.
Alaric.   507.

CLOVIS.

Cotemporary PRINCES.

Clovis. This prince subdues the whole country from the Loire as far as the Pyrenees.

508. 509.

Clovis makes himself master of Angouleme, but Theodoric defeats his army before Arles. A peace concluded between the Franks, the Visigoths, and Burgundians. The Visigoths had been settled about a hundred years, not only in Spain, but in that part of Gaul, called Septimania *; and had a king who resided at Toulouse, as the Ostrogoths had another in Italy. Clovis receives of Anastasius, emperor of the east, the title and ensigns of patrician, consul, and even of emperor. Paris is made the capital of the kingdom.

Pope.
Symmachus. 514.
Emperor of the East.
Anastasius I. 518.
King of Italy.
Theodoric. 526.
Kings of the Goths in Spain.
Gesalric. 511.

510.

Cruelties practised by Clovis against several princes, his relations; among others, against Sigebert, who reigned at Cologne, and his son Chloderic; against Chararic, king of the Morini; against Ragnacharius, king of Cambray; and against Regnomer, king of Mans; by which means he makes himself master of all those petty kingdoms.

511.

The council of Orleans, in which we find the true principles of the *Regale*. The different systems concerning the origin of the *Regale* † are well known; some attribute this right to the quality of our kings, as founders of those benefices which are subject to such a claim; others

---

* An ancient name of the province of Narbonne, so called from the following seven towns, Toulouse, Beziers, Nîsme, Agde, Maguelone, Lodeve, and Usés.

† The *Regale* is a right, by which the king enjoys the revenues of the archbishoprics and bishoprics of the kingdom, and confers benefices during the vacancy of the sees, till the incumbent has taken the oath of allegiance, and got it registered in the *chamber of accounts*.

CLOVIS.

to the right of patronage; others to the nature of the feudal law; others to the right of guardianship and protection; others, in short, to the claim of spoils, &c. But they do not seem to consider, that these principles tend equally to render the right of *Regale* common to all crowned heads, which is false, since the kings of France alone enjoy it; and to diminish the noble antiquity of its original, since it could be traced no higher than the end of the second race, by imputing it to the feudal law; whereas the above right having been solemnly acknowledged in a council by bishops, the just opposers of such pretension, and afterwards by councils and by popes, this acknowledgment no longer limits its original, but throws the first fruits of the bishopric at each vacancy into the hands of the king, by a prerogative at all times annexed to the dignity of his throne. The Salic law digested by Clovis. The death of St. Genevieve, who was interred in the church of St. Peter and St. Paul, which since that time hath taken her name.

Clovis dies at the age of forty-five years, of which he had reigned thirty: he was buried in the church of St. Genevieve, then known by the name of St. Peter and St. Paul. He left four sons behind him, THIERRY, by a concubine; CLODOMIR, CHILDEBERT, and CLOTHARIUS, all three by Clotilda. Audigier in his treatise on the *origin of the French*, pretends that Thierry was born in lawful wedlock. Clovis is likewise said to have had a daughter named Theodechilda, and an elder son named Ingomerus, who lived but eight days.

The bishops, out of hatred to Arianism, had favoured Clovis's conquests; and the gratitude

Cotemporary PRINCES.

Pope.
Symmachus. 514.
Emperor of the East.
Anastasius I. 518.
King of Italy.
Theodoric. 526.
King of the Goths in Spain.
Gesalric. 511.

CLOVIS

of that prince, in return for those services, is the real source of the authority which they have so long preserved in France.

The infantry in those days constituted the principal strength of their armies. The Gombette law enacted in 501 by Gundebald, king of Burgundy. This prince's barbarous code makes mention of duels; for he allows a single combat to those who will not be determined by an oath (art. 45.) However, if this law was the same as that of the Lombards, it is not so cruel as may perhaps appear at first sight. For the combats were fought with baston and buckler, *cum fustibus & clypeo*; and we meet with a capitulary of Charlemain, agreeable to the Lombard law.

The Theodosian code, reformed by count Goiaric, who is supposed to have been chancellor to Alaric; and by some authors erroneously attributed to Anianus, referendary to that prince (506.) In the year 529, April the 29th, was published the code of the emperor Justinian, about a hundred years after the compilation of the Theodosian code: the digest came out by order of the same Justinian, the 30th of December, 534. It has been affirmed by some writers, that this emperor was so very illiterate as not to know how to read; though he himself declares, that he perused his book of institutes more than once. We must do justice to the reputation of this great prince, whose learning was equal to his military skill; and who, by the blunder of a transcriber, has been confounded with his predecessor Justin I. the son of a cowherd, and the most ignorant of mortals. *Lex mundana* was composed of the Theodosian code for the use of the Romans; and of the national laws of the barbarians, for the trying of causes among

Cotemporary PRINCES.

Pope.
Symmachus. 514.
Emperor of the East.
Anastasius I. 518.
King of Italy.
Theodoric. 526.
King of the Goths in Spain.
Gesalric. 511.

CLOVIS.

among the latter: it was called *lex mundana*, or the *law of the world*, in contradistinction to the canon law. On this occasion, it is proper to observe, that Justinian's code has had the preference of that of Theodosius, because the former, who reigned a hundred years after the latter, inserted such constitutions as had been drawn up by the ablest statesmen, and by the most learned civilians, from the reign of Augustus down to Constantine: whereas Theodosius did little more than collect the constitutions of princes, who had governed the empire from the time of Constantine to his own reign; and those constitutions favoured of the decline of learning.

Is it not amazing that the Romans, whose empire embraced the whole globe, who were so great, so celebrated a nation, and among whom there was such a number of the most eloquent orators, should have been from the time of Romulus to Theodosius II. that is upwards of a thousand years, without a body of laws? True it is, that towards the year 303 of Rome, the republic had the famous laws of the twelve tables, ten of which were those they had collected in Greece; and the other two were composed of the customs, and of a small number of laws, at that time in force among the Romans. But what are these laws, and these foreign institutions, when compared to the necessities of a state? And yet so indifferent were those people in regard to this article, that three hundred years had elapsed from the reign of Romulus to the enacting of the laws of the twelve tables, and very near eight hundred years from that period to the reign of Theodosius, the author of the first code; unless we are willing to give the name of *code*, to a digest of the formulæ of civilians in

Cotemporary PRINCES.

Pope.
Symmachus. 514.
Emperor of the East.
Anastasius I. 518.
King of Italy.
Theodoric. 526.
King of the Goths in Spain.
Gesalric. 511.

CLOVIS.

the year 473 of Rome, under the title of *Flavian civil law*, *Flavian and Ælian law*, which would still leave an interval of upwards of six hundred years. The use of silk worms introduced from the East Indies.

The fourth century, namely, that which preceded our first kings, produced a greater number of learned men in Gaul, than had been known to have flourished before in this part of Europe: the chief seats of the muses were Treves, Bourdeaux, Toulouse, and Autun. Latin was the vulgar language of the country. But from that time, till the reign of Charlemain, learning was upon the decline. (*Literary History of France, Tom.* 1.)

Cotemporary PRINCES.

Popes.
Symmachus.
514.
Hormisdas. 523
John I. 526.
Felix IV. 530.
Boniface II.
531.
John II. 535.
Emperors of the East.
Anastasius I.
518.
Justin the cowherd. 527.
Justinian. 565.
Kings of Italy.
Theodoric. 526
Athalaric. 534.
Kings of the Goths in Spain.
Amalaric. 531.

THIERRY I. reigns at Metz.	CLODOMIR reigns at Orleans.	CHILDEBERT I. reigns at Paris.	CLOTHARIUS I. reigns at Soissons.
First years peaceable.	First years peaceable.	First years peaceable.	First years peaceable.
520. 521. This peace lasted only among the brothers; for Thierry was not able to defend part of his father's conquests against Theodoric. Thierry assists Herminfrid to strip his brother Balderic of part of Thuringia. Herminfrid breaks his word to him, at the time when he stands most in need of his assistance.	523. 24. &c. Clodomir wages war against Sigismund, king of Burgundy, whom he takes prisoner, and puts to death. He is slain himself at the battle of Veseronce, which he fought against Gondemar. The latter is proclaimed king of Burgundy, after the death of Sigismund, who is ranked in the list of saints.	523. 24. &c. Childebert joins Clodomir and Clotharius against Sigismund, the heir of Gundebald, who had been guilty of massacring the father and mother of Clotilda: they defeat Sigismund, but proceed no further.	523. 24. Clotharius joins Childebert and Clodomir against Sigismund.
531	535.	531.	531.

The FIRST RACE.

THIERRY I. reigns at Metz.	CLODOMIR reigns at Orleans.	CHILDEBERT reigns at Paris.	CLOTHARIUS I. reigns at Soissons.	Cotemporary PRINCES.
531. Thierry makes himself master of the kingdom of Thuringia, by defeating Herminfrid, whom he afterwards put to death: he is assisted in this war by his brother Clotharius, whom he endeavours to ensnare. 534. He dies, and leaves by Suavegotte, the daughter of Sigismund, no other issue than Theodobert and Theodechilde. THEODOBERT, his son, succeeds him. This young prince retook from the Visigoths, in the year 533, part of the conquests of Clovis, which that nation had seized, viz. Vellei, Rouvergue, and Gevaudan. He repudiates his wife Visegarda, to marry Deuteria, who was married already to another hus-	533. Two sons of Clodomir murdered at Paris in 526, by Childebert and Clotharius, who had already divided the kingdom of Orleans with Thierry. The third son, Clodoaldus, escaped, and was made a monk: he ranks as a saint, by the name of St. Cloud, a name which he has given to a village, that before was called Nogent-sur-Seine. Clodomir's wife was Ingonda or Gundoche, who was married a second time to Clotharius I. 543.	531. Childebert wages war against Amalaric, king of the Visigoths, who behaved extremely ill to his wife Clotilda, the sister of Childebert. Amalaric is overcome, and murdered by his own people. 534. Childebert and Clotharius use all their endeavours, upon the decease of Thierry, to dismember that prince's kingdom. Theodobert prevents their design, and enters into a close connexion with Childebert. Dissolution of the kingdom of Burgundy, by the defeat and death of Gondemar. Childebert, Clotharius and Theodobert, after having conquered that kingdom, divide it among themselves. Thierry had at first a share in this revolution. Childebert being frightened by	531. Clotharius accompanies Thierry in the war against the king of Thuringia, and escapes the snares, which had been laid for him by his brother. 534. Clotharius and Childebert endeavour to take advantage of the absence of Theodobert, (who happened to fall in love with a lady in Auvergne during the illness of Thierry his father) in order to dismember his dominions upon his father's decease. Theodobert returns in time, and defeats their designs. The kingdom of Burgundy had been founded near a hundred and twenty years in Gaul, when it was reunited to the French empire. This is the year	Pope. Boniface. II. 531. John II. 535. *Emperor of the East.* Justinian. 565. *Kings of Italy.* Amalasuntha. 534. Theodatus 537 *King of the Goths in Spain.* Theuda. 548.

THEODEBERT I. reigns at Metz.	CHILDEBERT I. reigns at Paris.	CLOTHARIUS I. reigns at Soissons.	Cotemporary PRINCES.
husband. He takes his wife again, and shares the kingdom of Burgundy with his two uncles. He had a third wife, whose name we do not find mentioned in history. 535. Justinian concludes a treaty with Theodobert and his uncles, in order to engage them in an alliance against Theodatus. The latter was raised to be king of the Ostrogoths by Amasuntha, who shared the empire with him, but was not his wife (notwithstanding what is asserted by a great number of historians) which is prov'd by the letters of this princess to Justinian (Cassiodorus). Vitiges, the successor of Theodatus, gains over Theodobert, and delivers up to the Franks, the cities possessed by the Ostrogoths in Gaul,	by a storm, which thundered upon his camp, agrees to a peace with Clotharius. Belisarius, Justinian's general, recovers Africa from the Vandals, who had been in possession of that country ever since the year 400.	year in which they place the establishment of the pretended kingdom of Yvetot *. * *Yvetot is a small district of Normandy, in the country of Caux, and neighbourhood of Caudebec, famous for a fabulous tradition, according to which the possessor of that lordship formerly bore the title of king, with the supreme authority. This fable was invented by Robert Gaguin the historian, and has been solidly refuted in a book printed at Paris in 1645, intitled* De falsa regni Yvetoti narratione ex majoribus commentariis fragmentum. *See also the Abbé de Vertot's dissertation on the same subject.*	*Popes.* Agapetus I. 536 S. Silverius. 540 Vigilius. 555. *Emperor of the East.* Justinian. 565. *Kings of Italy.* Theodatus. 537. Vitiges. 541. Ildebald. 542. Eraric. 542. Totila. 553. *King of the Goths in Spain.* Theuda. 548.
	544.	539.	

The FIRST RACE.

THEODEBERT I. reigns at Metz.		CHILDEBERT I. reigns at Paris.	CLOTHARIUS I. reigns at Soissons.	Cotemporary PRINCES.
Gaul, with the rights which they enjoyed there, as sovereign lords of the city of Rome.				Pope. Pelagius I. 559. Emperor of the East. Justinian. 565. King of Italy. Teias. 553. This was the last king of the Ostrogoths in Italy. King of the Gorbs in Spain. Athanagildus. 567.
539. Justinian brings Theodobert over again to his side, by granting him the same advantages as Vitiges had done; and this treaty is in regard to the Franks a further title of their property in Gaul. Ever since that time, says Procopius, the French were absolute masters of Provence and Marseilles, a colony of the Phacæans, and lords of that sea; which shews that we had already a navy. Theodebert dies (547). He is succeeded by his son THEODEBALDUS, whom he had by Deuteria his concubine.	543. The death of Clotilda, the widow of Clovis, at Tours. She is ranked among the saints, and lies interred at St. Genevieve. Some historians place her death in 548.	543. After having made a great progress in Spain, he is defeated before Saragossa, to which city he had laid siege. 555. Childebert, in his illness, is obliged to resign to Clotharius, his share of the succession of Theodebaldus. 556. Childebert, to be revenged of Clotharius, for extorting from him the abovemention'd cession, encourages the rebellion of Chram-	539. Clotharius makes an irruption into Childebert's territories. They conclude a peace. 543. Clotharius accompanies Childebert in this war. 555. Clotharius becomes master of the whole succession of Theodebaldus. He defeats the Saxons twice on the banks of the Weser. 556. Chramne, his natural son, rebels against him. 558.	
There is still extant a gold coin of Theodebert, where his image is stamped on one				

THEODEBALDUS reigns at Metz.		CHILDEBERT I. reigns at Paris.	CLOTHARIUS I. reigns at Soissons.	Cotemporary PRINCES.
one side, with the title of dominus noster, *which belonged to the emperors only; the reverse is* victory, *with the arms of the empire. He caused this coin to be struck, in order to humble the pride of Justinian, who had taken the title of conqueror of the French.* (Boutteroue). He raised a powerful army, and having made himself master of part of Italy, was preparing a little before his decease, to march to Constantinople, in order to attack Justinian, with whom he had quarrelled. The first maritime exploit we know of since the establishment of our kings on this side the Rhine, was this prince's expedition against Cochiliac, king of the Danes. Cochiliac's land forces were routed, while the French squadron, which arrived just at the same time, total *ly*		Chramne. 557. Pope Pelagius sends his confession of faith to Childebert. Boniface the VIIIth did the same thing in the reign of Philip the Fair in 1294. 558. The death of Childebert, who is interred at Paris, in the church of St. Germain des Prés, which he had built, by the name of St. Vincent. He leaves only two daughters by his wife Ultragotha, who was buried in the same church: the first instance of that fundamental law, which admits none but males to the crown.	558. By the death of Childebert, Clotharius reunites the whole empire of the French, and sends Ultrogotha with her two daughters into banishment.	*Popes.* Pelagius I. 559. John III. 572. *Emperor of the East.* Justinian. 565. *King of the Goths in Spain.* Athanagildus, 567. *England.* The Heptarchy begins in 559, and ends in 828 in the person of Egbert, who united the seven kingdoms.

THEODEBAL-DUS reigns at Metz.		*Cotemporary* PRINCES.
ly defeated the Danish fleet. Narses, Justinian's general, beats the French commanded by Bucelinus, on the borders of Casilinum, not far from Capua, in the year 553. Theodebaldus dies the same year, and his two great uncles succeed him.		*Popes.* John III. 572. *Emperor of the East.* Justinian. 565. *King of the Goths in Spain.* Athanagildus. 567. *England.* Heptarchy.

CLOTHARIUS reigns alone.

560.

HIS son Chramne rebels again, and enters into a league with Conober, count of Britany: for the chiefs of that province were stiled counts, and not kings; according to these words of Gregory of Tours, *nam semper Britanni sub Francorum potestate post obitum regis Chlodovechi fuerunt, & comites non reges appellati sunt.* Clotharius defeats his son in a pitched battle, and burns him, together with his whole family, in a cottage, to which he had fled for shelter.

562.

Clotharius dies at Compeigne in the one and fiftieth year of his reign, and is interred in the church of St. Medard of Soissons, which he had built himself. He is succeeded by his four sons. His wives were Ingonda, Aregonda, Chonsene, Radegunda, Condiucque, and Waldrada.

562.

CHEREBERT, king of Paris.	GONTRAN, king of Orleans and Burgundy.	SIGEBERT I. king of Austrasia.	CHILPERIC I. king of Soissons.	Contemporary PRINCES.
562. This prince had to his share the kingdom of Paris, in the manner his uncle Childebert possessed it at first; to which were joined by this partition the territories of Querci and Albigeois, and all that part of Provence, situate between the Durance and the sea.	562. This prince had the ancient kingdom of Orleans to his share, as it had been possessed by his uncle Clodomir; and in order to render this partition among the brothers equal, Gontran had also the kingdom of Burgundy, the territories of Vivarés, and the country situate beyond the Rhone, between this river and the Durance.	563. Whilst Sigebert was waging war beyond the Rhine, against the Huns, whom he defeated, Chilperic taking advantage of his absence, strips him of the city of Rheims, which he had made his capital. Sigebert upon his return, retakes this city, and dispossesses Chilperic of his dominions, which he afterwards restores to him, by the interposition of his two brothers.	562. Chilperic wants to have Paris for his share; his brothers oppose him: upon which they draw lots for the four kingdoms, and he becomes king of Soissons. He laid very heavy taxes upon his people: every acre of land * paid a hogshead of wine: and they likewise paid a capitation for their bondmen or slaves. The subjects oppressed, abandon their possessions.	Popes. John III. 572. Emperors of the East. Justinian. 565. Justin II. 573. Kings of the Goths in Spain. Athanagildus. 567. Liuba. 572. England. Heptarchy.
566. Cherebert dies, and is interred at Paris: his brothers divide his succession; but as each of them wanted to have the city of Paris, they agree to possess it all three in common, on condition that none of the three should enter it without the	568. Establishment of the kingdom of the Lombards in Italy, about sixteen years after the extinction of that of the Ostrogoths, in the person of Teias their last king. Alboin, king of the Lombards, invited, as it is sup-	565. He marries Brunechild, a younger daughter of Athanagildus, king of the Visigoths: she quitted the Arian errors, and embraced the catholic religion. 570.	568. Chilperic marries Golsonda, the eldest daughter of Athanagildus, and settled upon her for * That is, every *arpent*, or French acre, which is a measure of land, containing 100 perches square, of 18 feet each. her	

The FIRST RACE.

CHEREBERT, king of Paris.	GONTRAN, king of Orleans and Burgundy.	SIGEBERT I. king of Austrasia.	CHILPERIC, king of Soissons.	Cotemporary PRINCES.
the consent of the other two. This prince's wives were Ingoberga, Mirefleur, Theodegilda, and Marcouefe.	supposed, by Narses, who was dissatisfied with Justin, arrives in Italy, seizes Liguria, Milan, and Pavia, and in less than 4 years becomes master of Italy, except Rome and Ravenna. From thence those barbarians spread themselves over Burgundy, where they begin with laying the whole country waste; but being attacked by general Mummol, they are intirely routed. The beginning of the exarchate of Ravenna, under the patrician Longinus, deputed by the emperor Justin: it ended in 752, when Aistulphus, king of the Lombards, took Ravenna.		her dowry, according to the usage of that time, part of Cherebert's demesnes, which he had inherited. Golsonda is found dead in her bed; and Chilperic's mistress, Fredegunda, being suspected of the murder, this suspicion was confirmed, when Chilperic married her after the death of Golsonda. Her sister Brunechild revenges her death, and instigates her husband Sigebert, and Gontran, to take up arms against him. Chilperic loses part of his dominions, and at length obtains a peace, by quieting Brunechild with a present of those demesnes, which he had settled on Golsonda for her dower.	*Popes.* John III. 577. Benedict I. 577. *Emperor of the East.* Justin II. 578. *Kings of the Lombards in Italy.* Alboin. 571. Clephes. 573. Antharis. 590. *Kings of the Goths in Spain.* Athanagildus. 567. Liuba. 572. Leoviglidas. 585. *England.* Heptarchy.
		570. Sigebert availing himself of the distresses of his brother Gontran, king of Burgundy, fur-	570. 71. 72. Chilperic excited by Fredegunda, takes advantage of the quarrel between his two bro-	

The History of France.

GONTRAN, king of Orleans and Burgundy.	SIGEBERT, king of Austrasia.	CHILPERIC I. king of Soissons.	Cotemporary PRINCES.
	surprizes the town of Arles; but this advantage did not continue long, for Gontran's generals punished him, not only by retaking Arles, but by seizing on Avignon, which belonged to Sigebert, and which Gontran condescended to restore to him upon concluding a peace.	brothers, and sends his son Clovis against Sigebert, who is stripped of Tours and Poitiers: the two brothers coming to an accommodation, unite against Chilperic, and recover what had been unjustly taken from them. 573. 74. Sigebert and Gontran having quarelled again, about some point of ecclesiastic discipline, Chilperic, according to custom, takes advantage of this circumstance, and sends his eldest son Theodebert against Sigebert: Theodebert is victorious. Sigebert, terrified at these successes, brings foreign troops into France; Gontran joins with Chilperic to oppose these foreigners: Sigebert threatens to fall upon Burgundy; upon which Gontran remains neuter: Chilperic sues for peace, which Sigebert grants him.	*Popes.* John III. 572. Benedict I. 577 *Emperor of the East.* Justin II. 578. *Kings of the Lombards in Italy.* Alboin. 571. Clephes. 573. Antharis. 590. *Kings of the Goths in Spain.* Liuba. 572. Leovigildus. 585. *England.* Heptarchy.
	575.	575. Chilperic enters into a new confederacy with Gontran against Sigebert, and sends his son Theodebert to attack him; Theodebert is defeated, and slain in	
	Sigebert is murdered at the age of forty	battle. Chilperic, intimidated by this disaster,	

GONTRAN, king of Orleans and Burgundy.	CHILDEBERT II. king of Austrasia.	CHILPERIC I. king of Soissons.	Cotemporary PRINCES.
	forty, after having reigned fourteen years: he was a very accomplished prince. His body was interred at St. Medard of Soissons, near his father Clotharius. He left a son named CHILDEBERT, and two daughters, one of whom was married to Hermenigildus, the eldest son of Leovigildus, king of the Goths. His wife was Brunechild.	disaster, shuts himself up in Tournay. Brunechild sollicits her husband Sigebert, who did not want follicitation, to accomplish the destruction of Chilperic: accordingly Sigebert seizes on all his dominions, and lays siege to Tournay, where that prince had shut himself up, when two assassins, hired by Fredegunda, murdered him in his camp.	*Pope.* Benedict I. 577 *Emperor of the East.* Justin II. 578. *King of the Lombards in Italy.* Antharis. 590. *King of the Goths in Spain.* Leovigildus. 585. *England.* Heptarchy.
	576. Childebert, then only five years old, being kept under a strict guard at Paris by his uncle Chilperic, makes his escape by the management of duke Gondebald, and is crowned king of Austrasia at Metz on Christmasday. His mother Brunechild is imprisoned at Rouen by Chilperic, and her two daughters are confined at Meaux.	576. Chilperic, availing himself of the murder of Sigebert, gets away from Tournay, imprisons Brunechild, with her son Childebert, and her two daughters. Merovæus, the son of Chilperic, falling in love with Brunechild, marries her at Rouen, and sets her at liberty. Chilperic having advanced towards that city, in order to punish them, relents, and forgives them; but sends Brunechild into Austrasia, and obliges Merovæus to follow him.	
577. Gontran joins Childebert, whom he had adopted for his heir; and Mummol his general defeats Didier, Chilperic's	577. Brunechild engages her son Childebert to wage war against Chilperic.	577. Chilperic lays the blame of the defeat of his army on his son Merovæus, causes him to be ordained priest, and shuts	

GONTRAN, king of Orleans and Burgundy.	CHILDEBERT II. king of Austrasia.	CHILPERIC I. king of Soissons.	Cotemporary PRINCES.
peric's general. Death snatches away Gontran's two sons. He left two daughters behind him, Clodoberga and Clotilda.		shuts him up in the monastery of St. Calais from whence he makes his escape: but finding himself surrounded again in a farm near Terouanne, he prevails on his friend Guilene to put an end to his life. Prætextatus, bishop of Rouen, is deposed. 578. 79. 80. Fredegunda loses her three sons, who die of a dysentery.	*Popes.* Benedict I. 577. Pelagius II. 590. *Emperors of the East.* Justin II. 578. Tiberius. 586. *King of the Lombards in Italy.* Antharis. 590. *King of the Goths in Spain.* Leovigildus. 585. *England.* Heptarchy.
581. 82. 83. Gontran enters into an alliance with Childebert against Chilperic; and Childebert having afterwards concluded a treaty with Chilperic against Gontran, a bloody war breaks out among those princes.	581. Childebert unites at first with Gontran against Chilperic; and afterwards joins with Chilperic against Gontran: these princes enter into a bloody war against each other.	581. Fredegunda accuses Clovis, the last son of Chilperic by the first venter, of having poisoned her three sons, and causes him to be assassinated.	
		584. A peace is concluded among the three kings. Chilperic is murdered, upon his return from hunting. His wife Fredegunda, and Landry her gallant, were suspected of having had a share in the murder. He left a son behind him, only four months old, whose name was CLOTHARIUS, and who succeeded his father. His wives were Audovera, Golsonda, and Fredegunda. By the first, whom he	

Gon-   Chil-

The First Race.

GONTRAN, king of Orleans and Burgundy.	CHILDEBERT II. king of Austrasia.	CLOTHARIUS II. king of Soissons.	Cotemporary PRINCES.
Gontran, far from taking any advantage of the death of Chilperic, acts as a father to his son Clotharius, and defends Fredegunda against the just resentment of Childebert and Brunechild.	Childebert advances towards Paris, but Gontran had already entered that city, and espoused the cause of Fredegunda.	he repudiated, he had among other children Merovæus. Fredegunda, Chilperic's widow, prevails on Gontran to defend her against Brunechild and Childebert.	*Pope.* Pelagius II. 590. *Emperors of the East.* Tiberius. 586. Mauritius. 602. *Kings of the Lombards in Italy.* Antharis. 590. Agilulfus. 616. *Kings of the Goths in Spain.* Leovigildus. 585. Recaredus. 601. *England.* Heptarchy.
585. Gondebald, who pretended to be the son of Clotharius I. is crowned by some seditious persons at Brive-la-Gaillarde: but soon after he is assassinated by those very traitors before Carcassone, which was then besieged by Leudegesilus, general of Gontran's army. Childebert and Gontran promise sincere friendship to each other. Gontran appoints a council for young Clotharius, and obliges Fredegunda to quit Paris.	585. Gondebald, supported by Childebert, seized on the countries of Querci, Perigord, Angoumois, and part of Aquitaine, &c.	585. Recaredus, king of the Visigoths in Spain, and of Septimania in Gaul, quits the Arian tenets, and is converted to the Catholic religion: this was a prince worthy of the greatest encomiums. Fredegunda retires to Vaudreuil, where she is impatient under the loss of her authority.	
588. 89. Gontran declares war against Spain, to revenge the death of Brunechild's son-in-law, who was brother-in-law to Childebert; and to extend his dominions as far as the Pyrenean mountains. This war was not successful.	587. Childebert, by agreement with the emperor Mauritius, wages war in Italy against the Lombards; this war was not attended with success.	590. Fredegunda causes Prætextatus, bishop of Rouen, to be assassinated, and despises Gontran's menaces, who wanted to take cognizance of this crime. She makes several unsuccessful attempts against Childebert's life, and Brunechild's liberty.	
591. 92. Gontran wages war against Waroc, count of Britany, whom Fredegunda had	593.	593.	

GONTRAN, king of Orleans and Burgundy.	CHILDEBERT III. king of Austrasia.	CLOTHARIUS II. king of Soissons.	Cotemporary PRINCES.
had persuaded to take up arms. Waroc repairs to Guerrande, where he yields homage to Gontran in these terms: *We know, as well as you, that the Armorican towns (Nantes and Rennes) do belong to the sons of Clotharius; and we acknowledge that we ought to be their subjects.*			Pope. Gregory the Great. 604. Emperor of the East. Mauritius. 602. King of the Lombards in Italy. Agilulfus. 616. King of the Goths in Spain. Recaredus. 601. England. Heptarchy.
593. Gontran dies at the age of sixty, without leaving any issue. The church has given him the rank of a saint. He had declared his nephew Childebert heir to his kingdoms of Orleans and Burgundy. His wives were Veneranda, whom Gregory of Tours, and the author *de gestis Francorum*, look upon as a concubine; Marcatruda, whom he divorced upon suspicion of her having poisoned his son by Veneranda; and lastly Austregelda, by whom he had two sons that died young. Some authors pretend that his daughter Clotilda survived him. He kept his court at Chalons-sur-Soane, and lies interred in the church of St. Marcel of Soissons. The Gascons, or Was-	593. Childebert, in pursuance of the last will of king Gontran, re-unites the kingdoms of Orleans and Burgundy, and part of that of Paris, to Austrasia. We have a constitution of this prince (595) ordaining that murder shall be punished with death; whereas before it was subject only to a pecuniary fine. He creates Thassilo the first king of Bavaria. 595. Childebert overcomes the Varnes, a people of Germany, and destroys their kingdom. 596. Childebert dies of poison, leaving by his wife Faileube two	593. Clotharius and Childebert divide the city of Paris between them. Landry, who had the command of Clotharius's army, defeats Childebert in the neighbourhood of Soissons. The place where this battle was fought, then known by the name of *Trucciacum*, is the village of *Droissi*, within five leagues of Soissons, which together with *Bufanci, Chevrise, Nanteuil-sur-Muret*, and *Muret*, form a large plain, proper for a field of battle. (*Le Beuf.*) 594. Waroc, count of Britany, excited by Fredegunda, gives battle to Childebert's troops, on the side of Touraine: the engagement was very bloody, with equal loss on both sides. 597.	

The FIRST RACE.

THIERRY II. king of Burgundy.	THEODEBERT II. king of Austrasia.	CLOTHARIUS II. king of Soissons.	Cotemporary PRINCES.
Wascons, a barbarous nation, pass the Pyrenean mountains, and settle in *Novempopulania*, a province to which they give their name. By degrees they extend themselves as far as the banks of the Garonne.	two sons, who succeed him, under the direction of Brunechild their grandmother. THIERRY reigns in Burgundy, and THEODEBERT II. is king of Austrasia.		*Popes.* Gregory the Great. 604. Sabinian. 605. Boniface. IV. 614. *Emperors of the East.* Mauritius. 602. Phocas. 610. *King of the Lombards in Italy.* Agilulfus. 616. *Kings of the Goths in Spain.* Recaredus. 601. Liuba II. 603. Witteric. 610. *England.* Heptarchy.
	597. Brunechild cements a peace on all sides, in order to establish her power. She likewise promotes the conversion of the kingdom of Canterbury to the Christian religion.	597. The death of Fredegunda.	
599. Brunechild flies for shelter to her grandson Thierry, who gives her a kind reception.	598. The nobility of Austrasia, tired of Brunechild's oppressive administration, prevail on her grandson Theodebert to banish her.		
600. Thierry's army, joined with that of Theodebert, falls upon Clotharius, and gains a complete victory over him.	600. Theodebert having joined Thierry, defeats Clotharius.	600. Clotharius is vanquished by Theodebert and Thierry.	
601. 602. Thierry, having joined Theodebert, defeats the Gascons.	601. 602. Theodebert having joined Thierry, defeats the Gascons, and appoints Genialis their duke, who was the first that took the title of duke of Gascony.	603. Clotharius, seeing the two kings employed against the Gascons, sent two armies to invade their territories; that which Landry commanded under Me-	

THIERRY II. king of Burgundy.	THEODEBERT II. king of Austrasia.	CLOTHARIUS II. king of Soissons.	Cotemporary PRINCES.
605. 6. 7. 8. &c. Brunechild debauches Thierry's morals, in order to preserve her authority over him; and sets him against his brother Theodebert, so far as to persuade him that Theodebert was not the son of Childebert.	Adaluald is declared collegue of the kingdom of the Lombards. Theodebert grants him his daughter in marriage.	Merovæus, the son of Clotharius, is defeated by Thierry; and they both lost their lives: Theodebert spares the other army, from a jealousy he had conceived against his brother.	Popes. Gregory the Great. 604. Sabinian. 605. Boniface. IV. 614. Emperors of the East. Phocas. 610. Heraclius. 641. King of the Lombards in Italy. Agilulfus. 616. Kings of the Goths in Spain. Liuba II. 603. Witteric. 610. Gundemar. 612. Sisebutus. 612. England. Heptarchy.
	612. Theodebert is defeated by Thierry, taken prisoner at Cologne, and sent to Chalons-sur-Saone to Brunechild, by whose order he is assassinated. His wives were Bellichild, whom he caused to be strangled, in order to marry Theudechild.	611. Clotharius promises Thierry to remain neuter, during the war, which the latter is upon the point of waging against his brother Theodebert, upon condition that he will cause the whole country that had been taken from him in the last war, to be restored to him.	
613. Thierry dies at Metz of a dysentery, just as he was upon the point of waging war against Clotharius, who called upon him to perform the promise he had made of restoring the countries wrested from him; and he leaves four sons. Brunechild put to death, by Clotharius's command. This princess's tomb is to be seen in St. Martin's church at Autun. (Martene's literary journey.) Cor-	*Count Romulphus, a powerful lord, was involved in the calamities of this reign; and his son Romaricus, being convinced of the vanity of human grandeur, made a donation of his whole estate to the famous abbey of Remiremont, called Romarici mons: this was the time of church foundations: and it is amazing that there had been some already in the dutchy of Lorrain (which was called the kingdom of Austrasia) in Alsace, on the mountains*	613. Clotharius put two of Thierry's sons to death; the eldest had been acknowledged king of Austrasia, by the name of Sigebert II. and reigned but a very short time: a third son made his escape; and he granted a fourth his life, but obliged him to turn monk: hereby Clotharius re-united the whole French monarchy in his own person.	

		CLOTHARIUS II.	*Cotemporary* *PRINCES.*
Cordemoy has undertaken the apology of this princess in his history of France.	*tains of Voges, in the country of Lucquois, at present the diocese of Toul, Luxeuil, Estival, Moyen Moustier, S. Dié, Senone, Bon Moustier, &c.*		Popes. Boniface IV. 614. Deusdedit. 617. Boniface V. 625. Honorius I. 638. *Emperor of the East.* Heraclius. 641. *Kings of the Lombards in Italy.* Agilulfus. 616. Adaluald. 626. *Kings of the Goths in Spain.* Sisebutus. 621. Recaredus II. 621. Suintilla and his brothers. 631. England. Heptarchy.

CLOTHARIUS II. reigns alone.

613. 614.

The power of Clotharius excites the envy of the grandees, in consequence of which he becomes more moderate. He suffers Austrasia and Burgundy to continue to have their mayors, whose authority, not unlike to that of viceroys, began now to shew itself in France, and who at length concluded with seizing the sovereignty of the kingdom.

615.

The fifth council of Paris, composed of bishops and great lords: many such were held afterwards by Charlemaign, and by the succeeding kings, wherein ordinances or decrees were passed for the whole kingdom, which ordinances bear the name of *Capitularies*, as having been made in the assemblies of the nation.

616. 617. &c.

Clotharius holds a kind of moveable parliaments, called *Placita*, from whence come the word *pleas*.

622. &c.

Clotharius settles Austrasia and Neustria on his son Dagobert with the title of king. The commencement of the Mahometan æra, which they call the *Hegira*; that is, the date of the flight of Mahomet from Mecca: he died of poison in 632.

625.

CLOTHARIUS II. sole king of France.

625. 626. &c.

Dagobert, son of Clotharius, is married at Clichi: these two princes had some dispute in regard to Austrasia. The Gascons revolt; but this war is attended with no great consequence.

628.

Clotharius II. dies, regretted by all his people, as a lover of justice and peace; he was buried at Paris in the church of St. Germain-des-Prez, and was then forty-five years of age. Three things may be observed in regard to this prince; he is the third king that united the whole monarchy: he is the second of the name; and, by a kind of destiny annexed to the name, though he had only the kingdom of Soissons to his share, which was the least considerable of the whole, yet he re-united the intire monarchy, as his grandfather Clotharius had done before him. His wives were Haldetrudis, Bertrada, and Sichilda. He left two sons, Dagobert and Charibert.

Cotemporary PRINCES.

Popes.
Boniface V. 623.
Honorius I. 638.
Emperor of the East.
Heraclius. 641.
Kings of the Lombards in Italy.
Adaluald. 626.
Ariowald. 638.
Kings of the Goths in Spain.
Suintilla and his brothers. 631.
England.
Heptarchy.

DAGOBERT I. king of the rest of the French empire.

628. 629.

DAGOBERT's morals being corrupted, he repudiates his first wife, and marries three, all living at the same time, without reckoning concubines.

The relations of the magnificence of that age are hardly credible. St. Eloy, a native of the province of Limousin, was in the former part of his life a famous goldsmith; he used to wear a belt, set with diamonds, when he came to court in Clotharius's reign. He made for that prince a chair of massive

CHARIBERT I. king of part of Aquitaine.

628. 629.

CHARIBERT obtains part of Aquitaine from his brother, rather as a kind of appanage (though this name was not known till a long time after) than as a partition of the crown: yet he took the title of king, and the public acts were dated from his reign. He makes Toulouse his capital.

630. 31.

Charibert dies at Blaye: Childeric, his eldest son, as yet an infant, succeeds him, and is acknowledged king. His uncle Dagobert causes him

DAGOBERT I. king of the rest of the French empire.		Cotemporary PRINCES.

massive gold, and an entire throne of the same metal for Dagobert. These riches were owing to the Levant trade, which had been opened to the French by means of the negociations with the emperors of Constantinople: they likewise were owing to the spoils of Italy, from whence the French always returned loaded with booty, even when they were beaten out of that country. St. Eloy was afterwards treasurer to Dagobert, and bishop of Noyon: he built St. Paul's church without the walls of Paris, towards the year 640.

him to be poisoned; and in him ended the kingdom of Toulouse: but Charibert had two other sons, Boggis and Bertrand, who survived him. The former, to whom Dagobert gave Aquitaine as an hereditary dukedom, was the stem of a long succession of princes, whose posterity continued down to Lewis of Armagnac, duke of Nemours, slain at the battle of Cerignolles in 1503. (*Vaisette, History of Languedoc.*)

Popes.
Honorius I. 638.
Severinus. 640.
John IV. 641.
Theodore. 649.
Emperors of the East.
Heraclius. 641.
Constans. 668.
Kings of the Lombards in Italy.
Ariowald. 638.
Rotharis. 654.
Kings of the Goths in Spain.
Rechemer. 633.
Sisenandus. 636.
Suintilla. 640.
Tulga. 642.
England.
Heptarchy.

DAGOBERT, sole king of France.

632. 633.

The war against Samon, who from a merchant, rose to be king of the Sclavonians: it was not concluded till the coronation of Sigebert, the son of Dagobert, whom this prince creates king of Austrasia: this induced the Austrasians to carry on the war against those Barbarians with greater vigor.

634.

Dagobert helps to make Sisenandus king of the Goths in Spain, in prejudice to the son of the lawful sovereign: this crown was elective.

635.

The war against the Gascons, which is not of long continuance. Dagobert holds a general assembly in the palace of Gorges, not far from Versailles: there he makes his will, by which he bequeaths eight thousand pounds of lead to the abbey of St. Denis, in order to cover that church. 636.

DAGOBERT, sole king of France.

636. 637. 638. &c.

St. Eloy prevails on Judicael, a prince of Britany, to satisfy the king for the incursions he had made on the frontiers, and to acknowledge him for his sovereign.

Dagobert dies at Epinay: this prince caused the church of Strasburg, where Clovis had laid the first stone, to be erected into a bishopric: he is interred at St. Denis, which was his own foundation. He leaves two sons behind him, Sigebert II. king of Austrasia, and Clovis II. king of the remainder of the French empire. His wives were Gomatrudis, Nantilda, Ragnetrudis, Wilfegunda, and Berthilda.

The royal power is absorbed by the authority of the mayors of the palace.

Cotemporary PRINCES.

Popes.
Theodore. 649.
Martin I. 654.
Eugene I. 656.
Emperor of the East.
Constans. 668.
Kings of the Lombards in Italy.
Rotharis. 654.
Rodoald. 659.
King of the Goths in Spain.
Recesuindus. 672.
England.
Heptarchy.

SIGEBERT II. or III. king of Austrasia.	CLOVIS II. king of Burgundy and Neustria.
644. &c.	644. &c.
PEPIN, mayor of the palace under Dagobert, continued in that post under Sigebert, whom his father Dagobert had made king of Austrasia in 632. Pepin died in 639, and his son Grimoald succeeded him in that office.	CLOVIS reigns under the tutelage of his mother Nantilda, who administers the government, in conjunction with Ega, mayor of the palace.
646. &c.	646. &c.
The royal authority begins to decline. Sigebert, who fixed his residence at Metz, without concerning himself in the administration of his dominions, spends his whole time in founding, or reforming monasteries: some pretend to say, that he promised Grimoald to adopt his son, in case he had no issue of his own.	After the decease of Ega, Erchinoald, called also Archambaud, is created mayor of the palace in Neustria, and Flaochat in Burgundy.
654.	651.

SIGEBERT II. or III. king of Austrasia.	CLOVIS II. king of Burgundy and Neustria.	*Cotemporary* PRINCES.
654. 55. 56. Sigebert dies at Metz, and leaves by his wife Imnichildis a son named DAGOBERT, whom he recommends to Grimoald. But Grimoald causes him to be shaved, and sent to Ireland; then spreading a report of his death, he procures his son to be proclaimed king. Archambaud, mayor of the palace under Clovis, opposing this step, the usurper is dethroned. Childeric, a son of Clovis II. succeeds in the kingdom of Austrasia.	651. Clovis, to maintain the poor, had stripped the church of St. Denis of the gold and silver, with which the shrines of St. Denis and his companions were covered: as an indemnification to this abbey, he procures it, at an assembly of bishops, an entire exemption from all episcopal jurisdiction, which was confirmed by Landeric, bishop of Paris. 656. &c. Clovis II. dies soon after his brother, and leaves three sons behind him, of whom the third, named Thierry, had no partition: the eldest, CLOTHARIUS III. succeeds to his father's kingdoms: the second, whose name was CHILDERIC, had already succeeded to the throne of Austrasia, upon the deposition of Grimoald's son, and the false report of the death of Dagobert, the son of Sigebert. His wife's name was Batilda.	*Popes.* Theodore. 649. Martin I. 654. Eugene I. 656. Vitalian. 669. *Emperors of the East.* Constans. 668. Constantine Pogonatus. 685. *Kings of the Lombards in Italy.* Rotharis. 654. Rodoald. 659. Aripert. 661. Gundebert. 662. *King of the Goths in Spain.* Recesvindus. 672. *England.* Heptarchy.

CLOTHARIUS III.
king of
Burgundy and Neustria.

BATILDA, mother of CLOTHARIUS III. who was then only five years of age, has the direction of affairs under her son, and behaves with great prudence.

She retires out of devotion to the abbey of Chelles, which had been founded by herself, and leaves the kingdom to the discretion of Ebroin, mayor of the palace, whose violent measures she had

CHILDERIC II. king of Austrasia.	CLOTHARIUS III. king of Burgundy and Neustria.	*Cotemporary* PRINCES.
	had hitherto opposed. She likewise founded the abbey of Corbie; and the church has declared her a saint.	*Popes.* Vitalian. 669. Adeodatus. 676. Domnus I. 678. Agatho. 682.
670. Childeric becomes king of the whole realm of France, by the death of Clotharius III. and by Thierry's involuntary retreat to a monastery. Childeric resigns part of Austrasia to Dagobert II. the son of Sigebert. So long as Childeric followed the counsels of Leger, bishop of Autun, he behaved himself extremely well; but as he swerved from those rules, he fell into contempt. This prelate, whom the church has canonized as a martyr, was assassinated in 678, by Ebroin's order, in a forest of Artois, which still goes by his name. 673. Bodillon, a great lord among the Franks, having been basely used by Childeric, for his free remonstrances in regard to the danger of an exorbitant tax, which he wanted to lay on his people, assassinates this prince in the forest of Livri, together with his wife queen Bilichilde, and his son Dagobert. Childeric left a son, named DANIEL, who did not succeed him. THIERRY was taken from the abbey of St. Denis, and placed upon the throne. Childeric was interred in the church of St. Germain-des-Pres.	670. Clotharius III. dies, and is interred in the abbey of Chelles; Thierry, his second son, who had no share assigned him, in the succession, is made king in his room, by means of Ebroin. But the aversion which the people had conceived against this minister, fell upon the king himself; so that Thierry was shut up in the abbey of St. Denis. DAGOBERT II. king of part of Austrasia. Dagobert II. that same son of Sigebert, who had been sent away to Ireland, comes back, and reigns in Austrasia, part of which had been resigned to him by Childeric.	Leo II. 684. Benedict II. 685. John V. 686. Conon. 687. Sergius I. 701. *Emperors of the East.* Constantine Pogonatus. 685. Justinian II. 711. *Kings of the Lombards in Italy.* Garibald. 675. Partharit. 691. *Kings of the Goths in Spain.* Recefwindus. 672. Bamba. 680. Ervigius. 687. *England.* Heptarchy.

THIERRY III. king of Burgundy and Neustria.	DAGOBERT II. king of Austrasia.	Cotemporary PRINCES.
673. &c. THIERRY had already begun to reign in 670. Ebroin, the same who had been mayor of the palace under Clotharius II. obliges Thierry, by force of arms, to continue him in that office.	673. 674. &c. Dagobert, who had already the sovereignty of part of Austrasia, makes himself master of the rest of the kingdom, where Ebroin had obliged the people to swear allegiance to a false Clovis, who was pretended to be the son of Clotharius III. 678. &c. Dagobert II. is assassinated: his death ought naturally to have rendered Thierry sole master of the monarchy; but Austrasia dreading to fall under the power of Ebroin, mayor of the palace, refused to acknowledge any more kings: upon which Pepin and Martin got themselves declared dukes or governors of that country. (*Memoirs of the academy of belles lettres, tom.* 6.)	*Popes.* Adeodatus. 676. Domnus I. 678. Agatho. 682. Leo II. 684. Benedict II. 685. John V. 686. Conon. 687. Sergius I. 701. *Emperors of the East.* Constantine Pogonatus. 685. Justinian II. 711. *Kings of the Lombards in Italy.* Garibald. 675. Partharit. 691. Cunipert. 701. *Kings of the Goths in Spain.* Bamba. 680. Ervigius. 687. *England.* Heptarchy.

THIERRY III. reigns alone.
The beginning of the indolent kings.

688. &c.

Ebroin is assassinated, and several mayors succeed him. Bertaire, the last mayor, perished in the revolution which was brought about by means of Pepin. Duke Pepin Heristel was grandson of Pepin the elder, father of Charles Martel, and grandfather of a third Pepin, called *Brevis* or the *Short*, king of France, and head or founder of the Carlovingian race. He had already made himself master of Austrasia, at the time when Dagobert, the son of Childeric, was murdered; and in some measure was sovereign of that country, though still in appearance under the authority of king Thierry. They who
were

THIERRY III. reigns alone.

were dissatisfied with Thierry's government, removed to Austrasia, and Pepin, who wanted only a pretext for going to war, espoused their cause: Thierry was for calling him to an account; and a battle decided the dispute.

690. &c.

Thierry was defeated, and Pepin usurped the whole authority under the title of mayor of the palace.

Pepin subdues the several provinces bordering upon France, that had revolted during the weakness of the preceeding reigns. Thierry dies; but his decease makes no more noise than that of a private person: his wife's name was Clotilda, and he left two sons who succeeded him. He was interred in the church of St. Waast at Arras, of which he was the founder.

CLOVIS III.

692. &c.

PEpin continues to reign under the name of Clovis III. son of Thierry, and extends his conquests.

695. &c.

Clovis dies, after a reign of five years.

CHILDEBERT III. surnamed the Just.

PEpin, who continued to reign under the name of Childebert, the brother of Clovis III. makes his eldest son duke of Champagne, and his younger son mayor of the palace to Childebert. Both his sons die; and he founds the celebrated abbey of Fleury.

711. &c.

Childebert III. departs this life, after a reign of sixteen years. He was interred at Choisi, upon the river Aisne, and left a son, who succeeded him.

Cotemporary PRINCES.

Popes.
Sergius I. 701.
John VI. 705.
John VII. 707.
Sisinnius. 708.
Constantine. 714.
Emperors of the East.
Justinian II. 711.
Philippicus. 713.
Anastasius II. 714.
Kings of the Lombards in Italy.
Partharit. 691.
Cunipert. 703.
Luitbert. 704.
Aripert. 712.
Ansprand. 712.
Luitprand. 744.
Kings of the Goths in Spain.
Egica. 701.
Vitiza. 711.
Roderic, the last king of the Goths in Spain. 712.
England.
Heptarchy.

DAGO-

DAGOBERT III.

714.

THIS prince has very little authority. Pepin makes his grandson Theodebald, as yet an infant, mayor of the palace to Dagobert III.

The death of Pepin: this man was very useful to the state, at the same time that he subverted the regal power.

Theodebald, an infant, is mayor of the palace, under the guardianship of his mother; Charles, afterwards called Charles Martel, son of Pepin by a concubine named Alpais, is imprisoned by Theodebald's mother.

715. 16. &c.

So strange a government cannot subsist long; the people rise up in arms; Theodebald makes his escape, and his office is conferred on Rainfroy.

The Goths, who had driven the Romans out of Spain, are dispossessed of that country in their turn by the Saracens: these people had been invited over by count Julian, to be revenged of Roderic, who had violated his daughter. The Spanish Christians, who submitted to the Moors, and preserved their religion, were called *Mosarabians*.

The enemies bordering on France take advantage of these troubles; Charles Martel escapes out of prison, and appears in Austrasia: the Austrasians receive him with as much kindness as they would have shewn to his father Pepin himself, and acknowledge him as duke of that country.

Dagobert III. dies, and leaves a son called THIERRY, who did not succeed as king this time; for DANIEL, the son of Childeric II. was taken out of the monastery, and named CHILPERIC.

Cotemporary PRINCES.

Popes.
Constantine. 714.
Gregory II. 731.
Emperors of the East.
Theodosius III. 716.
Leo Isaurus. 741.
King of the Lombards in Italy.
Luitprand. 744.
King of the Goths in Spain.
Pelagius. 737. This prince concealing himself amidst the rocks of Asturia, preserved the regal name, and indeed continued that dignity among the Christian princes, who at length ejected the Moors in the reign of Philip III.
England.
Heptarchy.

CHILPERIC II.

THIS prince ought not to be ranked among the *lazy* or *indolent* kings. Rainfroy, promoting his service, opposes Charles Martel.

719.

In this reign the same thing came to pass, as had happened to Pepin under Thierry III. Charles Martel defeats Chilperic in several engagements; Rainfroy loses his post; and, what is very extraordinary, Charles substitutes in the room of Chilperic, another very obscure king, who was called CLOTHARIUS IV. This Clotharius dying soon after, Chilperic is recalled by Charles Martel from Aquitaine, whither he had fled for refuge: Charles uniting the whole authority of the French empire, chose nevertheless to be only mayor of the palace to Chilperic.

720. &c.

Chilperic II. dies at Noyon: he is succeeded by THIERRY of Chelles, the son of Dagobert III.

THIERRY IV. surnamed of Chelles.

725. &c.

CHARLES MARTEL undertakes to wage war against the nations bordering on France.

731.

Eudes, duke of Aquitaine, having twice violated the peace concluded with France, is twice defeated. This Eudes was of the blood royal, being the son of Boggis, and the grandson of Charibert (*see the year* 630.)

732.

Abderaman, king of the Saracens, passes the Garonne, in order to fight Eudes, duke of Aquitaine, who had encouraged an insurrection in one of his provinces. Eudes calls Charles Martel to his aid, and the Saracens are intirely discomfited between Tours and Poitiers; in this engage-

---

Cotemporary PRINCES.

Popes.
Gregory II. 731.
Gregory III. 741.
Emperor of the East.
Leo Isaurus. 741.
King of the Lombards in Italy.
Luitprand. 744.
King of Spain.
Pelagius. 737.
England.
Heptarchy.

THIERRY IV. surnamed of Chelles. | *Cotemporary* PRINCES.

engagement they were said to have lost upwards of three hundred thousand men.

733.

Charles Martel subdues the Frisons, converts them to the Catholic religion, and unites their country to the crown.

734. 735.

Eudes, duke of Aquitaine, happening to die, Charles Martel grants to Herald, that duke's son, the enjoyment of his father's demesnes, upon condition of yielding homage to him, and to his sons, without making any mention of king Thierry.

736.

The Saracens invade the territories of Herald, duke of Aquitaine, ravage Languedoc, and make themselves masters of the fortresses, which this prince possessed in Provence.

737.

Thierry dies; and Charles Martel continues to reign under the title of duke of the French, without nominating a new king.

739.

The Saxons revolt, and are again subdued.

Charles Martel drives the Saracens out of Provence, and recovers the towns, which those infidels had wrested from the duke of Aquitaine.

740.

Charles Martel sits down in peace, and enjoys the fruits of his valour, the fame of which had rendered him the arbiter of Europe.

Disturbances in Italy occasioned by the errors of the Iconoclasts, who were supported by the emperor Leo. Gregory II. had used his utmost endeavours to prevail on Charles Martel to oppose the progress of this heresy; but Charles constantly avoided giving him any assistance; whe-

Contemporary Princes:
Pope.
Gregory III. 741.
Emperor of the East.
Leo Isaurus. 741.
King of the Lombards in Italy.
Luitprand. 744.
Kings of Spain.
Pelagius. 737.
Favila. 739.
England.
Heptarchy.

INTER-REGNUM.

ther it was becauſe Gregory's offers did not appear ſufficient to him; or that he did not chuſe to give umbrage to the king of the Lombards, by whom the pope was alſo rendered very uneaſy. Gregory III. ſucceeded Gregory II. and made more advantageous propoſals to Charles; viz. that he would withdraw himſelf from the emperor's juriſdiction, and proclaim Charles conſul of Rome. This is the real epocha of the temporal grandeur of the popes, a propitious omen that the imperial dignity would be transferred to the houſe of France.

741.

The death of the pope, of the emperor Leo, and of Charles Martel; the latter is interred at St. Denis. Carloman and Pepin, the ſons of Charles Martel, ſhare the government of the kingdom between them, and keep cloſely united.

742.

Pepin thinks it more advantageous to put an end to the inter-regnum; and therefore fills up the throne with Childeric.

CHILDERIC III.

CHILDERIC III. the ſon of Chilperic II. is proclaimed king in that part of France governed by Pepin, that is in Neuſtria, Burgundy, and Provence; for Auſtraſia had no other maſter than Carloman.

743.

The council of Leſtines, in the preamble to which Carloman expreſſes himſelf like a ſovereign; this is the firſt council, in which they began to reckon the years from the incarnation of our Lord. The author of this æra was Dionyſius Exiguus in his cycle of the year 526, and

Cotemporary PRINCES.

Pope.
Zachary I. 752.
Emperor of the Eaſt.
Conſtantine Copronymus. 775.
King of the Lombards in Italy.
Luitprand. 744.
King of Spain.
Alfonſo I. 757.
England.
Heptarchy.

CHILDERIC III.

and venerable Bede made use of it afterwards in his history.

Pepin and Carloman defeat the Bavarians, the Alemans, the Saxons, and the Sclavonians.

744. &c.

Pepin vanquishes the duke of Aquitaine, who had revolted again; and these princes are reconciled.

746.

Carloman resigns the government of Austrasia, and retires to Rome, where he embraces a monastic life: he leaves behind him a son named Drogon, whom Pepin confines to a monastery.

747. 48. 49.

Griffon, the son of Charles Martel, but not by the same venter with Pepin, takes up arms against this prince, in order to assert the rights which he had derived from his father. Pepin marches against him, and defeats him several times: Griffon casts himself into the arms of the duke of Aquitaine.

750.

Childeric III. is dethroned, shaved, and shut up in the abbey of Sithiu, now St. Bertin, where he died in 754. He had a son named Thierry, who was sent to the monastery of Fontenelle in Normandy, and brought up there in obscurity.

The end of the race of the Merovingians, after a space of 270 years, computing from Clovis.

Contemporary PRINCES.

Pope.
Zachary 2. 752.
Emperor of the East.
Constantine Copronymus. 775.
Kings of the Lombards in Italy.
Hildebrand. 744.
Rachisius. 750.
Aistulphus. 756.
King of Spain.
Alfonso I. 757.
England.
Heptarchy.

PARTICULAR REMARKS.

DIFFERENT authors have written differently in regard to th
beginning of our monarchy, such as Mezeray, Daniel
Boulainvilliers, and the abbé du Bos : we shall venture to
give our opinion concerning their several systems.

We think contrary to M. de Boulainvilliers, that the Franks
had real kings, that Clovis was such, and not a chief of adventurers, as this author pretends ; that the Franks did not break
into Gaul by a sudden irruption, and reduce the inhabitants to
servitude, according to the practice of barbarous nations: therefore we are far from adopting any part of this author's system.

We think with father Daniel, that Clovis conquered Gaul
but we differ from him, inasmuch as we believe that the Frank
were settled there a considerable time before Clovis, and that thei
connexions with the Romans contributed to the facility of tha
conquest.

With Mezeray we can conclude nothing, because he had
very confused idea of things, and has but lightly touched upo
the several systems without embracing any, or without letting u
know the essential points about which the historians were di
vided.

We believe with the abbé du Bos, that Clovis was possess
of employments in the Roman empire ; that he availed himse
of this authority, even against the Romans themselves; that th
bishops and the cause of religion greatly contributed to his su
cess : but we do not think that the people of Gaul, exceptin
the Armorici, submitted voluntarily to his laws, and invit
him to the Gallic throne. We are of opinion, that he took a
vantage of conjunctures, of the disposition of the public,
the posts he occupied, of the aversion of the people to tyrant
and of the dread they entertained of other neighbouring prince
and that he made use of these several means, either to redu
the Gauls under his obedience, or to maintain his authority o
them, after he had brought them into a state of subjectio
and therefore that there was no one part of Gaul, which
did not conquer, and take possession of by force of arr
In a word, if I may venture to tell my opinion, I thi
th

PARTICULAR REMARKS.

that Clovis was more a conqueror than a politician; whereas the abbé du Bos makes him rather a politician than a conqueror.

Clovis said to the Gauls: the Romans oppress you, but afford you no protection; your estates are exhausted by the impositions with which you are burdened, and by the depredations of the Burgundians and Visigoths. Let me conquer you, and I will secure you from pillage: you shall pay no more than moderate taxes. The bishops enforced these arguments among the people; Clovis backed them by force of arms; the Roman troops defended themselves; the people tamely expected the event; and Clovis's good fortune performed the rest: after having really conquered a country, which did not make a voluntary submission to him, he took upon him the glorious title of deliverer of Gaul, instead of the odious appellation of conqueror. The like instances occur frequently in history, when princes, desirous of subduing a nation, have spread manifestoes among their enemies, with a view of disposing the people to submit to the fortune of war, in case it should favour their cause: the prince is then really a conqueror, but conceals himself in the disguise of a deliverer, and the prospect of a milder government gains the people, who are ever fond of novelty. Shall we say, for all this, that he has not conquered the nation, which he has made subject to his authority? This would be absurd and foolish: but he has not brought it under his yoke; he is a new master, and not a tyrant; the people are sensible that they have changed their sovereign, without altering their situation; at the same time the conqueror abides by the engagements of his predecessor, and maintains the laws which he finds established in the country: in short, the new king has acquired subjects by force, but preserves his sovereignty by lenity and moderation. Such is the history of what happened to Clovis. And this is what the abbé du Bos has explained extremely well: but as he was the first that discovered this truth, he was obliged perhaps, in order to destroy inveterate prejudices, to stretch a little too far on the opposite side: he has been shocked, and with good reason, at the violent irruption of the Franks, admitted and believed by the

PARTICULAR REMARKS.

torrent of historians; therefore, in order to confound them, he has presented us with a different picture, that of a sage and moderate king, the fame of whose virtues made him master of a powerful nation, without striking a single stroke: the medium between these two systems appears to us the most probable and the best founded.

The mayors of the palace were originally the same officer as our present lord steward; and the person invested with this dignity was called *major domus regiæ, palatii gubernator, præfectus,* &c. Thus when Chilperic sent Waddon to attend his daughter into Spain, where she was to be married to Recaredus, he gave him the title of *mayor of the palace* to the princess; and this is the notion we ought to entertain of all the mayors of the palace mentioned in history, before the death of Dagobert I. The power of the mayors began to increase upon the decease of that prince, from whence we may date the declension of the regal authority. Their office at first was temporary, afterwards for life, and at length they made it hereditary: at first they had the direction of the king's household, then they became prime ministers, and at length they were seen at the head of the armies: hence their titles were changed, and in process of time the mayor was called *dux Francorum, dux & princeps, sub-regulus.* It was Grimoald that first began to carry this dignity to the highest pitch in the reign of Sigebert II. king of Austrasia. *(Mem. of the acedemy of belles lettres, tom.* 10.)

The office of great referendary answered to that of the present chancellor: this office, which became more considerable under the princes of the second race, is now the first in the state since the suppression of that of constable. The count of the palace was greatly inferior to the mayor, yet he was judge of the king's household, and performed the functions of all the other offices which have been since erected, as butler, chamberlain, &c. This employment continued under the second race, whereas that of mayor was abolished: under the kings of the third race, the post of seneschal supplanted that of count of the palace, some resemblance of which is still preserved in

PARTICULAR REMARKS.

the office of great provoſt of the houſhold. The conſtable, who was inferior in dignity to the count of the palace under the ſecond race, became the firſt perſon in the adminiſtration under the third, and the office of ſeneſchal ended in 1191.

Very grave authors affirm, that under this firſt race the females had the property of that ſhare of the eſtate, which they inherited from the kings their fathers; that even the wives of our kings had the property of the eſtates which their huſbands aſſigned for their dower *(Gregory of Tours)* and that this property, in failure of iſſue, went to their collaterals: but this opinion is ſtrongly combated in a memorial of M. de F. *(Mem. of the academy of belles lettres, tom. 8.)*

Under the ſame race, our kings generally had the nomination of biſhops, excluſive of the people and the clergy.

The kings of the kings, and the princes of their blood, wore their hair long, and thereby were diſtinguiſhed from their ſubjects, *principes & ornatiorem capillum habent* (Tacit. de nor. Germ.) which ſerves to explain the practice, when they wanted to render a king incapable of wearing the crown; they ſhaved his head, and from that moment he was reduced to the level of a ſubject.

The hierarchy was formed at the time of Conſtantine the Great, upon the plan of the civil government; ſo that by following the rank and dignity of the cities and provinces of the empire, a new diſcipline was introduced upon the model of the ſecular magiſtrates. Then were ſtarted the titles of metropolitans, primates, patriarchs, &c. and this regulation was adopted by all Chriſtian princes. *(Dupin.)*

Benedict produced a kind of revolution in the weſt, by founding the monaſtic order, as Baſil had done in the eaſt. (Both of them have been canonized.)

St. Benedict founded his order upon mount Caſſino; from whence it diffuſed itſelf over Europe, and has been the model of all the religious orders eſtabliſhed ſince that time, ſuch as the monks of Clugny, of Gramont, the Carthuſians, Ciſtercians, &c. In thoſe early times the monks were ſubject to the authority of the biſhops; there was no ſuch thing as privileges and exemptions, granted since by popes, and in process of time so greatly multiplied.

It is a question whether the name of Merovingians came from Merovæus: and indeed it is somewhat extraordinary, that the Franks should prefer the name of Merovæus to that of Clodion his father, who, by Gregory of Tours, is stiled a king that consulted the good of his people. Was it that Merovæus pretended to be the son of Clodion and of a sea monster, which was considered as a deity; and that the Franks, being mostly Pagans, and fond of a marvellous original, chose to perpetuate its memory, by giving the appellation of Merovingian to their race of kings? But the absurdity of this fable is obvious. M. Gibert *(Mem. of the academy of belles lettres)* derives the name from *Maraboduus*, a king of the Germans, from whom the Franks deduce their original; and he forms from thence the name of Merovæus, by the analogy of the Germanic language rendered into Latin. M. Freret on the contrary *(ibid.)* after attempting to shew that the name of Merovingians was not known till the beginning of the second race, (which M. Gibert denies) when it was become necessary to distinguish the reigning from the abdicated family, restores Merovæus, the grandfather of Clovis, to the honour of having given his name to our first race of kings: and his reason why this race had not taken the name of any other prince before Merovæus is, that, according to Gregory of Tours, some people doubted whether Merovæus was the son of Clodion, and only looked upon him as a relation of that prince, *de stirpe ejus*; whereas, after Merovæus, the succession of that line was never interrupted. This is a dispute that remains as yet undecided between those two literati.

The Franks and the Gauls reckoned by days and not by nights, *nec dierum numerum ut nos, sed noctium computant*. (Tacit.) If a person living according to the Salic law, lost his slave, his horse, or his ox, the proprietor has the term of forty nights allowed him, to recover his property. *(Salic law, T. 50. de filtortis.)*

MINISTERS,

The First Race.

MINISTERS, WARRIORS, MAGISTRATES, EMINENT and LEARNED MEN,

Who flourished from the year 480 to 751, which includes the whole period of the first race.

MINISTERS.	WARRIORS.	MAGISTRATES.	EMINENT and LEARNED MEN.
Mayors of the palace, ranged according to the order of the reigns of kings. Reign of CLOVIS I. *who died in* 511. Lando. Reign of CLOTHARIUS I. *who died in* 562. Theodoric. Badegesilus. Gondoland. Landregesilus. Reigns of CHARIBERT, *who died in* 566, *and of* CHILPERIC I. *who died in* 584. Landregesilus. Cuppa. Landri. Chrodin. Gogon. Radon. Reign of CLOTHARIUS II. *who died in* 628. Landri. Florentian. Wlfoad. Warnachaire. Berthoald. Protadius. Claudius. Licin. Gondebald. Waraton. Carloman. Gondoald. Reign of DAGOBERT I. *who died in* 638. Gondoald. Sadregesilus. Arnoul. Ar-	*Generals of Armies.* Syagrius. Mummol. Didier. Leudegesilus Landri.	*Referendaries.* The names of the referendaries of this first race, who were the chief magistrates of that time, are so uninteresting, and what could be said concerning them is so very uncertain, that we chuse to confine ourselves to a simple note. The functions of the referendary, who was called the great referendary, were to seal the public acts with the royal seal, and to sign the diplomas. Besides the great referendary, there were other officers subordinate to him, who bore also the title of referendaries; their business was to draw up and to digest the letters royal; and sometimes they exercised the office of great referendary. Du Cange in his Glossary has given us a long list of those magistrates: Tesserau and du Chene have also taken notice of them.	Agathias, died towards the year 660. Alcimus Avitus. 520. S. Anthelmus, towards the year 709. Bede. 735. S. Benedict. 543. Boetius. 524. Cassiodorus. 575. S. Columbanus. 615. Dionysius Exiguus before 556. S. Eloi. 665. Ennodius. 521. S. Epiphanius. 496. Fortunatus, towards 600. Fredegarius, towards 658. S. Fulgentius, towards 533. Gennadius, towards 494. Gregory of Tours 595. John Climacus. 606. Jornandes, towards 552. Malculfus, towards 660. Marius of Avenche. 596. Procopius, towards 520. S. Remigius, towards 535. Salvianus. 490. Sidonius Apollinaris. 482. Symmachus. 514. Zo-

MINISTERS.	WARRIORS.	MAGISTRATES.	EMINENT and LEARNED MEN.
Archambaud. Pepin the elder. Cogon Neran. Ega. *Reign of* CLOVIS II. *who died in* 660. Archambaud. Bertinoald. Ebroin. Almaric. Flaochat. Martin. Grimoald. Adalgifus. *Reign of* CHILDERIC II. *who died in* 673. Ebroin. Robert. Wlfoald. S. Leger. *Reign of* THIERRY III. *who died in* 690. Ebroin. Leudefilus. Waraton. Gilimer. Bertaire. *Reign of* CLOVIS III. *who died in* 695. Pepin Heriftal. *Reign of* CHILDEBERT III. *who died in* 711. Pepin Heriftal. Dreux. Grimoald. Nordebert. *Reign of* DAGOBERT III. *who died in* 715, *and of* CHILPERIC II. *who died in* 720. Grimoald. Theobald. Rainfroi. Charles Martel. *Reign of* THIERRY IV. *who died in* 736. Charles Martel. *Reign of* CHILDERIC III. *who was shaved in* 750. Pepin the short.			Zozimus, towards 503.

A Chro-

A Chronological Abridgment

OF THE

HISTORY of FRANCE.

THE SECOND RACE.

WITHOUT adopting any particular fyftem concerning the fucceffion to the throne, it is fufficient to obferve in an hiftorical way, that the acceffion of Pepin was the firft inftance, in which the crown was transferred to a ftrange family. During the whole time of the firft race, it was worn only by the defcendants of Clovis; indeed without any right of feniority, or diftinction between legitimate and natural fons; and with the circumftance of partition: it was poffeffed in the fame manner, under the fecond race, by the fons of Pepin; but as this prince dethroned the lawful heir, his defcendants underwent the fame fate. At length, under the third race, the hereditary right was fo well eftablifhed, that our kings have it no longer in their power to change the order of fucceffion; fo that the crown devolves to their eldeft fon by an eftablifhed cuftom, *which,* as Jerome Bignon obferves, *is much ftronger than any law, being ingraved not on marble or brafs, but in the heart of every Frenchman.*

Accession to the crown.

REMARKABLE EVENTS.

PEPIN, *furnamed the* SHORT, *the first king of the second race, son of Charles Martel, comes to the crown in the year* 751, *about the age of thirty-seven. He is the first of our kings that chose to be crowned and anointed with the rites of the church. This ceremony was performed in the cathedral of Soissons, by St. Boniface, the pope's legate, and archbishop of Mentz.*

751. 52.

PEPIN is proclaimed king of France at Soissons: he was encouraged in this great enterprize by pope Zachary, and by S. Boniface, bishop of Mentz, who stood in need of his assistance against Constantine Copronymus, the protector of the Iconoclasts, and against the Lombards, the enemies of the holy see: yet not long after, he desired pope Stephen to absolve him from the crime of violating his allegiance to his lawful sovereign. (*Mem. of the Acad. of belles lettres.*) Pepin receives the submission of several lords, who had made themselves masters of Septimania, and unites it to the crown.

753. 54. 55.

Pepin defeats the Saxons, who, notwithstanding the treaties concluded with that prince, refuse to acknowledge his authority.

Aistulphus, king of the Lombards, seizes on the exarchate of Ravenna, and thereby deprives the emperor of the East of one of his principal possessions in Italy. He attempts next to make himself master of Rome. Pope Stephen comes to France to implore the assistance of Pepin, who marches twice over the Alps, recovers the exarchate, which he bestows on the pope, and lays the first foundation of the temporal power of the court of Rome. How could Leo IX. who was reckoned a man of learning, have recourse three hundred years after, to the pretended donation of Constantine, and make use of an imaginary title, when he had one at his hand, so authentic and well founded? True it is, that in the year 321 Constantine published that famous constitution, the source of ecclesiastic opulence, whereby the cathedral churches

The Second Race. 45

WIVES.	CHILDREN.	768. DEATH.	Cotemporary PRINCES.
Bertha, or Bertrada, daughter of Charibert, count of Laon, died in 783. There are three different opinions concerning this princess: Du Tillet says, that Bertha was the daughter of Ærarchia, emperor of Constantinople: we find in a paper of M. Smith's, inserted in the memoirs of Nevers, that she was daughter of the king of the Alemans: and lastly the annals of St. Bertin make her the daughter of the count of Laon, which is the opinion of Mezeraye and of father Anselme.	CHARLEMAIN, CARLOMAN, } who succeeded their father. Charlemain had Austrasia and Neustria, with some provinces of ancient Germany. Carloman had Burgundy, Provence, Septimania, Alsace, and what we now call Germany, which at that time was only the other part of Charlemain's share. Pepin, Rothaide, Adelaide, } died young. Gille. Giselle: she had like to have been married to the prince of the Lombards; and afterwards to the emperor Leo; but she concluded at last with turning nun.	PEPIN dies of a dropsy at St. Denis, the 24th day of the month of September 768, aged fifty-four, in the seventeenth year of his reign. This prince had all the great qualities of a hero: his tomb is remarkable for its epitaph; *Pepin, father of Charlemain:* as if he had derived more glory from his son, than from his own exploits.	*Popes.* Zachary. 752. Stephen II. 752. Stephen III. 757. Paul I. 767. Stephen IV. 772. *Emperor of the East.* Constantine Copronymus. 775. *Kings of the Lombards in Italy.* Aistulphus. 756. Desiderius. 774. *Kings of Spain.* Alfonso I. 757. Froila. 768. *England.* Heptarchy.

churches were permitted to acquire landed estates, and private people were suffered to make testamentary bequests to them: very likely this is what gave rise to the supposition of Constantine's donation.

756. 57.

The death of Aistulphus, king of the Lombards, renders the pope more powerful: he encourages the ambition of Desiderius, general to Aistulphus, by assisting him to become king of the Lombards, in prejudice to Aistulphus's brother. Desiderius, out of gratitude, ratifies and enlarges the donation made by Pepin. The first organ ever seen in France, was sent in 757 by Constantine Copronymus to Pepin, who being then at Compiegne, made a present of it to St. Cornelius's church in that city.

758. 59. 60. 61. 62. 63. 64. &c.

Pepin makes war against the Saxons, the Sclavonians, the Bavarians, and the duke of Aquitaine, who had given shelter to his brother Griffon. He drives the Saracens out of the country formerly held by the Goths; and is victorious on every side.

767. 68.

The duke of Aquitaine is vanquished by Pepin, and assassinated by the treachery of one Warnston, who imagined he should thereby oblige this prince. Pepin unites that dutchy to the crown. This duke of Aquitaine's name was Waifre; he was the grandson of Eudes, and descended from Charibert, the second son of Clotharius II. The Gascons submit to Pepin.

A strange revolution at Rome upon the death of Paul I. A layman, named Constantine, is made pope; the people rise up against him, and pull out his eyes: upon which, Stephen IV. is exalted to the pontificate.

The general assemblies, which under the kings of the first race were held in March, began in this prince's reign to be kept in May; because the use of cavalry being introduced into the armies, the finding of forage made it necessary to defer the assembly till the month of May.

Our kings of the second race kept their court-days on the festivals of Christmas and Easter.

768.

The Second Race.

Ministers.	Warriors.	Magistrates.	Eminent and Learned Men.	
Fulrad, high chancellor.	Walter, of Alsace. Gerard, of Rouffillon, count of Provence.	*Arch-chancellors.* S. Boniface. 755. Franco. Wolfrad. Bodillon.	S. Boniface.	755.
			S. Chrodegand.	767.
			S. Pirmin.	758.

768.
Acceſſion to the crown.

CHARLE-MAIN *and* CARLOMAN *ſucceed their father, king Pepin, in* 768.

REMARKABLE EVENTS.

768. 69. 70.

CHARLEMAIN and CARLOMAN ſucceed Pepin, their father: their ambition creates an uneaſineſs between them, on account of the apportionment of their dominions: Deſiderius, king of the Lombards, and the duke of Bavaria, encourage this miſunderſtanding.

771.

Carloman dies at Samoucy, and is interred at Rheims: his deceaſe renders Charlemain ſole maſter of the French monarchy.

772. 73.

Charlemain enters into a war againſt the Saxons, which laſts thirty years: he defeats them in the neighbourhood of Paderborn, and plunders their famous temple, where the idol Irminſul was worſhipped. It is thought that this was a ſtatue, which they had erected to Arminius, the avenger of their liberty.

774.

The extinction of the kingdom of the Lombards (which had laſted 206 years) in the perſon of Deſiderius, who wanting to make himſelf maſter of Italy, and to prevent Charlemain from oppoſing his deſign, cuts out work for that prince at home, by aſſerting the rights of the two ſons of Carloman his ſon-in-law, to whom he grants ſhelter. Charlemain paſſes mount Cenis, beats Deſiderius, takes him priſoner, and is crowned king of the Lombards. Giannone affirms, that the kingdom of the Lombards contributed to the happineſs of Italy; and he proves it by the wiſdom and lenity of their laws, which ſubſiſted long after the extinction of their government. The famous decree of Adrian I. by which he acknowledges Charlemain as king of Italy, and patrician of Rome. This prince
con-

The Second Race. 49

Wives.	Children.	814. Death.	Cotemporary PRINCES.
Himiltrudis, divorced in 770.	Pepin the baſtard. 811. Rothais.	Charlemain dies of a pleureſy, the 28th of Jan. 814. at the age of 74, in the forty-ſeventh year of his reign, the ſcrtieth ſince the conqueſt of Italy, and the fourteenth ſince he had been crowned emperor; he was interred at Aix-la-Chapelle.	*Popes.* Stephen IV. 772. Adrian I. 795. Leo III. 816. *Emperors of the Eaſt.* Conſtantine Copronymus. 775. Conſtantine VI. 797. Irene. 802. Nicephorus. 811. From this prince's reign begins *the empire of the Greeks,* called *the lower empire.* Stauracius. 811. Michael Curopalates. 813. Leo Armenus. 820. *Kings of Italy.* Deſiderius, vanquiſhed by Charlemain, who put an end to the kingdom of the Lombards in 574. This kingdom laſted 205 years. Charlemain, emperor. 814. *Kings of Spain.* Aurelio. 774. Silo. 783. Mauregat. 788. Veremund I. 791. Alfonſo the chaſte. 844. *England.* Heptarchy.
Hermingardis or Deſiderata, daughter of Deſiderius, king of the Lombards, alſo divorced in 771.			
Hildegardis. 783.	Charles, king of Eaſtern France. 811. Pepin, king of Italy. 810. Lewis, the Debonnaire, emperor and king of France. Lotharius, died young. Rothrudis. 810. Bertha. 853. Hildegardis. } died Adelais. } young.		
Faſtrada. 794.	Theodrada, abbeſs of Argenteuil. Hiltrudis or Rothrudis, abbeſs of Farmoutiers.		
Luitgardis. 800.			
	Natural children. Charlemain had by *Regina.* Hugh, the abbot. 844. Drogo, biſhop of Metz. 844. Adalinda. By *Adalinda.* Thierri. By *Gerſwinda.* Adeltrudis.		
	Some authors ſay, that this prince had another daughter named Emma, and that he married her to Eginhard, after diſcovering the intrigue between him and that princeſs. It is cuſtomary with		

confirms the donations made to the holy fee, referving to himfelf the fupreme jurifdiction. This is fully proved by the coins which he caufed to be ftruck at Rome, as fovereign, and by dating the public acts from the year of the emperor's reign, *imperante domino noftro Carolo*.

775.

Adrian I. grants to Charlemain, in a council held at Rome, the right of ordering, and confirming the election of popes. *(Chron. Albert. ann. 775.)*

New commotions in Saxony, where the inhabitants maffacre a body of French troops. Charlemain haftens thither from Italy, and obliges them to fue for pardon.

776. &c.

A fon of Defiderius, named Adalgifus, who fled to Conftantinople, keeps up a correfpondence in Italy. Adrian gives notice thereof to Charlemain, who marches himfelf to quafh thofe difturbances, and orders the duke of Friuli to be beheaded.

The famous affembly of Paderborn, where Charlemain concludes a treaty with the Saxons and Saracens, which gives him an opportunity of marching an army into Spain.

778.

He undertakes an expedition into Spain, in order to fettle Ibinalarabi in Saragoffa: by the way he receives the homage of the feveral princes, whofe territories were fituated between the Pyrenean mountains and the river Ebro. Lupus, duke of Gafcony, beats the rear of Charlemain's army in the valley of Roncevaux, where fell the famous Rowland, whofe name has been immortalized by our earlieft romances. Charlemain reftores the ancient kingdom of Aquitaine in favour of his fon Lewis, marches back into Germany, and defeats the Saxons in the country of Heffe.

779.

Charlemain celebrates the feaft of Eafter at Heriftal, where he publifhes a capitulary.

780. 81. 82. 83. &c.

He undertakes a fecond expedition to Rome, and makes a kind of triumphant march through Italy. His two eldeft fons, with us to give the name of *natural children*, to those who are born of concubines. But we are to observe, that what is called *concubinage*, and seems at present repugnant to civil and ecclesiastic law, was at that time a kind of marriage, less solemn indeed than the other, but equally legitimate. The women bore the name of *wives of the second order*. See the year 1021.

REMARKABLE EVENTS under CHARLEMAIN.

sons, Pepin and Lewis, accompanied him on this occasion: having made the pope crown one of them king of Lombardy, and the other king of Aquitaine, he left Pepin in Italy.

Witekind, the Saxon general, excites that people to revolt; and Charlemain's generals are vanquished at the battle of Sintal. Charlemain takes a severe revenge of them, and at length obliges Witekind to submit to baptism. The Saxon hero, whose frankness was equal to his valour, gave signal proofs of the sincerity of his conversion: for from that time he shewed himself a most zealous protector of the Christian religion. Charlemain subdues the people of Britany.

787. 88.

The dutchy of Bavaria is united to the crown of France, in consequence of the infidelity of Tassilon, duke of that province, who at length obliged his cousin, Charlemain, to put him and his son Theudon under an arrest, and to thrust them both into a convent. Charlemain's generals rout the Huns and the Abares, who had penetrated into Italy by the way of Friuli: they likewise defeat an army of Greeks, commanded by Adalgisus, of whom we find no mention afterwards.

789. 90. &c.

Charlemain introduced the Gregorian song into France: and by establishing a school within his palace, which became a model to several others, he merited the title of restorer of learning. Each member of this school or academy went by a particular name, and Charlemain himself, who looked upon it as an honour to be a member, took that of David. He sent to England for the famous Alcuinus. Peter of Pisa, who had been grammar-master to the king, assisted at all his conferences, together with the archbishops of Treves and Mentz, and the abbot of Corby, &c. The royal taste, as it generally happens, rendered learning fashionable; nay, the very ladies followed the example, and one in particular distinguished herself in the science of astronomy. Charlemain forms a grand project to open a communication between the ocean and the Euxine sea, by digging a canal which should

join

The Second Race.

Ministers.	Warriors.	Magistrates.	Eminent and Learned Men.
Eginhard, son-in-law, as some pretend, of Charlemain, was living in 840. Adelhard.	Gerard of Roussillon, count of Provence. Radulphus, or Ralph. Frederic, eldest son of the duke of Mosellana. Bouchard. Valac.	*Arch-chancellors.* Ithier. Radon. Luitbert. Ludebert. Archambaud. Luitgard.	Alcuinus. 804. Amalarius. 814. S. Angilbert. 814. Ansbert or Antpert. 778. Leidrade lived in 816. Ludger. 809. S. Lulle. 786. Paulus Diaconus. 801. S. Paulinus, patriarch of Aquileia. 804. Theodulphus, towards 802. Tilpin or Turpin. 800. Usuardus. 806.

REMARKABLE EVENTS under CHARLEMAIN.

join the Rhine to the Danube. In a capitulary of this year we meet with an important fact, in regard to what they call *sortes sanctorum,* or *the saints lots.* " Let no one, says the emperor, " have the temerity to predict or tell fortunes, by the psalter or " gospel." In the reign of Clovis we mentioned the *ot of the apostles,* which is the same thing; so that the councils had been beforehand with the emperor in condemning this practice. This folly, which began in the church towards the third century, is almost as old as the creation: and every body has heard of *sortes Homericæ, sortes Virgilianæ.* The pagans looked into Homer and Virgil to know their fortunes; and the Christians for the same purpose looked into the Bible.

794. &c.

The council of Frankfort, one of the most famous that ever was held in the west. Charlemain, as emperor, exercises the same authority in that assembly, as the emperors of the east had formerly shewn in the general councils, after they had embraced the Christian religion. The fathers of this council, at the same time that they condemned the doctrine of Nestorius, which some had attempted to revive, were led into an error, by the producing of spurious acts against the second council of Nice, in which the empress Irene had justly procured the condemnation of the Iconoclasts: they rejected this council of Nice, which was afterwards acknowledged as œcumenical, when the genuine acts were produced. Among several regulations made in the council of Frankfort, we should take notice of that which ordains, that the estates possessed by bishops before their promotion, shall revert to their relations; but those which they acquire during their episcopal dignity, shall belong to the church.

796. &c.

Charlemain transplants the Saxons from their own country, to prevent any farther revolts, and distributes them in different parts of his kingdom, some in Flanders, others in Helvetia, &c. Their country was repeopled by the Adrites, a nation of Sclavonia.

A let-

REMARKABLE EVENTS under CHARLEMAIN.

A letter of Leo III. to Charlemain, which proves that the pope yielded homage for all his poffeffions to the king of France. Charlemain makes himfelf mafter of the kingdom of the Abares, formerly the Huns, that is of Auftria and Hungary. A Parliament held at Aix-la-Chapelle; where it is enacted that no bifhop fhall ordain a bondman unlefs he has been firft enfranchifed, nor a freeman without the permiffion of the prince. This city was built by Charlemain with the greateft magnificence, and now became his ordinary refidence.

A revolution at Conftantinople. Upon the death of Copronymus, his fon Leo IV, who married Irene, afcended the imperial throne. Irene, after her hufband's deceafe, was entrufted with the regency during the minority of her fon Conftantine: but as this young prince wanted to ftrip her of her authority, when he came of age, fhe put him to death; by which means the empire fell under petticoat government.

799.
Charlemain feizes the iflands of Majorca and Minorca.

800. &c.
Charlemain is crowned emperor of the weft by Leo III. Thus this empire, which expired in the year 476, in Auguftulus, the laft emperor of the weft, and which was afterwards filled by the Heruli, by the Oftrogoths, and the Lombards, revived again in Charlemain, and continues to this day. The king of Perfia refigns the holy land to this prince, by his ambaffadors. The capitularies of Aix-la-Chapelle, the execution of which is committed to the *Miffi Dominici*; there are fome articles againft the counts, who no longer would adminifter juftice, without a bribe.

Lewis (afterwards called the Debonnaire) who had been proclaimed king of Aquitaine in his cradle, and who kept his court at Touloufe, the capital of his dominions, from whence he waged war againft the Saracens, makes himfelf mafter of Barcelona, which continued in the hands of the French till the reign of St. Lewis.

REMARKABLE EVENTS under CHARLEMAIN.

803. &c.

Nicephorus is crowned emperor of the eaſt (this is what we call the empire of the Greeks, or the lower empire) and Irene, whom Charlemain had demanded in marriage, is exiled to the iſle of Leſbos, now Mitylene. Nicephorus acknowledges Charlemain as emperor of the weſt. The limits of the eaſtern and weſtern empires ſettled between the two emperors. New regulations made at Mentz, relative to the laws by which the ſeveral people in Charlemain's dominions were governed, and many of which were added to the Salic law.

Charlemain, in order to complete the reduction of the Saxons, deprives their children of their paternal ſucceſſion. He likewiſe ſubdues the people of Pannonia, the Sclavonians, and the Huns. The Venetian ſtate at that time had two dukes, who were dependent on both empires. The cuſtom of the judgment of the croſs: it conſiſted in determining the cauſe in favour of one of the two parties, who held his arms extended in the form of a croſs, for a longer ſpace of time than his antagoniſt. A general law againſt private wars. *(Du Cange 26th Diſſertation on Joinville.)*

805. 6.

The grand capitularies drawn up at Aix-la-Chapelle, and remarkable in this, that many of them were revived by Lewis XIV.

An aſſembly (806) in which Charlemain divides his dominions among his three ſons, and makes a will for this purpoſe, which is confirmed by the French lords and by pope Leo: but what is very remarkable, he leaves thoſe people at liberty to chuſe themſelves a maſter after the deceaſe of the princes his ſons, provided he be of the blood royal.

807. 8. 9. &c.

About this time the barbarous nations of the north, the Normans, Angles, Danes, &c. begin to make themſelves known by their piratical deſcents upon the coaſt of France. Charlemain with great concern foreſaw the ravages they were one day likely to commit, and therefore endeavoured to prevent them: with this view he viſited his harbours, and built a number of ſhips of war, to be always manned and ready to put to ſea; and what appears

REMARKABLE EVENTS under CHARLEMAIN.

pears incredible, he had them stationed from the mouth of the Tiber to the extremity of Germany, that is, as far as Denmark. The nobility on those occasions had orders for personal service, the same as in land armies. Some articles to this purpose are extant in the capitularies. He made Boulogne one of the chief stations for his navy, and restored the ancient Pharos of that town, which had been destroyed by time.

The office of constable begins to be a considerable dignity. The emperor Nicephorus is slain by the king of the Bulgarians; Michael Rangabe succeeds him, in prejudice to the son of Nicephorus, and acknowledges Charlemain as emperor of the west. The latter loses his two sons, Pepin and Charles, and proclaims Bernard, the son of Pepin, king of Italy.

813.

Charlemain makes his son Lewis his collegue in the empire.

This great prince, says Eginhard, *wore only a plain doublet in winter, made of an otter's skin, a woollen tunic fringed with silk, and a blue coat or cassock; his hose consisted of transverse bands or fillets of different colours.* He would march with the greatest rapidity from the Pyrenean mountains into Germany, and from Germany into Italy. The whole world echoed his name. He was the tallest and strongest man of his time. In this respect, he resembled the heroes of fabulous story: he differed from them as he thought that force is of use only to conquer, but laws are necessary to govern. Accordingly he enacted several after the form observed in those days, that is, in mixt assemblies, composed of a number of bishops and the principal lords of the nation.

Charlemain, besides, was a lover, encourager, and protector of the arts and sciences; for this is a circumstance ever annexed to real greatness. To him we are indebted for the manner of computing by livres, sous, and derniers, such as is observed at present in France, with this difference, that the livre was then really a pound weight, whereas with us it is only numerical.

The first sumptuary laws, to regulate the price of cloths, and to distinguish the condition and rank of private people by their dress.

814.

REMARKABLE EVENTS.

814. *Acceſſion to the crown.*

LEWIS I. ſurnamed the DEBONNAIRE, emperor and king of France, aſcends the throne in the year 814; at the age of thirty-ſix, is proclaimed emperor at Aix-la-Chapelle, and crowned in 816 at Rheims by pope Stephen.

814. &c.

CHARLEMAIN's apparent zeal for religion greatly added to his power; but the ill-judged devotion of Lewis the Debonnaire, degraded his authority. This prince being too much employed in reforming the church, and too little in governing his dominions, incurred the hatred of the clergy, and loſt the eſteem of the laity. Yet he deſerves commendation for removing the princeſſes his ſiſters, and the ladies of their retinue, from court, where they had long behaved in a ſcandalous manner. He conciliates the affections of the Saxons, by reſtoring them to the right of ſucceſſion, of which they had been deprived by Charlemain. He sends his eldeſt ſon Lotharius into Bavaria, and Pepin into Aquitaine, in order to govern thoſe provinces, but keeps Lewis, his youngeſt ſon, at home. The council of Aix-la-Chapelle, (816) where regulations were made for the canons of cathedral churches, and for religious women. Thoſe dignitaries being tired of living in community, divided the revenue of the chapter among them, and went to live in private houſes: canons regular were ſubſtituted in their ſtead.

The emperor concludes a peace with Abderamen, king of the Saracens.

817.

He makes Lotharius his collegue in the empire, creates Pepin king of Aquitaine, and Lewis king of Bavaria. It is obſervable in this partition, that every freeman, or perſon not ſubject to a lord, is permitted to declare himſelf the vaſſal of which of the three princes he chuſeth: this ſhews that there were allodial or free lands at that time in France.

The SECOND RACE.

WIVES.	CHILDREN.	840. DEATH.	*Cotemporary* PRINCES.
Irmingardis. 818.	Lotharius I. emperor, and king of Italy. 855. Pepin, king of Aquitaine. 838. Lewis, king of Bavaria. 876. Gisela, married to count Eberhard, mother of Beranger, king of Italy, living in 876. Alpais, wife of Beggo, count of Paris. Hildegardis, wife of count Thierry, alive in 824.	LEWIS the DEBONNAIRE *dies in an island of the Rhine in the neighbourhood of Mentz, the 23d of June, 840. He lies interred in St. Arnoul's church at Metz.*	*Popes.* Leo III. 816. Stephen V. 817. Paschal I. 824. Eugenius II. 827. Valentine. 827. Gregory IV. 843. *Emperors of the East.* Leo Armenus. 820. Michael Balbus. 829. Theophilus. 842. *Emperor of the West.* Lewis the Debonnaire. 840. *King of Spain.* Alfonso the Chaste. 844. *Kings of England.* The heptarchy ended towards the year 828, when Egbert united the seven kingdoms. Egbert. 837. Ethelwolf. 857. *Kings of Sweden.* Biron III. towards the year 816. In the reign of this prince, Charlemain sent Herbert to preach the gospel in Sweden. Bratemund. 827. Siward II. towards 834. Heroth. 856.
Judith, daughter of count Welphus, a Bavarian lord.	CHARLES the BALD.		

REMARKABLE EVENTS under LEWIS I.

An ordinance exempting religious houses from *presents*, and from *military service*.

The emperor confirms the donations made to the popes, notwithstanding Stephen V. and Paschal I. had taken possession of the pontificate, without waiting, as had been the custom, till their election was confirmed.

818. 19. &c.

Lewis having vanquished the Gascons, Bretons, and Hungarians, marries a second wife, (819) Judith, a Bavarian princess, whose gallantry and ambition proved the source of all his misfortunes.

Bernard, provoked that his grandfather should confer the imperial dignity on Lewis the Debonnaire, in preference to himself, who was the issue of the eldest son, and seeing the new disposition made by Lewis the Debonnaire in favour of Lotharius, (in 830) had recourse to arms: the emperor marched against him, took him prisoner, and caused his eyes to be put out: Bernard died of the operation; and the kingdom of Italy was re-united to the crown of France. There are authors who pretend that this kingdom, which had been founded by the Lombards, was never annexed to the Gallic crown, but that it only continued to be dependent on it: and one of their proofs is, that the succeeding emperors took the iron crown of the kingdom of Italy, or Lombardy, independently of the imperial crown of Rome, or that of Germany. (*Sigonius. Muratori*). The title of *Vicount* began to be known in the person of Cixilane, vicount of Narbonne, who had hitherto taken only the appellation of *vidame*, *vice dominus*.

822.

The emperor does public penance at Attigni, to expiate Bernard's death. He thought proper to give this mark of repentance to the discontented prelates, whose influence on the minds of the people was all-powerful. We are surprized to see the bishops possessed of so great an authority; but it is for want of recollecting that this very authority was most serviceable to our kings at the beginning of the monarchy.

" The bishops, says the abbé du Bos, had a great share in the ma-
" nagement of public affairs, and presided at the deliberations of
" the

The SECOND RACE.

WARRIORS.	MAGISTRATES.	EMINENT and LEARNED MEN.
Gourdon Baulande. Charles of Argies. William Roſtrenan. Adhalard. Betheric. Bernard of Vincro.	*Arch-chancellors.* Hiliſachar. Fridegiſe. Theudo. Hugh.	S. Adalhard. 826. S. Agobard. 840. Amalarius, deacon of Metz. 837. S. Benedict, abbot of Anian. 821. Dodana, dutcheſs of Septimania, and wife of count Bernard, towards 842. Dungal. 834. Eginhard, towards 840. Theodulphus, biſhop of Orleans. 821.

REMARKABLE EVENTS under LEWIS I.

"the people, and in all their undertakings, not as chiefs of the Christian religion, but as principal citizens." The decline of the Roman empire, rendered the nations, hitherto subject to that government, sensible of the necessity of looking out for a new master; the Gauls, surrounded by Arian princes, had reason to be jealous both of their liberty and religion: and then it was that Clovis made his appearance: "The clergy, if they "must have a barbarian for their master, would prefer a pagan "prince to an heretic; the pagan religion was visibly on the "decline; and it was more probable to expect the conversion of "an idolatrous prince, than of one that professed the errors of "Arianism. Besides, as there was no affinity between the pagan "and Christian religion, the heathen priests could not desire "their princes to put them in possession of the churches built "and endowed by Christians; but this is what the bishops "had most to apprehend from the Arians." Thus their interest and credit jointly co-operated with the arms of our first king. The beginnings of a monarchy are generally so feeble, as to stand in need of the hand that assisted in laying the foundation and Clovis had too much sense not to let the bishops preserve that authority over the minds of the people, which had turned so greatly to his advantage: hence it is that the clergy continue to preserve such an influence in matters of state.

Further, the power which the bishops possessed in France became much greater in Germany, and was better preserved. As the German bishops, for the most part, were either sovereigns or great lords, it is incredible how much they were encouraged by the first emperors of that nation, from a persuasion that it was the best way of securing the fidelity of their subjects. From the same principle they created new bishops in conquered countries, imagining they should exalt the spiritual power, by the splendor of temporal authority.

Lewis sends his son Lotharius to command in Italy.

823. 24. 25. &c.

Lotharius is crowned emperor on Easterday by pope Paschal.

The northern nations continue subject to the emperor, and the Danes receive a king (Harold) from his hand. Pope Eugen

) to accept of the confirmation of his elec-
ius makes high complaints againſt this be-
igious ſtorm of hail, (825) followed by
h was generally felt in France and Ger-

827. &c.

eſires the emperor to confirm his election:
ove what M. de Marca has advanced againſt his
ly, that although the king remitted the power
: clergy and the people, yet the confecration
deferred till he had given his confent. *(Mar-*
.)
Navarre, whom the emperor had neglected to
eir neighbours, chufe for themſelves a king
the foundation of the kingdom of Navarre and
erity, after expelling the Moors and Saracens,
spaniſh monarchy under Charles the Fifth.
early as the year 800 was poſſeſſed of Weſſex,
ngdoms to which the Heptarchy was reduced,
rovinces of Great Britain*, under the title of
which put an end to the heptarchy.

830.

d, the emperor's fon by his fecond wife Judith,
re in the former partition, obtained Alemania,
ætia, and part of Burgundy, which were dif-
the dominions of his three brothers. Theſe
nded at this diviſion; and alledged as a reafon,
f their ſtep-mother, who, they faid, was guilty
vith Bernard, count of Barcelona: they pre-
the honour of their father, who, infenfible of
family, had conferred the principal employ-
ngdom, together with his whole confidence,
brought difgrace upon his name. But inſtead
:aufe, they ſtripped him of his dominions. Pe-
far as Verberie †, obliged his father and his wife

tain, but the fouth part of the ifland only, for he had no do-

†, a royal feat in Valois, on the river Oife, and in the diocefe

Judith,

Judith to retire to a monastery, and with great difficulty complied with their request for allowing them some time, before they put on the religious habit; a delay which contributed to their restoration.

The jealousy of the three brothers, and the haughtiness of Lotharius, saved Lewis the Debonnaire, who with the assistance of Gombaud the monk, is restored to his crown in a diet held at Nimeguen, where Lotharius was excluded from his partnership in the imperial dignity.

831. &c.

The emperor takes his wife out of the convent, in which she had been forced to assume a religious habit; and both for his own honour, as well as for Judith's, he makes her swear that she is innocent of all the crimes laid to her charge, besides submitting herself to the *Ordeal*, or trial by fire.

It is proper to mention a word or two, in regard to these *Ordeals*, which appear so absurd to us at present, and shew the weakness of the human understanding. This was the method our forefathers contrived to ascertain the truth of facts. The person accused had several ways to clear himself; the easiest was his oath: indeed, if the judge paid no regard to that, he gave orders for combat; the vanquished person was judged guilty, and underwent the punishment due to the crime, of which he had been accused, or been the accuser. But what is more extraordinary, when the parties did not chuse to defend their cause themselves, there were professed bravos, called champions, into whose hands they committed their fate. Another trial was that of hot iron: the iron was blessed, and carefully preserved in some religious houses; for all of them were not honoured with this privilege. There was likewise the trial of boiling and cold water; but this was only for the common people. So far in regard to criminal cases. But who could imagine, that in civil matters, and such as related to the police, they should have recourse to this manner of decision? In Germany, if they want to know whether the representation ought to take place in a direct line, opinions are divided, and the point must be determined by combat. In Spain, if the question is, which of the two deserves

REMARKABLE EVENTS under LEWIS I.

ferves the preference, the Roman or the Mofarabic office, it is decreed, that a combat fhall end the difpute. This decifion appeared extravagant, and with good reafon; but the other method was equally ridiculous; namely, their decreeing that the two liturgies fhould be thrown into the fire, and that which ftood the violence of the flames, fhould have the preference.

833. 34.

The emperor's three fons confpire againft him a fecond time; and join their troops in a plain between Bafil and Strafburg, fince called the *field of lies*: pope Gregory IV. having, according to feveral authors, efpoufed their caufe, and confented to follow their camp, they feized the emperor's perfon, who finding himfelf deferted by the whole army, was obliged to abdicate: from thence they conducted him to St. Medard at Soiffons, where he was clad in a penitential habit; Judith they banifhed to Tortona, and confined young Charles to the abbey of Prum. But new divifions among the three brothers (834), preferved the emperor once more; fo that he was reftored to his crown in the church of St. Denis, and had alfo the pleafure of being reftored to his wife. Lotharius, refufing to approve of this refettlement, retires into Burgundy, where he affembles a few troops, but at length is obliged to fubmit to his father, who forgives him.

835. 36. 37. &c.

The emperor finding himfelf infirm and declining, makes a new partition among his children, ftill without nominating a fucceffor to the empire. To Lotharius he gives Italy, to Lewis Germany and Saxony, to Pepin Aquitaine, and to Charles France and Burgundy; this divifion gave frefh offence to the three eldeft brothers, with whom he was obliged to renew the war. Pepin dies (838), and the emperor to punifh that prince's two fons, for the faults of their father, or rather, to pleafe Judith, gives Pepin's fpoils to his fon Charles, in prejudice to his grandchildren. The nobility of Aquitaine could not bear fo flagrant an act of injuftice: the emperor marched an army into their country, and obliged them to fubmit; while his fon, Lewis of Bavaria, taking advantage of this diverfion, feized all the towns that suited his conveniency. Lewis, however, was obliged to turn back, in order to stop the course of his father's conquests.

840.

This expedition of Lewis the Debonnaire against his own son, the king of Bavaria, proved fatal to the unfortunate father. He had conceived a dislike to this last journey, and was greatly shocked at the unnatural behaviour of his children, with whom he was obliged to be perpetually at war : a total eclipse of the sun happened upon his march, which terrified him to the highest degree, his imagination being already weakened by his misfortunes and by superstition, so that he died at length with vexation and fasting, after an illness of forty days.

Among the capitularies of this prince, we meet with a constitution concerning the monasteries, which obliges them to assist in relieving the necessities of the state.

Lewis the Debonnaire restored to the clergy of his kingdom the liberty of elections, and only reserved to himself the right of confirming them. He did more in favour of the popes; for he allowed them to take possession of the supreme pontificate, without waiting for his confirmation. Upon which occasion Pasquier makes the following remark : *The Italians, while they aggrandized themselves at our expence, were not sparing of fine words, but attributed this to piety and devotion, and therefore honoured him with the Latin epithet* Pius : *in France the men of sense and knowledge of the world, imputed it to want of courage, and for this reason called him the* Debonnaire, *covering his pusillanimity with another name. And now I am upon this subject, I remember to have heard Henry III. frequently declare, that one could not offend him more than by giving him the title of* Debonnaire, *because this word implied stupidity or foolishness.* Henry III. had reason to be afraid of such a reproach. It was the misfortune of both those princes to live at a time, when courage and resolution would have been more serviceable to them, than some other qualities, for which they were worthy of esteem.

Lewis the Debonnaire was reckoned a good astronomer : he is said to have been the first who discovered a comet, that appeared

REMARKABLE EVENTS under LEWIS I.

peared towards the year 837. He was indeed a very learned prince for his time, and deeply verfed in the laws. His death being occafioned, as it is faid, by the terror of an eclipfe, is not at all inconfiftent with his knowledge of aftronomy; the human mind is fufceptible of every abfurdity; this prince might believe that a particular event was connected with a natural caufe; and befides, the underftanding and the imagination are independent of each other. M. Pafchal ufed to fancy himfelf always clofe to a precipice.

In order to judge of the price of gold and filver at that time, it will be fufficient to mention two facts. At the council of Touloufe held in 846, the contribution which every parifh prieft was obliged to give to his bifhop, viz. a bufhel of wheat, a bufhel of barley, a meafure of wine, and a lamb, was valued at two fous, which the bifhop might take in lieu of the above articles. The fecond fact is, that Charles the Bald publifhed an edict at Poiffy in 864, in an affembly of the people (for thus we are to underftand thefe words *ex confenfu*) ordaining a new coinage; and as the old money was cried down by this edict, he ordered fifty livres (or pounds) of filver to be taken out of his coffers, for the circulation of commerce. Thefe facts are the more deferving of notice, as we obferved in 628. 29. the magnificence of the court of king Dagobert: and one would imagine that gold and filver, inftead of diminifhing, ought to have been more common in France fince the reign of Charlemain, whofe increafe of power muft have undoubtedly extended the commerce of his fubjects. This would be a proper matter of differtation, but the form of our prefent work will not admit of it.

Some writers pretend, that Lewis the Debonnaire had a natural fon, named Arnoul, whom he created count of Sens: but father Anfelme takes no notice of him.

840.

REMARKABLE EVENTS.

840.
Accession to the crown.

CHARLES II, *surnamed the* BALD, *son of Judith, the second wife of Lewis the Debonnaire, ascends the throne at the age of seventeen, in the year 840, and was crowned at Rome, by pope John VIII, the 25th of December, 875.*

840. 41.

CHARLES the Bald and Lewis of Bavaria enter into an alliance against the emperor Lotharius, who wants to encroach upon them. Pepin's son attempts to recover Aquitaine from Charles the Bald, whose tranquillity is likewise disturbed by the Bretons and by the Normans.

Lotharius having in vain endeavoured to attack his brother Lewis, king of Bavaria, falls upon Neustria, obliges Charles the Bald to yield up part of that province, and conclude a truce with him. The battle of Fontenay in Burgundy, in which Charles the Bald and Lewis of Bavaria are victorious over Lotharius and young Pepin: but they do not improve their victory. Some authors pretend, that in order to repair the loss of the nobility, who perished on that fatal day, it was established by the ancient customs of Champagne, that henceforward the *venter*, that is the mother, should ennoble the children, though their father was a peasant, or plebeian. This manner of ennobling rendered the issue capable of feudal tenures; but there was still this difference between them and the gentlemen by *parage*, that is *by the father*, that they could not be knighted like the latter (*Beaumanoir.*) This same battle gave occasion to another law, that the nobility should not be obliged to attend the king in the field, except in case of defending the state against a foreign invasion. (See the *Spirit of laws.*)

842. 43. 44.

Lotharius misses the opportunity of cutting Charles's army in pieces. At length the three brothers conclude a peace: Charles the Bald keeps Aquitaine and Neustria; Lewis has
Germany

The Second Race. 69

Wives.	Children.	877. Death.	Cotemporary Princes.
Hermintrudis. 899.	LEWIS the Stammerer. Charles. 865. Lotharius. 866. Carloman, who had his eyes put out by order of his father. 866. Judith, married first to Ethelwolf, king of England, and afterwards to Baldwin I, earl of Flanders, having been sent back, according to the English historians, by her first husband's son, to whom she had been joined in second wedlock. Her first marriage with Ethelwolf was not consummated, upon account of her youth.	CHARLES the BALD died in repassing the Alps, poisoned by his own physician Zedechias, the 5th or 6th of October 877, at the age of fifty-four; he had been king of France 38 years, and 2 years emperor; his bones were interred at St. Denis, of which monastery he had been abbot.	*Popes.* Gregory IV. 843. Sergius II. 847. Leo IV. 855. Next to this pope used to be placed pope Joan. Benedict III. 858. Nicholas I. 867. Adrian II. 872. John VIII. 882. *Emperors of the East.* Theophilus. 842. Michael. 867. Basil I. 886. Constantine VIII. 878. Leo VI. 911. *Emperors of the West.* Lotharius. 855. Lewis II. 875. Charles the Bald. 877. *Kings of Spain.* Alfonso II. 844. Ramir. 851. Ordugno. 862. Alfonso the Great. 910. *Kings of England.* Ethelwolf. 857. Ethelbald. 860. Ethelbert. 865. Ethelred. 872. Alfred the Great. 899. *Kings of Scotland.* Kenneth II. 855. Under this prince the kingdom of Scotland was enlarged by the destruction of that of the Picts. Donald V. 858. Constantine II. 874. Ethus. 875. Gregory. 892. *Kings of Sweden.* Heroth. 865. Charles VI. 868. Biorn IV. 883.
Richildis, sister of Boso, king of Arles or Provence, for this country had not as yet taken the name of kingdom of Arles. (D. Planchet.)	Pepin, Dreux, Lewis, Charles, } died young.		

REMARKABLE EVENTS under CHARLES the Bald.

Germany, whence he was called *Germanicus*; and Lotharius, the elder brother, had together with the title of emperor, Italy, and (in express terms) the city of Rome; he likewise was possessed of Provence, Franche Comté, the Lyonnois, and other countries inclosed by the Rhone, the Rhine, the Saone, the Meuse, and the Schelde. Bernard, count of Barcelona, so well known for his attachment to the empress Judith, and to her son Charles the Bald, is put to death at Toulouse by that very same Charles, against whom he had taken up arms.

845. 46. &c.

Pope Sergius II. is consecrated, without waiting for the confirmation of the emperor. The bishops would not approve of the consecration, till they had made a rule, that this should not be a precedent.

Nomenoe, who had been instituted duke of Britany by Lewis the Debonnaire, availing himself of the disturbances in France, obtains considerable advantages over Charles the Bald, and takes the title of king. He is succeeded in this kingdom by his son, Herispoe, in spite of Charles the Bald, who was able to preserve no more than the supreme jurisdiction or right of homage over this province. Salomon, cousin and successor of Herispoe, whom he murdered, continues to pay tribute to king Charles for Britany, *pursuant to ancient custom*; which are the words of the annals of St. Bertin. Some pretend that Nomenoe did nothing more than restore things to their former state; that Britany was not a fief originally detached from the crown, nor usurped from our kings, like the other provinces of France, which the governors converted into seignories or lordships, and over which in process of time they made themselves sovereigns; and therefore that when Britany became a fief dependent on the crown, the princes of that country still were possessed of the sovereignty, which being originally independent, could not be subject to re-unions, as was the case of fiefs usurped by subjects: be that as it may, the dispute is a matter of no consequence in our times, and may, in my opinion, be sufficiently decided by a passage out of Gregory of Tours, the father of our history, who says, *that the Bretons were always subject*

Ministers.	Warriors.	Magistrates.	Eminent and Learned Men.
Robert le Fort, or the Valiant.	Bouchard. Protade. Grillon. Hadige. Robert, earl of Anjou. Remelus.	*Arch-chancellors.* Ebroin, bishop of Poitiers. Lewis, son to a natural daughter of Charlemain. Gaucelin.	Ado. 874. Florus. 855. Freculfus, towards 852. Gotescalchus, towards 870. Hilduinus. 842. Jonas, bishop of Orleans. 842. Lupus. 853. Methodius. 847. Nithardus. 859. Pascasius Ratbertus. 865. Rabanus Maurus, archbishop of Mentz. 856. Ratramne, towards 868. Walefridus. 859.

REMARKABLE EVENTS under CHARLES the Bald.

subject to the power of the French after the death of *Clovis*, and their chiefs were called counts, and not kings.

850. &c.

Lotharius wages war with the Moors and Saracens, who were become masters of Benevento. Charles the Bald being engaged against the Normans, who had made irruptions into his kingdom, is dispossessed once more of Aquitaine by Pepin: but this prince is soon stripped of his conquest, and Charles orders him to be shaved, and shut up (852) in the abbey of St. Medard at Soissons.

Pope Leo IV. not only exhibits signal instances of his courage in defending Rome against the Saracens, but enlarges and embellishes that capital: he gave his name to a quarter of Rome, which was called the Leonine city. A modern author of universal history draws a beautiful character of this pontiff: " He
" shewed himself, by defending Rome, worthy of being its sove-
" reign. He was a Roman by birth; and the courage of the
" early ages of the republic seemed to be revived in him, at a
" time of cowardice and corruption : like one of the noble
" monuments of ancient Rome, which are sometimes found
" among the ruins of the modern city *."

853. 54.

The Normans commit horrid ravages in France.

Pepin having made his escape out of prison, returns to Aquitaine, where he is taken prisoner: he was conducted to Charles the Bald, who ordered him to be confined at Senlis, and at the same time caused all his sons to be shaved.

The people of Aquitaine having no longer Pepin to set up in opposition to Charles the Bald, invite the son of Lewis the Germanic: Charles vanquishes them, and sends his son, as yet an infant, into their country, in order to keep them within bounds; but they rebel against him.

855. &c.

The emperor Lotharius dies, after putting on the monastic habit in the abbey of Prum, hoping thereby to make the world

---

* Voltaire, Universal history, vol, 1, c, 18.

forget

REMARKABLE EVENTS under CHARLES the Bald.

forget that he had treated his father in a barbarous manner, that he had insulted religion, that he had persecuted his brothers, and been the cause of almost all the misfortunes with which Europe had been long afflicted. He leaves three sons behind him. Lewis II, whom he had made his collegue, succeeds him in Italy and in the imperial dignity; Lotharius in the kingdom of Lorrain, which took its name from this prince; and Charles in the kingdom of Provence. The death of Ethelwolf, king of England, who having made a journey to Rome some years before, subjected his kingdom to the tribute called Peter's pence. The popes afterwards demanded it as their due, and it was not suppressed till the reign of Henry VIII.

Lewis the Germanic seeing his brother Charles employed in opposing the Bretons, falls upon him unawares, and makes himself master of part of Neustria. Charles recovers this country again, and these two princes conclude a peace by the mediation of young Lotharius, their nephew, king of Lorrain.

Robert *le Fort* or the *Valiant*, whose original has given rise to so many different opinions, the great grandfather of Hugh Capet, obtains the government of what was then called the dutchy of France. Baldwin, great forester or ranger of France, runs away with the daughter of Charles the Bald, and widow of a king of England; after a good deal of difficulty, he gains the king's permission to marry her, and is made earl of Flanders. Lotharius, king of Lorrain, puts away his wife, to marry his concubine, Waltrada. This prince had reason to be jealous of both his uncles, who only waited for an opportunity to invade his dominions. Nicholas I. taking advantage of these circumstances, threatens to excommunicate Lotharius, unless he breaks off with Waltrada.

867. 68. &c.

Nicholas I. dies; and Adrian II. is moved by the submission of Lotharius, who goes to Rome to demand absolution. The schism of the Greek church. The cause of this separation was the chimerical claim of superiority, which the patriarch of Constantinople formed over the see of Rome. This mighty dispute had been decided at the council of Constantinople under the

REMARKABLE EVENTS under CHARLES the Bald.

the emperor Theodofius, but the bifhops of that city revived their pretenfions from time to time: at length Photius the eunuch, who intruded himfelf into the fee of Conftantinople in the room of the patriarch Ignatius, finding a favourable opportunity, renewed the attempt once more, and, confcious that he fhould never be able to obtain the precedency, endeavoured to render his fee independent. This he effected by feparating himfelf from the communion of Rome; which was productive of what we call the Greek fchifm. Photius experienced great viciffitudes of fortune, for the fee of Conftantinople was as tottering at that time as the throne: and he died at length in exile. His death only fufpended, but did not extinguifh the divifion: it was renewed feveral times, till the throne of Conftantinople was poffeffed by the Latins: then the emperor Baldwin having procured the election of a Latin patriarch, the eaftern and weftern churches were united. But this union lafted only during the Latin empire, that is, the fpace of fifty years; at the expiration of which the emperor Paleologus, having retaken Conftantinople in 1261, feparated himfelf again from the Roman communion. This renewal of the fchifm was of long continuance, and did not terminate till the year 1439, at the council of Florence. And even then the union of the two churches, being founded on the diftreffes of the Greek emperor, who wanted the pope's affiftance againft the Turks, was difavowed by the whole empire; fo that it can hardly be faid to have taken place: however fuch was the ftate of the Chriftian religion in the eaft, when it was banifhed from thence by Mahomet II, who made himfelf mafter of Conftantinople in 1453. From that period Mahometifm has been the eftablifhed religion of Afia; Chriftianity has ever fince been only tolerated; and the Greek patriarchs have continued fchifmatics.

Lotharius, king of Lorrain, dies (869) without legitimate iffue, and by his death the kingdoms of Lorrain and Provence, which he had inherited of his brother, are become vacant. The emperor is not in a fituation to make good his claim to his brother's fucceffion, his hands being full in Italy. His uncles, Charles the Bald and Lewis the Germanic, take advantage of this conjuncture.

875.

REMARKABLE EVENTS under CHARLES the Bald.

875. 76. 77.

The emperor Lewis II. dies at Milan, without male issue, and is followed soon after by Lewis the Germanic, one of the most virtuous and greatest princes that ever reigned in Germany. Charles the Bald marches into Italy, and obtains the imperial crown, notwithstanding the strong opposition of Carloman, the son of Lewis the Germanic, who was obliged to abide by his father's partition, the particulars of which are still extant in the famous map, published by father Sirmond, and justly esteemed by the literati the most valuable remains of geography in the middle age. The continuators of Eutropius, and not Eutropius himself, as father Daniel observes, are the only writers who advance, that Charles the Bald purchased the imperial crown, by renouncing, in favour of the Roman see, his right to that part of Italy, which was dependent on the western empire, such as the dutchies of Benevento and Spoleto, and likewise by relinquishing his right of presiding at the papal elections. True it is, he agreed to date the commencement of his reign from the day on which he was crowned by the pope; *(Labbe's councils)* an epoch which afterwards turned out so greatly to the advantage of the see of Rome. *(See the year* 1336.) Charles the Bald gets the daughter of Lewis II. into his possession, and marries her to Boso, his brother-in-law. The three sons of Lewis the Germanic share the kingdom of Bavaria among them: Charles the Bald, attempting to profit by their father's decease, and to recover what he had ceded in the last partition of the kingdom of Lorrain, is defeated by Lewis, the second son of the deceased king.

The chroniclers of the time take notice that the fair of *Landi*, which had been established by Charlemain at Aix-la-Chapelle, was transferred by Charles the Bald to St. Denis, and they have been followed by all modern writers. But the abbé de Beuf has discovered that the fair of *Landi*, called originally the Indiction, was instituted in the year 1109.

Under the reign of this prince has been usually placed the fable of pope Joan, between the pontificate of Leo IV. and that of Benedict III, an absurd fable, which destroys itself, and which no body will be any longer at the trouble of refuting.

REMARKABLE EVENTS under CHARLES the Bald.

Charles the Bald died at Brios, a village on this side of mount Cenis, poisoned by a Jew physician, named Zedechias, in whom he had reposed an entire confidence. History does not inform us whether this physician was ever punished; neither do we know what could have been his instigation to commit such a crime. This prince, who knew not how to maintain the rights of his crown against the see of Rome, was as much at a loss to defend them against his own subjects, and he gave a deadly blow to the royal authority, by rendering dignities and titles hereditary.

He was buried in the priory of Nantua, in the diocese of Lyons, and seven years after his bones were removed to St. Denis, where he desired to be interred, because he had been abbot of that place.

The council of Savonnieres, in 859, gives this prince the title of the *Most Christian King:* pope Stephen II. had already conferred the same on Pepin in 755: but it did not become the peculiar appellation of our sovereigns till 1469, when it was claimed by Lewis XI. exclusively of other princes. And now we are upon this subject, it may be observed, that Pepin and Charlemain called themselves kings by the *Divine Clemency*, whereas our princes of the third race stile themselves in their ordinances, *Kings by the Grace of God*, not only from their regard to religion, but moreover to signify their independency on the pope, who used formerly to claim the right of disposing of crowns.

877.

REMARKABLE EVENTS.

877.
Accession to the crown.

LEWIS II, *surnamed the* STAMMERER, *son of Hermintrudis, the first wife of Charles the Bald, ascends the throne, about the age of thirty-one, in the year 877. He was crowned at Compiegne by Hincmar, archbishop of Rheims.*
He was crowned emperor by pope John VIII.

877. 78. 79.

DISPUTES arise about the imperial dignity between Lewis the Stammerer and his cousin-german, Carloman, eldest son of Lewis the Germanic. Lewis the Stammerer is crowned king of France anew, in a council held at Troyes by John VIII, who escaped into France, after having in vain endeavoured to support Lewis's right to the empire. Richildis, the second wife of his father, Charles the Bald, joined those who grumbled for not having had a share in the largesses, which this prince had inconsiderately bestowed upon his accession to the crown. Of these Boso, the brother of Richildis, was the most formidable. In order to reconcile the minds of the malecontents, Lewis found himself under the necessity of dismembering great part of his demesnes; and from thence arose so many seignories, dutchies and counties possessed by private persons. This is believed to be the original of the counts of Anjou, of whom Ingelger was the founder; of the dukes of Britany, whose founder was Alain the Great; and of the dukes of Burgundy and counts of Provence, who sprung from Boso. Lewis the Stammerer at his death left his second wife pregnant of a son, who was Charles the Simple.

The duke of Spoleto and the marquis of Tuscany contributed greatly to raise Carloman, the son of Lewis the Germanic, to the imperial dignity, if it can be said that this prince was ever emperor, *for history makes but very obscure mention of it (Daniel).* This however is certain, that after his death, his brother, Charles the Fat, was emperor; and the latter was succeeded by Arnulphus, the bastard son of Carloman.

The end of this race affording nothing but a scene of trouble and confusion, we have changed the form

The Second Race.

WIVES.	CHILDREN.	879. DEATH.	Cotemporary PRINCES.
Anſgardis, a woman of mean extraction, from whom Lewis the Stammerer was divorced by order of his father, Charles the Bald, though he had two ſons by her, who ſucceeded to the crown. Adelaid, by whom he had a ſon, who did not ſucceed immediately.	LEWIS. CARLOMAN. Theſe two princes divide the monarchy between them. Carloman ſurvived Lewis. CHARLES the SIMPLE.	LEWIS the STAMMERER dies on the 10th of April, 879, at Compiegne, aged about three and thirty. He is interred in the abbey of St. Corneille.	*Pope.* John VIII. 882. *Emperors of the Eaſt.* { Baſil I. 886. { Leo VI. 911. *The empire of the Weſt conteſted by* Lewis the Stammerer. 877. and Carloman. 880. *King of Spain.* Alfonſo the Great. 910. *King of England.* Alfred the Great. 899. *King of Scotland.* Gregory. 892. *King of Sweden.* Biorn IV. 883.

of this abridgment, and resumed that which we observed in the history of the first race.

LEWIS III. and CARLOMAN.

879.

Lewis III. and Carloman, both of them sons of Ansgardis, whom Lewis the Stammerer had repudiated by order of his father, ascend the throne by means of Boso, who had married his daughter to Carloman: the two brothers shared the kingdom between them, and lived always in strict union. Lewis had Neustria, and part of Burgundy; Carloman had Aquitaine, and Septimania. There were some who stickled for the rights of Charles the Simple, a posthumous son; grounding his claim on the repudiation of Ansgardis: but the disturbances of the kingdom would not admit of an infant sovereign. This divorce of Ansgardis induced several to say, that Lewis and Carloman were bastards: it is mentioned in the genealogical history of the house of France, that their mother Ansgardis was the daughter of count Harduin; in proof of which the annals of St. Bertin, and Reginon are quoted.

Boso, brother-in-law of Charles the Bald, and son-in-law to the emperor Lewis II. establishes the kingdom of Arles, which comprehended Provence, Dauphiné, the Lyonnois, Savoy, Franche Comté, and great part of the dukedom of Burgundy.

Lewis and Carloman enter into an alliance against Boso, and vanquish him in several battles.

880. &c.

Lewis of Germany, the second son of Lewis the Germanic, makes war against Lewis and Carloman, who are obliged to resign to him that part of Lorrain, which had been enjoyed by Charles the Bald, and by Lewis the

Cotemporary PRINCES.

Popes.
John VIII.   882.
Marinus I.   884.
Adrian III. 885.
Emperors of the East.
{ Basil I.   886.
{ Leo VI.   911.
Emperor of the West.
Charles the Fat. 888.
King of Spain.
Alfonso the Great. 910.
King of England.
Alfred the Great. 899.
King of Scotland.
Gregory.   892.
Kings of Sweden.
Biorn IV.   883.
Ingellus.   891.

LEWIS III. and CARLOMAN.

the Stammerer. By the death of the emperor Carloman, his brother Charles the Fat succeeds to the imperial crown. The Normans continue their ravages in France; but Lewis III. gains a victory over them on the banks of the Schelde.

882. &c.

Lewis III. dying without issue, is interred at St. Denis, and leaves his brother Carloman sole king of France. This prince and Charles the Fat unite against the Normans, who desolated the kingdom by continual irruptions; but they are forced to grant some advantages to those invaders.

884.

Carloman, who succeeded his brother Lewis III, is killed by a wild boar; the annalist of Fulda says it was by one of his guards; he lies interred at St. Denis. Charles the Fat inherits the kingdom of France.

Some pretend that this was only a regency, which is the reason that I have not called him Charles III.

CHARLES the Fat.

CHARLES the *Fat*, son of Lewis the Germanic, and uncle, as we now phrase it, after the custom of Britany, to Charles the Simple, was already possessed of the imperial crown, when he was made king of France, in prejudice to Charles the Simple, and enjoyed almost as great an extent of dominions as Charlemain; but being too weak to bear such good fortune, he sunk under its weight.

885. &c.

The Normans undertake the siege of Paris, which lasts two years: Charles concludes an ignominious treaty with them, in consequence of which they raise the siege.

888.

Cotemporary
PRINCES.

Popes.
Adrian III. 885.
Stephen VI. 891.
Emperors of the East.
{ Basil I. 886.
{ Leo VI. 911.
Emperor of the West.
Charles the Fat. 888.
King of Spain.
Alfonso the Great 910.
King of England.
Alfred the Great. 899.
King of Scotland.
Gregory. 892.
King of Sweden.
Ingellus. 891.

CHARLES the Fat.

888.

Charles dies without issue, the scorn and contempt of his people. He was interred in the abbey of Richenaw, *Augia dives*, situate in an island of the lake of Constance. He had been solemnly divested of the imperial dignity. Arnold, a bastard son of the emperor Carloman, succeeds him in the imperial crown, to the prejudice of Charles the Simple, who saw himself excluded from every throne under pretence of his tender age; for which reason he did not succeed this time to Charles the Fat, in the kingdom of France.

EUDES.

888. &c.

EUDES, count of Paris, and son of Robert le *Fort*, is proclaimed king at an assembly held in Compiegne, and crowned by Walter, archbishop of Sens, to the prejudice of Charles the Simple. Goslin, bishop of Paris, had gained great honour, by his gallant behaviour in assisting Eudes, to defend that city against the Normans. Rodolphus, son of Conrad, count of Paris, erects the second kingdom of Burgundy, called *Burgundia Transjurana*, which comprehended the western part of Swisserland, from the river Russ, with the country of Valais, Geneva, Savoy, and Bugey. Boson had before erected the first kingdom, called *Burgundia Cisjurana*. Besides there was the dukedom of Burgundy, which we must not confound with the other two kingdoms. Eudes not having united the suffrages of the whole nation in his favour, is cited to Worms before the emperor Arnold, who is content with his submission, and leaves him in peaceable possession of the kingdom.

892.

Cotemporary PRINCES.

Popes.
Stephen VI. 891.
Formosus. 896.
Boniface VI. 896.
Emperor of the East.
Leo VI. 911.
Emperors of the West.
Charles the Fat. 888.
Arnold. 899.
King of Spain.
Alfonso the Great 910.
King of England.
Alfred the Great. 899.
Kings of Scotland.
Gregory. 892.
Donald VI. 903.
Kings of Sweden.
Ingellus. 891.
Olaus, towards 900.

EUDES.

892. &c.

Eudes routs the Normans, and yet is obliged to grant them advantageous conditions. He attacks the malecontents in the city of Laon, who wanted to proclaim Charles the Simple king. Fowk, archbishop of Rheims, reconciles the two princes. Eudes kept the provinces between the Seine and the Pyrenean mountains; while the country between the Seine and the Meuse, was left in possession of Charles the Simple: still these two princes continued to wage war against each other.

The body of pope Formosus is taken out of the grave (896), and undergoes a form of trial, under pretence that he had been transferred from a bishopric to the popedom, a thing, as they said, altogether unprecedented. Yet so early as the third century, we find that Alexander, bishop of Jerusalem, set the first example of a translation from one see to another, as well as of a co-djutor to a living prelate.

898.

Eudes dies at la Ferre, at the age of forty, and lies interred at St. Denis.

CHARLES III, surnamed the Simple.

898. &c.

AS the legitimacy of Lewis and Carloman was contested, because their mother had been repudiated, the like contest was raised, and perhaps with better foundation, against the birth of Charles the Simple, under pretence that his father had begot him by a second wife, while the first was yet living.

Charles the Simple, who had been crowned king so early as the year 893, begins to be despised, for not

---

Cotemporary PRINCES.

Popes.
Formosus. 896.
Boniface VI. 896.
Stephen VIII. 900.
Emperor of the East.
Leo VI. 911.
Emperors of the West.
Charles the Fat. 888.
Arnold. 899.
King of Spain.
Alfonso the Great 910.
King of England.
Alfred the Great. 899.
Kings of Scotland.
Gregory. 892.
Donald VI. 903.
Kings of Sweden.
Ingellus. 891.
Olaus, towards 909.

CHARLES the Simple.

not making a proper use of the advantages he had obtained over Zuentibold, duke of Lorrain, a bastard son of Arnold. The emperor Arnold dies, and is succeeded by his son Lewis IV.

901. 2. 3. &c.

Intestine wars break out among the nobility of the kingdom, which the king is unable to prevent.

910. 11.

William, count of Auvergne, and duke of Aquitaine, founds the abbey of Cluny.

912. &c.

The Normans, enticed by the hope of plunder, continued to make descents upon France, and to commit depredations. King Charles, moved by the representations of his people, who sighed for peace upon any condition whatever, at length concluded the famous treaty of St. Clair upon the Epte; whereby he gives his daughter Giselle in marriage to Rollo, the chief of those barbarians, with part of Neustria, which had already taken the name of Normandy, and of which this Rollo was the first duke; upon condition that he should yield homage to him for that province, and embrace the Christian religion. Rollo likewise demanded that the direct and immediate lordship of Britany should be yielded to him, subject however to the supreme jurisdiction of the crown of France; to which it became a rear-fief or mesne-tenure, by virtue of that treaty. But Britany having been afterwards erected into a dutchy and peerage by Philip the Fair in 1297, in favour of John II, ceased, according to the nature of peerages, to be a mesne tenure; so that it no longer depended on the king on account of Normandy, but on account of the crown. Some pretend that this judiciary clause, the

Cotemporary PRINCES.

Popes.
Stephen VIII. 900
Romanus. 900
Theodore. 901
John IX. 905
Benedict IV. 907
Leo V. 907
Christopher. 907
Sergius III. 910
Anastasius III. 911
Lando. 913
John X. 921

Emperors of t. East.
Leo VI. 911
Alexander. 911
Constantine IX. 961

Emperors of t West.
Lewis IV, the la emperor of t French. 911
Conrad I. 911
Henry I. 931

Kings of Spain.
Alfonso the Great 911
Garcia. 911
Ordugno II. 911

King of England.
Edward the Eld. 921

Kings of Scotla.
Donald VI. 901
Constantine III 911

Kings of Swee.
Ingo II. towa 911
Eric VI. towa 911
Eric VII. towa 911

CHARLES the Simple.

the *cry of Haro*[*], is derived from Rollo, whose equity was not inferior to his valour, and whose very name had an effect upon his subjects after his decease. The emperor Lewis IV. departs this life, and the imperial dignity is transferred from the house of France, through the weakness of Charles the Simple; who finding himself reduced to a small patrimony, in consequence of the usurpations of the nobility of his kingdom, had it not in his power to assert his right to the empire. The imperial dignity from that period became elective, and the dignities, or great offices, which before had been only commissions, were rendered hereditary, because the empire had ceased to be such, and a prince elected must submit to the conditions imposed upon him by the electors. Conrad, duke of Franconia, is made emperor, after this dignity had been refused by Otho, duke of Saxony. His authority was not acknowledged in Italy, where the popes were grown powerful, and the government had been usurped for above these sixty years by petty tyrants, such as Guido, Lambert, Berenger, &c. This occasions great confusion in the present period of history, and has been the reason that several authors have not acknowledged Conrad, nor even Henry I, as emperors; but have begun to date the new imperial family from the reign of Otho. This prince, who was called Otho the Great, the son of Henry I, having been crowned at Rome in 962, after the example of Charlemain, united the kingdom of Italy to that of Germany: a king of Germany, they say, could not be acknowledged as emperor, till

Cotemporary PRINCES.

Pope.
John X. 928.
Emperor of the East.
Constantine IX. 960.
Emperors of the West.
Lewis IV. 912.
Conrad I. 919.
Henry I. 936.
King of Spain.
Garcia. 913.
King of England.
Edward the Elder. 925.
King of Scotland.
Constantine III. 943.
Kings of Sweden.
Eric VI. towards 917.
Eric VII. towards 940.

[*] The *clameur de Haro*, or *cry of Haro*, is derived from Raoul, the French name for Rollo, because this prince having administered justice with great exactness, those who had damage done them, used, even after his death, to cry out *A Raoul*. By virtue of this cry, the person who meets his adverse party, obliges him to go before the judge, who decides the difference between them, at least provisionally.

G 5

CHARLES the Simple.

he had been at Rome, to receive the imperial crown from the pope.

920. &c.

Henry, furnamed the Fowler, fon of that Otho who refufed the imperial dignity on account of his great age, is made emperor after the death of Conrad.

922.

Robert, the brother of Eudes the late king, forms a powerful party againſt Charles the Simple, and fets up for king: he is crowned at Rheims; but Charles the Simple marches an army againſt him, and kills him in battle. Yet Charles did not gain the victory, but was beaten, and obliged to fly for fhelter to Herbert, count of Vermandois, who confined him to the caſtle of Peronne, where he died a few years after (the year 929). Here end the capitularies of our kings. The moſt ancient inſtruments relative to the good order and welfare of the kingdom that we know of, fince the capitularies do not afcend higher than Lewis the Grofs in the year 1100; and even till the reign of St. Lewis, they confiſt only of private charters, granted to churches or communities, and no way appertaining to the government, except however the ordinance of Philip Auguſtus in the year 1190. This ordinance is indeed a treafure: it regards the royal bailiffs, who increafed in number in proportion as the royal demefne was enlarged, and who by the way of appeals accuſtomed the people gradually to acknowledge the regal jurifdiction. "They were ordered to receive the "complaints of the king's fubjects every month "at the feffions, and to do them fpeedy juſtice, "to watch over the conduct of the provoſts of the "nobility, and to contain them within their duty; "laſtly,

CHARLES the Simple.

" lastly, to give an account of their behaviour
" and province every fourth month to the king's
" council."

The wife of Charles the Simple makes her escape into England, where she is received by her brother Athelstan; she takes her son Lewis along with her, who for that reason was surnamed the Transmarine.

RODOLPH.

HUGH the GREAT refuses to accept of the crown of France; but his brother-in-law, Raoul, or Rodolph, duke of Burgundy, is elected king and crowned at St. Medard of Soissons. This prince is obliged to distribute great part of the crown lands among the grandees, in order to gain them over to his side. This may be looked upon as the æra of the first institution of fiefs, though we perceive long before some feint traces of this form of government. If monarchy is the properest state for maintaining the stability of empires, and procuring the tranquillity of individuals, we ought to look upon the establishment of feudal tenures as equally fatal to both, since nothing could be more opposite to the authority of the sovereign. The king's vassal had a right to refuse to obey him; and the rear vassals of the crown, subject at the same time to the king, and to his immediate vassal, were in an uncertain state, not knowing whom they should obey. Happily for us the times are changed; the name of fief is continued, but the thing itself is almost abolished: and except the yielding of fealty and homage, which is now become no more than an empty name; and some privileges belonging to the lord paramount, we perceive no longer

Cotemporary PRINCES.

Popes.
John X. 928.
Leo VI. 929.
Stephen VIII. 931.
John XI. 936.
Emperor of the East.
Constantine IX.
Emperor of the West.
Henry I. 936.
Kings of Spain.
Ordugno II. 923.
Froila. 924.
Alfonso IV. 931.
Ramire II. 953.
Kings of England.
Edward the Elder. 925.
Athelstan. 940.
King of Scotland.
Constantine III. 943.
King of Denmark.
Harold IV. the history of whose ancestors is fabulous, was converted to Christianity, and began to reign 930, and died in 980.
King of Sweden.
Eric VII. towards 940.

RODOLPH.

longer any difference between feudal tenure, and soccage.

924. 25. 26. &c.

The Normans continue their depredations. Rodolph is at war with the Hungarians, who penetrate as far as France: but he sends them back by dint of money.

928.

Herbert, count of Vermandois, prevails on Rodolph to grant him the county of Laon; and upon this condition he promises not to restore Charles the Simple to his liberty.

929. 30. 31. &c.

Charles the Simple dies at the age of fifty, at Peronne, where he lies interred. He was thrice married; by his first wife, whose name we know not, he had Giselle, who was married in 912 to Rollo, the first duke of Normandy; by the second, whose name was Frederuna, and who died in 917, it is doubted whether he had any issue; by the third, named Edgina, he had Lewis, afterwards surnamed *Transmarine*. This Edgina, daughter of Edward the Elder, king of England, after having given signal marks of fortitude and resolution, during almost the whole course of her life, concluded at last, after her husband's decease, with marrying Herbert, count of Troyes, the second son of Herbert, count of Vermandois, who had kept her husband in confinement during the last seven years of his life.

It is proper to observe, that the southern provinces never acknowledged Rodolph's authority.

This prince, standing no longer in fear of the count of Vermandois, strips him of all the territories which he had ceded to him before by treaty. The nobility submit to Rodolph. Divers wars between the Normans and the Bretons, who were at length subdued by William *Longsword*,

Cotemporary PRINCES.

Popes.
Stephen VIII. 931.
John XI. 936.
Emperor of the East.
Constantine IX, 960,
Emperor of the West.
Henry I. 936.
Kings of Spain.
Alfonso IV. 931,
Ramire II. 950.
King of England.
Athelstan. 940.
King of Scotland.
Constantine III. 943.
King of Denmark.
Harold VI. 980.
King of Sweden.
Eric VII. towards 940,

RODOLPH.

sword, Rollo's successor. War between the Bulgarians and Hungarians.

936.

Rodolph dies at Autun, without issue, and is interred at Sens. Otho the Great is elected emperor after the death of Henry his father. We are to observe, that Henry I. took upon him only the title of king of Germany, and did not assume that of emperor, till the pope proposed to him to receive the imperial crown in Rome, and to rescue Italy from a number of tyrants, who successively lorded it over that country, in the quality of kings of Lombardy. At that time the ceremony of coronation was considered, pursuant to what we have already observed, as a condition necessary for assuming the imperial title.

Hugh, duke of France and Burgundy, count of Paris and of Orleans, surnamed the *Great*, the *Abbot*, and the *White*, and whose present fortune seemed to be a presage of the grandeur of his posterity, did not think proper as yet to seize the crown; but in order to pave the way for this great revolution, which he had been long meditating, he sends for Lewis *Transmarine*, who had been conveyed by his mother into England.

Cotemporary PRINCES.

Popes.
John XI. 936.
Leo VII. 939.
Emperor of the East.
Constantine IX. 960.
Emperors of the West.
Henry I. 936.
Otho I. 973.
King of Spain.
Ramire II. 950.
King of England.
Athelstan. 940.
King of Scotland.
Constantine III. 943.
King of Denmark.
Harold VI. 980.
King of Sweden.
Eric VII. towards 940.

LEWIS IV, surnamed Transmarine.

LEWIS TRANSMARINE, the son of Charles the Simple, ascends the throne about the age of sixteen, and is crowned at Laon by Artaud, archbishop of Rheims. He makes preparations (938) to rescue Lorrain from the emperor Otho, at the invitation of the Lorrainers themselves, who were tired of the German yoke. In order to accomplish his end, he marries (939) Gerberga,

LEWIS TRANSMARINE.

Gerberga, daughter of Henry I, surnamed the Fowler, sister of the emperor Otho I, and widow of Gilbert, duke of Lorrain. Otho is alarmed at this marriage. Lewis makes some progress in Lorrain; but Otho marches an army into that country, defeats the rebels, and obliges Lewis to retire.

940. 41.

Lewis Transmarine going to war with the grandees of his kingdom, is defeated, and afterwards concludes a peace, by the mediation of the pope, and of the emperor Otho, who had the generosity to declare himself against the rebels in France, although they had acknowledged him for their king.

942. 43. 44.

William, duke of Normandy, the son of Rollo, is assassinated by order of Arnold, earl of Flanders. Lewis Transmarine takes advantage of this conjuncture, and seizes on the dukedom of Normandy, in prejudice to young Richard, the son of William.

945. 46. 47. &c.

Lewis having forfeited his word to Hugh the Great, count of Paris, to whom he had promised a share of Normandy, to prevent his disturbing him in that expedition, loses that province, by the valour and conduct of this count. Hugh, having taken the king prisoner, obliges him to restore Normandy to Richard, and refuses to set him at liberty till he had extorted from him the entire cession of the county of Laon. He continues (946) to carry on a most obstinate war against the king, who was supported by the emperor Otho, and by the earl of Flanders. This was concluded at length by the authority of the pope, who having excommunicated

---

Cotemporary PRINCES.

Popes.
Stephen IX. 943.
Marinus II. 946.
Agapetus II. 955.
Emperor of the East.
Constantine IX. 960.
Emperor of the West.
Otho I. 973.
Kings of Spain.
Ramire II. 950.
Ordugno III. 955.
King of England.
Edred. 955.
King of Scotland.
Malcolm. 958.
King of Denmark.
Harold VI. 980.
King of Sweden.
Eric VIII. 980.
Poland.

This monarchy began in the year 550, in the person of Lechus: after his decease, it was governed by 12 dukes or palatines till the year 700, when the Poles nominated a prince. From this period they reckon fourteen princes down to Micislaus, the first Christian prince of Poland in 964. Deceased in 999.

Philip, the stem of the barons of Pernstein, from whom the house of Leczinski derives its origin, introduced the Christian religion into that kingdom.

LEWIS TRANSMARINE.

municated Hugh by means of his legates, in two councils held at Treves and Ingelheim, obliges him to make peace, and to restore the county of Laon.

954.

Lewis Transmarine dies at Rheims of a fall from his horse: he is interred in that city, and leaves, among other issue, Lothaire, and Charles, duke of Lorrain. He had taken the precaution to associate his son to the crown three years before his death.

LOTHAIRE.

954. &c.

LOTHAIRE, the eldest son of Lewis Transmarine, and of Gerberga, sister-in-law to Hugh, succeeds to the crown, at the age of fifteen. He is king under the protection of Hugh the Great, who had only one step more between him and the throne.

The crown ceases to be partitioned among brothers.

956.

Hugh the Great, otherwise Hugh the Abbot, departs this life, and leaves several children behind him: the eldest, Hugh Capet, was king of France; his younger brothers, Otho and Henry, were successively dukes of Burgundy; he married his two daughters, Emma to Richard duke of Normandy, and Beatrix to Frederic the first duke of Upper Lorrain.

957. &c.

This reign does not afford any considerable event. The king's demesne being reduced almost to the town of Laon, he did not concern himself in the wars, which his vassals waged among themselves.

961.

Cotemporary PRINCES.

Popes.
Agapetus II. 955.
John XII, named Octavian; this was the first pope that changed his name; he was elected at eighteen years of age. 964.
Emperor of the East.
Constantine IX. 900.
Emperor of the West.
Otho I. 973.
Kings of Spain.
Ordugno III. 955.
Sancho. 967.
Kings of England.
Edred. 955.
Edwy. 957.
King of Scotland.
Malcolm. 958.
King of Denmark.
Harold VI. 980.
King of Sweden.
Eric VIII. 980.
Prince of Poland.
Micislaus. 999.

LOTHAIRE.

961. &c.
Lothaire makes some attempts upon Normandy, which do not succeed.

965. &c.
The king attacks Arnold II, who refused to pay him homage, which he pretends to be his due, and wrests several towns out of his hands.

973.
The death of the emperor Otho, surnamed the Great. This prince seeing the doctors puzzled to know whether the representation ought to take place between grandchildren and uncles, ordered a single combat to decide the question, and in the event the representation took place. Under this prince the Roman crown was again annexed to the empire, by a concordate between him and pope Leo VIII.

974. &c.
The emperor Otho II, in order to hinder the kings of France from ever recovering Lorrain, and to create a jealousy in the kingdom, divided Lorrain into two parts; the Upper, which is the present, he took to himself; and the other he gave to Charles, the brother of Lothaire, upon condition of yielding him homage for it.

978. &c.
Lothaire in vain endeavours to recover Lorrain; though he is victorious over Otho II, yet he concludes a peace with that prince, and resigns the abovementioned province to him, on condition of his holding it as a fief of the crown of France. This same Otho had received in dower with his wife Theophania, daughter of the emperor of the east, the lower part of Italy, which, together with the exarchate of Ravenna, formed the remainder of the possessions of the eastern emperors in Italy. But this dower, if the fact be true, did not continue long in his
hands;

Cotemporary PRINCES.

Popes.
Benedict VI.　974.
Boniface VII. 975.
John XIV.　985.
John XV.　996.
Emperors of the East.
John Zimisces.　975.
Basilius III.
Constantine X.　1025.
Emperors of the West.　1028.
Otho II.　983.
Otho III.　1002.
Kings of Spain.
Ramire III.　982.
Veremund II. 999.
Kings of England.
Edgar.　975.
Edward II, called the *martyr*. 978.
Ethelred.　1016.
Kings of Scotland.
Culenus,　976.
Kenneth III. 984.
Constantine IV.　985.
Grime.　993.
Kings of Denmark.
Harold VI.　980.
Sweno.　1014.
Kings of Sweden.
Eric VIII.　980.
Olaus, the first Christian king of Sweden　1019.
Prince of Poland.
Micislaus.　999.

LOTHAIRE.

hands; for the battle in Calabria in 982, against the Greeks and Saracens, bereft him of those provinces.

The dignity of hereditary great seneschal, annexed to the family of the counts of Anjou, in the person of Geoffery Grisegonnelle.

Lothaire dies of poison at Rheims, at the age of forty-five, and leaves by his wife Emma, daughter of Lothaire, king of Italy, a son named Lewis V, whom he had associated to the crown, and who afterwards succeeded him. Lothaire was a prince of great courage; and it is thought that he was poisoned by his wife Emma.

LEWIS V, surnamed the Slothful.

Lewis V, surnamed the SLOTHFUL, *juvenis qui nihil fecit*, son of Lothaire and of Emma, succeeds to the crown, at the age of twenty. He married Blanche, daughter of a great lord of Aquitaine, by whom he had no issue.

987.

Lewis V. reigned but one year, and died of poison at Compiegne, in the same manner as his father: it is believed that he was poisoned by the queen his wife, who did not love him, and who had parted from him at one time, to return back to Aquitaine.

His uncle Charles should by right have succeeded him, but Hugh Capet seized the crown.

The end of the Calovingian race, which lasted two hundred and thirty-six years.

Cotemporary PRINCES.

Pope.
John XV. 996.
Emperors of the East.
Basil III. 1025.
Constantine X. 1028.
Emperor of the West.
Otho III. 1002.
King of Spain.
Veremund II. 999.
King of England.
Ethelred. 1016.
King of Scotland.
Grime. 993.
King of Denmark.
Sweno. 1014.
King of Sweden.
Olaus I. 1019.
Prince of Poland.
Micislaus. 999.

PARTICULAR REMARKS.

AMONG the different opinions concerning the manner, in which the Franks were possessed of landed estates under the first and second race, the following seem to be the best founded.

The estates possessed by the Franks after their entrance into Gaul may be divided into *Salic lands*, and *military benefices*.

The Salic lands were those which fell to their share by conquest, and were hereditary: military benefices, which had been instituted by the Romans before the conquest of the Franks, were a gift of the prince, and only for life; from thence came the name of *benefices* possessed by the clergy. The Gauls on the other hand, being united under the same government, continued to enjoy their possessions in full liberty, as under the Romans; except the Salic lands, which the Franks had seized, and could not be any great matter, considering the small number of the Franks, and the large extent of the monarchy. People of both nations, how obscure soever their birth, were capable of public offices and governments, and employed in war, under the authority of the prince. " Such is the excellency " of the French constitution, that it has never excluded, " even the meanest subject, from the highest dignities and " employments." (*Matharel*, answer to *Hotman*'s book, entitled FRANCO-GALLIA.)

Towards the end of the second race, a new kind of possession was established, under the name of *fief*. The *dukes* or governors of provinces, the *counts* or governors of towns, and other officers of inferior order, taking advantage of the enfeebled state of the royal authority, rendered those titles hereditary in their families, which had been hitherto only possessed for life; and having usurped both the lands and the *jurisdiction*, they erected themselves into lords and proprietors of places, where they had been only magistrates, either military or civil, or both. Thus a new kind of authority was introduced into the kingdom, to which the French gave the name of *Suzeraineté*, (sovereign, yet subaltern jurisdiction); a name says Loyseau, as barbarous, as the thing itself is absurd.

The

PARTICULAR REMARKS.

The nobility of families, a thing unknown in France till the time of the fiefs, began with this new kind of feignory; fo that it was the poffeffion of lands that conftituted the nobility, as it gave them a fort of fubjects called *vaffals*, who had other vaffals under them by *fubordinate infeoffments*: and fuch was the authority of thofe lords, that their vaffals were obliged in certain cafes to ferve under them againft the king himfelf. Knight fervice was alfo another fource of nobility. (*See the year* 1270).

It is difficult to know from whence the fiefs derived their origin: to me it feems that this kind of poffeffion, in the beginning, was no more than a cuftom or unwritten law of the Lombards; and upon this account fome authors have ftiled it *the child of Time*, which indeed is the cafe of all cuftoms. It was Conrad the Salic (who died in 1039) that firft thought of giving it a greater extent, and of reducing it to a written law.

The Romans were ftrangers to fiefs, fo that when any of them happened to be invefted with thofe poffeffions, they were obliged to follow the difpofition of the laws of the Lombards.

But it is obfervable, that the law of fiefs or feudal tenures among the Franks, was different from that of the Lombards. Only the eldeft fons inherited the fiefs in France, in order to preferve their original fplendor. (*Cujas lib.* 1. *de feud. tit.* 9. *in fin.*) whereas the fiefs were fplit among the Lombards. It is likewife proper to remark, and it is to our prefent point, that the *cuftom* of fiefs among the Lombards, was antecedent to the law of the Franks: but that this fame cuftom among the Franks was antecedent to the firft written law, becaufe the feudal law was not eftablifhed in Italy till the eleventh century, and fiefs were known in France fo early as the 10th.

All origins are obfcure; hence we have no law nor title relating to the firft infeoffments; and our kings confented to them only by a general toleration: but when the great fiefs came to be re-united to the crown, thofe which the king left in the hands of private perfons, were poffeffed by new grants. Our kings did not think of extinguifhing them all; nay, they thought proper to grant fome new infeoffments. They did more; for at different times they permitted the union of feveral of thofe feignories, in order to form very large eftates,

which

PARTICULAR REMARKS.

which they afterwards erected into dukedoms, counties, or marquisates: so that the ancient dignities still subsisted; but with this essential difference, that the primitive seignories were the effect of force and rebellion, whereas the new titles were derived from the royal authority. The king then ran no risk of rendering any of his subjects too powerful; the form of government being changed; on the contrary, those who had distinguished themselves by their services, he attached more particularly to his interest.

The church having been received by the state under Constantine, introduced her worship, which she held of God alone; but could not exercise it in public without the emperor's permission: it was he that assembled the councils; and when the Christian religion came to spread itself wider, each sovereign exercised the same authority in ecclesiastic matters within his own dominions, as had been enjoyed by the emperor. Thus the council of Orleans was convoked by the authority of Clovis: councils were also convened by Carloman, and by his brother Pepin, when they were only mayors of the palace.

The meeting of general councils was an affair, in which the authority of secular princes was too much interested, not to create a jealousy with regard to the manner of convoking them. For the sake of harmony, it was necessary there should be one common center of unity, founded in religion, on which all other churches depended, itself entirely independent: this is what at length rendered the popes, as common fathers of the faithful, masters of this convocation, but with the just and necessary concurrence of the respective sovereigns. The legates afterwards extended the rights of the holy see in this respect too far; and Charles the Bald authorized their encroachments; so that there were frequent instances of their assembling national councils in the kingdom to which they were deputed, without consulting the sovereign.

With regard to the elections of bishops, the discipline of the church has not been always the same. So long as the primitive Christians held their assemblies in private, or did not form a society under the sanction of the secular power, they chose their own pastors independently of the prince: but when once the emperors favoured them with the public exercise of their religion,

the

PARTICULAR REMARKS.

the elections sometimes depended on the prince, and other times on the clergy and people, but always with mutual pretensions, which occasioned an infinite deal of trouble and vexation: hence those quarrels about investitures, equally hurtful both to church and state, where the two powers, for want of understanding one another, greatly exceeded their just bounds, the emperor by encroaching on the spiritualities, and the pope on temporalities.

There were but few festivals at this time, such as Easter-day, Whitsun-day and Christmas-day; for it is not supposed that the latter feast was the most ancient, since it did not come from the apostles, who established no festivals, but in commemoration of mysteries, to which themselves had been eye-witnesses. The nobility of each diocese were obliged to celebrate these solemnities in the chief city; and the kings themselves made it a point of duty, to assist there in person, as well as their meanest subjects. We find in the centuriators of Magdeburg, the famous constitution of Charlemain, containing the list of festivals observed in his time, which even then were marked in red letters, viz. Christmas-day, St. Stephen, St. John the Evangelist, Holy Innocents, Circumcision, the Epiphany, the octave of the Epiphany, the purification of the Virgin Mary, eight days at Easter, Rogation-days, Holy Thursday, Whitsun-day, St. John Baptist, St. Peter, St. Paul, St. Martin, and St. Andrew.

Under the reign of Clovis we took notice of the different laws by which the Franks were governed, it remains for us now to mention a word or two in regard to the Capitularies.

Without entering into the question, concerning what influence the people had in the debates of the field of Mars, where the *Capitularies* were drawn up, we shall only quote the following words of Charles the Bald. *Such are,* says this prince, *the Capitularies of our father, which the French have thought proper to acknowledge as a law, and which our liege subjects have resolved in a general assembly, for ever to observe.* These were laws passed in the *Parliament* or *Sessions,* at which both clergy and laity assisted: which is the reason that Reginon sometimes calls them *Synodus*, other times *Placitum*, because the concur-

PARTICULAR REMARKS.

rence of both orders of the state, when ecclesiastical and temporal affairs were equally discussed, did to all effects render them both *Councils* and *Parliaments*, parliaments from the summons, and councils from the occasional debates. *(Literary history of France.)*

The empire of the West, founded by Charlemain, was hereditary in his family, because he had conquered it; and it did not become elective, till transferred to the Germans: the house of France was dispossessed of the imperial dignity by the weakness of that prince's descendants, and by the partitions among his posterity. Had the imperial title continued annexed to the French monarchy, without introducing a division of those dominions, the empire would have been perpetuated in the house of France, and what change soever might happen, people would have respected the imperial dignity, as inherent in their sovereign. But the partitions of Lewis the Debonnaire having divided the minds of his children, so as to cause animosities and wars between them, and of course between the subjects in each of those divisions, after a very little time they became strangers to one another.

In the ninth century the monks inherited from their relations, and were allowed to have property: it was not the same with the laity, for these could not inherit from monks. *(Pref. towards an ecclesiastic and civil history of Britany.)*

The use of cuirasses and helmets, as well as that of bows and arrows, which had been hardly known under the first race, became a military law under the second *(Capit. of Charlem.)* Chivalry at this time began to be introduced: the knight, who was called *Miles*, held a rank in the army, independent of his military employment.

The barbarous custom of doing justice to one's self by force of arms, and of associating the whole family in pursuit of revenge, had passed from Germany into Gaul, where it maintained its ground upwards of six hundred years. The French, intirely bred to the profession of arms, and jealous of their liberty, could not resolve to break themselves of a custom, which they erroneously considered as the privilege of nobility, and the characteristic of independence. It is observable, that if any one of the family thought the pursuit

PARTICULAR REMARKS.

suit and revenge of the injury too dangerous, in such case by the Salic law he was at liberty to desist publickly from that private war; but at the same time this very law, title 63, deprived him of the right of succession, as one that was become a stranger to his own family, and in punishment for his pusillanimity. A preposterous and barbarous law, which encouraged, or rather was derived from the ferocity of the nation. What streams of blood have flowed from this unhappy prejudice, of which neither the Greeks nor Romans had any idea! Yet these combats afterwards required the express leave of the prince; so that it was high treason to appoint place and time for fighting, to challenge or send challenges and defiances, without the sanction and authority of the sovereign: whereas, when there was gage or pledge adjudged by the king, according to their manner of phrasing it in those days, that is, when the king looked upon the provocation or offence sufficient to merit a duel, it became lawful, and was frequently honoured by the king's presence; nay the very bishops themselves sometimes assisted at this spectacle, as in the case between the dukes of Lancaster and Brunswic. It has been since pretended, that this approbation of the prince was so far from rendering duels more frequent; that on the contrary they multiplied greatly after the express prohibition against them by Henry II. And the reason given is, that as every man then began to judge of the offence according to his own fancy or prejudice, it was looked upon as a dishonour to hesitate a moment about fighting upon the least pretence. By the same principle they maintain, that those combats in which they fought it out, that is, where one of the combatants was necessarily to perish, were an infallible way to render them less frequent. This is what the marshal de Brissac did in Piedmont: seeing to what excess the madness of duels was carried, he resolved to tolerate them, but with such circumstances of horror, as soon extinguished this brutal desire: he ordered that the combatants should decide their quarrel upon a certain bridge, inclosed within four pikes, and that the person overcome should be thrown into the river, and the conqueror by no means permitted to grant him his life. A remedy most cruel, and worse than the disease! Our

PARTICULAR REMARKS.

Our kings have from that time directed their attention to suppress so barbarous a custom; but the laws upon this subject were multiplied to no purpose, since the reign of Henry II, for want of abilities to put them in execution. How great our obligations to the prince (Lewis XIV.) who utterly abolished a practice, which his predecessors with so many edicts had attacked in vain!

Marriages in those days were under happy regulations: criminal connexions were not treated as bagatelles; infidelity to the marriage bed was called adultery. " Manners, says Tacitus, had more influence with them, than laws with other nations." *Plus ibi boni mores valent quam alibi bonæ leges.* So great an union might proceed from this, that husbands did not receive any dower or fortune: it is true, the wife brought some arms, or military present with her, which savoured of the rudeness of those early times; but there was no such thing, as the husband's receiving any lands or money. His disinterested choice convinced the wife of his affection, and at the same time kept her in dependence. Nay more; so far were the women from bringing with them any portion at their marriage, that they received a dower from their husbands. At the abbey of St. Peter in Vallée there is a register, at least seven hundred years old, in the opinion of M. le Laboreur, where we find a donation to this convent by Hildegardis, countess of Amiens, and widow of Valeran, count of Vexin. This lady declares, in the title of the deed, that she has bestowed upon the abbey of St. Peter a freehold estate, which she had received of her consort upon her marriage, pursuant to the Salic law, which, she says, obliges the husband to endow his wife.

Latin was as yet the vulgar tongue in France, that is, the language used by every body, under the first race: but it ceased to be such at the beginning of the ninth century. It was succeeded by the *Romance* tongue, that is, a mixture of the Frank dialect and of bad Latin, which is become the French language. There was also the Tudesque or Teutonic introduced by the Franks: this appears very clearly by a treaty between Charles the Bald, and Lewis the Germanic; here the two languages
are

PARTICULAR REMARKS.

are very diſtinct, the *Tudeſque* is for the Germans, and the *Romance* for the Franks: this is the moſt ancient record in France.

The Benedictine authors of the *Literary hiſtory of France* (Tome VI. and VII.) affirm, that the French began to write romances in the tenth century: they likewiſe give a very good refutation of le Maire, of the abbé Fleury, of Calmet, and of the laſt hiſtorian of the city of Paris, who make them of a later date by two hundred years. They obſerve farther, that among the Greeks, fictions were the fruit of politeneſs and learning; whereas among the Franks, they were the offspring of ignorance. As the *Romance* language was at that time more generally underſtood, the authors of thoſe compoſitions preferred it to any other, for publiſhing their ingenious tales, which from thence took the name of *Romances*.

The ſame hiſtorians make a very judicious reflection on the eighth century: *this century is the laſt term of the decline of learnin Gaul; and at the ſame time the æra of the firſt endeavours towards reſtoring it to its former flouriſhing ſtate.*

Nothing can be more precarious, than what has been written towards the beginning of the ſecond race, concerning the tranſactions that happened under the firſt: the hiſtorians were all devoted to the reigning family, and endeavoured to juſtify its uſurpation, by attributing to Pepin's anceſtors the whole good that was done while they diſcharged the office of mayors of the palace, and by laying the whole blame of what the ſtate had ſuffered, upon the laſt kings of the firſt race. We muſt therefore, in regard to this period, abide by cotemporary writers, and afterwards proceed to thoſe, who like Aimonius, wrote, it is true, under the third race; but wrote without prejudice or intereſt: even the teſtimony of the abovementioned author muſt be uſed with caution; and we are to remember, moreover, that his hiſtory concludes at the forty-firſt chapter of the fourth book, as father le Cointe has obſerved, and not confound what was written by him, with what has been added by his continuators.

MINISTERS, WARRIORS, MAGISTRATES,
Eminent and Learned Men,

Who flourished from the commencement of the reign of Lewis the Stammerer, in the year 877, to the end of the second race, in the year 987.

Ministers.	Warriors.	Magistrates.	Eminent and Learned Men.
Anscheric.	Renaud of Saluces.	*High chancellors.*	Abbo. 892.
Ebles.	Eudes, count of Paris.	Urgard.	Anastasius the librarian. 887.
Seulf.	Robert, count of Paris.	Foulk.	Eudes or Odo of Cluni. 942.
	Hugh the Great.	Anscheric.	Flodoardus. 966.
	Otho.	Ernuste.	Hincmar. 882.
		Malhute.	Luitprand. 970.
	For this column of the second race, as well as for that of the first, we have singled out only such as were the most celebrated at that time; but it is obvious that this list might have been easily enlarged.	Herveus.	Radulphus. 910.
		Roger.	Reginon. 908.
		Luitgard.	Joannes Scotus. 883.
		Ebles.	Suidas, *who is believed to have flourished in this century.*
		Adalgaire.	
		Abbo.	
		Ansegise.	
		Eric.	
		Hugh of Vermandois.	
		Artaud.	
		Adalric.	
		Adalberon.	

A Chronological Abridgment

OF THE

HISTORY of FRANCE.

THE THIRD RACE.

*T*OWARDS *the end of the second race*, says Mezeray, *the kingdom was held by the law of feudal tenures; and governed rather as a great fief, than as a monarchy*: hence this same author calls the government under the third race, the time of the *Grand Polities*. And indeed it was under the third race that our kings recovered their authority, after it had been almost annihilated at the expiration of the second. We must confess, that Hugh Capet was indebted to this very diminution of power, for the revolution in his favour, exclusive of the legitimate heirs: but when once he established himself on the throne, he and his successors, animated by the same spirit, and wisely adhering to the same principle, from which they never deviated, by degrees resumed all that had been usurped by the great lords; and did not take a single step but what tended to this end, till at length they recovered the full rights and prerogatives of the crown.

987.
Accession to the crown.

HUGH CA-PET *comes to the crown, at about forty-five years of age; and is crowned at Rheims the 3d of July,* 987, *by the archbishop Adalberon. He is the founder of the third race of our kings.*

He made a church of his palace (now St. Bartholomew). There is extant an original seal of this prince's, and it is the first on which we see what the French commonly call the *hand of justice* *; he holds it with his right hand, and a globe with his left; on his head he wears a crown ornamented with flowers; he is represented in this seal with short hair, and a long forked beard: round it is this inscription, *Hugo Dei misericordia Francorum rex.*

* It is a kind of sceptre, with a little ivory hand at the top.

REMARKABLE EVENTS.

987.

CHARLES, duke of Lower Lorrain, son of Lewis Transmarine, and uncle to Lewis V, the last king of the second race, was the only legitimate heir to the crown, but happened to be excluded by several circumstances from the succession. While the last descendants of Charlemain were fallen into a kind of contempt, those of Robert *Fortis,* or the *Strong,* had raised themselves to the highest degree of power, by the services done to their country: the people were disgusted with Charles, for his weakness in yielding homage to the emperor Otho: nay, they went so far as to start some doubts concerning his title, from the suspicions formerly raised in regard to the legitimacy of Charles the Simple; in short, the whole nation united in favour of Hugh Capet, duke of France, and great grandson of Robert.

988. 89. 90. 91.

Hugh Capet causes his son Robert to be crowned at Orleans, in order to secure the throne to him.

Charles determining to maintain his right to the sovereignty, lays siege to Laon, and takes it; he likewise gains a victory over Hugh, who attempted to recover the town. Not long after this, Hugh retakes Laon, by a correspondence with the bishop of that place, the 2d of April, 991, on Thursday night in passion-week, and takes Charles prisoner, together with his wife, and Arnold, archbishop of Rheims, who had been treacherous to Hugh, though he was indebted to this prince for his archbishopric.

This Arnold, the natural son of king Lothaire, is deposed, in a council held at the abbey of St. Basil, in the neighbourhood of Rheims, after having acknowledged his treasonable behaviour

The THIRD RACE. 105

WIVES.	CHILDREN.	996. DEATH.	Cotemporary PRINCES.
Adelaid, daughter, as is supposed, of William III, surnamed *Towerhead*, duke of Guyenne, and count of Poitou.	ROBERT. *Haderwinds*, or *Havide*, wife of Raginerus IV. count of Hainault; and afterwards of Hugh III. count of Dasbourg. Adelaid, of whom father Anselm takes no notice. She was married to Renaud, count of Nevers. Goslinda or Giselle, wife of Hugh I, to whom she brought the seignory of Abbeville. *Natural son.* Goslinus archbishop of Bourges. 1029.	HUGH CAPET *departs this life Octob. the 24th,* 996, *aged about* 55 *years, and is interred at St. Denis.* He follows the example of Clovis, in fixing his residence at Paris, which had ceased to be the seat of our kings, during the whole time of the second race, and under the princes of the first, commonly called the *lazy kings.*	*Popes.* John XV. 996. Gregory V. 999. *Emperors of the East.* { Basil III. 1025. { Constantine. 1028. *Emperor of the West.* Otho III. 1002. *King of Spain.* Veremund II. 999. *King of England.* Ethelred. 1016. *Kings of Scotland.* Grime. 993. Malcolm II. 1023. *King of Denmark.* Sweno. 1014. *King of Sweden.* Olaus. 1019. *Prince of Poland.* Micislaus. 999.

REMARKABLE EVENTS under HUGH CAPET.

viour to the king. The person chosen to succeed him, was Gerbert, who had been preceptor to king Robert, and was afterwards known by the name of pope Silvester II. Pope John XV. disapproves of Arnold's deposition, and obliges the king to agree to the convening of a new council at Aix-la-Chapelle, which was afterwards held in 995 at Mouzon. As there was only a very small number of bishops in this assembly, the affair was referred to a council, to be held at Rheims the first day of the following July. The decision of these prelates having had no effect, Gerbert continued in possession of his see during the life of Hugh Capet; so that Arnold was not restored till the next, and without the interposition of any council.

This Gerbert is supposed to have introduced the Arabic or Indian ciphers into France; for the Arabians had borrowed this kind of notation from the Indians, and Gerbert might have learnt it of the Saracens in a journey, which he once undertook to Spain. *(Le Beuf, literary history of France.)* He was also the person that constructed the first clock, whose movement was regulated by a balance, which practice subsisted till the year 1650, when they began to make use of pendulums.

992. &c.

Charles dies, and leaves children behind him, that had no posterity, so that the war is concluded, after a continuance of four or five years. The duke of Guyenne, the counts of Flanders and Vermandois, who had favoured Charles's pretensions, are obliged to submit.

Hugh Capet, having just reason to apprehend some further incursions from the Danes and Normans, by the mouth of the Somme, ordered fortifications to be erected round Abbeville in Ponthieu, which at that time was only a farm, called *Abbatis villa*, dependent on the abbey of St. Riquier. The government of this country he conferred on a lord named Hugh, who from *Advowée* of St. Riquier, became count of Ponthieu: such was the original of the counts of that name.

It is generally believed, that the peerage of France may be dated from the beginning of this century; but at the same time we must observe, that the peers are of greater antiquity than the peerage: the latter, le Laboureur says, did not begin to be real both in name and effect, till the fiefs became hereditary

and

REMARKABLE EVENTS *under* HUGH CAPET.

and patrimonial, whereas at all times the peers were judges of their fellow citizens. This is corroborated from the following circumstance, that when the cities acquired the rights of commoners, or of a third estate; in several places, and particularly in Picardy, they called their judges by the name of *city peers*. We ought likewise to take notice, that after the usurpation of fiefs from the crown, the peerage became more or less considerable, according to the greater or lesser degree of power in the lord paramount; so that the peers of the king of France were greater lords than those of the count of Champagne; and for the very same reason the principal peers were characterized by their dependance on the crown. Thus the duke of Britany, whose power was equal to that of the duke of Normandy, was nevertheless inferior to him in dignity, for this reason that originally he did not hold of the crown, but of the king only, as duke of Normandy; and Normandy having been alienated, he was consequently no more than a rear-vassal. Hence even to this very day, a seignory, dependent on a particular lord, or even on the king, by virtue of his private domain, is released from that dependance, in order to hold only of the crown, whenever the seignory is erected into a dutchy and peerage. The introduction of this new dignity procured the crown to Hugh Capet. At that time there were seven lay peers of France, that is, seven lords, whose seignories were held immediately of the king: these elected from among their own body the person, capable of annexing the greatest number of provinces to the regal dignity, and of preventing the peers from making encroachments upon one another: by this choice the peerage of Hugh Capet was united to the crown, so that there remained no more than six peers.

There are different opinions in regard to the original of peerage: that which traces it up to Charlemain, is romantic: that which dates it from the reign of Lewis the Young, gives it only a momentary existence, for this is the very æra of the reunion of those same peerages to the crown. Others, as Favin, believe that the peerage was instituted by Robert, " who " devised a kind of council of state, composed of six eccle- " siastics, and of six great feudatory lords of Burgundy, Aqui- " taine, Normandy, Flanders, Champagne, and Toulouse, ho- " nouring them with the title of peers: this institution is dated

" from

REMARKABLE EVENTS under HUGH CAPET.

" from the year 1020, and the twenty fourth of his reign." Favin does not support this opinion by any authority; besides, he forgot that there were not six ecclesiastic peers at that time, since we find that the bishop of Langres still depended on the duke of Burgundy in the reign of Lewis VII; and that it was this king who engaged the duke of Burgundy to unite the county of Langres to the bishopric, and make that prelate hold of the king, with a view of causing his son Philip Augustus to be crowned, and of rendering this ceremony memorable by the convening of twelve peers.

As the form of this work will not admit of dissertations, we must be satisfied with proposing our opinion, but hope that by no means we shall be suspected of attempting to decide. I apprehend therefore that the peerages and feudal tenures have one common original; because the introducing of those new seignories, at that critical time, gave a deadly blow to the royal authority. This seems to be sufficiently explained by Viguier. " Before the reign of Lewis the Stammerer, the whole kingdom
" was in some measure a royal demesne .... and the king
" granted what part thereof he pleased to his subjects; but in the
" reign of Charles the Simple, it was divided into seven large
" provinces .... and into several lesser counties, some of
" which depended on the seven large provinces, in the nature
" of subaltern fiefs, as the counties of Touraine, Anjou,
" Blois, and others, on the county of France; which makes
" me suspect it to be the cause, why the counts of Anjou did
" not rank among the peers, since the time of Hugh Capet, nor
" the counts of Champagne, in right of their county of Tours:
" .... with regard to the great provinces, the first and chief
" of the seven, was that to which they gave the name of France
" and of Paris .... so that if Hugh Capet had thought proper
" to grant the dutchy of France to any of his children, without
" reuniting and incorporating it into the royal demesne, we
" should have had seven peers, because there were seven great
" princes before."

Besides these, the king had ecclesiastic peers; but we do not find that the other peers of France had ecclesiastics of that appellation, but most of them had more lay peers than the king. These

were

REMARKABLE EVENTS under HUGH CAPET.

were judges in the courts of juſtice belonging to the nobility; and it was neceſſary there ſhould be two at leaſt, with their lord at their head, to paſs judgment: the lord who had no peers, borrowed them of his paramount. Beaumanoir in his cuſtoms of Beavoiſis obſerves, that the lords could not ſit in judgment, in a cauſe where they themſelves were a party concerned. In vain did the peers of France attempt to make uſe of this law againſt the king, who aſſiſted at thoſe trials, and whoſe duty it was ſo to do, for by defending his own rights, he maintained thoſe of the ſtate.

The count of Paris was inveſted with the adminiſtration of juſtice, with the direction of the police and of the finances, and with the command of the armies: ſubordinate to him was the viſcount. When Hugh Capet attained the regal dignity, he annexed the county of Paris, which he poſſeſſed by feudal tenure, and which Hugh the Great had received of Charles the Simple; he annexed it, I ſay, to the crown. Thus the title, as well as office of count, being reunited and ſuppreſſed, there remained the viſcount, who adminiſtered juſtice under the count: the officer whom the king appointed to repreſent the viſcount, was called the provoſt, (and we ſtill retain the name of the provoſt of Paris) who in proceſs of time ceaſed to exerciſe the functions of a magiſtrate, but continued ſtill to be at the head of the Chatelet *, where he gives his vote without collecting thoſe of the other judges, for their preſident is the lieutenant civil †.

The firſt canonization made by the papal authority, was that of St. Udalricus in 993. Before this time, that is, during the nine firſt centuries, it was ſettled, that all biſhops had an equal power in regard to the canonization of ſaints: but the authority of the pope, as well as the number of canonizations, having increaſed ſince that time, people began to have recourſe to the ſee of Rome, in order to give a greater ſolemnity to the affair. Hence we find that Alexander III. iſſued out a decree, declaring, that the canonization of ſaints was one of thoſe higher cauſes, reſerved to the apoſtolic ſee. Boniface pretended the ſame thing; and Urban VIII.

---

* The Guildhall or ordinary Seſſions houſe for civil and criminal cauſes.
† A judge of ordinary controverſies between party and party.

ſtrictly

strictly forbid any reverence or worship to be given to those, who died even in reputation of sanctity, before they had been beatified or canonized by the church of Rome. The custom was for the pope to consult the cardinals on this occasion; yet Sixtus V. dispensed with this ceremony, as we find by a letter of cardinal de Joyeuse to king Henry III. " On Wednesday " the 9th of this instant March, his holiness issued out a bull " declaring St. Bonaventure a doctor of the church, without " taking the opinion of the cardinals."

This was the age of ignorance: so profound it was, that scarcely did kings, princes, and lords, much less the common people, know how to read. They were acquainted with their possessions by usage, but they seldom thought of defending them by registers, since they were strangers to the practice of writing. To this it was owing that marriages in those days were frequently declared void: for as those marriages were concluded at the church door, and subsisted only in the memory of such as had been present, they could not recollect either their alliances or degrees of kindred, so that relations were often married without the necessary dispensations. Hence arose so many pretences, in case of dislike, or for reasons of state, to part from one's lawful wife; hence also the great influence which the clergy began to obtain in temporal affairs, because they were the only persons that had some knowledge of letters. " As the Druids, says Pasquier, kept the " keys of their religion and of letters, so did our priests en- " gross both these articles to themselves .... our nobility " not troubling their heads at all about so important a subject. " Now from this ancient stupidity (of our nobles) it came to " pass, that we give several meanings to the word *clerk*, which " in its genuine and original signification belongs only to ec- " clesiastics. And as none but themselves made profession of " letters, so by way of a metaphor, we called a man of letters " a *great clerk*, a stupid blockhead a *bad clerk*; and learning went " by the name of *clerkship*."

The revenue of our kings consisted in their *demesnes*, which may be divided into nine species; the *produce* of the royal bailiwicks and provostships, which our princes sometimes farmed out

REMARKABLE EVENTS under HUGH CAPET.

to the bailiffs and provosts; the *produce* of the crown lands received likewise by bailiffs and provosts; the *jurisdiction of woods and forests*; the *quit rent*, and other duties or acknowledgments of seignory; these were so much the more considerable, as since the establishment of feudal tenures every thing was held in fee, because our kings found it more advantageous to grant lands in that manner, than to hold the property of them in their own hands; the *regale*; the duties of *import* and *export*, received on the frontiers of the kingdom; the *coinage*; the *droit de gite*, or power to lie at the house of a tenant or vassal; and *the taxes on the Jews*: without reckoning the rents or duties for the right of *commons*, and what went by the name of *voluntary customs*; this was a rent or duty paid by the vassals in four extraordinary cases, namely, when the king made his eldest son a knight, when he married his eldest daughter, when a war broke out, or when he happened to be taken prisoner. The feudal lords had likewise the same power over their tenants. The persons entrusted with the receipt of the king's revenue, brought it to Paris in three terms, St. Remy, Candlemas, and Holy Thursday: there was a time when the monies so received, were deposited into the hands of a knight templar, who was the king's treasurer, and made out the receipts and discharges to the provosts and other persons concerned. This was the civil list, or support of our king's houshold; for by means of the knight services, to which every immediate vassal of the crown was bound, the king was at no expence in going to war. True it is, that he depended in some measure on his vassals, who would frequently leave him in the middle of a campaign, when the time of their service was expired.

Could any one imagine, that there was so little intercourse in those days between the several provinces of France, that an abbot of Cluni, having received an invitation from Bouchard count of Paris, to bring some of his monks to *St. Maur des Fosses*, excuses himself by saying, he is afraid to undertake so long a journey to a strange country, where he was not at all acquainted?

REMARK-

REMARKABLE EVENTS.

996.
Accession to the crown.

Robert succeeds to the crown, in the year 996, at the age of about five and twenty. He was born, baptized, and crowned, at Orleans.

996. 97. &c.

Robert having kept Arnold, archbishop of Rheims, under confinement, restores him to his liberty, and grants him the peaceable enjoyment of his archbishopric, in expectation that this complaisance would induce the pope to confirm his marriage with his kinswoman Bertha, whom he had married without a dispensation. Gerbert, being stripped of his archbishopric, retired into Germany to the emperor Otho: he was afterwards made archbishop of Ravenna, and at length was raised to the pontificate by the name of Silvester II.

The king cannot prevail on the pope to approve of his marriage with Bertha. Gregory V, in a council held at Rome in 998, declared the marriage void, and if they would not agree to a separation, he excommunicated them, together with Archambaud, archbishop of Tours, by whom they had been married. The king refused to obey. All the bishops concerned in the marriage, repair to Rome, and make their submission to the pope; the people and even the courtiers desert the king; his domestics, who are obliged to attend him, make every thing he had touched, pass through the fire, in order to purify it. Robert at length complying, Bertha is dismissed, and in a short time after he marries Constantia, daughter of William count of Provence and Arles.

The emperor Otho III. erects Poland into a kingdom, in favour of Boleslaus prince of Poland; and the pope makes Hungary a kingdom, to oblige Stephen duke of Hungary.

Crescentius, consul of Rome, having about the same time procured a very rich Greek, whose name was Arnolph Arbacius, to be chosen pope,

by

The Third Race.

WIVES.	CHILDREN.	1031. DEATH.	Cotemporary PRINCES.
Bertha, a relation of Robert, and widow to Eudes I. count of Blois. Pope Gregory V. by his excommunications obliged him to part with her; and he took for his second wife, Constantia, daughter of the count of Provence and Arles, she died in 1032. Dom Vaissette makes her the daughter of William Taillefer, or *it iron*, count of Toulouse.	Hugh, died before his father. HENRY I. Rob. I. duke of Burg. Eudes. Adelaid, wife of Renaud, count of Nevers; she was living in 1063. Adela, or Alisa, wife of Richard III, duke of Normandy, and afterwards of Baldwin, count of Flanders. 1079. It appears beyond all doubt from a passage of Hugh of Fleury, that Adela was never married to any other husband than Baldwin, and this is Mezeray's opinion. Yet Dom Luc d'Achery maintains the contrary, from a deed of 1026, and is followed by father Daniel, though this deed contains only a nuptial present made by Richard to Adela *his future spouse*. In short, father Simplician seems to resolve the difficulty, by saying that Adela had been promised to Richard, but was never married to him.	Robert departs this life at Melun the 20th of *July* 1031, aged sixty years. He was interred at St. Denis. The register of the dead, belonging to the collegiate church of Lisle, places this death on the 26th of June VI. *Kal. Julii obitus Dom. Roberti Francorum regis*. And by a charter of Baldwin count of Flanders, in the year 1066, taken from the register of the same church, this death is fixed to the 29th of June: *Unoquoque anno Canonici XII. solidos recipiant in die solemni Apost. Petri & Pauli, quia eadem die celebrabunt anniversarium diem Roberti Francorum regis*. Nevertheless, the day of celebrating the anniversary ought not to determine the day of his death; since, according to Baillet, they chose for that ceremony, the feast that was nearest the time of the decease, in order to render the anniversary more solemn.	Popes. Gregory V. 999. Silvester II. 1003. John XVI. called the XVIII. 1003. John XVII. called the XIX. Sergius IV. 1012. Benedict VIII. 1024. John XX. 1023. *Emperors of the East.* Basilius III. 1025. Constantine X. 1028. Romanus Argyrus. 1034. *Emperors of the West.* Otho III. 1002. St. Henry, surnamed the Lame. 1024. Conrad II. surnamed the Salic. 1039. *Kings of Spain.* Veremund II. 999. Alfonso V. 1028. Veremund III. 1037. *Kings of England.* Ethelred. 1016. Edmund Ironside. 1016. Canute the Great. 1036. *Kings of Scotland.* Malcolm II. 1023. Duncan. 1030. Macbeth. 1047. *Kings of Denmark.* Sweno. 1014. Canute the Great. 1036. *Kings of Sweden.* Olaus. 1019. Amundus. 1035. *Kings of Poland.* Boleslaus, first king. 1025. Micislaus. 1034.

VOL. I. I

by the name of John XVII, in prejudice to Gregory V, who was obliged to withdraw from Rome, the emperor Otho III. restored the lawful pope, and Crescentius was killed; the antipope had his eyes pulled out, and afterwards was hanged.

1001. 1002. &c.

Henry, duke of Burgundy, brother of Hugh Capet, and uncle to Robert, dies without legitimate issue, and bequeaths his dukedom to the king. The bequest is contested by Landri count of Nevers, and by Adelbert son to the dutchess of Burgundy. Robert obliges them to submit, annexes this dutchy to the crown, and invests his second son Henry with it; who upon his accession to the throne, cedes it to his younger brother Robert. This Robert is the founder of the first royal branch of the dukes of Burgundy, which lasted near three hundred and sixty years, till this dutchy was reunited to the crown in the year 1361 by king John, who gave it to his fourth son Philip the Hardy, founder of the second house of Burgundy, which ended in Charles the Bold, slain before Nancy in 1477.

The reason why we find no letters patent of the ancient peerages, is that they were erected by the peers themselves; on the contrary, we meet with letters of peerage granted to Philip the Hardy, the stem of the second house of Burgundy, because he had been raised to this dignity by his father king John. But how comes it then that we find no letters patent granted to Henry duke of Burgundy, since he arrived to that honour merely by the liberality of Robert his father, who gave him the abovementioned dutchy and peerage? or at least that we do not meet with those, which were granted by that same Henry, when upon his accession to the crown, he resigned Burgundy to Robert his younger brother?

Saint Romuald began towards the year 1009, to found the monastery of the Camaldulenses in Italy. The death of Otho III. without issue, at the age of 29. His decree enacting that the emperors should be elected by Germans, who were to give their suffrages to princes of the Germanic nation only, delivered Italy from those petty tyrants, that alternately usurped the imperial title.

The THIRD RACE.

Ministers.	Warriors.	Magistrates.	Eminent and Learned Men.
Seneschals. William living in 1060.	Foulk Nerra, count of Anjou. 1040. Manasseh, count of Damartin, living in 1028. Burcard, count of Melun and Corbeil. Bouchard, lord of Montmorency, living in 1028.	*Chancellors.* Abbo. Arnoul, living in 1019. Roger, living in 1024. Franco, living in 1028. Baldwin. 1059.	Abbo, abbot of Fleury. 1004. Ademar, towards 1029. Aimonius, towards 1008. Arnould. 1023. Burchard, bishop of Worms. 1024. Ditmar, bishop of Wurtsburg. 1019. Fulbert. 1028. Gerbért, pope by the name of Silvester II. 1003.
Eudes, count of Chartres. 1037.			

REMARKABLE EVENTS under ROBERT.

The edict of the emperor Henry II. published at the pope's request, in order to give the force of law throughout the empire to the decree made at Pavia. The purport thereof was, that the clergy should have neither wives nor concubines, and that the sons of clergymen should be villains or bondmen to the church in which their fathers officiated, though their fathers themselves were free. The prohibition of concubines, in regard to the clergy, shews that those concubines were not what we understand at present by that name; since the divine law, by which all Christians are restrained from that kind of carnal commerce, would have been abundantly sufficient.

This indeed is a point of too great curiosity not to enlarge upon it as much as the nature of this work will permit, by abstracting a passage from Giannone, which will give a general idea of the matter. " Some writers have censured those
" laws which permit *concubinage*, and only forbid people not to
" have a wife and a concubine at the same time. But we shall
" be no longer surprised at those institutions, when we consider
" that among the Romans concubinage was a legitimate union
" not only tolerated, but authorized: for which reason they gave
" it the name of half-marriage, *semi-matrimonium*, and to the
" concubine that of half-wife, *semi-conjux*. They might have
" either a wife, or a concubine, provided they had not both at
" the same time. This usage continued afterwards, when the
" emperors embraced Christianity. Constantine the Great gave
" a check to concubinage, but did not abolish it; for it sub-
" sisted several years in the church. Of this we have a very
" authentic proof in one of the councils of Toledo, which or-
" dains, that every man, whether of the laity or clergy, ought
" to be satisfied with one companion only, wife or concubine
" without being allowed to have both at the same time . . . .
" This ancient custom of the Romans was preserved in Italy
" not only among the Lombards, but afterwards when the
" French established their dominion in that country. There
" were also some other nations, who considered concubinage a
" a legitimate union; and Cujas assures us, that the Gascon
" and other people bordering on the Pyrenean mountains, ha
" not relinquished this custom in his time." This would be
prop-

REMARKABLE EVENTS under ROBERT.

proper place for a dissertation; but I leave it to some person more capable of handling the subject than myself.

1022. &c.

A meeting of Manicheans is discovered in Orleans, whither the king and queen repaired with several prelates, in order to prevent the spreading of some errors, which a woman from Italy had propagated in that city. On this occasion divers heretics were burnt. Simony had reached to such a pitch, that episcopal sees were made a condition of matrimonial contracts, and likewise assigned for dowers: nay, there was such a relaxation of discipline, that bishoprics were conferred on children, and a pope was elected only at eighteen years of age.

A famous interview at Yvoie between Robert and this emperor Henry II, stiled the saint, who at first had only the title of king of Germany, and did not assume that of emperor, till he had been crowned at Rome. These two princes having a great esteem for each other, and being equally zealous in the cause of religion and peace, entered on this occasion into the proper measures for preserving harmony both in church and state.

Helgaud, a monk of Fleury, mentions in the life of this king, that to hinder his subjects from committing perjury, and consequently from incurring the penalties due to that crime, he made them swear on a relick-box, out of which he had taken care to remove the relicks; just as if the intention did not constitute the perjury: but in those days they knew no better.

1026. 27.

Robert having lost his eldest son Hugh, whom he caused to be crowned at Compiegne in 1017, procures his second son Henry I. to receive the regal unction at Rheims, in spite of queen Constantia, who wanted to prefer her youngest son Robert.

About this very time the Norman name began to be famous in Italy. This country was then divided between the emperors of the east and west, except the south part, which was possessed by several petty princes, Greeks, Lombards, and Italians, too near neighbours to agree, and incessantly infested by their common enemy the Saracens, who reigned in Africa, and had made themselves masters of Sicily. Forty Normans returning

REMARKABLE EVENTS under ROBERT.

from Palestine, landed in Italy just when the Saracens were attacking the town of Salerno; their courage alone preserved that place, which duke Gaimar was no longer able to defend; and the Saracens were cut in pieces. Content with the glory of this enterprize, the Normans refused the settlements offered them in Apulia, and returned to their native country. But the fame of their valour followed them wherever they went; and the gratitude of the Italians, who had loaded them with magnificent presents, excited the rest of their countrymen to signalize themselves by the like exploits. In this conjuncture the sons of Tancred of Hauteville set out for Italy, where they met with such extraordinary good fortune, as to found a flourishing empire. Tancred was twice married, and had twelve sons, with whose fame all Europe resounded, and whose history, though strictly true, has the air of a romance. William, surnamed *Bras-de-fer,* or Iron-arm, Drogo, and Hunifrid, were the three first counts of Apulia; Robert Guiscard was duke of Apulia and Calabria; his son was Boemund father of Tancred: Roger the youngest brother, made himself master of Sicily, and founded that monarchy towards the year 1129. The two Sicilies were possessed by his son Roger II. His successors were William I, William II, Tancred bastard of Roger II, and lastly William his son, whose eyes Henry VI. caused to be pulled out, in order to possess himself of those kingdoms, in right of Constantia his wife, daughter of Roger II. Such were the sovereigns of Naples and Sicily, who after expelling the Greeks and Saracens out of Italy, and seizing the territories of the Lombards and of the petty princes, governed that country before the emperors of the house of Swabia, who were succeeded by the house of Anjou.

Robert was a learned prince for his time, humane, and affable. He composed some hymns, which are still sung in churches. He had made several pilgrimages, among others one to Rome towards the year 1016, or 1020. He refused the imperial dignity, and the kingdom of Italy, which was offered him by the Italians.

REMARKABLE EVENTS.

1031.
Accession to the crown.

Henry I. succeeds to the crown, July the 20th 1031, aged about 27 years. He had been crowned at Rheims in his father's life time.

1031.

Constantia, Henry's mother, still desirous of preferring her younger son Robert to Henry, excites a rebellion, in which she is supported by Eudes count of Champagne, and Baldwin count of Flanders. Robert, surnamed the Devil, duke of Normandy, assists Henry in subduing the rebels: the count of Champagne received three different defeats.

Henry pardons his brother Robert, and gives him the dutchy of Burgundy, from whence began, as we have above observed, the first race of the dukes of Burgundy of the blood royal.

The queen dies.

1032. &c.

Henry, to acknowledge his obligations to the duke of Normandy, confers upon him the towns of Gisors, Chaumont, Pontoise, and the whole district of Vexin.

1037. 38. 39.

Eudes count of Champagne is slain in an engagement, in which the duke of Lorrain is conqueror. This war was occasioned by the succession to the kingdom of Burgundy, which consisted of a considerable part of Provence, of all Dauphiné, the provinces of Lyonnois, la Bresse, and Bugey, with the remainder of the country extending as far as mount St. Claude. This was called the second kingdom of Burgundy, and ended at length by the death of Rodolphus III, who died without issue in 1033, having bequeathed his dominions to the emperor Conrad II, surnamed the Salic. Conrad annexed as much as he could of this kingdom to the empire; hence the border of the Rhone on the side of Dauphiné and Provence, still goes by the name of Imperial land; the

remainder

The Third Race.

Wives.	Children.	1060. Death.	Cotemporary Princes.
Matilda, daughter of Conrad, one of the greatest princes that sat on the imperial throne since the reign of Charlemain, betrothed but not married to Henry I.		Henry I. departs this life towards the close of the year 1060. at Vitri in Brie, aged fifty years. He is buried at St. Denis.	*Popes.* John XX. 1033. Benedict IX. ordained in 1033. retires for the 3d time. 1048. Greg. VI. retires. 1046. Clement II. 1047. Damasus II. 1048. S. Leo IX. he is the first that used a coat of arms. 1054. Victor II. 1057. Stephen X. 1058. Nicholas II. 1061.
Anne, daughter of Jaraslaus, king of Russia, was married to Henry, in the year 1044. After the king's decease, she was married again to Raoul of Peronne, count of Crepi and Valois. Marriages of this kind were not considered at that time as degrading: upon the death of her second husband, she went to end her days in her own country.	Philip. Robert. 1060. Hugh, who married Adelaid the daughter of Herbert, and by this marriage became count of Vermandois. 1002. *This Hugh, according to some people, was the grandfather of a prince named Hugh, deceased in 1212, who associating with John of Matha, founded the order of Mathurins: through humility he changed his name from Hugh to Felix, and is now enrolled in the list of saints, by the name of St. Felix of Valois. But M. Baillet thinks this St. Felix was only a private person, born in the district of Valois, from whence he took his name.*		*Emperors of the East.* Romanus Argyrus. 1034. Michael IV. 1041. Mich. Calaph. 1042. Constantine XI. 1054. Zoe and Theodora. 1056. Mich. VI. depos. 1057. Isaac Comnenus. 1059. Constan. Ducas. 1067. *Emperors of the West.* Conrad II. 1039. Henry III. surnamed the *Black*. 1056. Henry IV. 1106. *Kings of Spain.* Veremund III. 1037. Ferdin. the Great. 1065. *Kings of England.* Canute the Great. 1036. Harold. 1040. Hardiknute. 1042. Alfred. 1043. Edward the Confessor. 1066. *Kings of Scotland.* Macbeth. 1047. Malcolm III. 1084. *Kings of Denmark.* Canute the Great. 1036. Harold his broth. 1040. Hardiknute. 1042. Magnus. 1048. Sweno II. 1074. *Kings of Sweden.* Amundus. 1035. Edmundus. 1041. Haquin. 1059. Stenchil. 1061. *Kings of Poland.* Micislaus II. 1034. Casimir. 1058. Boleslaus II. 1079.

remainder was dismembered: but of the ruins of this kingdom were formed the counties of Provence, Burgundy, Viennois, and Savoy.

1040. 41. &c.

Eudes, the younger son of Robert, conspires against Henry; Stephen and Thibaud, sons of the count of Champagne, support him in his revolt: they are defeated; and Galeran, count of Meulan, having joined them, forfeits his estate, which is confiscated to the king's use, and united to the crown.

The lord's truce, established in 1041. This was a law by which single combats were prohibited from Wednesday evening till Monday morning, out of respect to those days which Christ had consecrated by the last mysteries of his life. The royal and ecclesiastic authority could do no more, to hinder the king's subjects from destroying one another.

1047. 48. 49. 50. &c.

William the *Bastard*, son of Robert the *Devil*, who died in the year 1035, in his return from the Holy Land, had succeeded his father in the dukedom of Normandy. The possession of this country was disputed with him by several lords, descendants of the dukes of Normandy. Henry I, dubious which side to take, and tempted to benefit himself by these divisions, was still restrained by the promises he had made to Robert in favour of his son, and concluded at last with assisting him to gain the battle of Val-des-Dunes, where Henry was in danger of his life. At length started up another pretender, named William of Arques, son of Richard II. duke of Normandy, and cousin of Robert the *Devil*; he was assisted by Henry I, who grew jealous of William the Bastard; but William triumphed over this new enemy towards the year 1047. This prince was afterwards surnamed the Conqueror, from having subdued England, after Edward the Confessor had appointed him his successor.

The first errors concerning the real presence in the sacrament, broached by Berenger, archdeacon of Angers.

1056. 57. 58. 59. 60.

The emperor Henry III. procures his son Henry IV, only three years old, to be declared king of the Romans, and his

The THIRD RACE.   123

MINISTERS.	WARRIORS.	MAGISTRATES.	EMINENT and LEARNED MEN.
Seneschals. William, living in 1060. Jeffery Martel, count of Anjou. 1061.	*Constables.* Alberic, living in 1060. The office of constable, which before his time extended only to the king's stables, became now a state employment, and rose at length to be the first dignity in the kingdom next the sovereign, in the person of Matthew II. of Montmorenci. Foulk Nerra, count of Anjou. 1040. Jeffery Martel, count of Anjou. 1061. Hugh I, count of Dammartin, towards 1081.	*Chancellor.* Baldwin.	Avicenna. 1036. Stephen king of Hungary. 1038. He wrote two books, one on morality, the other on laws. Glaber Radulphus, towards 1050. Guido Aretinus, towards 1050. Helgaud, towards 1050. Humbert, cardinal, towards 1063. John, the king's physician. St. Odilo. 1049. To him we owe the institution of the feast of All Souls, which has been adopted by the church.

REMARKABLE EVENTS under HENRY I.

successor to the empire, with the consent of the lords assembled at Tribur.

The emperors begin to have their sons chosen kings of the Romans. This distinction of titles might be owing to the desire those princes had, of perpetuating the imperial dignity in their family: and as the emperors of the east with this same design caused their eldest sons to be declared *Cæsars*; in like manner the western emperors, not chusing to make use of the word *Cæsar*, which was fallen into oblivion, adopted the title of *king of the Romans*, in imitation perhaps of what really happened to Charlemain, who had been king of Italy before he was raised to the imperial throne. But what is very extraordinary, after they had been dispossessed of Italy, they still preserved the name of *king of the Romans*, with the same view no doubt of rendering the imperial crown hereditary; of adopting a title, which no longer implied any real power, but only pointed out the persons that were to fill the vacant throne; and of gradually reconciling the public to a lineal succession of princes.

Henry causes his son Philip to be crowned at Rheims in 1059, at seventeen years of age, and appoints Baldwin, count of Flanders, his guardian.

In this reign we find the beginning of the present house of Lorrain in Gerard of Alsace; and of the house of Savoy, in Humbert *with the white hands*, count of Maurienne. Gerald, count of Geneva, who lived in the reign of Rodolph III, king of Arles, is the founder of this family; and supposed to be the Berthold so celebrated in romance.

The Romans elect consuls, which weakens the authority of the pope.

The Italian cities begin to render themselves independent on the emperor; they likewise elect consuls, who are still represented in some parts of Italy by the *Podestas*.

Nicholas II, in a council held at Rome in the year 1059, confirms the emperor's right to the chusing of popes and to the investiture of bishops: the emperor was then a minor. Berenger appeared in this assembly, where he threw his writings into a fire, lighted with his own hands, and signed a confession

of

REMARKABLE EVENTS under HENRY I.

of faith, which he afterwards retracted: it is said however that he sincerely repented his errors before his decease. The same pope invested Robert Guiscard, the eldest son of Tancred, with the territories of which he was possessed in Italy: this is the foundation of the papal pretensions, to the supreme jurisdiction of the two Sicilies.

By a letter from this pontif to the clergy of Sisteron, it appears plainly that they did not confer baptism in those days, except in cases of necessity, at any other time than on the eves of Easter and Whitsunday.

1060.
Acceſſion to the crown.

Philip I. aſcends the throne in the year 1060, at eight years of age. He had been crowned at Rheims in his father's life time. This is a longer reign than any of the preceding, except that of Clotharius; and than any of the following, except that of Lewis XIV. This ſame reign is famous for ſeveral great events, in which however Philip I. had no ſhare; and he appeared the more contemptible to his ſubjects, as this century had been fruitful of heroes. Hence the royal authority was weakened greatly in his hands.

REMARKABLE EVENTS.

1060. 61.

BAldwin, count of Flanders, the king's brother-in-law, was appointed by that prince to the guardianſhip of his ſon in preference to his wife Anne, becauſe of her being a foreigner, and very little reſpected; and to the duke of Burgundy, by reaſon of his influence in France, and his having formerly pretended to the crown.

1062. 63. 64. 65. 66.

Baldwin diſcharges his truſt with honour, and ſubdues the Gaſcons, who were diſpoſed to revolt. A revolution in England (1066) upon the death of Edward the Confeſſor, who leaving no iſſue, appointed William the Baſtard, duke of Normandy, to ſucceed him.

1067. 68. 69. 70. 71. 72. 73. 74. &c.

Baldwin dies, when the king is but fifteen years of age. This prince makes war in Flanders, where he is beaten in the neighbourhood of St. Omer by Robert, the younger ſon of Baldwin, who ſeizes Flanders in prejudice to his nephews, the ſons of his elder brother, ſlain in this war.

Gregory VII, in the famous *Dictatus*, of which he is ſaid to be the author, eſtabliſhed it as a maxim, that the pope has a right to depoſe the emperor, and to releaſe his ſubjects from their oath of allegiance. (*Father Harduin's councils, the year* 1075.) Some hiſtorians pretend that this work is not his; be that as it may, there is no doubt but the principles of this pontif were the ſame as thoſe of the *Dictatus*; ſince he has advanced the like doctrine in his thirty fifth letter to Roderic, biſhop of Chalons; in his letter to Heriman, &c. But what is very ſingular, this ſame Gregory began his reign with

aſking

The THIRD RACE. 127

WIVES.	CHILDREN.	1108. DEATH.	Cotemporary PRINCES.
Bertha, daughter of Florentius count of Holland, whom Philip I. divorced. 1093.	Lewis VI, furnamed *Craſſus* or the *Groſs*. Henry died young. Charles. Conſtantia, married to Hugh, count of Troyes, and afterwards to Boemond, prince of Antioch. *Natural Children.* Philip I. had by *Bertrada of Monfort, wife of the count of Anjou,* Philip, count of Mante, lord of Mehun. Florus, or Fleury. Cecilia, married to Tancred, nephew of Boemond: afterwards to *Pontus Toloſanus*, count of Tripoli. Euſtache, wife of John count d'Etampes, *of whom father Anſelm makes no mention.*	Philip I. dies at Melun in his fifty ſeventh year; July the 29th 1108. His body was removed to the abbey of St. Benedict on the Loire, where he had choſen to be interred.	*Popes.* Nicholas II. 1061. Alexander II. 1073. Gregory VII. 1085. Victor III. 1087. Urban II. 1099. Paſchal II. 1117. *Emperors of the Eaſt.* Conſtantine Ducas. 1067. Romanus Diogenes. 1071. Michael VII. depoſed. 1078. Nicephorus depoſed. 1080. Alexius Comnenus. 1118. *Emperors of the Weſt.* Henry IV. 1106. Henry V. 1125. *Kings of Spain.* Ferdinand the Great. 1065. Sancho II. 1073. Alfonſo VI. 1109. *Kings of England.* Edward the Confeſſor. 1066. Harold. 1066. William the Conqueror. 1087. William Rufus. 1100. Henry I. 1135. *Kings of Scotland.* Malcolm III. 1084. Duncan II. 1084. Edgar. 1095. Alexander. 1114. *Kings of Denmark.* Sweno II. 1074. Harold VII. 1085. St. Canute. 1086. Olaus II. 1086. Nicholas. 1135. *Kings of Sweden.* Stenchil. 1061. Ingo III. 1064. Halſtan. 1080. Philip. 1110. *Kings of Poland.* Boleſlaus II. 1079. Ladiſlaus. 1162. Boleſlaus III. 1139.

REMARKABLE EVENTS under PHILIP I.

asking the emperor's approbation upon his exaltation to the pontificate. Historians are much divided in their opinion concerning this pope, who was canonized by Gregory XIII.

Matilda, countess of Tuscany, (1077) grants all her territories to the holy see. Foulk, count of Anjou, makes a donation (1079) to the king, of the country of Gatinoy, which was annexed to the crown. Foundation of the order of Carthusian monks (1086).

William the Conqueror departs this life at Rouen the 9th of September 1087, and is interred at St. Stephen's in Caen. This prince took care to provide the churches in his dominions with good pastors: he was likewise an encourager of learning, which stood in need of such a protector, at a time when books were so scarce, that Grecia, countess of Anjou, gave for a collection of homilies, 200 sheep, a measure * of wheat, another of rie, another of millet, and a number of sables. He was a great lover of public justice. He ordered the laws of England to be written in French, the language of his court, which he wanted to introduce into schools. Godfrey of Bouillon afterwards made the same regulation in Palestine, upon his accession to that crown; and we have the *customs* otherwise called the *assizes and good usages of the kingdom of Jerusalem*, written in the Romance language.

William settled Normandy upon his eldest son Robert; England upon his second son William; and to his third son he gave the estate of his mother Matilda.

1088. &c.

The kingdom of Portugal is founded by Henry of Burgundy, who married one of the daughters of Alfonso VI, king of Castile, by whom he had been created count of Portugal.

1092. 93. 94. 95. 96. 97. 98. 99.

Philip having in 1091 repudiated his wife Bertha, by whom he had several children, marries Bertrada of Monfort, whom he inveigles away from her husband Foulk Rechin, count of Anjou,

---

* In the original it is *muid*, a French measure, containing five quarters, a comb, and a bushel.

and

The Third Race. 129

Ministers.	Warriors.	Magistrates.	Eminent and Learned Men.
Seneschals. Raoul, living in 1067. Frederic, living in 1075. Robert, living in 1079. Gervase, living in 1086. Guy of Montlherri. 1108. Hugh of Montlherri, living in 1118.	*Constables.* Balderic, living in 1068. Walter, living in 1069. Aleaume, living in 1074. Adam, living in 1079. Thibaud of Montmorenci, living in 1090. Walo. 1097. Matthew, living in 1097. Gaston of Poissy, living in 1107. Hugh of Chaumont. 1138. *Chiefs of the first crusade.* Hugh the Great, count of Vermandois. Robert, duke of Normandy. Robert, count of Flanders. Raymond, count of Toulouse. Bohemond. Godfrey of Bouillon, with his brothers Baldwin and Eustace. Stephen, count de Chartres. Hugh, count de St. Pol.	*Chancellors.* Gervase. 1084. He performed the ceremony of the king's coronation, as archbishop of Rheims, and pretended that the dignity of chancellor of France was annexed to his see: he is said to have succeeded in his pretension, both in favour of himself and the church of Rheims. Indeed he was the third archbishop since Herveus, that possessed the dignity of chancellor; but we do not find that since his time, this high office has been annexed to that see. Baldwin II. living in 1063. Peter Loiseleves. 1082. William, living in 1074. Roger. 1095. Godfrey of Boulogne, living in 1092. Ursion, living in 1090. Hubert of Boulogne, living in 1092. Stephen of Senlis. 1140.	Adam of Bremen, towards 1075. Adelmannus. 1062. Berengarius. 1088. Berto. 1100. St. Bruno. 1101. Drogo. 1098. Guitmund, towards 1080. Lambert, bishop of Arras, towards 1077. Lanfrank. 1089. Gilbert Maminot, bishop of Lizieux, first physician to William the Conqueror. Marianus Scotus. 1086. Odo, bishop of Cambray, was living in 1090. He was of the sect of the *Realists.* Petrus Damianus. 1072. Radulphus Ardens, towards 1100. Raimbert presided in the schools of the chapter of Lisle, founded in 1055. He was of the sect of *Nominals.* Lewis XI. was obliged to publish an edict for suppressing the ridiculous sects of Nominals and Realists.

Vol. I.   K

REMARKABLE EVENTS under PHILIP I.

and is excommunicated (1094) by pope Urban II. This count of Anjou had been divorced from two wives, when he married Bertrada; and the second wife was wedded again to another husband. The death of Bertha made the king flatter himself, that the pope would approve of his marriage with Bertrada; but he was excommunicated once more (1095) in the council of Clermont.

The first crusade was determined in this council, under the pontificate of Urban II. (The bishops as yet had the precedency of cardinals.) In this assembly the name of pope was for the first time given to the head of the church, exclusively of the bishops, who used to assume that title; and here also Hugh, archbishop of Lyons, obtained of the pope a confirmation of the primacy of his see over that of Sens. Godfrey of Bouillon is appointed to command this expedition: he was made king of Jerusalem in the year 1099, at the end of this first crusade; though he chose only to be called the advocate, or defender of the holy sepulchre. The chief persons concerned in this enterprize, were Hugh the king's brother, Robert duke of Normandy, Raymond count de Touloufe, Bohemond, Baldwin, Godfrey of Bouillon, Stephen count de Boulogne, father of the king of England of that name, &c. Bohemond, son of Robert Guiscard, went in search of adventures, and gained the principality of Antioch, together with the honour of marrying a daughter of France. Hugh, king Philip's brother, sought for an opportunity to signalize himself, and to remove from a country, where he partook of the ignominy of a king, who was a slave to all his passions, and had degraded himself in the opinion of his people, by his vices; but still more so by his shameful submission to ecclesiastical penances. But as for Robert, duke of Normandy, as he had been excluded from the crown of England by his brother William Rufus, was it not his interest to try to recover so rich an inheritance? Instead of that, he mortgaged the dukedom of Normandy, the only possession left him, to this very William, in order to defray the expence of his pilgrimage. And if we come to old Raymond, count de Touloufe, what business had he, who was master of almost all Languedoc,

and

REMARKABLE EVENTS under PHILIP I.

and part of Provence, to go a crusading at his time of life, at the head of a hundred thousand men? Little did he foresee that this example would be turned one day against himself; and that his own family would shortly be sacrificed to another crusade. But, in truth, they were both determined by the general bias, which had set all Europe in motion.

The crown of Jerusalem devolved, for want of male descendants, from Godfrey to the house of Anjou, and from thence to Guy of Lusignan, who after the fatal battle of Tiberiad, was no longer able to defend himself against the count de Montferrat. John de Brienne was afterwards raised to that throne: but this whole succession of regal titles served only to add splendor to families, without any great advantage or profit. The emperor Frederic, having married the daughter of John de Brienne, was invested with all her rights, which he did not think it worth his while to assert; and the conquest of Jerusalem being no longer an object of ambition, after the misfortunes of the holiest of our kings, this city became, what it had been before Godfrey's expedition, a place of pilgrimage. It was upon the occasion of those wars, that the orders of the Hospitallers, the Templars, and the Teutonic knights were instituted. The founders of the two last could hardly be able to know their successors. But as for the knights Hospitallers of St. John of Jerusalem, they have preserved the spirit of their first institution, and still continue to defend their religion against the Turks. Philip (1096) dismisses Bertrada, and is reconciled to the church; but relapses to his former scandalous life (1097). The order of Citeaux, founded by some monks of the order of St. Benedict, belonging to the abbey of Molesme.

1100. 1. 2.

Philip is excommunicated anew in the council of Poitiers. England and Normandy are reunited under Henry I. upon the decease of William Rufus, who had already possessed himself of Normandy, though he had no other right to that province, than by a mortgage from his brother Robert, at his setting out for Palestine. Robert upon his return recovered Normandy by an accommodation with Henry; but the two brothers having afterwards quarrelled, the former was defeated by the latter in 1106, at the battle of Tinchebray [*], and Normandy annexed to the crown of England. Arpin fells his vicounty of Bourges to Philip, who orders homage to be yielded in his name to the count of Sancerre, for a spot of land dependent on that nobleman. Amazing! that the king should pay homage to his subjects: but this custom was wisely abolished by Philip the Fair in 1302, who changed the homage into an indemnity.

1103. 4. 5. &c.

Lewis the *Gross*, having been associated to the regal dignity by his father, quells some disturbances in the kingdom. An assembly of bishops convened at Baugency by Richard, legate of the holy see: the king was present at this meeting, in company with Bertrada, but they could not agree as to the conditions, upon which he was to receive absolution. King Philip at length is absolved at Paris, by Lambert bishop of Arras, the pope's deputy, and promises, in the presence of several prelates, to break off all acquaintance with Bertrada. He did not however observe his promise; for we find in a roll of St. Nicholas's at Angers, that in the year 1106, on the sixth of the ides of October, Bertrada was in that city in company with Philip, to pay a visit to Rechin her former husband; that Rechin gave them a sumptuous entertainment; and Bertrada waited upon them both at table. In all probability the count of Anjou had consented to this second marriage; for we learn from Suger, in the life of Lewis the Gross, that Bertrada's two sons were declared capable of succeeding to the crown, which makes us presume, that the pope at length approved of their nuptials. Bertrada had a dower granted her upon the royal demesnes, which was the estate of Haute-Bruyere, in the neighbourhood of Montfort, and diocese of Chartres, where she founded a priory; and died not long after, having taken the veil as a nun of Fontevrault from the hands of Robert of Arbrissel. About this time the popes began to shake off their dependance on the

---

[*] A large town in the Lower Normandy.

emperor

REMARKABLE EVENTS under PHILIP I.

emperor. The quarrel in regard to investitures continued. A schism arises between the priesthood and the empire, which proved equally destructive to the emperor Henry IV, and to pope Gregory VII: during this celebrated contest, both the emperor and the pontif, for want of understanding each other, exceeded the limits of their respective jurisdiction, the church endeavouring to encroach upon the state, and the state upon the church: in the issue, the emperor was stripped of his imperial dignity, and Gregory VII. of the pontificate. To this purpose we might apply a passage of the Greek history: take heed, said a person one day to the Athenians, lest your care of celestial concerns, do not make you lose your earthly possessions; for at that time they were ruining themselves in sacred edifices. The like advice might have been given to the pope: have a care that your greediness for earthly possessions, do not make you forfeit heaven: your spiritual power will be disputed presently, if you persist in usurping the temporal. The times are now altered: matters have been cleared up; and each party is in the peaceable enjoyment of his rights and privileges. But what is very well worth observing, the emperor, who exceeded his power in this controversy with the pope, was ignorant of his own prerogative, as plainly appears from a letter addressed to Gregory by the assembly of Worms, where we find these words: "that according to the tradition of the fathers, a sovereign prince has God alone for his judge; so that he cannot be deposed for any crime, unless he *apostatizes* from the faith." Just as if subjects could be discharged from their oath of allegiance, because their king was become a heretic. The council of Troyes (1107) restrains the clergy from marrying.

Philip is the first of our kings, who, to give sanction to his charters and letters patent, ordered them to be signed by the great officers; on which occasion they were also subscribed by the king's preceptors. At the dedication of the priory of St. Martin's in the fields, after the names of the king, of Hugh his brother, of Baldwin count of Flanders, regent of the kingdom, and of his son Baldwin of Mons, we read in the month of May 1067, *Ingelramus pædagogus regis*. In like man-

REMARKABLE EVENTS under PHILIP I.

ner in a charter granted to Melun the same year, in favour of the abbey of Fleury, we find Ingelram stiled *Magister Regis*; and Marcellin *master* of Hugh the king's brother: the king's confessor sometimes enjoyed the same honour.

The foundation of the order of Fontevrault, the head of which is a woman.

The death of the emperor Henry IV, at the age of fifty five. It is as difficult to point out the virtues and vices of this prince, as those of the pontif, who was the cause of all his misfortunes. Conrad, his eldest son, rebelled against him, and made himself king of Italy; his second son poisoned him, and seized the imperial crown, by the name of Henry V.

1108.
Accession to the crown.

LEWIS *VI, surnamed* CRASSUS, *or the Grofs, succeeds to the crown in* 1108, *aged about thirty years. The ceremony of his coronation was performed at Orleans by the archbishop of Sens, because at that time there was a schism in the church of Rheims, in consequence of two pretenders to that archbishopric.*

He had been associated to the crown in 1099, during his father's life time.

REMARKABLE EVENTS.

1108.

THE demesnes immediately belonging to the king, were at that time no more than the dutchy of France, which comprehended the city of Paris, with a few other towns, and about thirty seignories. The remainder was the property of the king's vassals, who indeed yielded homage to him for their fiefs, but in every other respect acted as masters on their own estates, and exercised a kind of sovereignty.

The most turbulent among these were the counts de Corbeil and Mante, the lord of Puiset in the country of Beauce, with those of Coucy, Montfort, Montlherri, Rochefort, &c. whose fiefs being intermixed with the royal demesnes, divided the sovereign's forces, and at the same time supported each other. The possession of the dutchy of Normandy had rendered the king of England a near neighbour, who was always sure to assist the rebels: hence arose these petty wars between the king and his subjects, in which the latter part of the reign of Philip I, and the beginning of that of Lewis the Grofs, were so greatly entangled. The single castle of Puiset held out three years against this prince.

The misfortunes of the times may justify the crusades, which the kings made subservient to their interest, by employing their brave vassals in distant countries.

1113. 14. 15.

The beginning of the wars betwixt France and England; which did not terminate till the reign of Charles VII.

Lewis the Grofs too late perceived his mistake in suffering the English to get footing in France, when he might have opposed Henry I, king of Eng-

The Third Race.

WIVES.	CHILDREN.	1137. DEATH.	Cotemporary PRINCES.
Adelaid, daughter of Humbert, count of Maurienne and Savoy, married to Lewis in 1115. She was married again, after the death of Lewis, to Matthew of Montmorency, constable of France, and died in the year 1154. This princess founded the abbey of Montmartre. *Lewis the Gross married Luciana in 1104, daughter of Guido le Rouge, count of Rochford. This marriage, having never been consummated, was declared null and void, at the council of Troyes in 1107, on account of consanguinity.*	Philip associated to the kingdom; he died before his father of a fall from his horse. 1131. LEWIS THE YOUNG. Henry, canon of the church of Notre Dame of Paris, afterwards monk of Clairvaux, then bishop of Beauvais, and lastly archbishop of Rheims. Hugh died young. Robert, founder of the house of Dreux, whose grandson Peter, surnamed *Mauclerc*, was count of Britany, in right of Alice his wife, heiress of that county, from whom Anne of Britany descended. Robert had also a granddaughter, named *Alice*, who was married to Rainard III, lord of Choiseul, the stem of the house of Choiseul. Philip, archdeacon of the church of Paris, having been chosen bishop of that city, resigned this dignity, through modesty, to Peter Lombard, surnamed *master of the sentences*. Peter, who married Isabella, daughter and heiress of Renaud, lord of Courtenay. 1183. Constantia, married to Eustace of Blois, crowned king of England in 1152, during the life of his father Stephen, and by whom she had no issue; married afterwards to Raymond count de Toulouse, who was living in 1176.	LEWIS the GROSS dies at Paris the first of August, 1137, aged about sixty years. He is interred at St. Denis. The last words of Lewis the Gross are very remarkable: *Remember, my son, and have it always before thine eyes, that the regal dignity is only a public trust, of which thou art to give a strict account after thy decease.*	*Popes.* Paschal II. 1117. Gelasius II. 1119. Calixtus II. 1124. Honorius II. 1130. Innocent II. 1143. *Emperors of the East.* Alexius Comnenus. 1118. Johannes Comnenus. 1143. *Emperors of the West.* Henry V. 1125. Lotharius II. 1138. *Kings of Spain.* Alfonso VI. 1109. Alfonso VII. 1137. Alfonso VIII. 1157. *Kings of England.* Henry I. 1135. Stephen. 1154. *Kings of Scotland.* Alexander I. called the Fierce. 1114. David I. 1143. *Kings of Denmark.* Nicholas. 1135. Eric III. 1138. *Kings of Sweden.* Philip. 1110. Ingo IV. 1129. Ragwald. 1140. *King of Poland.* Boleslaus III. 1139.

REMARKABLE EVENTS under LEWIS the GROSS.

England, to prevent his making a conquest of Normandy, and wresting it from Robert his elder brother, to whom that province in right belonged, according to their father's testament.

Henry refuses to sequestrate the fortress of Gisor, or to raze it to the ground, pursuant to agreement; because this place was upon the frontier of France and Normandy. Lewis declares war against Henry, which was remarkable for a great number of battles, the vassals joining with either party, according to their interests: it was concluded in 1114 by a treaty, which left Gisors in possession of the English on condition of homage. St. Bernard founds the abbey of Clairvaux.

1116. 17. &c.

Lewis the Gross being desirous at length to repair the damage, which his father's ill policy had occasioned, and was likely still more to occasion to France, undertook to protect William Clito *, surnamed *Courtecuisse*, or *Short-thigh*, son of Robert, whom Henry had kept in prison ever since the battle of Tinchebray; and to restore him to the dutchy of Normandy, which had belonged to his father. But it was now too late, for Henry was grown too powerful; so that Lewis the Gross was beaten at the battle of Brenneville in 1119.

Henry strengthens his interest by marrying two of his daughters, the one, named Matilda or Maud, to the emperor Henry V; the other, also Maud †, to Conan, son of the duke of Britany; and makes the latter yield homage to him for this dutchy. His claim was founded on this, that as Neustria had been ceded to the Normans, and Britany, according to him, did depend on that province, it ought therefore to be held in fee of the new dukes of Normandy. Their grandson was Conan IV, father of Constance, the widow of Geoffrey of England, count of Anjou, by whom she had no issue; but by Guy, count

---

* The English historians call him William Crito; and according to them, he was surnamed *Courte-hose*, either from wearing his breeches very short, or because his legs were disproportioned in length to the rest of his body.

† This was a natural daughter. He was twice married, first to Maud, daughter of Malcolm, king of the Scots; and afterwards to Adelaid, daughter of Geoffrey count of Lovain, by whom he had no issue; but by his first wife he had William, who was drowned, and Matilda, who was married to the emperor Henry V, and afterwards to Geoffrey Plantagenet.

- de

REMARKABLE EVENTS under LEWIS the GROSS.

de Thouars, she had Alice, wife of Peter of Dreux, the great grandson of Lewis the Grofs, and through him Britany devolved to the house of France, in which it is likely for ever to continue.

The king's affairs obliging him to be reconciled to his chief vassals, he restores the count of Anjou to the place of seneschal. This office had been hereditary in the house of Anjou, ever since the reign of Lothaire: but either the declension of the royal authority, made those lords think it beneath them to officiate in person; or they were excluded from this service, by waging war against the king. For which reason, the Garlandes, ministers, and favourites of Lewis the Grofs, exercised that employment in their stead. This count, however, apprehending that his right would be extinguished, resumed his post; and afterwards consented that William de Garlande should continue in the discharge thereof during his absence, on condition of his holding it in fee, and yielding homage to him for it. This is not the only great office, which the lords proprietors granted in fee to persons of inferior rank and authority.

Lewis the Grofs favours the monks of *St. Maurdes Fossés*, with the privilege of ordering single combats between their villains and freemen.

1120. &c.

St. Norbert institutes the order of Premonstratenses.

A peace is settled between Lewis and Henry, who renews his homage for Normandy.

The king of England meets with a terrible misfortune in his family; his son, and the flower of the nobility, having been cast away within sight of the harbour of Barfleur, where they had but just embarked on their return to England *.

This event revives the interests of William Clito; several lords, as well Normans as French, declare themselves in his favour, and are privately supported by Lewis the Grofs. Henry gains the advantage in this war, and stirs up the emperor against the king.

* In this shipwreck perished his legitimate son William duke of Normandy, his natural son Richard, Matilda his natural daughter, his niece Lucia, the earl of Chester, &c. with a hundred and forty officers and soldiers, fifty sailors, most of whom were in liquor, which was the occasion of their running upon the rocks near Barfleur. This misfortune had such an effect upon the king, that he was never seen to laugh after it.

REMARKABLE EVENTS under LEWIS the GROSS.

The emperor Henry V. makes preparations for invading Champagne, in order to be revenged of an affront, which he pretended to have received in the council of Rheims, where he had been excommunicated on account of the inveftitures. The king affembles all his vaffals; even the clergy marched on this occafion; and Suger, abbot of St. Denis, joined his fovereign with the *fubjects* of the abbey * : the army was upwards of two hundred thoufand ftrong; fo that the emperor durft not venture an engagement againft fo confiderable a force. Lewis might have eafily marched his troops forthwith againft the king of England, and recovered Normandy; were it not that his vaffals, who followed his banner againft a foreign prince, would have deferted him, if he had attacked the duke of Normandy, it being their intereft to preferve a balance between thofe two powers.

The quarrel about inveftitures ended in 1122, by the treaty between Calixtus II. and Henry V; in which this prince refigned great part of his prerogative. The fubftance of the accommodation was, that the emperor fhould agree not to confer the inveftiture any longer, but by the *fceptre*; whereas before he ufed to deliver it with the *crofs* and *ring*.

The archbifhop of Vienne forms pretenfions to the primacy of France, founded on a bull of Calixtus II. in the year 1120.

The clergy of Rome are declared to have the fole right of chufing the pope, without the confent or confirmation of the emperor.

1127. 28. 29.

Lewis avenges the parricide committed upon the perfon of Charles the Good, count of Flanders, who was affaffinated in the church of St. Donatianus at the time of divine fervice. The king adjudges this county, vacant in failure of iffue, to William Clito, nephew of Henry I, who ftill affumed the title of duke of Normandy. Charles the Good was of the houfe of Denmark, fon of Canute, and count of Flanders by his mother

---

* On this occafion we firft hear of the Oriflamme, which was, ftrictly fpeaking, the banner of the abbey of St. Denis, being a crimfon flag fixed to a gilt lance, from whence it derived its name; and from its being carried on this occafion before the king, it came in procefs of time to be confidered as the royal ftandard of France.

The THIRD RACE. 141

MINISTERS.	WARRIORS.	MAGISTRATES.	EMINENT and LEARNED MEN.
Seneschals. Anseau de Garlande. 1118. William de Garlande, who yielded homage for this office to Foulk, count of Anjou, afterwards king of Jerusalem. 1120. Stephen de Garlande. 1150. Raoul of Peronne, count of Vermandois. 1152. Suger. 1152. Stephen of Senlis, bishop of Paris. 1140. Algrin, who is stiled the king's secretary.	Hugh de Chaumont. 1138. Thibaud, count de Chartres. 1152. Thomas de Marle, lord of Coucy. Hugh de Crecy. 1112. Amalarius de Montfort. Hugh lord of Puiset. Guido of Rochefort. 1112. Milo, vicount of Troyes.	*Chancellors.* Stephen of Senlis. 1140. Stephen de Garlande. 1150. Simon, living in 1130. Algrin, living in 1137.	Anselm of Canterbury. 1109. Stephen of Autun. 1138. Eudes of Cambray. 1113. Guibert, abbot of Nogent. 1124. William of Champeaux. 1121. Hildebert, bishop of Mans. 1132. Ivo Carnotensis. 1115. Leo Ostiensis, towards 1112. Marbodus. 1123. St. Norbert. 1134. Robert of Arbrissel. 1117. Roscelin. 1110. Rupertus. 1135. Sigebert. 1113.

REMARKABLE EVENTS under LEWIS the GROSS.

Adela, heirefs of Robert the Frifon. Lewis affociates Philip, his eldeft fon, and caufes him to be crowned.

Thierry of Alface, fupported by Henry I, attacks William Clito, and is beaten; but William receiving a wound *, which proved fatal to him, Flanders remained in Thierry's poffeffion, and Henry ceafed to have a competitor for the dukedom of Normandy.

1130. 31. 32. 33. 34.

A frefh fchifm between Innocent II. and Anacletus. The former is acknowledged legitimate pope in the council of Etampes, where the matter is referred to St. Bernard. During this conteft, Roger, a Norman prince, founded the kingdom of the two Sicilies: he received the inveftiture thereof from the antipope Anacletus II, whofe election he had acknowledged as legitimate; and it was granted him anew by Innocent II. in 1139. The young king Philip having been killed by a fall from his horfe, Lewis the Grofs caufed his fecond fon Lewis the Young to be crowned at Rheims (1131) by pope Innocent II.

1135. 36. 37.

Henry I, king of England, dies without any other iffue than Matilda, widow of the emperor Henry V, whom he had married again to Geoffrey Plantagenet, fon of the count of Anjou, and made his heir. Stephen count of Boulogne, nephew of Henry I. by his fifter Adela, was preferred by the Englifh to Geoffrey; which occafioned great difturbances in that kingdom: but after Stephen's deceafe, Henry II, the eldeft fon of the count of Anjou, afcended the throne.

Full homage or allegiance began to be known by the charter of inveftiture, which Lewis the Grofs granted to Foulk count of Anjou.

Lewis the Grofs departs this life. He is the firft of our kings that went to take the holy ftandard, called *Oriflamme*, from the abbey of St. Denis; and he founded St. Victor. He was a prince refpectable for his gentle manners, and for every royal virtue: but he was a bad politician, which rendered him always a dupe to Henry I. king of England.

---

* At the fiege of Aloft, which Thierry had undertaken to raife.

REMARKABLE EVENTS under LEWIS the GROSS.

And yet this prince began to recover the authority usurped by the vassals; which he accomplished partly by establishing the commons, or third estate; partly by enfranchising the villains or bondmen; and partly by diminishing the exorbitant authority of the seignioral jurisdictions: it is true, this was not so much owing to the king, as to the four brothers the Garlandes, and to the abbot Suger, his ministers. With regard to the article of the judiciary power, it was recovered in this and the succeeding reigns, in the following manner.

The first thing our kings did, was to send commissaries into the provinces, formerly called *Missi Dominici*, and afterwards *judges of the exempt or privileged:* they inquired into the conduct of the dukes and counts; received the complaints of such as had been oppressed by those officers; and in cases where they did not pronounce sentence themselves, they referred them to the king's great assizes, or parliament, stiled in the capitularies of Charlemain, *Mallum Imperatoris*.

The next step they took, was to create successively four great bailiffs throughout their demesnes, who by the privilege of *Royal cases* became sole judges in a great number of causes, exclusive of the lords: these same bailiffs being grown too powerful, the judiciary power was extended to their lieutenants. In consequence of this, the king obliged the lords to resign this power also to their officers. And at length the appeals from those seignioral courts to the royal judges, intirely put an end to the exorbitant power of private jurisdiction; and therefore, says Loyseau, *this right or privilege of determining appeals, is the surest support of the sovereign authority.*

REMARKABLE EVENTS.

1137.
Accession to the crown.

LEWIS *VII*, furnamed THE YOUNG, ascends the throne the first of August 1137, aged eighteen years. He was surnamed the Young, to distinguish him from his father, with whom he had reigned in conjunction for some years.

La Roche Flavin assigns another cause for his being surnamed the *Young*, namely, for having restored Guyenne to Eleanor.

1137. 38. 39.

AS the authority of our kings of the thir[d] race grew more settled, they believed the[y] might act with less caution in regard to securin[g] the crown in their families: for which reaso[n] Lewis the Young did not follow his father['s] example in the ceremony of a second coronation[,] nor did Philip Augustus think it necessary to hav[e] his son crowned in his life-time.

Lewis the Young, a brave prince, but per[-]haps indiscreetly devout, had like to have lo[st] his dominions: his marriage with Eleano[r] daughter and heiress of William duke of Aqu[i]taine, rendered him very powerful; yet the no[-]bles, whose pride had been so well humble[d] by Lewis the Gross, began to raise their head[s] at the instigation of Thibaud count of Cham[-]pagne.

The code of laws compiled by order of Theo[-]dosius the younger, towards the year 435, a[nd] introduced by the Romans into France, was lo[st] towards the end of the second race. The co[de] published by Justinian in 529, and to which [we] had been entire strangers, was found in Apul[ia] towards the year 1137, and brought to Franc[e] where it is become our written law. (The B[e]nedictine fathers, in *their literary history of Fran*[ce] pretend that this event happened at least [a] century later.) Cujas has since restored t[he] Theodosian code; but at present it is on[ly] used for consulting.

1140. 41.

The doctrine of Abelard is censured at t[he] council of Sens. Abelard himself had been [al]ready stigmatized at the council of Soissons, 1121, from whence he appealed to the pope, wh[o]

The THIRD RACE. 145

WIVES.	CHILDREN.	1180. DEATH.	Cotemporary PRINCES.
Eleanor, whom Lewis repudiated. She married a second husband, Henry count of Anjou, who afterwards succeeded to the crown of England. 1204.	Mary married to Henry I. count of Champagne: 1198. Alice, married to Thibaud, count of Blois, living in 1183.	LEWIS the YOUNG dies at Paris, the 18th of Sept. 1180, aged about 60 years, of a palsy by a pilgrimage to St. Thomas of Canterbury's tomb, in order to obtain the recovery of his son Philip's health. He found his son recovered at his return, but fell ill himself of the distemper, of which he died. He was interred in the abbey of Barbeaux, near Melun.	*Popes.* Innocent II. 1143. Celestin II. 1144. Lucius II. 1145. Eugenius III. 1153. Anastasius IV. 1155. Adrian IV. 1159. Alexander III. 1181. *Emperors of the East.* Johannes Comnenus. 1143. Emmanuel Comnenus. 1180.
Constantia, daughter of Alfonso VIII. king of Castile. 1160.	Margaret, married first to Henry the Young, surnamed *Courtmantel*, son of Henry II. king of England; and secondly to Bela III. king of Hungary. 1197. Alice died young.		*Emperors of the West.* Lotharius II. 1138. Conrad III. 1152. Frederic I. 1190. *Kings of Spain.* Sancho III. 1158. Ferdinand II. 1175. Alfonso IX. 1214. *Kings of Portugal.* Alfonso I. proclaimed king of Portugal in 1139. died in 1185. He was son of Henry of Burgundy, grandson of Robert of France, whom Alfonso VI. created count of Portugal. *Kings of England.* Stephen. 1154. Henry II. 1189. *Kings of Scotland.* David I. 1143. Malcolm IV. 1155. William. 1214. *Kings of Denmark.* Eric III. 1138. Eric IV. 1147. Sweno & Canute. 1155. Waldemar I. 1182. *Kings of Sweden.* Ragwald. 1140. Swercher. 1160. Eric IX. 1162. Charles VII. 1168. Canute. 1192. *Kings of Poland.* Boleslaus II. 1139. Ladislaus. 1146. Boleslaus IV. 1173. Micislaus deposed and restored. 1202. Casimir II. 1194.
Alice, daughter of Thibaud, count of Champagne. 1206.	PHILIP AUGUSTUS. Alice contracted to Richard I. king of England, and afterwards married to William count of Ponthieu. 1195. Agnes, wife of young Alexius Comnenus, the son of Emmanuel, emperor of Constantinople. She was married the second time to Andronicus, who dethroned Alexius; and her third husband was a lord of Adrianople.		

VOL. I. L

REMARKABLE EVENTS under LEWIS the YOUNG.

whom he was also condemned: but as he was going to Rome, in order to pursue his appeal, Peter the Venerable prevailed on him to stay at the abbey of Cluny, where he died two years after, that is, in 1142, having edified that monastery by his humility and retractation. Eloisa, whose mournful tale is so well known, survived him two and twenty years, for she did not depart this life till 1163. Abelard's body was removed to the monastery of Paraclet *, of which Eloisa was abbess.

The beginning of the Guelfs and Gibellines, two factions into which Italy was long divided. The former were attached to the pope, the latter to the emperor.

1142. 43. 44.

Disputes between the king and the court of Rome, fomented by Thibaud count of Champagne. Innocent II. had obligations to the king, since this pontif had been preferred to his competitor Anacletus II, in a council held at Etampes. This however did prevent his laying the king's demesnes under an interdict, on account of the archbishopric of Bourges, where Innocent II supported the person elected by the chapter, though the king, in virtue of his prerogative, had opposed this election.

Lewis the young, in order to be revenged of Thibaud, puts the inhabitants of Vitri in Pertois to the sword, and sets the town on fire (1143).

1145. 46. 47.

St. Bernard advises the king to undertake a crusade in person, in order to expiate that crime. The abbot Suger strongly opposes this step, and endeavours to persuade him only to send a body of troops; but St. Bernard's counsels were received as inspirations from heaven. It was the peculiar felicity of this extraordinary man to sway the human mind one moment he concealed himself in the recesses of his solitude the next he shone in the magnificence of a court; never out of his place; yet without a title or public character; and deriving from his personal merit a degree of estimation, superior to all authority: though he was but a poor monk of Clairvaux, he enjoyed more power than the abbot Suger, the first minister of

---

* A famous monastery in the diocese of Troyes in Champagne, situate on the little river Ardue, in the parish of Quincy, within a league of Nogent sur Seine.

The THIRD RACE.

WARRIORS.	MAGISTRATES.	EMINENT and LEARNED MEN.
Constables.	*Chancellors.*	Abelard. 1142.
ugh of Chaumont. 1158.	Noel, living in 1142.	St. Bernard. 1152.
Iatthew of Montmorenci. 1160.	Cadurc. 1198.	Arnold of Brescia. 1155.
mon de Neaufle, living in 1150.	Bartholomew, living in 1147.	Eloisa. 1163.
ioul, count of Clermont. 1191.	Simon, living in 1152.	Gilbert of Poirée. 1154.
	Alderic.	Gratian. 1151,
	Hugh de Chamfleuri. 1175.	Hugo de St. Victor. 1140.
	Hugh de Puiseaux. 1185.	Goscelin. 1152.
		Otho of Freisingen, brother by the same venter to Conrad III. 1158.
		Peter the notary, *vacante cancellaria*, living in 1157.
		Petrus Lombardus. 1164.
		Peter, surnamed the *Venerable*, abbot of Cluni. 1157.
		Richardus de St. Victore. 1173.

REMARKABLE EVENTS under LEWIS the YOUNG.

France; and he preserved over his disciple pope Eugene III. an influence, which did honour to them both. St. Bernard however was no great politician, though conspicuous for sanctity and learning. His sermons are master pieces: M. Henry de Valois, the ornament of the last century, preferred them to all the discourses of the ancients, whether Greek or Latin; and indeed he is stiled the last of the fathers. In the preface to an edition of his works, we find a curious dissertation on the question, whether his sermons were pronounced in French or in Latin. What seems to prove that he pronounced them in French, is, that illiterate monks assisted at his conferences, and Latin was no longer understood by the vulgar: besides, these discourses are extant in old French, in the library of the *Feuillans*, *rue St. Honoré* at Paris; and the manuscript seems to have been written about St. Bernard's time. He died in the sixty third year of his age.

The motive of this second crusade was the taking of Edessa by Noradin, who threatened to fall upon the several conquests made by the Christians. The king sets out (1147) with Eleanor his wife, and an army of fourscore thousand men. Conrad duke of Swabia, who had been elected emperor, leads a considerable body of troops upon the same expedition. The abbot Suger is made regent of the kingdom of France, in conjunction with Raoul count of Vermandois, the king's brother-in-law, who married Eleanor's sister.

The people of Rome pretending that the pontifical power does not extend beyond spiritual affairs, revive the dignity of senator, which weakens the papal authority.

1148.

The emperor had been defeated the preceding year by the treachery of the Greeks. The king is also beaten by the Saracens. The European Christians lay siege to Damascus; but are obliged to raise it, by the treachery of the Christians of Syria. This indeed is the stile, in which most of the cotemporary historians express themselves: yet to judge of this crusade from the former; and if we can give any credit to the princess Anna Comnena, daughter of the emperor of Constantinople, who wrote the history of those calamitous times, her father acted just

prince would have done in his place. His
-run by upwards of seven hundred thousand
anded provisions with as much insolence, as a
ommands contributions; and when there was
omplying, they laid waste his territories: even
d the avarice of the chief crusaders, who found
ess difficulty in a conquest of this nature, than
 distant province, where religion only was in
e the object seemed of less importance, in
hey drew nearer to it. Alexius laid these
udent behaviour, so that he found means at
 those dangerous guests. The soldiers trans-
w climate, and unwilling to check their in-
tes, died of distempers; and thence it pro-
: emperor Alexius and the Greeks were ac-
oisoned the wells and springs. There is still
om Stephen count de Boulogne, to the countess
i he commends the kind behaviour of Alexius,
had received more magnificent presents, than
e Conqueror, upon his marrying that prince's
t not the same prejudice have given rise to the
uccessors of Alexius held a correspondence with
order to destroy the troops commanded by the
 and Lewis the Young?
f Rheims, summoned by Eugene III. in the king's
a numerous concourse of prelates sufficient to
œcumenical, this undoubtedly would have been
reckoned no less than eleven hundred, among
primates of England and Spain, with the pope
Yet Eugene III. himself, in his letter to the
 avenna, stiles it only an assembly of Cisalpine
oves that there were very few Italian prelates,
ability was one reason that hindered this from
 a general council. In this assembly a certain
?, imagining himself to be pointed out by these
 qui venturus est, was condemned to close im-
ne would hardly conceive that such a wretch
ad any followers; and yet he had many.

This

REMARKABLE EVENTS under LEWIS the YOUNG.

This council contains seventeen canons, commonly called the canons of Eugene III, most of which are inserted in the body of the canon law. We may take notice of the sixth, by which the advowees, or patrons of churches, are forbid to receive, either by themselves, or by their inferiors, more than their ancient dues, upon pain of being deprived of ecclesiastical burial: the seventh restrains bishops, deacons, sub-deacons, monks, and nuns, from marrying: the twelfth prohibits tilts, and tournaments, &c. (which had their rise in France, and were spread over all Europe) upon pain to those who lost their lives in those sports, of being buried in unconsecrated ground, &c. In this council was likewise determined the metaphysical dispute of Gilbert of Porée, bishop of Poitiers, concerning the Trinity. But what is chiefly worth our observation, upon the separation of the prelates, the pope called a congregation, in which the cardinals pretended, that the French bishops had no right to judge of doctrinal points; but that this privilege was reserved to the pope alone, in consistory. And indeed the profession of faith made by the bishops of France, was not inserted in the acts of the council, which are preserved in the Vatican library; but the French prelates took care to place it in the copies of this council, drawn out for their own use. St. Bernard makes a considerable figure in this assembly. *(The pontificate of Eugene III. by Dom. Delannes, page* 161.)

1149.

Robert, count of Dreux, returning from Jerusalem before the king his brother, endeavours to create disturbances, by imputing the ill success of the crusade to the ignorance of Lewis VII, and representing him as incapable of public affairs, with a view to seize the administration, and perhaps the crown. Suger assembles the states of the kingdom. Eugene III, upon his return to Rome, did the king great service by his letters to the French clergy; so that the public tranquillity was no way interrupted.

The king in his return to France is taken prisoner at sea by the Greeks, and rescued by an officer belonging to Roger king of Sicily. It is amazing that this prince was not surfeited with crusades; instead of that, he was meditating another: but when he came to propose it to the parliament at Christmas, he found

REMARKABLE EVENTS under LEWIS the YOUNG.

found the minds of his subjects so averse, that he relinquished the project. It is very probable, the armorial scutcheons, which belong to the nobility only, were introduced in the time of the crusades, for the use of persons, who being cased over with iron, could hardly be distinguished without some external mark. The knights were known by their coat armours; and the different fur linings of these coats, which the French put over their cuirasses, formed the several colours, since received in their armorial ensigns, which are easily distinguished, such as ermine, vaire, sable, vert, &c. To these they sometimes added other ornaments, borrowed also from their dress, as the *fesse* from their girdle, the *pale* from the spear or javelin; the *saltire* from the stirrup; the *mascle* from the links that formed the coats of mail, &c. (Du Cange.)

Spain had its crusade as well as Asia; for much about the same time a numerous fleet, manned with Germans, English, and Flemings, sailed up the Tagus, to assist the king of Portugal in recovering the city of Lisbon, at that time possessed by the Saracens: he afterwards made it his capital, instead of Coimbra, which had been hitherto the chief city of that kingdom.

1150. 51. 52. &c.

Lewis the Young repudiates Eleanor, upon suspicion of her having been guilty of an intrigue in Syria with his uncle the prince of Antioch, and with a young Turk, named Saladin: under the pretence of consanguinity he obtains a divorce, and leaves her in possession of Guyenne and Poitou. The abbot Suger opposed a step so prejudicial to the state, and it was not put in execution till after that minister's death.

This was a very different kind of a man from St. Bernard: though the church has not given him a rank in her calendar, his name will be immortal in history. Suger, from the condition of a private monk of St. Denis, rose to be abbot of that place by his great abilities. St. Bernard having rebuked him for his secularity, or attention to the things of this world, for his sumptuous habit, and numerous retinue, no way suitable to a person of his condition, he altered his manner of life, and reformed his monastery. In this house, says St. Bernard, was transacted the business of the court and of the army; the cloyster was often crowded with

REMARKABLE EVENTS under LEWIS the YOUNG.

with foldiers, and refounded with lawyers; even the women were fometimes admitted. But this is not at all furprizing, for the monks in thofe days, being more learned than other people, had a confiderable fhare in public affairs: their houfes were as much defigned for the education of youth, as for the reception of monks; and Lewis the Grofs himfelf was brought up at St. Denis. There he became acquainted with Suger; and he employed him afterwards in the moft important affairs. Suger died in his feventieth year. He was a mean looking man, and of low extraction. We might apply to him that expreffion of Tiberius concerning Curtius Rufus: it is a fine thing to be felf-born, *Curtius Rufus mihi videtur ex fe natus* (Tacitus). The place of his nativity is not known: fome fay it was St. Denis, and others St. Omer. He built the prefent church of St. Denis, except the portal and the two towers adjoining, which are venerable monuments of the ancient church, erected by Pepin and Charlemain: and what does equal honour to his memory, he is fuppofed, with very high probability, to be the author of the compilement of the great chronicles, known by the name of St. Denis. (*Memoirs of the Acad. of belles lettres, tome* 15. *page* 591.)

Eleanor was married again, as Suger had forefeen, fix weeks after her divorce, to Henry, count of Anjou and duke of Normandy, next heir to the crown of England, to which he fucceeded by the name of Henry II. After this marriage he was duke of Normandy and Aquitaine, and count of Anjou, Poitou, Touraine, and Maine.

This year was publifhed Gratian's decretal *, which has never been intirely purged of its errors; the falfe decretals compiled by Ifidorus, beginning from St. Clement, and ending with pope Syricius, where Dionyfius Exiguus, a judicious author, begins his collection, are inferted here as an authentic work. The death of the emperor Conrad, who is faid to have been poifoned by Roger king of Sicily: he defigned his nephew Frederic fhould fucceed him in the imperial dignity, though he had a fon alfo named Frederic, whom he confidered as too young for fo heavy a burden.

* A collection of canons, compiled by Gratian a Benedictine monk.

REMARKABLE EVENTS under LEWIS the YOUNG.

1154. 55.

Lewis marries Conſtantia, daughter of Alfonſo king of Caſtile, in the city of Orleans, where ſhe was crowned by the archbiſhop of Sens. He undertakes a pilgrimage to St. James of Compoſtella.

Stephen, king of England, departs this life, after having adopted Henry, who ſucceeded to the crown. This adoption muſt have been made with great reluctancy by Stephen, ſince he left a ſon named William, who was count of Boulogne. Euſtace his eldeſt ſon, whom he had aſſociated to the crown in 1152, and who died before this adoption, would have not ſubmitted to ſuch a regulation ſo patiently as William.

1156. 57. 58. 59. 60.

A war between France and England, occaſioned by the county of Touloufe. Henry II. was obliged to raiſe the ſiege of that city. A truce between the two kings renewed ſeveral times. This ſouthern part of France was continually the theatre of private wars among the ſeveral princes and lords, who diſputed every inch of it, ſuch as the counts of Toulouſe, Provence, Barcellona, Montpellier, Carcaſſonne, Beſiers, Narbonne, Alais, &c. all of them vaſſals of the crown; but our kings were too weak at that time to check their inſolence.

Alexander III. grants the excluſive right of pontifical elections to the cardinals. The marquiſate of Auſtria is erected into a dutchy (1156) by Frederic Barbaroſſa, in favour of Henry, ſurnamed of *Jaſamergott*, marquis of Auſtria.

1161. 62. 63. 64. 65. 66.

Letters patent, by which Lewis beſtows the revenue of the biſhopric of Paris, during the vacancy of that ſee, on the nuns of the abbey of Hieres: (a proof of the right of regale.)

The famous conteſt betwixt Thomas Becket, archbiſhop of Canterbury, and king Henry, concerning eccleſiaſtical immunities.

1167. 68.

Geoffrey, ſon of Henry II, marries Conſtantia, daughter of Conan, count of Britany, who brings him this province for her dower. Henry ſeizes the whole country in his ſon's name. Single combats are laid under ſome reſtriction, being no longer permitted for a debt under five ſous.

1169.

REMARKABLE EVENTS under LEWIS the YOUNG.

1169. 70.

A peace concluded at Montmirail between Lewis and Henry. The latter marries his son Henry to Margaret the daughter of Lewis.

Thomas archbishop of Canterbury, at his return from France, where he had been in exile seven years, is assassinated in his own church: perhaps he stretched the ecclesiastical privileges too far, in opposition to the royal prerogative.

1171. 72. 73. 74. 75. 76. 77. 78.

The war breaks out again with England, and is concluded by a promise of marriage between Richard the second son of Henry, and Alice the second daughter of Lewis the Young, upon her coming to age.

The end of the schism (1157), which began in 1159, with two competitors to the holy see, Alexander III. and Victor IV, the antipope. Victor was succeeded in the countries, which acknowledged the legality of his election, by Paschal III. and Calixtus II. At length Alexander III. was universally proclaimed the lawful pope. The emperor Frederic, who had encouraged the schism, was obliged to conclude a peace, with the loss of the battle of Lignano.

1179. 80.

Lewis pays a visit of devotion to the tomb of St. Thomas of Canterbury in England: at his return, he takes care to have his son crowned at Rheims, and adjudges the privilege of performing this ceremony, which had been hitherto undecided, to this archiepiscopal see, because it was then filled by his brother-in-law, the cardinal of Sabine. The peers took their seats at this ceremony: Henry, king of England, assisted also on this occasion as duke of Normandy; and Philip, count of Flanders, bore the royal sword, as peer of France: this is the first time that the counts of Flanders assumed this title.

Alfonso II. count of Barcellona in right of his father, and king of Arragon in right of his mother, causes a declaration to be made in the council of Tarragon (1180), *that the public acts which used to bear date in Catalonia from the year of the reigns of the kings of France, should thenceforward be dated only from the Christian æra.* (Ferreras.)

The

REMARKABLE EVENTS under LEWIS the YOUNG.

The Lateran council, reckoned the æra of the laws relating to the impropriation of tythes.

In this century, we perceive the first traces of theatrical representations. A monk of the name of Geoffrey, who was afterwards abbot of St. Albans in England, being employed in the education of youth, made them exhibit a species of devotional tragedies upon a stage, with theatrical dresses. The subject of the first piece were the miracles of St. Catharine. This is a good deal prior to our representations of mysteries, which did not begin till 1398, when a stage was erected at Paris in the hotel of the Trinity.

The twelfth century is remarkable for the schools established in the cathedral churches and monasteries: not that we can set any value on the works composed there, such as the chronicles, legends, scholastic treatises, verses, &c. but we are indebted to those seminaries for preserving almost all the works of the ancients. The monks transcribed the books: this was their daily employment, and perhaps if it had not been for them, we should have lost the whole treasure of Greek and Roman antiquity. These schools served likewise for the instruction of youth; but they were soon laid aside, upon the erecting of colleges. Robert, count of Dreux, the king's brother, founded a house of this kind, by the title of St. Thomas of Canterbury; and this is now called St. Thomas of the Louvre. There was likewise in the same city a college of English, and another of Danes. Paris was become the chief seat of learning, being frequented by young people from all parts of Europe, so that the number of students was equal to that of the other inhabitants; and indeed they were always a formidable body in case of tumults or insurrections. The quarter afterwards known by the name of the university, became the best inhabited, the professors of the several arts and sciences having given it the preference, on account of its purer air: at length they were obliged to enlarge the town, which was become too small for so numerous a people.

1180.
Acceſſion to the crown.

PHILIP II, ſur-named AUGUS-TUS, ſucceeds to the crown in 1180, at the age of fifteen. He had been crown-ed at Rheims, in his father's time. Hugh abbot of St. Ger-main des Prez, Her-vé abbot of St. Vic-tor, and Eudes ab-bot of St. Gene-vieve, were his godfathers; Con-ſtantia, ſiſter of Lewis VII. wife of the count of Tou-louſe, and two wi-dows of the city of Paris, were his god-mothers.

REMARKABLE EVENTS.

1180. 81. 82. 83. 84. 85.

THIS is one of our moſt victorious princes. He checked the outrages and depredations of the nobility, and expelled the Jews, releaſing his ſubjects from any debts due to thoſe people; an action flagrantly iniquitous, being contrary to the law of nature, and conſequently to religion. Such was the opinion of a great pope (Gregory the Great): notwithſtanding his zeal for the converſion of the Jews, he could not ſuffer them to be treated unjuſtly; and therefore he ordered the Jews of Palermo to be reimburſed the full value of the ſynagogues that had been taken from them: and indeed the Jewiſh annals have cele-brated the moderation and equity of this holy pontif.

The king's mother wanted to prevent her ſon from marrying the daughter of Baldwin, count of Hainault, leſt this match ſhould increaſe the authority of her uncle the count of Flanders, guardian to the young king, and diminiſh that of her brother, the count of Champagne, by whom ſhe expected to govern. She therefore retires to Champagne, and prevails on the king of England to join her brother againſt France. Philip, without being in the leaſt daunted at this revolt, begins with chaſtiſing the count de Sancerre, one of the ringleaders, celebrates his marriage, obliges Henry II. king of England to ſue for peace, and fo-ments the diviſion between that prince and his ſons. Henry, eldeſt ſon to the king of England, departs this life *, expreſſing great ſorrow for his undutiful behaviour to his father. The county of Vermandois is annexed to the crown, in ſpite of Philip, count of Flanders, by the deceaſe of

---

* At the caſtle of Martel in Quercy in Guienne, of a ſlow fever, June the firſt, in the 28th year of his age.

Eliza-

The THIRD RACE.

WIVES.	CHILDREN.	1223. DEATH.	Cotemporary PRINCES.
Isabella, daughter of Baldwin, count of Hainault. 1190. Ingeburga, daughter of Waldemar, and sister of Canute, kings of Denmark. Philip II. put her away; but Innocent III. obliged him to take her again. 1236. Agnes of Merania, daughter of the duke of Dalmatia, repudiated by Philip; this broke her heart, and she died in 1211. Repudiations must have been a very common thing in those days, for we find in the marriage contract of Peter, king of Arragon, in the year 1204, a clause that would surprize us greatly in the present age: viz. this prince promises solemnly never to repudiate Mary of Montpellier; and still further never to marry any other person during her life.	Lewis VIII. Philip count de Boulogne. Mary, wife of Philip, count of Namur, afterwards of Henry I. duke of Brabant. These children were legitimated by the pope, though he had declared this marriage void, and the king had taken Ingeburga, his second wife, again. This legitimation, says Rigord, gave offence to a great many, because of the authority which the pope assumed in the affair. The pope proceeded on this foundation, that these children were born of a marriage, which was deemed bona fide, to be valid, till that of Ingeburga was reestablished; and so far appears very right: but what is somewhat surprising, when the lord of Montpellier wanted to avail himself of this example, they made answer, that there was a wide difference betwixt the king of France and him. Philip Augustus had also by an unknown person, a son, named Peter Charlot, to whom William the Breton dedicated his Philippids, and who died in 1229 in a voyage beyond sea, attending St. Lewis.	Philip Augustus dies at Mantes the 14th of July, 1223, aged fifty nine years, of which he had reigned forty three. He is interred at St. Denis. Annales Victoriani (ad annum 1223.) hoc anno obiit Philippus, rex Francorum, ab aliquibus Augustus cognominatus, hujusce nominis secundus, vir fortunatissimus, qui regnum Francorum duplo ampliavit; hic in omnibus actibus Felix, ecclesiarum et religiosarum personarum amator et fautor, & specialiter ecclesiarum sancti Dionysii, et sancti Victoris Parisiensis.	Popes. Lucius III. 1185. Urban III. 1187. Gregory VIII. 1187. Clement III. 1191. Celestin III. 1198. Innocent III. 1216. Honorius III. 1227. Emperors of the East. Alexius Comnenus. II. 1183. Andronicus I. 1185. Isacius Angelus. 1204. Alexius III. 1203. Alexius IV. 1204. Murzuphilus. 1204. Empire of the Latins. Baldwin. 1205. Henry. 1216. Pet. of Courtenay. 1220. Rob. of Courtenay. 1229. Emperors of the West. Frederic I. 1190. Henry VI. 1198. Philip. 1208. Otho IV. 1218. Frederic II. 1250. Kings of Spain. Alfonso IX. 1214. Henry I. 1217. Ferdinand III. 1252. Kings of Portugal. Alfonso I. 1185. Sancho I. 1212. Alfonso II. 1223. Kings of England. Henry II. 1182. Richard I. 1199. John Lackland. 1216. Henry III. 1273. Kings of Scotland. William. 1214. Alexander II. 1249. Kings of Denmark. Waldemar I. 1182. Canute VI. 1202. Waldemar II. 1241. Kings of Sweden. Canute. 1192. Suercher. 1211. Eric X. 1218. John I. 1223. Kings of Poland. Casimir II. 1194. Lescus. 1226.

REMARKABLE EVENTS under PHILIP AUGUSTUS.

Elizabeth of Vermandois his wife, without issue. This county came to the house of France, by Hugh, the third son of Henry I, who married the heiress.

Maurice de Sully began to rebuild the church of Notre Dame at Paris, and the great altar was finished in 1182. About this same period, were erected the churches of Cluny, St. Remy at Rheims, St. Genevieve, &c. While architecture was thus raising its head, painting, sculpture, &c. began also to revive. Such is the fate of the polite arts, that they go hand in hand; after they have been involved in general darkness, they suddenly, and, as it were, with one united effort, recover their former lustre.

A most strange revolution happened in the empire to Henry, surnamed the Lion, duke of Saxony, Bavaria, Westphalia, &c. and son-in-law to Henry II, king of England: his territories extended from the Adriatic gulph to the Baltic. This unfortunate prince was stripped of all his dominions by the emperor Frederic; and of all his former grandeur nothing more remained to his family, than the dutchy of Brunswic, which they possess to this day *.

Richard, the second son of Henry II, was at war with the count of Toulouse, having some pretensions to that province as duke of Aquitaine. Philip defended his vassal, so as to reap the whole benefit of this contest, which ended in the death of prince Henry: Richard then being the eldest son, changed sides, and joined with Philip.

1186. 87. 88.

Philip wages war against Henry II. to recover the towns in the Vexin, which had been given in dower to his sister Margaret, upon her marriage with Henry, and ought to have reverted to him at her decease without issue. Richard, being now the next heir to the crown by the death of Henry, joins with Philip, because his father Henry had refused to let him be crowned in his own life-time, as he had granted to his elder brother; and likewise debarred him from marrying Alice, Philip's sister, to whom he had been affianced: but it is thought that Henry himself was in love with that princess.

* From this duke Henry by Matilda, is descended his present majesty king George III.

Saladin

The Third Race.

Ministers.	Warriors.	Magistrates.	Eminent and Learned Men.
Seneschals. Thibaud I. of Blois. 1191. The office of seneschal ended with him. — William of Blois, called the cardinal of Champagne. 1202. Robert Clement. 1181. Giles Clement. 1182. — Guerin, bishop of Senlis, afterwards chancellor. 1230. He founded the church of the abbey of Victoire, near Senlis, which the king had made a vow to erect, if he proved victorious at Bouvines.	*Constables.* Raoul, count of Clermont. 1191. Dreux of Mello. 1218. Matthew of Montmorenci, who raised this above all other military offices. 1230. *Marshals of France.* Alberic Clement, who began to raise this dignity, and to render it a military employment. 1191. Nevelon d'Arras, living in 1217. Henry Clement. 1214. John Clement, living still in 1260. Simon of Montfort. 1218.	*Chancellors.* Hugh de Puiseaux. 1185. Hugh de Bethisi, living in 1186. Guerin, bishop of Senlis, knight of the order of Jerusalem. 1230.	Arnulfus. 1182. Guy d'Aties, keeper of the seals, living in 1201. Averroes. 1206. Peter of Corbeil. 1222. St. Dominic. 1221. Stephen of Tournay. 1203. Eudes of Sully. 1208. Foulk, curate of Nulli, 1202. Godfrey of Viterbo. 1186. William the Breton, living in 1223. William of Tyre, towards 1180. Helinand. 1212. John of Salisbury. 1182. Joachim, deceased towards 1214. Maurice of Sully. 1196. Petrus Comestor. 1198. Peter of Blois. 1200. Villehardouin, towards 1212.

REMARRKABLE EVENTS under PHILIP AUGUSTUS.

Saladin retakes Jerusalem, eighty nine years after the French had erected that kingdom.

The emperor Frederic I. marries his son (Henry VI.) to Constantia, aunt and heiress to William king of Sicily.

1189. 90.

Philip and Richard take the town of Mans. Henry II. concludes a peace, and dies * : he is succeeded by Richard, surnamed *cœur de Lion*, or the *Lion's heart*. Henry II, the first king of England of the race of the Plantagenets, was possessed of a greater extent of territory than any prince that ever sat on the British throne: but his disappointments were equal to his successes. His wife Eleanor was a slave to her passions; she had dishonoured her first husband's bed, and disturbed the second with her jealousy and ambition. Henry's sons, elated with their father's great fortune, wanted to partake of it in his life-time; and the famous quarrel with the archbishop of Canterbury, made the clergy his enemies. Besides England, to which he annexed Ireland, he was possessed of Guyenne, Poitou, Xaintonge, Auvergne, Limosin, Perigord, Angoumois, Anjou, Maine, Touraine, and Normandy, to which he likewise added Britany, by the marriage of one of his sons to the heiress of that province. He wrote his will in the romance language, which sufficiently proves it to have been then the vulgar tongue, and that Latin was understood only by the learned.

Lusignan, king of Jerusalem, having been defeated at the battle of Tiberiad † in 1187, this misfortune was attended with the loss of Jerusalem, which determined the European princes to undertake another expedition into Asia. The emperor Frederic set the example, at the head of a hundred and fifty thousand men; but this unfortunate prince was drowned in crossing the Cydnus (the same river in which Alexander the Great had like to have lost his life by bathing). He was succeeded by his son

---

* At Chinon in Touraine, on the 6th of July, and the 57th year of his age. His death was owing to his grief, upon discovering that his favourite son John had been concerned in all his brother's plots to dethrone him.

† A famous city of Galilee, situate towards the south extremity, and upon the west bank of the lake of Genezareth, otherwise called the sea of Tiberiad. Josephus says it was built in honour of Tiberius, by king Herod Agrippa.

EVENTS under PHILIP AUGUSTUS.

'ranconia, who died soon after. Philip and
a third crusade.
will, in which, among other precautions for
state, he settles the regale, in case of vacant
d laid the tenth penny already on the clergy
 tax was called *Saladin's tithe*, being raised on
ade.
away his time in Sicily, and does not reach
iths after king Philip. By the way he takes
 from Isaac Comnenus, and yields the sove-
Guy of Lusignan. The Venetians and the
rive their rights and pretensions to this island,
ints of the said Guy, whose posterity kept pos-
he year 1458. James, the bastard of John
ietor, married Catharine Cornaro, a Venetian
d this island to the Venetians: but Selim II.
em in 1571. Charles, duke of Savoy, had as
yprus as the republic, by a grant from Char-
daughter of that same John III, who had been
's uncle: yet Victor Amadeus was the first of the
iat assumed the title of king of Cyprus (1633).

1191.

the French: the conquest of this town was of
he crusaders, than that it enabled them to lay
i; but intestine divisions prevented their taking

iis of Montferrat, distinguished himself in the
ern christians. The dejection of the troops,
tle of Tiberiad, had no way disheartened him;
n Guy of Lusignan as cast from the throne,
the death of his wife, from whom he de-
title, he got himself proclaimed king of Je-
:ing of France espoused his cause; and Ri-
 embraced the side of Lusignan. The duke,
Austria, being left at the head of the Ger-
ins with Philip Augustus, under pretence of
 some insult from Richard. These divisions
lose sight of the chief object of the crusade,
e end of so formidable an armament. The
king

REMARKABLE EVENTS under PHILIP AUGUSTUS.

king being seized with a distemper, which made his hair and nails fall off, was obliged the next year to retire from Syria. After the departure of this prince, Richard performed prodigies of valour, which only added to his glory; and the conquests of the crusaders in Palestine were confined to the taking of Acra, otherwise named Ptolemais. This excepted, the Christians were left in as bad a situation as before the arrival of the two kings: Conrad, marquis of Montferrat, in whom they had placed their whole hopes, was assassinated; the count of Champagne was elected king of Jerusalem in his stead; and Lusignan went to take possession of the isle of Cyprus.

The first mention we find of the dignity of marshal of France, was during the present war; but this officer had not as yet the command of armies.

1192.

The king upon his return from Asia, seizes part of Normandy, in the absence of Richard.

The reunion of the county of Artois, which the king acquired by his marriage with Isabella, daughter of Baldwin, count of Flanders and Hainaut.

1193. 94. 95. 96. 97. 98. 99.

Differences with the court of Rome, in regard to the divorce of Ingerburga. Richard, in his return from Asia, was shipwrecked in the Adriatic gulph: there he took the road of Germany, hoping he should not be known; but it was his fate to fall into the hands of Leopold, marquis of Austria. This prince had not forgot the indignity with which Richard treated him at the siege of Acra, by pulling down the Austrian standard from the top of a tower, and erecting his own in its stead. He therefore sold him to the emperor Henry VI, who kept him prisoner the space of fifteen months. Richard did not survive his confinement above five or six years; and the remainder of his days was one continued series of disasters; so that he may be said to have left all his glory in Asia. The disturbances of his kingdom, and the successes of Philip Augustus, embittered the rest of his life; and he was killed in 1191 before Chalus, a small castle in the neighbourhood of Limoges, to which he had laid siege, with a view of possessing himself of a treasure, which was said to have been lately found

REMARKABLE EVENTS under PHILIP AUGUSTUS.

found in that neighbourhood, and depofited in the caftle *.

The foundation of the order of Redemption of captives, in 1198, by John de Matha.

1200. 1. 2. 3.

John, furnamed *Lackland*, brother of Richard, fucceeded that prince, to the prejudice of his nephew Arthur, fon of Geoffrey of Britany, his elder brother: he pretended that in England the right of reprefentation, in a lineal defcent, did not take place; and moreover, that the nation had a power of chufing out of the reigning family, which prince foever fhe thought proper for her king; and this was his ftrongeft plea. Arthur has recourfe to arms, affifted by Philip; but John defeats him in Poitou, feizes his perfon, and puts him to death. This prince, after repudiating Avifa, daughter of the earl of Gloucefter, marries Ifabella of Angouleme, though contracted to the earl of Marche, to whom fhe was afterwards married, upon the death of the king her hufband.

John *Lackland* was fo called, according to du Chefne, from his having received no appanage or fettlement, during the life of his father Henry II: the reafon of which was his being yet a minor; and the laws of feudal tenures ordained that even the nobility themfelves fhould not be poffeffed of fiefs, unlefs they were able to difcharge the duties annexed thereto, and had attained the age of one and twenty, the term required for feudal majority, (as that of roturiers, or peafants, was fourteen, becaufe they were then capable of tranfacting bufinefs). Philip the Hardy, founder of the fecond houfe of Burgundy, was alfo furnamed *Lackland*, before king John of France had given him the county of Touraine and the dutchy of Burgundy for his appanage: the fame name was likewife conferred on Philip, count of Brefcia, who became duke of Savoy in 1496, by the death of his grand nephew duke Charles John Amadeus, from his having no lands fet apart for his ufe, till he was two and twenty years of age. Yet we are to obferve, that according to the eftablifhments of

---

* He was wounded with an arrow, fhot by a crofs-bow man, named *Bertrand*, and died the 11th day after, on the 6th of April, the 10th year of his reign, and the 42d of his age. Chalus was taken before he expired. He was interred at Fontevraud.

REMARKABLE EVENTS under PHILIP AUGUSTUS.

St. Lewis, when a gentleman married his son, or made him a knight, he was obliged by custom, to grant him one third of his estate.

John is summoned before the court of peers of France, to be tried for the murder of prince Arthur, and in default of appearance is declared a rebel. In consequence hereof his lands are confiscated, and he himself is condemned to death, for murdering his nephew within the jurisdiction of the king of France. Philip seizes Normandy, and annexes it to the crown, about three hundred years after its first separation: the same he did by Touraine, Anjou, Maine, &c. so that nothing more remained to king John, but Guyenne, out of all his possessions in France.

1204. 5.

The fourth Crusade. Boniface of Montferrat had the command of this expedition, in the room of the count of Champagne, who died in 1201. Baldwin count of Flanders, Eude duke of Burgundy, &c. set out upon the same errand, with permission from the king, so early as the year 1202. The pretended object of the crusaders was still the deliverance of the Holy land; but their real design being to search after adventures, the first opportunity of that kind put the Holy land quite out of their heads. True it is, that this was productive of a very extraordinary revolution, no less than the founding a new empire, namely, that of the Latins. The whole event is related in a curious letter from the emperor Baldwin to the archbishop of Cologne, which we meet with in several historians. I shall give the following extract of it. "While the crusaders "were at Venice, Alexius Comnenus, son of Isaac Angelus "came to implore their assistance against the tyrant, his uncle "Alexius, who had caused the emperor's eyes to be put out, "and usurped the imperial throne. He promised to pay the Ve"netians for the ships, which they should lend the crusaders to "transport them to Asia, and that he would assist them with his "whole force to conquer the Holy land, and to reduce the Greek "church to the pope's obedience. The French, persuaded by "these promises, set sail for Constantinople, in conjunction with "the Venetian troops, and their duke d'Andolo, who resolved "to join in this expedition: they attacked the capital, and "ma

REMARKABLE EVENTS under PHILIP AUGUSTUS.

"made themselves masters thereof in six days. Isaac was restored to the throne, and died shortly after; his son Alexius
succeeded him, but neglected to perform his promise to the
French, who withdrew from thence, highly displeased with
his behaviour.

"The French having committed great excesses at the taking
of Constantinople, the Greeks conceived a prodigious aversion
against Alexius, who had invited them into their country: so
that as soon as those strangers were gone, the inhabitants rose
up in arms against their sovereign. Alexius Ducas, surnamed
Murziphilus, from his large eyebrows, a person of mean extraction, whom young Alexius had raised to high dignities, appeared at the head of the rebels: having seized Alexius, he
caused that prince to be put to death, and himself to be elected
emperor. This usurper, desirous of pleasing the populace of
Constantinople, declared war against the French, who still
remained in Greece. In consequence hereof, the French
army laid siege to Constantinople a second time, and notwithstanding the obstinate resistance of the Greeks, carried the
city by storm. Murziphilus endeavouring to escape by sea,
was taken prisoner, and put to death, as he deserved.

"The French being thus masters of Constantinople, chose
Baldwin, count of Flanders, to be emperor of the Greeks,
the second Sunday after Easter, in the year 1204; and laying
aside all thoughts of the expedition to the Holy land, they
turned their attention towards preserving their new conquest."
This was called the *empire of the Latins*, which lasted no more
than fifty years. The Greeks revolted, and after expelling the
French, chose Michael Paleologus for their emperor. This
government continued about two hundred years, to the taking
of Constantinople by the Turks.

There still remained some princes of the imperial family of the
Comneni, who were not disheartened at the destruction of their
empire: one of them, whose name was also Alexius, escaped
with a few ships to Colchis, and there, between the sea and mount
Caucasus, formed a petty state, on which the Greeks bestowed
the magnificent title of the empire of Trebisond. This new

REMARKABLE EVENTS under PHILIP AUGUSTUS.

settlement continued till the invasion of the Turks, who put a final period to the eastern empire in 1453.

1206. 7. 8. 9. &c.

The king publishes an edict in favour of the Jews. Disturbances occasioned by the Albigenses: a crusade is formed on this account, and an army sent to extirpate them. Innocent III. spirited up this barbarous war; Dominic was the apostle, the count of Toulouse the victim, and Simon, count of Montfort, the conductor or chief. The Albigenses were the remains of the sect of Manicheans, whose doctrine had been revived by a heretic, named Henry, from whence they had been called *Henricians*, till a council was held against them at Lombez in the country of the Albigeois*, where they were distinguished by the denomination of Albigenses. Henry VI. died in the year 1198, and left his son Frederic, only nine months old, under the tuition of his brother Philip, after he had taken care to see him crowned emperor. The tender age of this prince was the cause of setting him aside, and Philip pursuing his private interest, got himself elected emperor at Erfurt. But Otho duke of Saxony, having been also chosen to the imperial dignity by the pope's interest, the two princes came to an accommodation, and Otho consented to resign the empire to Philip, whose daughter he had married, on condition of being appointed his successor. In this agreement there was no mention made of Frederic, who did not recover the imperial crown, till after Otho had been defeated at Bovines by Philip Augustus. According to several writers, upon the death of Philip in 1208, the number of electors was fixed to seven, in the diet of Franckfort. This æra, in the opinion of others, is not so ancient: it is proper however to know, that the right of suffrage at the imperial election is at present annexed to the great offices of the empire, such as those of high steward, high cup-bearer, &c. settled upon the great or Aulic fiefs; whereas before this period, that is, during the interregnum of 1270, and for some time afterwards, the princes did not assist at the imperial diets by virtue of their *office*, but in right of their lands.

* So called from the city of Alby, in the province of Languedoc, situate on the river Tarne.

REMARKABLE EVENTS under PHILIP AUGUSTUS.

A memorable victory over the Moors (July the 12th, 1212) obtained by Alfonso IX, king of Castile, Peter king of Arragon, and Sancho king of Navarre, in the neighbourhood of Tolosa*: it is said, that above two hundred thousand infidels were left dead on the spot.

Disturbances in England, occasioned by the election of an archbishop of Canterbury. The pope lays the kingdom under an interdict: John, instead of supporting himself against the encroachments of Innocent III, by the influence and affection of his clergy, confiscated all the church livings, and alienated the minds of his subjects; nay he went further, for he is said to have courted the Miramolin of Africa, offering to become his vassal, and to embrace his religion; but the barbarian treated him with contempt. (St. Romuald.) Rapin takes no notice of this fact. The pope proceeded from an interdict to excommunication, and released his subjects from their oath of allegiance, giving the crown of England to the king of France. John seeing himself deserted by the whole nation, resolved to submit to the pontif, by yielding him homage for his kingdom, and rendering it tributary to the holy see.

The legate, content with king John's submission, wanted to dissuade Philip from insisting on the papal donation; but Philip having made the preparations for this great enterprize, gave orders for his fleet to set sail from the mouth of the Seine: this fleet is said to have consisted of seventeen hundred ships, a prodigious number for that time; which makes us doubt the truth thereof, especially as there had been no mention made as yet of a French navy, under the princes of the third race. Philip, before he made a descent in England, was for subduing the earl of Flanders, the only French vassal that opposed this war; and accordingly, he seized Flanders. In the mean time, no less than five hundred ships set sail from England, and joining those belonging to the earl of Flanders, surprized, and intirely destroyed the French fleet.

---

* Some stile it the battle of Muradal, from the pass of that name through the Sierra Morena, and others, the battle of Losa, from a great rock of that denomination; but it is most commonly called the battle of *navas de Tolosa*, from a little town of that name, in the open country, beyond the mountains.

REMARKABLE EVENTS under PHILIP AUGUSTUS.

This exertion of the French naval force, is sufficient to astonish us, unless we explain it with the *author of the marine of the ancients*, by saying " that in proportion as their ships were more
" clumsy and ill shaped, they became more numerous, though
" in all probability they were ill built and ill manned: in
" short, they reckoned to make amends by their numbers for
" their slight and irregular construction. On the contrary,
" as the art of navigation improved, the number of vessels
" diminished; but they increased in strength and magni-
" tude."

The council of Paris (1210), in which Aristotle's metaphysics are condemned to the flames, left the refinements of that philosopher should have an ill effect on weak understandings, by applying those subtleties to matters of religion.

1214.

Philip had very soon his revenge for the defeat of his fleet, by the battle of Bovines, where, with an army of fifty thousand men, he obtained a compleat victory, though not without great danger of his life, over the combined forces of the emperor Otho and his allies, consisting of more than a hundred and fifty thousand men. The earls of Flanders and Boulogne were taken prisoners. The chevalier Guerin, nominated to the bishopric of Senlis, had the command of the king's army, *not in order to fight, but to animate the barons, and other knights, in honour of God, the king, and kingdom, and in the defence of their sovereign lord.* Matthew de Montmorenci, who was constable four years after, had a considerable share in this victory. Lewis, the eldest son of Philip, beats the king of England at the same time in Poitou. This was the first campaign in which a marshal of France was seen to command an army; his name was Henry Clement. There are two things observable on this subject: 1°. there were four marshals of France successively in this family: 2°. John Clement, the son of Henry, though an infant, was made marshal of France upon the death of his father, as if this office had been then hereditary: for which reason Lewis VIII. took care to get a declaration from John Clement when he came of age, acknowledging that it was not an hereditary employment. This precaution was necessary, to avoid the inconveniency that happened

pened in the office of feneschals, which the counts of Anjou had rendered hereditary in their family. The abbey of *Victoire* is founded in memory of these important successes. The emperor engaged in this war, not so much out of regard to his uncle the king of England, as to be revenged of Philip, who had formerly treated him with some contempt, and to disable him from assisting Frederic II, who had been his competitor to the empire, ever since the decease of the emperor Philip, uncle to Frederic. The battle of Bovines destroyed Otho's party, and this prince dying four years after, Frederic became master of Germany. The king began to have regular troops.

1215. 16. 17. 18. 19. 20. 21. 22. 23.

The fourth general Lateran council, convoked by Innocent III. The acts of this assembly contain seventy canons: the primacy was determined in favour of the patriarch of Constantinople, preferably to the other three patriarchs of Alexandria, Antioch, and Jerusalem, though the council of Nice had regulated otherwise, and granted the precedency to the patriarch of Alexandria. The county of Toulouse was adjudged by these prelates to the count of Montfort. We may observe, on this occasion, that Innocent III. thought it beneath his dignity to wear a cross, by which he was confounded with other bishops; yet there is no doubt but the popes used to wear this outward mark, as may be proved from the conclusion of Luitprand's history, where Benedict renouncing the pontificate to which he had been called without the emperor Otho's consent, delivered up his cross into the hands of Leo VIII, the legitimate pontif, who broke it in the presence of the emperor, prelates, and people.

The order of *Preaching brothers*, called Dominicans, confirmed by the pope in 1215. They had been instituted ever since the year 1206.

The first statutes of the university, drawn up by Robert de Courçon, otherwise called the cardinal of St. Steven, legate of the holy see. It is said, that the university was founded by Charlemain; which only proves its high reputation, by referring it to so ancient an original. The above opinion is not attested by any cotemporary writer. In all probability, the first rise of the university was towards the end of the reign of Lewis the Young;
but

REMARKABLE EVENTS under PHILIP AUGUSTUS.

but the name itself did not begin to be used till the reign of St. Lewis, so that Peter Lombard may be looked upon as its founder. Then it was that colleges were erected, different from the schools belonging to the chapters, such as the school of St. Germain de l'Auxerrois, from whence the *Quai de l'école* derives its name. This institution was considerably increased during the reign of St. Lewis. Jane, queen of Navarre, founded the college bearing her name, in the reign of her husband Philip the Fair; and cardinal le Moine did the same by his in 1302, &c. But the most flourishing state of the university was under Charles VI; for two principal reasons, the schism of thirty eight years, and the differences betwixt the duke of Orleans and John the *Fearless:* both parties (which always happens in times of public calamity) began to lay hold of every advantage, and to strengthen themselves with the reputation of a society, that was never intended for state affairs. One cannot help being surprized at the privileges, enjoyed by the university and its scholars. The rector granted leave to preach; neither he nor his scholars contributed towards the support of the government; their causes were appointed to be heard before the provost of Paris, who was decorated with the title of *Conservator of the royal privileges of the universities of Paris*; the rector's signature was used in public acts and treaties; the university sent members to general councils; in short, learning seemed so great a prodigy in those days of ignorance, that it was imagined they could not shew too many favours to a community, in whose hands the sciences seemed to be deposited. Towards the end of the reign of Charles VI, the credit of the university began to decline, in consequence of the extinction of the schism, and the invasion of the English, who had no party to manage: and the troubles of the nation having subsided in the reign of Charles VII, it reverted to its natural state, that of presiding over the instruction of youth, and promoting polite literature. Not but that this learned body preserved for some time the remains of their ancient grandeur, which continued insensibly to diminish, till the reign of Lewis XII, when the cardinal d'Amboise having abolished their frivolous claims, it dwindled away to nothing, and our kings recovered their lawful authority. But while the university of Paris

REMARKABLE EVENTS under PHILIP AUGUSTUS.

Paris was divested of imaginary privileges, and reduced to its own natural strength, it acquired more real dignity and splendor. This mother of all other universities, has produced the greatest number of persons, eminent in every branch of literature; and although she has been the oracle even of councils themselves, still she preserves an inviolate submission to the holy see, whose pontifs have not disdained to consult her upon occasion; in short, she enjoys the empire of knowledge in the Christian world, an empire the more firmly established, as it is intirely owing to her own merit. About this same time the university of Toulouse was founded.

King John, by being reconciled to the pope, does not stand upon better terms with his subjects: he is obliged to grant them the famous charter called *Magna Charta*, which he afterwards revokes. The English no longer keep any measure with him, but revolt, and call in Lewis, son of Philip Augustus, under colour that the crown of England really belonged to him; that king John had usurped it from his nephew Arthur, and rendered himself unworthy of it by the murder of that prince; that in default of Arthur, Lewis was the lawful heir, in right of his wife Blanche of Castile, descended from a daughter of Henry II. Philip Augustus, willing to act cautiously with the pope, and at the same time to avail himself of the present disposition of the English, determines to assist the prince his son, without appearing in the affair himself. Lewis makes a descent upon England, is crowned at London, and defeats king John. The French prince is excommunicated by the pope; but this does not reverse the fate of John, who dies of chagrin. The resentment of the English nation ending with his death, they declare in favour of his son Henry III: then falling upon Lewis, they lay siege to London, and oblige this prince to depart from England. From that moment the English were reinstated in all their rights and privileges, which the Anglo-Saxons, invited over by Vortigern, had introduced into England in 449; privileges arising from the liberty enjoyed by those people, and so firmly established upon their possessing themselves of the island, that they are now become the fundamental laws of the kingdom. Edward, surnamed the *confessor*, reduced them into a code in 1040,

REMARKABLE EVENTS under PHILIP AUGUSTUS.

1040, called the laws of Saint Edward, or the common law; which underwent various revolutions, till the reign of king John, when the barons taking advantage of that prince's distress, insisted on the restoration of the Saxon laws, otherwise stiled the laws of St. Edward. John held out as long as he could; but was obliged at length to condescend, and to grant the two famous charters, namely, *that of liberty*, or *magna charta*, and the *charter of forests*. This is the æra of British liberty, or rather of British liberty restored; an æra to which the nation has ever since appealed, because these two charters are preserved, while the generality of ancient records are lost. The *magna charta* contains sixty seven articles, the charter of forests has but eighteen; they are dated in the year 1215, a year before the death of king John.

The origin of the *serjeants at arms*, the first guards of the kings of France, that can be proved from history. They distinguished themselves at Bovines, and prevailed on the king to build the church of *St. Catharine du val des escoliers*, in discharge of a vow they had made during this battle. They were all gentlemen, and whereas every other office used to die with the king, that of serjeants was for life. (Boutelier, du Cange.)

Philip subdued the provinces of Normandy, Anjou, Maine, Touraine, Poitou, Auvergne, Vermandois, Artois, Montargis, Gien, &c. and reunited them to the crown. He was surnamed *Augustus* from his conquests. After having reduced Normandy, he established the law of retaliation, which then obtained throughout the kingdom.

REMARK-

| 1223. Accession to the crown. | REMARKABLE EVENTS. |

LEWIS *VIII, surnamed* COEUR DE LION, *succeeds to the crown the 14th of July* 1223, *aged thirty six years. He is the first of the 3d race, that was not crowned in his father's life-time. Stephen, abbot of St. Genieve, afterwards bishop of Tournay, was his godfather, being only as yet an abbot.*

He was crowned at Rheims the 6th of August 1223.

1223. 24.

HENRY III, instead of assisting at the coronation of Lewis, according to his duty, demanded the restitution of Normandy. The king refused to comply; and being sensible that as soon as the truce between that prince and him expired, the English would renew the war, he entered into a treaty with the emperor Frederic, and several lords who might have joined with the king of England. Then issuing a proclamation, to confirm the confiscation, which his father had made of Normandy, as also of the several fiefs hitherto belonging to the kings of England, he determined to drive the English out of France; with which view he put himself at the head of a numerous army. In this expedition he dispossessed king Henry of Niort, St. John d'Angeli, and of all the country on this side the Garonne, besides the territories of Limousin, Perigord, and Aunis, together with Rochelle. There remained nothing further towards effecting the total expulsion of the English, but to make himself master of Gascony and Bourdeaux: but Lewis VIII. was ill advised; for instead of pursuing his conquests against Henry, he suffered himself to be persuaded by the pope to make war against the Albigenses. Two reasons determined him to take this step; one, that the pope permitted him to lay an extraordinary tax upon the clergy of France; the other, that young Amaury of Montfort resigned his right to all the conquests, with which Philip Augustus had invested his father in Languedoc. St. Lewis made the same Amaury of Montfort confirm this cession; and in return granted him the post of constable in 1230, upon the death of Matthew de Montmorency.

Maurice,

The Third Race. 175

WIVES.	CHILDREN.	1226. DEATH.	Cotemporary PRINCES.
Blanche of Castile, daughter of Alfonso IX. king of Castile, married to Lewis in 1200. 1252. Blanche had a sister named Berangere, wife of Alfonso king of Leon, by whom she had a son named Ferdinand. This prince was king of Castile to the prejudice of Lewis IX, the son of Blanche, who, according to some grave authors, was the elder sister. But what is very remarkable, both the sons of these princesses, Lewis and Ferdinand, were inrolled by the church in the list of saints.	Philip died young. ST. LEWIS. Robert count of Artois. Philip died young. John, count of Anjou and Maine, died young. Alfonso, count of Poitiers and Toulouse. 1271. Philip, surnamed Dagobert, died young. Stephen died young. Charles, count of Anjou and Provence, king of Naples. 1295. A daughter died young. Isabella died the death of a saint in the abbey of Louchamp, which she founded herself. 1269.	Lewis VIII. departs this life at the castle of Montpensier in Auvergne, in 1226, aged 39 years. He is interred at St. Denis.	*Pope.* Honorius III. 1227. *Emperor of the East.* Robert de Courtenay. 1229. *Emperor of the West.* Frederic II. 1250. *King of Spain.* Ferdinand III. 1252. *King of Portugal.* Sancho II. 1246. *King of England.* Henry III. 1273. *King of Scotland.* Alexander II. 1249. *King of Denmark.* Waldemar II. 1241. *King of Sweden.* Eric XI. 1250. *King of Poland.* Lescius. 1226.

REMARKABLE EVENTS under LEWIS VIII.

Maurice, bishop of Mans, and William of Beaumont, bishop of Angiers, take the oath of allegiance to the king. Bondonnet, in his account of the bishops of Mans, says, that before Maurice's time this oath was not required, and that it came to be used in consequence of an arret of parliament. I apprehend that Bondonnet is mistaken, and that the practice of taking the oath of allegiance is of a much earlier date, as appears by the 3d council of Tours in 817, and by the 2d council under Lewis the Debonnaire at Aix la Chapelle in 836. But independently of these authorities, since the bishops, from the first foundation of their sees, held whatever temporal power they exercised, of the king, there could be no manner of doubt but they were obliged in conscience to take an oath of fealty to the prince, whom they represented in their respective provinces.

An impostor pretending to be Baldwin, earl of Flanders and emperor of Constantinople, (who had been dead these twenty years) excites an insurrection in Flanders. Lewis VIII. sent for this man to Peronne, who refused to answer any question proposed: being ordered to depart from thence, he was seized by the Flemings, and hanged.

1225. 26.

The king renews the war against the Albigenses, and lays siege to Avignon, at the intreaty of pope Honorius III. Some say (*Matthew Paris*) that he died at this siege; others that he took the town, and departed this life a few months after. The latter opinion is the most general and most authentic. Thibaud, count of Champagne, who followed the king in this expedition, asks leave to return home, and departs without obtaining it, a circumstance which gave room to a malignant suspicion. The count of Champagne was suspected of having poisoned the king. This prince made his will, and ordered all the bishops and lords at court to be witnesses to it: he first declared Lewis, his eldest son, king; then he gave the county of Artois to his second son; Poitou to the third; Anjou and Maine to the fourth: this will was executed. It is observable, that in this settlement he determines the inclinations of his fifth son John, and of those that shall come after him, by commanding them *to enter into holy orders*. Well may we be surprised, that

Ministers.	Warriors.	Magistrates.	Eminent and Learned Men.
Guerin, bishop of Senlis. 1230.	*Constable.* Matthew de Montmorency. 1230. *Marshals of France.* John Clement, living in 1260. Robert de Coucy, living in 1226. Gautier de Nemours, living in 1230.	*Chancellor.* Guerin, bishop of Senlis. 1230. It was he who rendered this the first office of the state. He resigned it in 1228, together with his bishopric, and put on the habit of a Cistercian monk in the abbey of Chaalis. The establishing the treasure of the charters, was also owing to his advice. An arret published solemnly at Paris in 1224, by the king in his court of peers, in favour of the great officers against the peers of France, whereby it is declared, that according to ancient usage, and the practice observed a long time, the great officers of the crown, namely, the chancellor, butler, chamberlain, &c. ought to assist at the trial of a peer of France, in order to pronounce sentence on him, in conjunction with the other peers of the realm; in consequence of which they all sat upon the trial of the countess of Flanders.	St. Francis of Assisi. 1226. We may apply to him, what a poet says of Zeno, founder of the Stoics, *esurire docet, et discipulos invenit.* William of Seligni. 1223. Rigord, towards 1224.

REMARKABLE EVENTS under LEWIS VIII.

so religious a prince should make such a disposition: but without doubt it was to avoid the multiplying of appanages; or rather dismembering the demesnes, the property of which was invested in the eldest sons, for appanages were not well known at that time.

By another act, Lewis VIII. declares his wife, Blanche, queen regent.

This prince, adhering to the maxims of his predecessors, distinguished the commencement of his reign by enfranchising the villains, who were still very numerous in France.

1226.
Acceſſion to the crown.

LEWIS IX, called ST. LEWIS, ſucceeds to the crown the 8th of November, 1226, aged about twelve years. He was crowned at Rheims by James de Baſoche, biſhop of Soiſſons, the church of Rheims being then vacant: this was the third minority under the third race.

REMARKABLE EVENTS.

1226. 27. 28. 29.

QUEEN Blanche, the king's mother, was the firſt that had the united powers of guardian and regent. This whole minority was employed in ſubduing the confederate barons and princes; ſuch as Thibaud VI, count of Champagne; Peter de Dreux, ſurnamed *Mauclerc*, count of Britany, and grandſon of Robert de Dreux; Philip, count of Boulogne, the king's uncle; Hugh de Luſignan, count de la Marche; Jane, counteſs of Flanders; Enguerrand de Coucy; the counts of Ponthieu and Chatillon, &c. The queen was greatly aſſiſted in her adminiſtration by cardinal Romain, the pope's legate. Thibaud VI, count of Champagne, takes umbrage at this princeſs, and oppoſes her with open force. A penal law againſt heretics: the firſt enacted in France. St. Martin of Tours, who lived in the fourth century, refuſed to communicate with ſome biſhops, who had inſiſted on putting Priſcillian, the heretic, to death.

The count of Touloufe, who had ſupported the Albigenſes, makes his ſubmiſſion to the king and the pope: the principal condition of the treaty concluded with the king, was, that the daughter of the count of Touloufe ſhould be married to Alphonſus, the king's brother; and that in failure of iſſue from this marriage, the county of Toulouſe ſhould revert to the crown; which came to paſs. The country then poſſeſſed by the count of Touloufe, together with that which count Amaury reſigned to the king, began to take the general denomination of *Languedoc*.

The count of Champagne having been brought over by the queen, engages again with the male-contents, and concludes a marri-

WIVES.	CHILDREN.	1270. DEATH.	Cotemporary PRINCES.
Margaret, eldest daughter of Raymond II, count of Provence, married to St. Lewis in 1234. 1285.	Lewis died young. Philip the Hardy. John died young. John, surnamed Tristan, born at Damietta in 1250, died at Tunis in 1270. Peter, count of Alençon. 1283. Robert, count of Clermont in Beauvoisis. From this prince's marriage with Beatrix of Burgundy, daughter of John of Burgundy, and Agnes of Bourbon, is descended the branch of Bourbon, which came to the crown three hundred years after, by the succession of Henry IV. Blanche. 1243. Elizabeth, wife of Thibaud, king of Navarre, married to this prince the 6th of April 1255, died in 1271. Blanche the younger, born at Joppa, wife of Ferdinand de la Cerda, son of Alfonso X, king of Castile. 1320. Their issue were deprived of the crown by their uncle Don Sancho. Margaret, married to John duke of Brabant. 1271. Agnes, wife of Robert II, duke of Burgundy. 1327.	St. Lewis dies before Tunis the 25th of August 1270, aged fifty six years. His flesh and his bowels were removed to the abbey of Montreal near Palermo in Sicily, and there deposited in a marble tomb. His bones were carried to St. Denis. Pope Boniface VIII. canonized him at Orvieto the 11th of August 1297, and in the year 1298 his head was removed from St. Denis to the holy chapel. Lewis XIII. obtained of the pope, that the festival of this saint should be celebrated throughout the whole church.	*Popes.* Honorius III. 1227. Gregory IX. 1241. Celestine IV. 1241. Innocent IV. 1254. Alexander IV. 1261. Urban IV. 1264. Clement IV. 1268. He was the greatest civilian of his time, and had been married. His father, chancellor to Raymond VI, count of Touloufe, died a Carthufian. Gregory X. 1276. *Emperors of the East.* Robert de Courtenay. 1229. Baldwin II. 1261. *The Greek empire restored.* Michael Paleologus. 1283. *Emperors of the West.* Frederic II. 1250. Conrad. 1254. *Interregnum.* Henry of Thuringia. 1247. William, count of Holland. 1256. Richard. 1257. Alphonsus. 1284. *Kings of Spain.* Ferdinand III. 1252. Alfonso X. 1284. *Kings of Portugal.* Sancho II. 1246. Alfonso III. 1279. *King of England.* Henry III. 1273. *Kings of Scotland.* Alexander II. 1249. Alexander III. 1286. *Kings of Denmark.* Waldemar II. 1241. Eric VI. 1250. Abel. 1252. Christopher. 1250. Eric VII. 1286. *Kings of Sweden.* Eric XI. 1250. Waldemar. 1276. *King of Poland.* Boleslaus IV. 1279.

marriage with the daughter of the count of Britany. The queen gets timely intelligence of this step, breaks off the match, and detaches him from the rebellious party: the latter to punish him for his inconstancy, assert the rights of his cousin Alice, queen of Cyprus, to Champagne, (rights incontestable, if the legitimacy of this princess had not been disputed) and joining might to right, invade the territories of this prince. The king marches to his assistance; and having obliged the rebels to lay down their arms, he effectuates an accommodation between Alice and Thibaud, by means of a sum of money, which he advanced the latter, and for which Thibaud cedes to him the counties of Blois, Chartres, and Sancerre, with the viscounty of Chateaudun. Thus this prince is abused by the malecontents, and stripped by the king. The count of Britany, persisting in his revolt, has recourse to Henry III. king of England; but the queen-regent is said to have gained over Robert du Bourg *, that prince's minister, who kept his master in a state of inaction, or suffered him to act but faintly. The queen restores the earl of Flanders to his liberty, in order to match him against his enemy the count of Britany; and she draws the count of Boulogne into her interest, by inspiring him with a jealousy of Enguerrand de Coucy, who aimed at the regency, and perhaps at the crown.

The king lays siege to the castle of Bellesme in Perche, and takes it.

Italy was at this time most miserably torn with intestine divisions; the popes and the emperor were at war, the latter to maintain his possessions, the former to usurp them. Frederic II. had been raised to the Imperial dignity ever since 1215; he reigned upwards of six and thirty years, during which time he gained immortal honour by his valour, constancy of mind, and magnanimous enterprizes. Few emperors were possessed of such extensive dominions as this prince: he was king of Naples and Sicily, in right of his mother Constantia; king of Jerusalem by his second wife Yolante (a title preserved ever since by the kings of Sicily); he wrested Austria from the duke of that name

---

* Our historians call him *Hubert*. He was said to have taken a bribe of five thousand marks. M. Paris.

MINISTERS.	WARRIORS.	MAGISTRATES.	EMINENT and LEARNED MEN.
Peter of Vilebonne, living in 1270.	Matth. de Montmorenci. 1230. Amauri, count of Montfort. 1241. Humbert of Beaujeu. 1248. Giles of Trasegnies, called the *Brown*, living in 1272. Humbert of Beaujeu. 1285. *Marshals of France.* Henry Clement, lord of Argenton and Metz. 1265, Ferri Pasté, living in 1244. William of Beaumont, living in 1250. Gautier, sieur de Nemours, living in 1265. Renaud de Pressigni, living in 1270. Raoul de Sores, surnamed *d'Estrées*, living in 1281. Heric de Beaujeu, 1270.	*Chancellors.* Guerin, bishop of Senlis. 1230. John Allegrin, living in 1240. John de la Cour d'Aubergenville. 1256. Simon de Brion, who was pope by the name of Martin IV. 1285.	Accursius. 1229. Albericus, living in 1241. Alexander Halensis. 1245. Philip d'Antogny, C. S. St. Antony of Padua. 1231. Stephen Boileau, or Boylesve. Peter de Fontaines, towards 1270. He may be looked upon as the most ancient author, that has written upon the French laws. Giles, archbishop of Tyre, C. S. and confessor to St. Lewis. 1266. Gingiskan. 1227. Nicholas de Gros-Parmy, C. S. 1250. Raoul de Gross-Parmy, surnamed de Piris, C. S. 1270. William de St. Amour, towards 1270. William bishop of Paris. 1248. William de Lorris, towards 1265. Hugo Cardinalis. 1261. Matthew Paris. 1259. Peter des Vignes. 1249. Robert of Sorbonne, towards 1271. Vicent of Beauvais, towards 1264.

REMARKABLE EVENTS under LEWIS IX.

(this they call the firſt houſe of Auſtria; for the ſecond did not begin till the time of Rodolphus of Habſburg, by marriage); he took Sardinia from the Saracens; in a word, Frederic was equally formidable in the empire and in Italy. And yet the pope dared to enter the liſts with this mighty prince: and what is very extraordinary, this ſame pope, who oppoſed the power of a great emperor, had not a ſufficient degree of authority over his own ſubjects; for while he endeavoured to encroach upon Frederic, the Italians attempted to diveſt him of his rights. But Gregory IX. prevailed over the emperor, and the Romans. He began with cutting out work for Frederic; for which he had a good pretence, upon that prince's marriage with Yolante, heireſs of the kingdom of Jeruſalem. Frederic by his marriage contract had engaged to undertake an expedition to the Holy land, in order to poſſeſs himſelf of his wife's kingdom; and after having delayed this voyage for ſome time, without being in the leaſt affected with the pope's excommunications, at length he reſolved to embark. His abſence was of no long continuance; for when he had got himſelf crowned king of Jeruſalem, and concluded a treaty with the Saracens, he made all poſſible haſte to return, knowing that the pope had ſent him into Syria, only to diſtreſs him in Italy. But he ſoon recovered what Gregory had taken from him; and this pontif once more had recourſe to excommunications. Innocent IV, between whom and Gregory there was only a ſeventeen days pope, (Celeſtine IV.) and who before his exaltation to the pontificate, had been Frederic's friend, adopted the maxims of his predeceſſor; and Frederic, as we ſhall hereafter ſee more at large, was depoſed in the council of Lyons. The landgrave of Thuringia, and William count of Holland, were ſucceſſively choſen to ſucceed him; Frederic beat them both, but died in the midſt of theſe commotions: yet neither Italy nor the empire recovered their tranquillity.

1230. 31. 32. 33, &c.

Diſturbances in the univerſity of Paris; the Dominicans take this opportunity to eſtabliſh two profeſſorſhips of divinity.

REMARKABLE EVENTS under LEWIS IX.

The Inquisition instituted in 1204, and adopted by the count of Toulouse in 1229, was at length committed to the Dominicans by pope Gregory IX, in 1233.

The king of England makes a descent in Britany; but this does not hinder the king of France from carrying on his conquests in that province. Henry III. proceeds to Gascony, from whence he returns to Britany, and, after wasting his time in entertainments and diversions, he reimbarks for England. The king publishes a declaration, importing, that the count of Britany had forfeited his estate for high-treason: this was Peter Mauclerc, who notwithstanding he had the honour of being a *lord of the blood* (according to the expression of those days) entered into every plot and intrigue during the minority of St. Lewis. At length he was subdued, *and presented himself before the king*, says a cotemporary writer, *with a cord about his neck, and prostrating himself at his feet, asked forgiveness of his treason.* St. Lewis, according to the same author, received him very ill, and spoke to him in these terms: " Wicked traytor, although " thou hast merited an infamous death, yet I pardon thee in " consideration of thy noble blood; but I shall let thy son en- " joy Britany during his life only, and, after his decease, it is " my will, that the kings of France be masters of thy country." *If it be true*, says the abbé Vertot, *that this religious prince expressed himself in that manner, he must have been convinced that Britany, as well as every other fief, was originally a royal grant, since he had a power of annexing it to the crown.* This is the argument the abbé Vertot makes use of to support his system of the original authority of our kings over Britany; but independently of that ancient claim, did not our princes derive as good a title from the conquest of Armorica by Clovis? A truce of three years is concluded with the king of England. The minority of St. Lewis expires (1235) at the age of one and twenty. The old man of the mountain sends his emissaries to assassinate the king.*; but being afterwards affected with the fame of his virtues, he

---

* The *old man of the mountain* is a name well known in romance. He was king of the Assasinians, a people in the neighbourhood of Tyre in Phœnicia. They followed the Mahometan religion, and trained up young people to kill such persons, as the *old man of the mountain* had devoted to destruction.

gives

gives this prince notice to take care of himself. This fact is mentioned by all our historians, yet begins to lose credit: we are to observe however, that the reasons against it appear insufficient to the editor of the Mem. of the Acad. of Belles Lettres, t. xvi. p. 165.

1238. 39. 40. 41.

Thibaud, count of Champagne, wants to revoke the renunciations which he had made to the king; but no attention being paid him, he sets out in 1238 upon the crusade, at the head of several French lords. This expedition was unsuccessful. The king purchases the county of Mâcon, which had been subject to its own lords ever since the establishment of feudal tenures.

The plurality of benefices is condemned at an assembly of divines. The pope, having deposed the emperor Frederic, makes an offer of the imperial dignity to Robert, the king's brother: St. Lewis, far from being flattered with this dangerous proposal, peremptorily rejects it, saying, that it was sufficient for Robert to be brother to the king of France. He redeems our Saviour's crown of thorns from the Venetians, for the same sum as had been paid by them to Baldwin II, emperor of Constantinople. He likewise purchases the most valuable relics, remaining in the hands of the Latin princes; namely, a great piece of the genuine cross, our Saviour's robe, the sword, the lance, the sponge, and other instruments of his passion. It is believed, that this fragment of the genuine cross, is the same as was brought from Jerusalem by St. Helena to her son Constantine the Great. The king invests his brother Alphonsus with the counties of Poitou and Auvergne; the count de la Marche, as well as the other vassals, are obliged to pay him homage. The countess, his wife, upbraids him with this step as an act of cowardice; upon which he has recourse again to arms.

In the year 1241 the association of the *Hanse Towns* is said to have been originally formed by some cities of Germany, which entered into a confederacy for the encouragement and protection of their commerce. Hamburg and Lubec were the first that joined in this alliance.

The THIRD RACE. 187

REMARKABLE EVENTS under LEWIS IX.

1242. 43. 44.

The battle of Taillebourg *, and another the next day in the neighbourhood of Xaintes, in which the king is victorious over the count de la Marche, and over Henry III. king of England, to whom he grants a truce of five years. It cost the count de la Marche the town of Xaintes, and a part of Xaintonge, which Lewis annexed to the crown. The king falls dangerously ill, and makes a vow to set out for the Holy land.

The holy see having been vacant twenty months, by the detention of some cardinals, whom the emperor Frederic had caused to be imprisoned; at length the conclave was held at Anagni, where nine of the sacred college were present, and Innocent IV. was elected. This was the cardinal of Fieschi, a Genoese, of the illustrious family of la Vagna, which has given two popes to the church, besides a great number of cardinals. As this pontif before his exaltation to the triple crown had always expressed himself with moderation during the quarrels between Frederic and Rome, and had even shewn some marks of friendship for that prince, Frederic's ministers testified great joy at his election, expecting a perfect harmony between the church and the empire; but Frederic being better acquainted with mankind, said that he should only lose his friend the cardinal, and make a new enemy of the pope. In regard to this election, Matthew Paris relates a remarkable story; that when the cardinals shewed themselves so dilatory in proceeding to the nomination of a pope, they were given to understand, that if they did not put an end to the vacancy of the holy see, which proved detrimental to the tranquillity of the church, the French would find means to do without them, and to chuse a pope on this side the mountains. The same historian adds, that it was not an idle menace, but that our nation had a privilege of this kind, which had been formerly granted to St. Denis by St. Clement, upon investing him with the apostleship of the west. But this opinion of Matthew Paris is absolutely exploded.

---

* A town of France in the province of Guyenne, on the banks of the Charente. The English historians represent this as a skirmish, when Lewis pursued the rear of the English army in its retreat.

1245.

REMARKABLE EVENTS under LEWIS IX.

1245. 46. 47. 48.

The council of Lyons, in which the emperor Frederic II. is excommunicated, and deposed by pope Innocent IV. Frederic appeals to a future council. In this assembly the red hat was appropriated to cardinals. Charles, count of Anjou, the king's brother, marries Beatrix of Provence, who had been left under the tuition of Romec de Villeneuve, baron of Vence, and Albert of Tarascon. In consequence of this marriage, Charles becomes count of Provence, though his countess was the younger sister of Margaret, wife of St. Lewis. But such was the will and pleasure of their father, Raymond Beranger, who had a right to dispose of his estate according to his own fancy; and he chose rather that his subjects should have a prince that resided amongst them, than a king with whose presence they were not likely to be honoured. After the death of St. Lewis, who had acknowledged the validity of Raymond's will, his wife Margaret wanted to maintain her right of seniority; but the emperor Rodolph of Hapsburg, pretending to be the competent judge of this dispute, as lord paramount of the counts of Provence, (the kingdom of Arles, on which Provence depended, having been annexed to the empire) confirmed the right of Charles of Anjou. We are to observe here by the way, that this sovereignty of the emperors of Germany, as kings of Arles, expired with the emperor Charles IV. (Longerue). And in order to sum up the whole that is necessary to be known with reference to Provence, it had been originally subject to the kings of France, under the Carlovingian race; it fell afterwards under the dominion of Boso, brother-in-law of Charles the Bald, which Boso became king of Arles; upon his decease this province remained for some time in a state of anarchy, and exposed to the incursions of the Saracens; but another Boso, assisted by his son William, chased away those infidels; and this William is considered as the first count of Provence. The male line of the family happening to be extinct, the counts of Barcellona acquired this estate by marriage; and a princess descended from them, brought the county of Provence to the house of France, by espousing, as we have observed, the count of Anjou. The ordinance called the *king's quarantain*, by which the heirs of a person murdered, are forbid to take their revenge, before the expiration of forty days. The

REMARKABLE EVENTS under LEWIS IX.

The fifth crusade. St. Lewis embarks for the Holy land on Friday the 12th of June 1248, after Whitsunday. He was attended in this expedition by his three brothers, Robert count of Artois, Alphonsus count of Poitiers, and Charles count of Anjou, together with Hugh duke of Burgundy, William de Dampierre count of Flanders, and his brother Guy, Hugh de Chastillon count of St. Paul, his nephew Gaucher, Hugh count de la Marche, with his son, &c. Queen Blanche is made regent during the king's absence.

1249. 50. 51.

The death of Raymond VII, count of Toulouse, who was succeeded by his daughter Jane, wife of Alfonsus count of Poitiers, the king's brother. Thus with Raymond ended the male line of the counts of Toulouse, four centuries after Fredelo had been created count of that name in 849 by Charles the Bald.

Damietta in Egypt is taken by St. Lewis. The death of the count of Artois in Massora, where the king, and all the officers in his retinue, performed prodigies of valour. The French army is reduced by famine and sickness to great distress; and the king is made prisoner in the neighbourhood of Massora, together with his two brothers Alphonsus and Charles. He restores the city of Damietta, and pays four hundred thousand livres for his ransom: cotemporary historians say eight hundred thousand bezants, which they rate at a hundred thousand marks of silver; but the reader may see concerning this valuation, the twentieth dissertation of du Cange on the history of St. Lewis. The regent pressed the king to return to France; but notwithstanding her intreaties he went to Palestine, where he continued four years longer, with a view to repair the fortifications of Cæsarea, Philippi, Joppa, Acra, and Sydon: his residence in that country procured the liberty of upwards of twelve thousand Christians. (Joinville.)

1252. 53. 54.

The death of queen Blanche, who is interred at Maubuisson, an abbey of her foundation in 1242. Saint Lewis returns to Paris (1254) where Henry king of England pays him a visit. Matthew Paris, a cotemporary writer, giving an account of the entertainment which St. Lewis made for that prince, takes notice, that as he would have yielded the place of honour to king Henry, the latter

REMARRKABLE EVENTS under LEWIS IX.

latter refused to accept of it, saying, that it was better filled by the king of France; for, added he, *you are my lord paramount, and always will be such.*

Enguerrand de Coucy, and several other lords, are chastised for their oppression. The death of Thibaud I, king of Navarre and count of Champagne. The crown of Navarre, after having been four hundred years in possession of the house of Bigorre, which had filled all the Spanish thrones, fell at length to the house of Champagne, in the person of Thibaud VI, son of Blanche of Navarre, which Blanche had been married to Thibaud V, count of Champagne, and inherited the kingdom of Navarre upon the decease of her brother Sancho the *Strong* in 1234. Thibaud VI. had two sons, Thibaud and Henry, both of whom were kings, and survived him; the latter left an only daughter Jane, who was married to Philip the Fair.

The Carmelites settled in France.

An ordinance of St. Lewis, dated from St. Giles, (1254) by which it appears, that the three estates were consulted, in matters any way relative to the interest of the people.

1255. 56. 57.

The emperor Frederic II. departed this life in 1250. Conrad his son and successor died in 1254, poisoned, as it is said, by Manfred his natural brother, who seized the kingdoms of Naples and Sicily, which of right belonged to Conradin the lawful son of Conrad: the usurper, being desirous of securing these kingdoms in his family, gave his only daughter Constantia in marriage to Peter king of Arragon, with Sicily for her dower, reserving only the usufruct to himself. Urban IV. (the same who instituted the feast of the Holy sacrament) being an enemy, like all his predecessors, to the house of Swabia, excommunicates Manfred in 1263, and declares Charles of Anjou king of Naples and Sicily. Clement IV, adhering to the same principles, thundered out his excommunications in 1268 against Conradin, for attempting to assert his rights after the death of Manfred, who was slain in 1266 at the battle of Benevento. Conradin was vanquished by Charles of Anjou, who caused him to be beheaded, and became peaceable possessor of the throne of the two Sicilies. Charles had been honoured with the senatorian rank by the Romans, so early as

in

REMARKABLE EVENTS under LEWIS IX.

in the pontificate of Urban IV, which gave umbrage to the two popes; but their aversion to the house of Swabia stifled any jealousy they might conceive against this new dignity. With this prince began the first branch of Anjou, that reigned in Sicily; his successors were Charles the *Lame*, Robert, Johanna of Naples, dethroned by her cousin Charles of Anjou, surnamed the *Peaceful*; Charles the *Peaceful* had Ladislaus for his son, who was father of Johannilla, so infamous for her irregular life. Johannilla, finding herself attacked by Charles the Peaceful, called in Lewis duke of Anjou, the second son of John king of France, to undertake her defence, and to succeed to the crown: with him began the second house of Anjou, kings of Naples and Sicily; but neither he nor his successors were able to maintain themselves in the possession of those countries.

Alexander IV. unites several congregations of hermits (1256), and gives them the rule of St. Austin; three years after this the Austin friars came and settled in France.

A famous arret against the lord of Vernon, obliging him to indemnify a merchant, who had been robbed upon the high road in the open day, within his seigniory. Such was the custom in those times; the lords were obliged to keep a guard upon the roads from sun-rise to sun-set, because of the right of *peage* * which they enjoyed on this account. We meet with the like arret against the count of Artois in 1287 *(Bouchel)*. This was a very ancient regulation *(capit. of Charlemain, 812)*.

1258. 59. 60. 61. 62. 63. &c.

A treaty concluded between St. Lewis and James I. king of Arragon, upon the marriage between Philip (who was then St. Lewis's second son, but two years after became the eldest, and succeeded to the crown, by the name of Philip the Hardy) and Isabella, the youngest daughter of James, to whom her father gave the counties of Carcassonne and Besiers for her portion. The conditions of the treaty were, that St. Lewis should relinquish, in favour of the king of Arragon, the sovereignty which France preserved over Barcellona, Roussillon, &c. ever since she had conquered that country from the Saracens; and that the king

---

* A custom or toll paid for passage; which the lords of manors have a right to demand, within their jurisdictions.

of

REMARKABLE EVENTS under LEWIS IX.

of Arragon on the other hand should yield to the crown of France, all his pretensions either by the marriages of his predecessors, or by other titles, to the counties of Narbonne, Nismes, Alby, Foix, Cahors, and other districts in Languedoc, held as rear fiefs of the crown of France; as likewise all his right in Provence to the counties of Forcalquier and Arles, and to the town of Marseilles; without including however the barony of Montpelier, which did not revert to the crown till the reign of Philip of Valois. This appears to be a very prudent treaty; for the renunciation in favour of Arragon, related only to distant demesnes; whereas the cession made to France, was of districts situated within the kingdom. Yet it may be said, on the other hand, that the king parted with incontestable rights of sovereignty, uninterruptedly enjoyed by his predecessors, ever since the time of Charlemain; whereas most of the claims which James renounced, were ill founded. Hence there are many who deny the existence of this treaty, pretending that the original can no where be found; and that there is only a simple ratification of it at a time remarkable for forgeries, without either date, place, or name of the commissioners; all which looks very suspicious; and therefore they conclude, that the rights of France to Catalonia do still subsist in their full vigour.

The king of France concludes a treaty with Henry III. very different from that with the king of Arragon. He restores intire provinces to him, namely, the part of Guyenne beyond the Garonne, already possessed by Henry, with the Limousin, Perigord, Quercy, and Agenois, upon condition of yielding full homage to the kings of France; and the king of England renounces only the rights he might possibly have to Normandy, Maine, Anjou, &c.

St. Lewis is chosen arbitrator between the king of England, and the revolted barons *. The latter refusing to abide by the award, a civil war breaks out, and the earl of Leicester takes

---

* King Henry III. attended by prince Edward, met St. Lewis at Amiens, where the states of the kingdom were assembled. The sentence pronounced by Lewis was in favour of Henry.

REMARKABLE EVENTS under LEWIS IX.

he king prisoner *, but his son Edward sets him at liberty, and Leicester is slain. This Leicester was son by a second venter of he famous earl of Montfort, and heir in right of his grandmother to the estate of the Leicester family. The year 1264 is generally believed to be the æra of the admission of the commons into the parliament of England, the king having been compelled, during his imprisonment, to issue out a summons for four knights of every shire to assist at the next parliament †, in order to represent their respective counties. In like manner several authors date the admission of the third estate into the assembly of the states general, from the reign of Philip the Fair. St. Lewis being chosen umpire between the d'Avenes and Dampierres, sons of Margaret countess of Flanders and Hainault, by different husbands, determines that the d'Avenes shall have the county of Hainault, and the Dampierres that of Flanders.

The king's prohibition in 1260 against duels or gages of battle within his demesnes, instead of which he substituted the trial by witnesses; for (as Beaumanoir says, who wrote his *Practice* in 1283) *the holy king Lewis abolished them in his own court, but did not extend his orders to the courts of his barons.* Foundation of the hospital of *Quinze-vingt* ‡ the same year: it is said, though without proof, to have been erected in favour of some gentlemen, whose eyes had been pulled out by the Saracens.

The ordinance of 1262, in regard to the coinage, importing, 1°. that in districts where the barons had no mint, the king's coin alone shall be current: 2°. that where the barons had a mint, the king's coin should go for the same value as upon his own demesnes. At that time there were upwards of fourscore private lords, who had the privilege of coining; but the king alone had the prerogative of coining money of gold and silver. On one side was a cross, and on the other were pillars; hence to this very day

---

* At the battle of Lewes, on the 14th of May 1264; with the king was taken his son, his brother, and his nephew; and about 5000 persons fell on both sides. Prince Edward escaped out of prison, raised an army, and encountered the earl of Leicester at Evesham on the 5th of August 1265, where the earl lost his life.

† Each county was to send two knights; and each city and borough, as many citizens and burgesses.

‡ An hospital wherein three hundred blind people are relieved with bread, lodging, and about fourpence a day.

REMARKABLE EVENTS under LEWIS IX.

the different sides of a piece of money are called *cross* and *pile*

The king's ordinance against blasphemers, or, according to the expression of the time, against *those who shall swear a wicked oath* against God, the Virgin, and the Saints. It is proper to observe that before this ordinance, St. Lewis used to punish blasphemy with the amputation of some member; but now he became more moderate at the advice of pope Clement IV, and reduced the punishment to a mulct or fine, after the example of his royal predecessors.

1269. 70.

The sixth and last crusade projected in the year 1267. St. Lewis having committed the regency to Matthew, abbot of St. Denis, and to Simon de Clermont of Nesle (whose place in case of death was to be supplied by Philip bishop of Evreux, and John count of Ponthieu) returns to Africa, where he lays siege to Tunis. The plague reaches his camp, and he is carried off by the distemper.

The French navy, no sooner created than destroyed under Philip Augustus, recovered itself greatly in the reign of St. Lewis; if it be true what an historian observes, that this prince embarked sixty thousand men at Aigues mortes: we must own, that he borrowed a large number of ships of the Venetians and of the Genoese; yet the greatest part of the fleet consisted of French shipping. And in regard to the former expedition, Joinville says, that upon his departure from Cyprus for the conquest of Damietta, he had eighteen hundred vessels of all sizes. This same prince likewise equipped a considerable squadron for the defence of the coast of Poitou against the English fleet of Henry III; and his brother Charles of Anjou had no less than eighty sail, reckoning gallies and ships, at the time of his expedition to Naples.

The Sorbonne * was founded in this reign, by Robert Sorbonne, confessor of St. Lewis, as appears by letters patent, bearing date 1250.

General customs known by the name of the *establishments* of *St. Lewis*. In this compilation, St. Lewis inserted some of the laws of his predecessors, and several of his own enacting, so that

* A college for the study of divinity in the university of Paris, so called from its founder; it was rebuilt by cardinal Richelieu.

REMARRKABLE EVENTS under LEWIS IX.

...whole makes a kind of code, which he caused to be digested little before his second crusade. The pragmatic sanction in regard to ecclesiastic affairs: whence we may judge of the king's great attention in maintaining the liberties of the Gallican church. But it has been since questioned, whether this prince was the author of it. It was St. Lewis that built the *holy chapel* *. He likewise published several edicts for and against the Jews. Establishment of the *police* at Paris, by Stephen Bóileau, provost of that city, a magistrate worthy of the greatest encomiums. He began with the punishment of criminals: the *country provosts* had put every thing to sale, even the very liberty of trading; and the imposts on provisions were excessive; but he applied a remedy to both: he ranged all the chapmen and artificers into different companies, under the name of confraternities: he drew up the first statutes, and established several regulations with such equity and prudence, that whatever has been enacted since in regard to these companies, or to the erection of new societies of the same kind, has been transcribed or borrowed from those statutes. The family of Stephen Boileau, whose real name is *Boylesve*, continued afterwards to make a figure in the province of Anjou, where it subsists to this day.

To this reign we must refer, according to Joinville, the institution of masters of requests: at first there were no more than one; this number afterwards increased; and by the edict of 1742 it is fixed to fourscore.

Father Daniel is in the right: *St. Lewis was one of the greatest and most extraordinary men that ever existed.* He was a prince of experienced valour: but he exerted his courage only in matters of the highest concern. His soul was fired by noble objects, such as a regard to justice, and the love of his country: on every other occasion he seemed to be weak, simple, and pusillanimous. Hence it was, that he gave such signal instances of bravery, in fighting against rebels, against the enemies of his country, or against infidels: hence it was, that notwithstanding his piety and devotion, he had firmness sufficient to oppose the encroachments of popes and bishops, when he appre-

---

* A sacred structure in Paris.

hended

hended their raising any disturbances in his kingdom: hence was, that in the administration of justice, he behaved with a integrity worthy of admiration. But in his own domestic œco nomy, he made quite another figure; his servants were h masters, his mother had an absolute sway over him, and his tim was spent in the most simple practices of devotion. Indeed the practices were ennobled by virtues of the most solid kind, fro which he never deviated, and which properly formed his ch racteristic.

Joinville attributes the following instance of religious belief the count of Montfort, viz. his having refused, when in tl district of Albigeois, to go and see the consecrated host, whi was visibly changed into the body of our Lord; and the same a thor says, that he had heard the story from the king himself: y du Cange, in his observations on Joinville, says, that John V lani (book 6. chap. 7.) ascribes this fact to St. Lewis, and r to the count of Montfort.

The king being just ready to embark for the fifth crusa summoned all the barons of his kingdom to Paris, to ma: them swear, that if he should die abroad, they would ackno ledge the succession of his family to the crown. Joinvil, who without doubt was strongly attached to St. Lewis, ha pened to be summoned as well as the rest: *but for my pa,* says he, *as I was not his subject, I would not take the oath; a indeed it was not my intention to stay behind.* Upon which Cange, in his XIIIth and XIVth dissertations, shews very clear that this was a consequence of the feudal law, by which the rr vassals were forbid to take an oath, or to yield homage to tl r superior lord; and that they ought to pay obedience to their - mediate lord only, as being his special subjects. Such indd was the jurisprudence of that time: and this is corroborated y an article of St. Lewis's establishment, which he publishe a little before his last voyage to Africa: it declares, that the val is obliged, upon pain of confiscation of his fief, to follow his d to war, even against the king himself, in case the king ref d to do justice to his lord. This same Joinville, writing some the after to Lewis X, begs to be excused for calling him *his good* r only; because he owes the title of *monseigneur*, or *my lord*, to rn

REMARKABLE EVENTS under LEWIS IX.

t to the count of Champagne, his immediate lord (du Cange). moſt ſtrange effect of uſurped authority! yet it obtained in 1er countries, beſides France; ſince the emperor Frederic I, in ler to extirpate the like abuſe, mentions particularly in his linance from the camp of Ronſal, that it is his intention the peror ſhall be excepted by name, in the oath of allegiance, ich the vaſſal takes to his lord.

Inſtitution of the military order and knighthood of the ſhip I creſcent.

In this century the *golden legend* made its firſt appearance; it s a collection of the lives of ſaints, written in Latin by *Jaus de Voragine*, archbiſhop of Genoa. Melchior Canus, biıp of the Canaries, uſed to call it by a contrary name, *legenda rea* *.

* Or the *iron legend*.

1270. Accession to the crown.

PHILIP III, surnamed the HARDY, ascends the throne in 1270, at the age of five and twenty, and a few months. He was surnamed the HARDY, because it is said he was not intimidated at seeing himself exposed to a barbarous nation after the death of his father. But he did nothing afterwards to merit that title. He was crowned at Rheims in 1271 by Miles of Baroche, bishop of Soissons, the see of Rheims being then vacant.

REMARKABLE EVENTS.

1270. 71. 72.

PHILIP THE HARDY, being in Africa at the decease of his father St. Lewis, publishes an ordinance from the camp before Carthage, touching the majority of the king, which was fixed at fourteen: but it was not put in execution (*see the year* 1371). His uncle Charles, king of Sicily arrives with a fleet and army to his assistance and the infidels are defeated. The king concludes a truce with them for ten years, and returns to France with Thibaud count of Champagne and king of Navarre, and with Alphonsu count of Poitou, who die by the way. Alphonsu was also count of Toulouse; both he and his wife having died without issue, this county reverted to the crown, but was not reunited till 1361. Henry succeeds his brother Thibaud in the kingdom of Navarre.

The first letters of ennoblement in favour of Raoul the goldsmith. This new privilege, by which the *roturiers* or plebeians were raised from their low station, and placed upon a level with the nobles, did no more than restore things to their original state. The inhabitants of France, even after Clovis, under the first, and for a long time under the second race, were all of one condition, whether Franks or Gauls; and this equality, which lasted so long as the kings of France were absolute, was first interrupted by the rebellion and violence of those who usurped the great seignories. Not but there were some persons more powerful than others under the two first races; and indeed it would be difficult to comprehend how either Gauls or Franks, when invested with high dignities, could be of the same class as the rest of the inhabitants; but this only because we confound authority with the

The THIRD RACE.

WIVES.	CHILDREN.	1285. DEATH.	Cotemporary PRINCES.
Isabella of Arragon, married to Philip in 1262, died in 1271.	Lewis died young of poison. PHILIP THE FAIR. Charles, count of Valois, by whom the branch of Valois ascended the throne. Robert died young.	Philip the Hardy dies at Perpignan, in his return from the expedition of Arragon in 1285, aged forty years and some months. He was interred at St. Denis.	*Popes.* Gregory X. 1276. Innocent V. 1276. Adrian V. 1276. John XXI. 1277. Nicholas III. 1280. Martin IV. 1285. *Emperors of the East.* Michael Paleologus. 1283. Andronicus II. 1332. *Emperor of the West.*
Mary of Brabant married in 1274. 1321.	Lewis, count of Evreux, whose son, named Philip, was afterwards king of Navarre, in right of his wife Joan of France, only daughter of Lewis X. king of France and Navarre; their son was *Charles the Bad.* 1319. Margaret married to Edward I. king of England. 1317. Blanche married to Rodolphus, duke of Austria, eldest son of the emperor Albert I. 1305.		Rodolphus, count of Habsburg, founder of the house of Austria. 1291. *Kings of Spain.* Alfonso X. 1284. Sancho IV. 1295. *Kings of Portugal.* Alfonso III. 1279. Denis. 1325. *Kings of England.* Henry III. 1273. Edward I. 1308. *King of Scotland.* Alexander III. 1286. *King of Denmark.* Eric VII. 1286. *Kings of Sweden.* Waldemar. 1176. Magnus. 1290. *Kings of Poland.* Boleslaus IV. 1279. Leschus. 1289.
This princess was as great a lover of poetry as her father Henry duke of Brabant; she assisted a famous poet of that time, whose name was *y Reix Adenex*, to write the romance of Clemadez. This same poet had also celebrated the noble atchievements of ancient knights in rhime, among others those of Ogier the Dane, Bertrand du Bois, and Buenon de Commarchis.			

condition of persons. It cannot be denied but there were some men more respectable than others; but it did not follow from thence, that the rank or post they enjoyed, made them of a different nature, as it were, from the rest of their fellow-citizens. They were the first in the state, but not of a separate order; and the public offices were equally discharged by both, to the contrary of what afterwards happened, when the nobility obtained considerable advantages over the commonalty.

Such was my opinion, and I had taken it from M. de Valois, before that famous work appeared, which we shall call the *code of the law of nations*. What I read upon this subject in *the Spirit of Laws* (book 29. chap. 25.) contains, I own, very great difficulties, both from the known authority of the author, and because in matters relating to history, facts must preponderate over every other argument. For if we only reason upon the point, we should find it difficult to believe, that in such a nation as the *Franks*, the people were not all upon an equal footing: if they were so before the conquest, would they have lost their equality by being conquerors? " Let Tegan say to Hebo, whom the em-
" peror had emancipated, *the emperor has made you a free man, but
" did not ennoble you,*" (this is one of M. de Montesquieu's proofs). But does this shew that there were *nobles* in those days? And does the word *noble* answer to our present idea of a man of quality? when, according to the principles of our monarchy, no condition at all is equal; whereas in those days every man was upon a level. *The emperor has emancipated, but not ennobled you*; true: but the meaning is, the emperor's act can have no retrospect to your original servitude; just as the king by ennobling a person cannot cancel the obscurity of his birth: in a word, by infranchisement* a man was delivered from a servile state, but not raised to the condition of one that was free born. Thus I understood this passage: whenever the word *noble* happened to be mentioned in those early times, I conceived that it implied no more than a person free-born, and that freedom constituted the only and true nobility. This was the opinion of M. de Valois; and I might

---

* This answers to the distinction among the Romans of *ingenui* and *liberti*, the former were such as had been born free, and of parents that had been always free; the latter such as had been actually made free themselves.

The THIRD RACE.   201

MINISTERS.	WARRIORS.	MAGISTRATES.	EMINENT and LEARNED MEN.
Matthew of Vendome. 1286. Peter de la Brosse, hanged in 1276.	*Constable.* Humbert de Beaujeu. 1285. *Marshals of France.* Lancelot de St. Maard, living in 1276. Ferri de Verneuil, living in 1288. William, lord of Bec-Crespin, living in 1283.	*Chancellors.* Peter Barbet, archbishop of Rheims. 1298. Henry de Vezelai, living in 1279. Peter Challon, living in 1283.	Albertus Magnus. 1280. St. Bonaventure. 1274. Raymond of Pennafort, towards 1275. Roger Bacon, towards 1284. St. Thomas of Aquin. 1274. We must not omit a beautiful answer, which this saint made to Innocent IV. He happened to enter the pope's apartment, just when they were reckoning of money: the pope said to him, you see that the time is over, when the church used these words, *I have neither gold nor silver*, (Acts of apostles) to which the angelical doctor made answer, it is true, holy father, neither can she any longer say to the paralitic, *get up and walk*. Stephen Tempier. 1279. We find in the president Fauchet's *collection of the origin of the French poetry and language*, an extract of the works of a hundred and twenty seven poets, written before the close of the 13th century.

have been led into this way of thinking by the authority of so great a name: *In lege Sálica nobilium nulla fit mentio*, pag. 485. *In the Salic law there is no mention at all made of nobles*: the whole passage is equally clear; but we have already expatiated too much for an abridgment.

The king's commissioners take possession of the county of Toulouse: by the instruments drawn on that occasion, the province was continued in the possession of her ancient custom of settling the tailles and the subsidies, which it was to pay as a free gift to the king. This prince punished the rebellion of the count de Foix, by seizing his country, but restored it to him the year following.

1273.

The princes of Germany had elected Henry, landgrave of Thuringia, to the imperial throne, in preference to Conrad, to whom Frederic his father had bequeathed that dignity. Henry happening to die in 1247, they chose William count of Holland: this prince survived Conrad, who died in 1254. William breathed his last in 1256, in the midst of the troubles of the empire. After his decease, Richard count of Cornwall, and Alfonso king of Castile, were chosen by different parties. During this time of distraction, which was called the *Interregnum*, and continued till 1273, Rodolph count of Habsburg was elected emperor at Frankfort: he was the stock of the house of Austria, which subsisted till the last emperor Charles VI. Father Hergott, who published the genealogy of the house of Habsburg in 1737, and whose system appears preferable to the many different opinions, which have been adopted by the writers on the origin of this family, finds its real source in *Burgundia Transjurana*, in a district of Swisserland called *Argoia* or *Argew*. Here are demesnes with the title of county, which belonged to the house of Habsburg, before it took that title. It was not known by the denomination of Habsburg till the 12th century, when the lords began to assume the name of their seignories. In order therefore to investigate its original, we should ascend as high as those, who either governed as counts, before the counties were hereditary; or afterwards possessed those cantons *(Pagi)* in full property, which devolved to that house, as soon as the counties became patrimonial estates: and we may date the name of this

family,

REMARKABLE EVENTS under PHILIP III.

family, from the time that the custom of distinguishing the nobility by their possessions was first introduced. (See the three articles of the *Journal des Savans* of the year 1740, by M. de F. where this subject is exhausted.) During the interregnum, the first foundation of the territorial jurisdiction of the states of the empire was laid, and confirmed by succeeding emperors.

1274.

Philip declares war against Alfonso king of Castile, who had chosen his second son for his successor, in prejudice to the children of Ferdinand de la Cerda, his eldest son by Blanche the sister of king Philip. This war was but of short duration. The second council of Lyons, famous for the matters debated in that assembly, and among others for that of *the procession of the Holy Ghost*, the chief object of the Greek schism. We meet with a proof of the right of *joyful accession* * in an arret of parliament, published upon Candlemas of the year 1274; and confirmed in the subsequent reigns: which is a full refutation of those authors, who pretend that this right was unknown in France, before the reign of Henry III.

The king yields up the county of Venaissin to pope Gregory X.

1275. 76. 77. 78. 79. &c.

An ordinance in regard to the law of mortmain. Peter de la Brosse, formerly St. Lewis's barber, becoming a favourite of Philip the Hardy, and fearing lest his interest should be hurt by the attachment which the king had for the queen his wife, accuses this princess of having poisoned Lewis, the eldest son of Philip by the first venter. The calumny being discovered by a nun or beguine of Nivelle in Flanders, who was consulted on the occasion; la Brosse is hanged.

We are informed by an English lawyer, who in the reign of Edward I. wrote a practice of English law, by the title of *Fleta*, that a public assembly was held at Montpellier, where all the princes of Christendom agreed either by themselves, or by their ambassadors, that the lands belonging to their crown should be unalienable; and that the dismembered parts should be reunited. The above author has been contradicted by Selden in a learned

---

* A duty paid in France upon the accession of the king.

REMARKABLE EVENTS under PHILIP III.

differtation on the *Fleta*, who pretends that there never was any fuch affembly. Selden has been followed by Lauriere in the collection of ordinances, and by Dom. Vaiffette in his hiftory of Languedoc; yet all this makes but a fingle authority. And who knows but Selden had political reafons to deny the fact, without fupporting his opinion by any proofs; as he certainly had fome fuch reafons when he wrote his *Mare claufum*, in order to attribute the empire of the fea to England. I fhall further add, that about the time in which I mentioned this affembly of Montpellier, feveral princes of Europe had agreed, as it were by common confent, to declare their crown lands unalienable. See the particular remarks at the end of this work.

1282.

The Sicilian vefpers on Eafter-Sunday. This is the name given to the maffacre of all the French fubjects of the king of Naples, who were then in Sicily: it was committed by the direction of Peter king of Arragon, who afterwards feized that ifland; and his fucceffors have kept it ever fince. The emperor Rodolphus declares his fon Albert duke of Auftria, after recovering this province from Ottocares king of Bohemia, who had ufurped it from the houfe of Auftria: and from that time the counts of Habfburg have taken the name of this dutchy. Auftria had been erected into a dukedom by the emperor Frederic Barbaroffa in 1152, and according to feveral authors in 1156.

1283. 84. 85.

The law of *appanages* begins to be better known, by an arret concerning the county of Poitiers, which was adjudged to the king, in prejudice to his uncle Charles of Anjou. According to our prefent idea of *appanage*, it did not begin to be in full force till the reign of Philip the Fair; and before that time it had undergone feveral variations. During the two firft races, the king's children divided the crown equally among them: towards the beginning of the third, the inconveniency of thefe partitions produced the expedient of fetting apart fome portion of lands, for the younger fon to enjoy in full property.

But in proportion as the principles of true policy were improved, the inconveniency of difmembering the crown lands became more obvious; for which reafon the apportionments,

REMARKABLE EVENTS under PHILIP III.

which the possessors had a right to dispose of before as their own property, grew into a kind of intail, and were at length settled in such a manner, as to revert to the crown in default of *heirs*. This is properly the first beginning of appanages, which implied a kind of grant of a certain portion of the king's demesnes, only for a particular time, without extinguishing the property of the crown.

This law is fully established by the arret above mentioned. The dispute was between Charles of Anjou, king of Sicily, and Philip the Hardy his nephew, concerning the county of Poitiers. Charles claimed this estate as the next heir of Alphonsus the last deceased, who was his brother, whereas Philip was only his nephew. But the arret was given in favour of Philip, upon this principle, that whenever the king granted an estate or inheritance to one of his younger sons, and the donee came to die without heirs, the inheritance should revert to the doner, that is to the king, or to his next heir, and the brother of the deceased should have no sort of right or pretension.

Thus we find the appanages limited to the heirs of the person in whose favour they were originally created: but in these heirs not only males, but females were included; which was of dangerous consequence, because the portions assigned in appanage, might descend to foreigners by marriage. Philip the Fair remedied the latter inconveniency; for, according to du Tillet, he ordained by his codicil, or, according to Dupuy, by his letters patent, that the county of Poitou, which he had settled on his youngest son Philip of France, who afterwards ascended the throne by the name of Philip the Long, should revert to the crown, for want of *heirs male*, whereby the females were excluded. Such was the last state of this branch of jurisprudence.

Philip marries his eldest son to Jane queen of Navarre, heiress of that kingdom, and of the counties of Champagne and Brie, by the death of king Henry her father. In consequence of this marriage, Philip the Fair took the title of king of Navarre. Pope Martin IV. declares that the king of Arragon had forfeited his dominions, in punishment for the massacre called the Sicilian vespers, and granted the investiture thereof to Charles of Valois.

A war

REMARKABLE EVENTS under PHILIP III.

A war breaks out in Sicily between the king of Arragon, and Charles king of Naples, who raised the siege of Messina, and died in Apulia. Robert of Artois, son of him who deceased in Africa during the expedition of St. Lewis, was entrusted with the regency by this prince, who left his son Charles the *Lame* a prisoner, and his widow without a support. Philip wages war with the king of Arragon, in revenge for the enterprize in Sicily against his uncle Charles of Anjou, and to maintain the rights of Charles of Valois. Having made himself master of two towns in the kingdom of Arragon, he retired without attempting any thing further; and died at his return. The king of Arragon also departs this life during this war, and leaves James his second son king of Sicily, who afterwards ascended the throne of Arragon, by the death of his elder brother Alfonso. Then it was that the two kingdoms of Naples and Sicily were separated: Peter I. of Arragon was king of Sicily; and Charles the *Lame* succeeded his father in the kingdom of Naples, and in his pretensions to the other crown. Pope Clement IV. used to distinguish those two kingdoms by these words: *regnum Siciliæ citra & ultra Pharum.*

Philip, upon the occasion of his marriage with queen Mary, which he took care to have performed in the holy chapel by the archbishop of Rheims, notwithstanding the remonstrances of the archbishop of Sens, declared this church exempt from the jurisdiction of the metropolitan.

The foundation of the university of Montpellier.

During this reign disturbances were raised in Languedoc and in Guyenne, by the lords of that country, such as the counts of Foix, Armagnac, Narbonne, &c. who sometimes waged war against one another, and sometimes against the king: these troubles were the more dangerous, as the above lords assumed the air of sovereigns, and were relations or allies of the kings of Navarre, Castile, and Arragon. Philip the Hardy was incessantly employed either in reconciling them together, or in reducing them under his obedience.

The king of England, having hitherto dated the charters of Guyenne from the year of his own reign, is obliged to alter the date to king Philip's reign, being vassal to this prince for the dukedom of Aquitaine.

REMARK-

The HISTORY of FRANCE.

*1285.
Acceſſion to the crown.*

PHILIP IV, ſur-named the FAIR, king of France in his father's right, and king of Na-varre in right of his wife Jane, ſuc-ceeds to the crown in 1285, aged about ſeventeen years. He was crowned at Rheims the twelfth of January 1286 by Peter Barbet, archbiſhop of that city. He was called the falſe coiner, be-ing the firſt of our kings that debaſed the coin.

The ſilver mark, which at the be-ginning of this reign was at fifty five ſous ſix deniers tournois, was at eight livres ten ſous in 1305; which was done by the advice of the Florentines, Muſicbati & Bicbi.

REMARKABLE EVENTS.

1285. 86. 87. 88. 89. 90. 91.

EDward, king of England, yields homage to the king of France for Aquitaine. The Engliſh monarch having promiſed his daughter in marriage to Alfonſo king of Arragon, obtains of this prince, and of his brother James king of Sicily, that Charles the Lame ſhall be ſet at li-berty, upon condition of renouncing his preten-ſions to Sicily, and likewiſe prevailing on the count of Valois to relinquiſh his pretenſions to the kingdom of Arragon. But when Charles was releaſed, inſtead of keeping his promiſe with the king of Arragon, he went to Italy, where ſiding with the Guelfs againſt the Gibellines, he was crowned king of the two Sicilies by the pope; and after defeating the king of Arragon, he concluded a truce with that prince for five years. In 1290 happened the miracle of the conſecrated hoſt, known by the name of the miracle of the *Billettes**. A regulation in regard to the Exchequer, the anci-ent court of judicature of the dukes of Normandy. Upon the annexing of this province to the crown, the king ſent proper magiſtrates to adminiſter juſtice there in the laſt reſort. Robert of Artois returns to France. Philip the Fair enters into an accommodation with Don Sancho, king of Caſtile, at the expence of la Cerda: yet the king of Caſtile continuing to feel ſome inquietude on ac-count of the juſt pretenſions of the latter, his ſon Ferdinand IV. prevailed on la Cerda to ſubmit his demand to the arbitration of the kings of Arragon and Portugal, who adjudged two and thirty towns to him, which compoſe the dutchy of *Medina Cœli*, ſtill poſſeſſed by his deſcendants. Charles the Lame engages (1291) Charles of Valois to relinquiſh his pretenſions to Arragon, and gives

* A convent of Carmelite friars at Paris.

him

The THIRD RACE.

WIVES.	CHILDREN.	1314. DEATH.	Cotemporary PRINCES.
Jane, heiress and queen of Navarre, only daughter of Henry king of Navarre, married in 1284. 1304.	LEWIS X. PHILIP THE LONG. CHARLES THE FAIR. Rob. died young. Margaret. Isabel, married to Edward II. king of England. 1357. Blanche died young.	PHILIP THE FAIR *dies at Fontainebleau, the place of his nativity, the 29th of November 1314, aged forty six years. He was interred at St. Denis.*	*Popes.* Honorius IV. 1289. Nicholas IV. 1292. Celestine V. abdicates, 1294. Boniface VIII. 1303. Benedict X. or XI. 1304. Clement V. 1314. The holy see removed to Avignon. *Emperor of the East.* Andronicus II. 1332. *Emperors of the West.* Rodolphus. 1291. Adolphus of Nassau. 1298. Albert I. 1308. Hen. of Luxemburg. 1313. *Ottoman family. Commencement thereof.* Ottoman. 1326. *Kings of Spain.* Sancho IV. 1295. Ferdinand IV. 1312. Alfonso XI. 1350. *King of Portugal.* Denis. 1325. *Kings of England.* Edward I. 1308. Edward II. 1326. *Kings of Scotland.* Alexander III. 1286. John Baliol. 1303. Robert Bruce. 1329. *King of Denmark.* Eric VIII. 1321. *Kings of Sweden.* Magnus. 1290. Birger. 1326. *Kings of Poland.* Leschus. 1289. Primislaus. 1296. Ladislaus deposed. 1300. Wenceslaus. 1305. Ladislaus restored 1333. *Dukes of Russia.* Alexander. This prince established the Russian power, and fixed the seat of this government at Moscow; he died towards 1300. Daniel Alexandrowitz. 1327.

VOL. I.   P

him his daughter in marriage, together with Anjou and Maine. The king of Arragon deserts his brother James king of Sicily. Othelin, count of Burgundy, marries his daughter to Philip the Long, and gives his county to the king.

1292. 93. 94. 95.

A war arises betwixt France and England, from the seizing of some Norman vessels by the English. Philip demands satisfaction of Edward I, who refuses to comply; upon which he is summoned to the court of peers, in order to answer the charge of treason against his sovereign lord the king. The summons was performed by the bishops of Beauvais and Noyon: in process of time, none but knights were commissioned to make this kind of citation; and now it is done by the clerks belonging to the court. Edward refusing to appear, is declared guilty of treason, and the dutchy of Guyenne confiscated to the king's use; who deputes his brother the count de Valois, and Raoul count de Clermont, to take possession thereof in his name. The king imprisons Guy earl of Flanders, for siding with Edward. James king of Sicily, who succeeded his brother Alfonso in the kingdom of Arragon, without any regard to the rights of his brother Frederic, makes a surrender of Sicily to the duke of Anjou, dreading the power and intrigues of Philip the Fair. But Frederic knew how to assert his rights, so as to maintain himself in Sicily; and this is the æra of the real separation of that monarchy from the kingdom of Naples.

The troubles in Scotland (1295) occasioned by king John Baliol, prevent Edward from succouring Guyenne. The commencement of the quarrel between Boniface VIII. and Philip the Fair. This pope erects the bishopric of Pamiers without the king's consent, and thus divides the ancient diocese of Toulouse, under pretence of its too great extent. The bishopric of Toulouse was afterwards separated from the metropolitan church of Narbonne, to which it had been suffragan; and erected into an archbishopric by pope John XXII. in 1317.

La Thaumassiere has given us an ordinance of 1294, relating to *luxury*, extremely curious, from the king's entering into a minute detail of the state and condition of his subjects,
which

The Third Race.   211

Ministers.	Warriors.	Magistrates.	Eminent and Learned Men.
Enguerrand de Marigni, minister of the finances, hanged in the following reign at Montfaucon in 1315. The king's principal secretaries. Raoul de Perreau. Ames of Orleans. John de Belut. Philip de Marigni.	*Constables.* Raoul de Clermont de Nesle. 1302. Gaucher de Chatillon, count of Porceau. 1329. *Marshals of France.* John de Harcourt. 1302. Raoul le Flamene, living in 1287. John de Varennes, living in 1292. Simon de Melun. 1302. Guy of Clermont. 1302. Foucaude de Merle. 1314. Miles de Noyers. 1350. John de Corbeil. 1318.	*Chancellors.* John de Vassoigne. 1300. William de Crepi. 1300. Peter Flotte. 1302. Stephen de Suizi, cardinal. 1311. Peter de Mornai. 1306. Peter Belleperche. 1307. Peter de Grez. 1325. Peter de Corbeil. 1300. William de Nogaret. 1313. Giles Aicelin de Montagu. 1318. He founded the college of that name. Peter de Latilli. 1327. They who discharged the function of first presidents before the time of Philip of Valois, were called *masters in parliament*; among others, Hugh de Courci, William Bertrand, &c. went by that name. *The king's advocates.* John de Vassoigne. 1300. John Dubois practised in 1300. John Pastoureau practised in 1301.	John Cholet, founder of the college which goes by his name at Paris. 1293. William Durand. 1296. William de Nangis, living in 1301. Henry of Gaunt. 1293. John de Meun, towards 1310. Johannes Duns Scotus. 1308.

P 2

REMARKABLE EVENTS under PHILIP IV.

which affords a great infight into the mannners and cuftoms of that time.

1296. 97. 98.

The war in Guyenne, where the count de Valois has the command. Queen Jane marches againft the count of Bar, in order to defend Champagne, which was her own demefne; the count furrenders himfelf to this princefs, and does homage for his eftate. The death of John count of Holland: with him was extinguifhed the ancient houfe of the counts of Holland, who had borne this title the fpace of 437 years. John d'Avefne, count of Hainault, fucceeds to the inheritance of Holland and Frife-land.

A truce of two years between France and England: it was agreed, that the king fhould give his fifter Margaret in marriage to Edward I; and his daughter Ifabel to prince Edward, together with Guyenne for her dower, on condition of holding it by the fame tenure as his predeceffors had done; that is, as a vaffal of the French crown.

An ordinance publifhed in the parliament of All Saints, whereby the king prohibits all private wars, fo long as he is at war himfelf. In Languedoc he abolifhed all bodily fervitude for ever, and changed it into an annual *Cens* or quit-rent *.

The firft letters for creating a dutchy and peerage, granted to John duke of Britany, in 1297. The king, in all probability, wanted to replace the peerage of Champagne, which he had annexed to the crown, by his marriage with Jane the heirefs of that county. There was a like creation, of the fame date, in favour of the county-peerages of Anjou and Artois.

Adolphus of Naffau, being elected emperor after Rodolphus, is vanquifhed and depofed by Albert, the fon of Rodolphus, who is raifed to the imperial throne. The houfe of Auftria, ftrictly fpeaking, begins from this prince. The empire of the Turks is founded by Ottoman, from whom it has derived its name.

---

* The *Cens* fignifies the rent of affize, quit-rent, or chief-rent; and was the firft pecuniary charge laid on conquered lands, as a fign and acknowledgment of the direct feignory of him that grants it. This was impofed by the captains and leaders of the Franks, when they conquered Gaul, in imitation of the Roman *Cenfus*, and is ftill continued as a mark of bafe or fervile tenure.

REMARKABLE EVENTS under PHILIP IV.

1299. 1300. 1301.

Philip subdues all Flanders by means of his brother the count [de] Valois. Guy surrenders to this prince, who persuades him to come and treat with the king. Philip, refusing to abide by the agreement made with the count de Valois, detains the earl of Flanders and his two sons prisoners. Charles of Valois, offended at this behaviour, retires to Italy, where he marries the daughter of Baldwin emperor of Constantinople: the pope bestows this empire upon him, and makes him his vicar in Italy. A new form of jubilee, with indulgences, introduced by Boniface VIII. This was to be celebrated every hundred years; pope Clement VI. reduced it to fifty; pope Paul II. to twenty five, and there it stands. Some think the Christian jubilee was borrowed from that of the Jews, which is solemnized every fiftieth year; but father Pagi is of opinion that the Christians imitated the secular games of the ancients, which they sanctified by a different use, in order to convert the Pagans the more easily, by meeting them half way, when there was nothing criminal in the action. The same has been said of Moses; viz. that the intent of those rites ordained by the Deity, was to induce the Israelites to forget the Egyptian ceremonies. Charles of Valois makes war in Italy, and banishes the poet Dante. The order of Celestine monks, which had been instituted in 1244, is introduced into France in 1300.

1302.

The battle of Courtray, in which the French are defeated, and Robert of Artois is slain. Upon the news of this overthrow, the king summons the ban and rear ban, lays the fifth penny upon the estates of all his subjects, and raises the coin.

Guy of Lusignan, count of Angoulême, and lord of Coignac, devers up his lands to the king. Jane founds the college of Navarre at Paris. An ordinance concerning the reformation of the kingdom. Philip the Fair adjudges the county of Artois, vacant by the death of Robert II, to his daughter Maud, in preference to Robert of Artois, grandson of Robert II, and nephew to Maud; upon this pretence, that the representation of the next in blood did not take place in the county of Artois. When Robert of Artois came to age, he wanted to set aside this judgment; but he was obliged to approve of it in 1309, and continued to acquiesce

REMARKABLE EVENTS under PHILIP IV.

to it the remainder of this king's reign, and during that of his succeſſor Lewis X.

1303.

Edward deſerts the Flemings, and accommodates matters with Philip, from whom he recovers Guyenne, by a treaty concluded the twentieth of May.

The beginning of the famous conteſt between Boniface VIII. and Philip the Fair: the firſt cauſe of the pope's uneaſineſs, was that the king had given ſhelter to his enemies the Colonna's; but Philip had much more reaſon to complain of Boniface. This pontif, thinking himſelf authorized by the example of his predeceſſors, wanted to have a ſhare of the *decimes* or *tenths*, which the king had raiſed on the clergy of France: he is irritated at Philip's refuſal; and begins to ſhew his reſentment, by erecting, as we have already mentioned, the new biſhopric of Pamiers, without the concurrence of the royal conſent, neceſſary on that occaſion. Boniface does not ſtop here; but ſets the king at open defiance, by appointing that very man, named Bernard Saiſſetti, his legate in France, who had dared to be ordained a biſhop in ſpite of his ſovereign. Bernard, in virtue of his legatine powers, enjoins the king to embark in a new cruſade, and to ſet the earl of Flanders at liberty. The king cauſed Bernard to be arreſted; and delivered him into the hands of his metropolitan, the archbiſhop of Narbonne. The pope thundered out a bull, laying the whole kingdom under an interdict. Philip aſſembles the three eſtates of the kingdom (it is believed that this was the firſt time of the third eſtate's being admitted to this aſſembly) and agrees to call a council: notice thereof is given to the neighbouring princes, and the ſtates agree to appeal to a future council againſt every thing that had been done by the pope. Nogaret ſets out for Italy, in appearance to ſignify the appeal, but in reality to ſeize the pope's perſon. Sciarra Colonna and he ſurround the pontif in the city of Anagnia: Sciarra gives him a box on the ear, and would have killed him, but was prevented by Nogaret: the pope died ſoon after.

1304.

The battle of Mons in Puelle on Tueſday the 18th of Auguſt, in which Philip obtains a complete victory over the Flemings. In rememberance of this victory, an equeſtrian ſtatue of this prince was erected at Notre-Dame; and he likewiſe founded a yearly

income

REMARKABLE EVENTS under PHILIP IV.

income of a hundred livres to the church of Notre-Dame at Paris. There have been some mistakes concerning this monument, which some authors, and among the rest Nicholas Gilles, attribute to Philip of Valois: but in order to ascertain the fact, we need only to read the *Necrologium* * of the church of Notre-Dame at Paris, as well as the sixth lesson of the Paris breviary, where commemoration is made of this victory on the 18th of August, the day on which the battle of Mons in Puelle was fought; whereas that of Cassel happened the 23d. A treaty with the Flemings, by which their earl is set at liberty: this prince arrives at Compiegne, where he dies at the age of fourscore, and is succeeded by his son Robert of Bethune. Benedict XI. absolves the king from the censures of Boniface VIII, together with all those who had been included in the excommunication, excepting Nogaret.

1305. 6. 7. 8.

The prohibition of duels in civil causes.

Bertrand de Got, named Clement V, transfers the holy see to Avignon in 1308, where it continued till 1376, when Gregory XI. (this was the last French pope) withdrew from thence to Rome, where he arrived in 1377. There is some contradiction in authors upon this head, some dating the end of the translation from the pope's departure from Avignon, others from his return to Rome. The pope declares, that the bull *unam sanctam*, published by Boniface VIII. against Philip the Fair, shall not prejudice the liberties of France. The foundation of the university of Orleans, confirmed by the king in 1312. Some pretend that the parliament did not begin till this year to be sedentary. *It was the institution of parliaments,* says Loyseau, *that prevented our being cantoned out and dismembered, after the manner of Italy and Germany, and that maintained this kingdom intire.* Various are the opinions concerning the original of parliaments; what we may safely affirm, is that these courts, such as they continue to this day, existed so early as the year 1294, as appears by an ordinance of that year, mentioned by Budeus in his commentary on the Pandects. In this ordinance, which existed in his time, (he died in 1540) but is not come down to us, it is mentioned, contrary to an excellent principle, that

* A list, or account of deceased persons.

they

REMARKABLE EVENTS under PHILIP IV.

they will not reckon votes, but thefe fhall be weighed by the judges who fit in the upper tribunal, *in maximo tribunali*; and that the prefidents of the courts, *principes aut præfides curiæ*, fhall pronounce fentence according to the opinion of thofe, whom they think moft capable and beft qualified, *ex confentium gravitate et meritis*. (*Budæus in Pandectas*.) The king, upon rendering the parliament of Paris fedentary, imagined it would no longer be fufficient for the extent of its jurifdiction; and therefore he created about this time the parliament of Touloufe. Yet we are to take notice, that Philip the Hardy had erected a parliament at Touloufe fo early as 1279, which did not continue longer than the fortnight after Eafter. Neither are we to omit, that, under Alphonfus, count of Touloufe, this prince had his parliament attending his perfon; and their fittings were fometimes held at his court, fometimes at Vincennes, Longpont, &c. (*Hiftory of Languedoc*.)

The beginning of the Swifs republic, three cantons of which rife up in arms againft their fovereign of the houfe of Auftria, thefe were Uri, Underwalden, and Schweitz. The latter gave its name to the republic. This ftate increafed by the addition of ten other cantons, the laft of which, viz. Appenzel, joined them in 1513; and by the alliance of fome other feignories, fuch as S. Gall, Mulhaufen, the Grifons, the Valais, &c. Their fovereignty was recognized at the treaty of Munfter, by the empire and the houfe of Auftria; as that of the Dutch was by the crown of Spain. The king would fain prevail on Clement V, who was indebted to him for the pontificate, to procure the imperial crown, vacant by the death of Albert, for Charles of Valois. The pope privately follicits the electors to chufe a German prince; and Henry, count of Luxemburg, is elected. The time was not yet come, when the houfe of Auftria was to eftablifh itfelf on the imperial throne; for not till a hundred and thirty years after, upon the election of Albert II, in 1438, did the empire become in fome meafure hereditary in this powerful family. The death of Edward I. In regard to this prince we are to obferve, that he did a more important fervice than ever king of England had done that kingdom, by conquering the principality of Wales, hitherto governed by its particular fovereigns.

1309.

REMARKABLE EVENTS under PHILIP IV.

1309. 10. 11. 12.

Towards the beginning of the third race, the several functions of secretary and notary, centered in the chancellor. Guerin, bishop of Senlis, having been created chancellor of France, rendered this office of higher importance, so that the secretaryship was left to the king's notaries and clerks, and the chancellor only reserved to himself the power of inspection: but as the secretaries or clerks, who had immediate access to the king, grew also in process of time to be men of greater consequence, some of them were distinguished from the rest by the name of *clerks of the secret*; and this was the first origin of our secretaries of state. Philip declared in the year 1309, that there should be three clerks of the secret near his person, and seven and twenty clerks or notaries under them.

The knights of St. John of Jerusalem, under the command of their grand master Foulques de Villaret, wrested the isle of Rhodes from the infidels, (1310) whence they have been called the knights of Rhodes.

The order of knights templars abolished. This is a most shocking affair, whether the crimes were real, or invented by avarice. It is said that the templars, protesting their innocence, summoned pope Clement V. and king Philip the Fair to the divine tribunal; and that accordingly they both died at the time predicted. It is also observed, that, some years before, Ferdinand IV, king of Castile, was cited in the same manner by two gentlemen, whom he put to death, without hearing what they had to say in their justification; and that he died within thirty days of the *summons*, from whence he had the surname of Ferdinand the *Summoned*. The county of Lyons is annexed to the crown, by Lewis, the king's eldest son, who obtained it by conquest from Peter of Savoy, archbishop of Lyons; but this prelate and his chapter were permitted to retain the title of count of Lyons. Clement V, at the king's request, commences a process against the memory of Boniface VIII; but this pope is justified in the council of Vienne.

The king prepares to make war against Robert earl of Flanders, for non-payment of a debt of eight hundred thousand livres. Enguerrand de Marigny, under colour of this war, raises great sums of money. A considerable debasement of the coin; the sou

and

and the denier were reduced to two thirds of wh
worth in the reign of St. Lewis, and yet they v
for the fame intrinfic value. This was owing
fpecie in the kingdom, impoverifhed by the cru

The regulation of Paffi in the month of J
king ordains, that the *quinze-vingt* or *three hu*
belonging to the hofpital founded by St. Lewi
flower-de-luce on their clothes, to diftinguifh the
focieties of blind people of a more ancient foun

The bridge of *St. Efprit*, which had been fi
a building, was finifhed about the year 1309.
to the town, which before was called St. Satur
bitants had undertaken and executed the work,
tion of the prior of St. Saturnin, of the order of
lord of that town together with the king.

1313. 14.

Philip the Fair is not happy in his daughte
garet of Burgundy, wife of Lewis X, is conv
and ftrangled in prifon. Jane of Burgundy, v
Long, is likewife charged with adultery, but l
her again. Blanche, the wife of Charles the
of the fame crime, but faves her life, by pretenc
riage is void on account of confanguinity. Se
fiefs purchafed by *roturiers*. Some ennoblemen
and the fpecie of the kingdom, having been con
by means of the crufades; both thefe loffes we
ennobling was the way to effect the one, as far a
thing would admit; and commerce in time woulc
the other. But it is evident that no ennoblement c
or make a perfon noble by extraction, who was
plebeian by birth; and confequently the practice
of nobility, has not hindered the difference whi
fift, between nobility by birth and that by creati
has it then produced? It has removed the differ
the ftate or condition of perfons, and rendere
fame clafs or order; it has abolifhed feveral pri
nobles affumed over the *roturiers*; and thereby
the former, without giving any thing more t

the privilege of being raised to a rank, which they do not possess by birth. For it is true, that our kings are masters alike of all their subjects, but it is not in their power to hinder the antiquity of services, and the dignity of ancestors, from effecting that difference which constitutes real nobility. In short, ennoblements have exalted *roturiers*, and infected them with the luxury of the great: this has brought them both nearer to a level; so that luxury, which banished equality from among the Romans, has restored it among the French.

Philip the Fair is the first of our kings that restrained the appanages to the male heir only; *(see the year* 1283*)* as appears by his codicil in form of ordinance, dated the year 1314 *(du Tillet, du Puis, Hudson)*. It was occasioned by his giving the county of Poitiers to his son Philip the Long, on condition of furnishing a dower out of it to his sisters. This same king began to reduce the great lords to sell their right of coinage, by an edict in 1313, which laid so great a restraint upon the private mints, that they found it more advantageous to forego their privilege.

John de Monluc, register of the parliament of Paris, was the first who made a collection of arrets, which he bound up together, and called them the *regestum, quasi iterum gestum*, because they were copies; they are still deposited in parliament, and known by the name of *Olims*.

Looking over the ordinances of our kings, I find that those against usury were the most frequent, and almost the first in this king's reign; in all probability this was owing to the alteration in the coin. This prince likewise published several edicts against the Jews.

Upon the decease of Clement V, the 20th of April, 1314, the cardinals assembled at Carpentras, in order to proceed to the election of another pope; but not being able to agree, the holy see became vacant during the whole subsequent reign, and was not filled till Philip the Long came to the crown. The cardinals met at Lyons, but finding it difficult to fix upon a proper person, referred the election to the single vote of cardinal James d'Ossa, who nominated himself, and took the name of John XXII.

REMARKABLE EVENTS.

1314.

1314. Accession to the crown.

LEWIS X, *surnamed* HUTIN *(an old French word, signifying mutinous and quarrelsome) ascends the throne in the year* 1314, *at the age of twenty-three or twenty-five, (for historians are not agreed as to the date). He was crowned at Rheims in* 1315, *by Robert de Courtenay, archbishop.*

LEWIS X. deferred his coronation till the year following, because of the disturbances of his kingdom, and chusing to wait for his new wife. This however did not hinder him from taking the reins of government into his own hands, though the performing of this ceremony used to be considered as essential to the prince's authority. He had been already crowned king of Navarre in his father's life time, after the decease of Jane his mother, queen of Navarre.

1315.

Charles of Valois, son of Philip the Hardy, and uncle of Lewis X, having engrossed the whole power, although the king was of age, displaced several officers, in order to advance his own creatures: he had indeed a just pretence, from the oppressive duties, and debasement of the coin. There was not even money sufficient to defray the expences of the coronation; they laid the blame on Enguerrand de Marigny, prince Charles's enemy, and minister under the late king. Charles took care to have him sentenced to be hanged, which was accordingly executed at Montfaucon, on the very gibbet erected by himself. This minister was of a noble family in Normandy: his grandfather's name was Portier; but, having married the heiress of the family of Marigny, he transmitted the name to his descendants.

The council of Senlis, in which Peter de Latilly, bishop of Chalons, and chancellor of France, was charged with several crimes, among the rest, with having been accessary to the extortions and other misdemeanors of Enguerrand de Marigny, and with having poisoned his predecessor;

WIVES.	CHILDREN.	1316. DEATH.	Cotemporary PRINCES.
Margaret, daughter of Robert duke of Burgundy, and of Agnes daughter of St. Lewis, married in 1305. Lewis caused her to be confined, for incontinency, to the castle of Gaillard, and afterwards strangled in 1315.	Jane, heiress of the kingdom of Navarre, which she brought in marriage to her husband Philip, count d'Evreux, grandson of Philip the Hardy, and son of Lewis count d'Evreux, she died in 1349. The count d'Evreux, after the death of Philip the Long and Charles the Fair, took possession of the kingdom of Navarre, which belonged to his wife, as daughter and heiress of Lewis IX, because that kingdom might devolve to the female line in succession, whereas it was otherwise in regard to the kingdom of France, to which she laid claim as the daughter of Lewis X, but was excluded by the Salic law. Yet Philip the Long and Charles the Fair took the title of kings of Navarre. With regard to the counties of Champagne and Brie, to which Jane was also heiress, Philip of Valois kept possession of them by a private agreement, resigning some other lands to her in France. This treaty is dated 1336, and ought to be considered as the real epocha of the irrevocable union of Champagne and Brie to the crown.	LEWIS X. dies at the castle of Vincennes, Saturday the 5th of June 1316, by drinking cold water, when he was too warm. He was suspected to have been poisoned, and was buried at St. Denis.	Pope. The holy see, vacant during this whole reign. Emperor of the East. Andronicus II. 1332. Emperor of the West. Lewis V, duke of Bavaria. 1347. Ottoman family. Ottoman. 1326. King of Spain. Alfonso XI. 1350. King of Portugal. Denis. 1325. King of England. Edward II. 1326. King of Scotland. Robert Bruce. 1329. King of Denmark. Eric VIII. 1321. King of Sweden. Birger. 1326. King of Poland. Ladislaus. 1333. Duke of Russia. Daniel Alexandrowitz. 1327.
Clemence of Hungary, married in 1315, died in 1328.	John, a posthumous son, born in 1316, who lived only eight days, and for that reason has not been ranked among the kings of France. Lewis X. had a natural daughter, named Fideline, who became a nun.		

cessor; but he was acquitted the year following in another council held likewise at Senlis.

The king, having recalled the Jews into his kingdom for the space of twelve years, gives them leave to purchase lands held by socage. Whenever a Jew turned Christian, his effects were confiscated by the lord of the manor, under pretence that the lord was deprived of his property or right in the person of the Jew, who was now enfranchised: a very odd custom, and of dangerous consequence, for it often came to pass, that these new converts, finding themselves stripped of their all, and reduced to mendicity, returned to the Jewish religion. This custom was afterwards abolished by a declaration of Charles VI. in 1381. (*Brussel.*)

Letters patent, by which the king approves a constitution of the emperor Frederic, and orders it to be carried into execution. The eleventh article is of great importance; it strictly forbids the husbandmen to be disturbed in their business; or their goods, persons, tools, and oxen, &c. to be seized, under any pretence whatsoever, upon pain of paying fourfold damage, and of infamy.

1316.

The war begun in the preceding reign, against the count of Flanders, is continued unsuccessfully. Lewis X. raises the siege of Courtray. The people are oppressed with taxes under colour of this war, offices of judicature are sold, the tenths are raised on the clergy, the villains, of whom the king had a great number upon his demesnes, are compelled to purchase their liberty at the price of their moveable effects, which at that time they were allowed to dispose of.

We meet with a very extraordinary thing in regard to enfranchisements in the register of Champagne, which is extant in the charter rolls; viz. that Stephen, lord of Conflans, did, by an agreement with his mother in 1238, enfranchise Robert de Besil and his children, upon condition of a month's military service per annum, so that the villain held his liberty as it were in fee.

The Third Race.

Ministers.	Warriors.	Magistrates.	Eminent and Learned Men.
Charles of Valois. 1325.	*Constable.* Gacher de Chatillon. 1329. *Marshals of France.* John de Corbeil. 1318. John de Beaumont. 1318. Renaud de Trie. 1324.	*Chancellors.* One thing worthy of observation, is that Lewis made use of the same seal during his reign, which he had used before in his father's lifetime, as if he had foreseen his reign would be so short, that it would not be worth while to change his seal. Peter de Latilli. 1327. Stephen de Mornai. 1332. Peter d'Arablai. 1346. *The king's Advocates.* Paul de Brayeres practised in 1315. Raoul de Presles, appointed in 1315.	Giles Colonne. 1316. Raymundus Lullus. 1315.

1316.
Accession to the crown.

PHILIP V, sur-named the LONG, (so called, because of his high stature) count of Poitou, ascends the throne of France in the year 1316, after his brother Lewis X; on which occasion Jane, the daughter of Lewis X, was excluded. He was three and twenty years of age, and was crowned at Rheims, together with his wife Jane, the 9th of January, 1317, by Robert de Courtenay.

REMARKABLE EVENTS.

PHILIP the Long was at the same time regent of the kingdom of Navarre, during the minority of Jane of Navarre, his niece, daughter and heiress of Lewis X; and of the kingdom of France, till Clemence of Hungary was brought to bed. This princess was delivered of a prince named John, who lived but eight days. Upon his death, there were great contests about the succession.

Eudes of Burgundy, uncle of Jane, being brother to Margaret of Burgundy, that prince's mother, pretended that Jane had a right to the crown. The affair was long debated; Philip convened a great assembly on Candlemas day, where, in the presence of cardinal Peter d'Arablay, it was concluded, that, by virtue of the Salic law, females were not permitted to inherit the crown of France. This is the first time that our history makes mention of the Salic law. As there were many malecontents in the kingdom, Philip made presents to them all, in order to quiet them: to Eudes of Burgundy he gave Jane his eldest daughter in marriage, with the county of Burgundy for her dower; by which means Eudes became proprietor of both Burgundies. Charles, the brother of Philip the Long, understood his own interests so little as to espouse the party of Jane; and he is supposed to have taken this step, in order to obtain a better provision as a younger brother, seeing that Philip at that time had a son, and therefore there were no hopes of his succeeding to the crown. Robert of Artois revives his pretensions to the county of that name, and takes up arms with a view to recover it. A solemn arret in 1318, by which Matilda is confirmed in possession of the county-peerage of Artois, and Robert is obliged to submit. The king had a personal
interest

The THIRD RACE. 225

WIVES.	CHILDREN.	1322. DEATH.	Cotemporary PRINCES.
lane, countess of Burgundy, daughter l heiress to o, count of rgundy, and ttilda, countess of Artois, rried in 1306 d in 1329. *This countess Artois assisted the coronation of the king, her in-law, as ress of France, in conjunction with the peers, she held the crown the king's head, likewise assisted in the same lity at the ment given inst the earl Flanders.*	Lewis, died young. Jane, married to Eudes, duke of Burgundy. 1347. Margaret, wife of Lewis, count of Flanders. 1382. Isabella, married to Guigues VIII, dauphin of Viennois, and afterwards to John, baron of Faucogney in Franche Comté, living in 1345. Blanche, a nun. 1358.	PHILIP the LONG dies the 3d of January, 1322, aged twenty-eight. He is interred at St. Denis.	*Pope.* John XXII. 1334. *Emperor of the East.* Andronicus II. 1332. *Emperor of the West.* Lewis V, duke of Bavaria. 1347. *Turkish emperor.* Ottoman. 1326. *King of Spain.* Alfonso XI. 1350. *King of Portugal.* Denis. 1325. *King of England.* Edward II. 1326. *King of Scotland.* Robert Bruce. 1329. *King of Denmark.* Eric VIII. 1321. *King of Sweden.* Birger. 1326. *King of Poland.* Ladislaus. 1333. *Duke of Russia.* Daniel Alexandrowitz. 1327.

VOL. I. Q

REMARKABLE EVENTS under PHILIP V.

interest in this affair, having married Jane the daughter of Matilda countess of Artois, and of Otho count of Burgundy. This sentence was productive of a bloody war between Philip of Valois and Edward III. king of England, who espoused the party of Robert of Artois.

It may be observed here as a very singular circumstance, that the county of Artois should be given to Matilda, in preference to her nephew; while the Salic law was set up against Jane, the daughter of Lewis X, in favour of Philip the Long. Was not this a kind of contradiction, that the countess of Artois, in the character of a peeress of France, should support the crown on the head of a prince, who had lately stripped his niece of this very crown, under colour that females were incapable of the succession? Was not the Salic law of equal force in regard to the county of Artois, as to the kingdom of France? By no means. And the reason is, that the customs of each province determined the nature of the fiefs; now the crown was controuled by no custom, as not being held by feudal tenure. For though Mezeray says, that the kingdom was governed after the manner of a great fief, it is obvious he could not mean that France was a fief, since this supposeth a lord paramount and vassals; whereas the crown is held of God alone, and they who live under it are not vassals but subjects: it is true, the king had vassals also on his demesnes, but still they were his subjects, and his demesnes acknowledged no other superior but himself. *The kingdom does not devolve to females,* says Loisel, *though females are capable of all other fiefs.*

The duke of Britany, who did not assist at the king's coronation, nor send any apology, though he had been summoned, obtained letters of forgiveness for this default; *rex remittit defectum.*

The bull of John XXII, in 1316, by which the holy chapel is exempted from episcopal jurisdiction.

Sancho of Arragon, king of Majorca, comes to Paris to yield homage to the king for the town of Montpelier, which at that time belonged to the house of Arragon.

1319.

MINISTERS.	WARRIORS.	MAGISTRATES.	EMINENT and LEARNED MEN.
Gerard de la ...uette, died un-.r the torture. 1322.	*Constable.* Gaucher de Chatillon. 1329. *Marshals of France.* John de Corbeil. 1318. John de Beaumont. 1318. Renaud de Trie. 1324.	*Chancellors.* Peter de Chappes. 1336. John de Cherchemont. 1328. *Attorney general.* William de la Magdelaine, living in 1316.	Antony Andrew. 1320. Dante. 1321. John, lord of Joinville, towards 1318. His sister, named Isabel, was married to Ferri du Chatelet, son of Thierry d'Enfer, and grandson of Ferri de Bitche, duke of Lorrain (*Calmet's Genealogical History of the House of Chatelet.*)

REMARKABLE EVENTS under PHILIP V.

1319.

An ordinance excluding prelates from parliament, *because the* king *makes it a point of conscience not to hinder them from attending to their spiritual government*; yet he retains the prelates in his privy council.

1320.

The dispute betwixt France and Flanders is terminated, after a sixteen years war, by a peace signed the 2d of June. The Jews poison a great number of wells and springs, at the instigation of the kings of Tunis and Granada, who, being Mahometans, were afraid lest the king should undertake a new crusade.

Till the reign of Philip the Hardy, the Jews had inhabited several wards of what we call the *city*, such as the Jews street *(rue de la Juiverie)* the Jews island, *(l'isle aux Juifs)* which was on the very spot where now stands the statue of Henry IV, and where they had a mill called the Jews mill, *(le moulin des Juifs)* &c. There is still, within the inclosure of the *Palais*, a street known by the name of *Nazareth*, (in the new plan of Paris 1739) which was formerly called the *street of Galilee*; there likewise another that goes by the name of the street of *Jerusalem* the inclosure of the *Palais* having been formerly an asylum, which it was customary for the Jews to retire, with the permission of the keeper of the parliament jail.

1321.

Philip the Long had a notion, a little before he died, of settling the same weight, measure, and coin, throughout the whole kingdom of France. Lewis XI. had afterwards the like design.

The bulls of Clement V, stiled the *Clementines*, are received in France. The *sixth* of Boniface VIII. is not admitted in the number.

We find by letters patent, published by Philip the Long in 131 a custom that appears very extraordinary: at that time they used to give the religious veil to girls only eight years old, and perhaps earlier: though they had not received the solemn benediction nor made their vows; yet it seems that if, after the abovementioned ceremony, they quitted the convent with a view to marry they were obliged to take out letters of legitimation for their children, in order to render them capable of inheriting; from whence one would conjecture, that without those letters they would have been

REMARRKABLE EVENTS under PHILIP V.

en deemed as baftards. *(Regifter 53 of the charter roll, piece* 190.) ?ry different from this is another fact of an earlier date by upırds of 200 years, viz. towards 1109. St. Hugh, abbot of uny, in a fupplication to his fucceffors, wherein he recommends their care the nunnery of Marcigny, which he had founded himf, enjoins them not to fuffer any young perfon to be admitted o that houfe, under the age of twenty; and makes this injunction irrevocable point, as being fupported by the authority of the 1ole church. Neither ought we to omit, now we are upon the icle of religious women, a cuftom as ancient as the 12th cenry: it was requfite they fhould learn Latin, which had ceafed be the vulgar tongue; a cuftom that continued till the 14th ntury, and ought never to have been laid afide.

This reign is remarkable for a great number of good edicts. 1 ordinance made at St. Germains, from which, fays du Tillet, derived an excellent maxim, " that in matters of juftice, no ' regard is paid to miffive letters; a facred regulation of our ' kings, to guard againft furprize, in this their principal office." other ordinance, determining, that confifcations fhall be ap-1 ed to the difcharging either the perpetual annuities, or thofe ly for life: another annexing to the royal domain, fuch eftates the king poffeffed before his acceffion to the crown: another bidding the mafters in parliament, whether prefidents or others, interrupt the bufinefs of the court: another relating to the cipline or government of this body of magiftrates.

REMARKABLE EVENTS.

1322.
Accession to the crown.

CHARLES IV, surnamed the FAIR, comes to the crown by the death of his brother, in 1322, at the age of twenty-six, or thereabouts. He was crowned at Rheims by the archbishop, Robert of Courtenay. He took the title of king of Navarre, as Philip the Long had done, both as guardians of their niece Jane, daughter of Lewis X, to whom the kingdom of Navarre belonged in right of her mother.

1322. 23.

THIS prince, says du Tillet, *was a strict distributer of justice, taking care that every man enjoyed his right.* A general search after the farmers of the revenue, mostly Lombards or Italians. La Guette being put to the rack, in order to make a discovery of the immense treasure which he was said to have amassed in the administration of the late king's revenue, expires in the midst of torments. Jordain de Lisle, a famous freebooter, is hanged for killing an officer, who had summoned him to appear before the parliament. The imperial dignity, after the death of Henry VII, is contested by Lewis duke of Bavaria, and Frederic duke of Austria. Lewis vanquishes Frederic in 1322, and remains master of the imperial throne in spite of pope John XXII.

After the death of Robert of Bethune, earl of Flanders, a difference arises between Lewis his grandson, and Robert of Cassel his brother, who claimed the succession of Flanders, as nearer by a degree than Lewis.

This was a question of much the same nature, as that which had happened in regard to the county of Poitiers, between Philip the Hardy and his uncle Charles of Anjou: the parliament taking upon them to determine the cause, passed the same judgment, and Lewis was preferred. This prince being the king's nephew, and of course disliked by the Flemings, the enemies of France, was embroiled with those people; but the pope having laid their country under an interdict, and Lewis also receiving succours from Charles the Fair, the troubles were quieted.

1324. 25. 26. 27.

The war breaks out again between Charles the Fair, and Edward II, who had succeeded his father,

The THIRD RACE. 231

WIVES.	CHILDREN.	1328. DEATH.	Cotemporary PRINCES.
Blanche of Burgundy, youngest daughter of Otho IV, married in 1307, and divorced for her bad conduct. She was confined to the castle of Gaillard, with Margaret, her sister-in-law, and afterwards took the veil at Maubuisson. 1325. Mary of Luxemburg, daughter of the emperor Henry VII, married in 1322, died in 1323. Jane, daughter of Lewis, count d'Evreux, married in 1325. It is said, that she often went to visit the Carthusians, and dressed their victuals. 1370.	Philip, died young. Jane, died young. Jane, died young. Mary, 1341. Blanche, who was married to Philip, duke of Orleans, the youngest son of Philip of Valois.	CHARLES the FAIR dies at Vincennes the first of February, 1328, aged thirty-three years. He is interred at St. Denis.	*Pope.* John XXII. 1334. *Emperor of the East.* Andronicus II. 1337 *Emperor of the West.* Lewis V, duke of Bavaria. 1347. *Turkish emperors.* Ottoman. 1326. Orchan. 1357. *King of Spain.* Alfonso XI. 1350. *Kings of Portugal.* Denis. 1325. Alfonso IV. 1357. *Kings of England.* Edward II. 1326. Edward III. 1377. *King of Scotland.* Robert Bruce. 1329. *King of Denmark.* Christopher II. 1333. *Kings of Sweden.* Birger. 1326. Magnus. 1363. *King of Poland.* Ladiflaus. 1333. *Duke of Russia.* Daniel Alexandrowitz. 1327.

REMARKABLE EVENTS under CHARLES IV.

father, Edward I, but was poffeffed of none of his virtues. Montpefat was the caufe of this war, by defending a caftle againft the French, which he pretended to be held of the king of England. Charles of Valois marches into Guienne, and wrefts feveral towns from the Englifh. The death of Charles of Valois. The remorfes which this prince felt in his laft hours, for the execution of Enguerrand de Marigny, juftified the memory of that minifter, who had received fentence unheard; his memory was reinftated, and his effects were reftored to his family. Charles the Fair is the firft of our kings that granted the tenths to the pope; after having refufed them for a long time, he confented at length, upon condition of being admitted to his fhare. Ifabella, queen of England, fifter of Charles the Fair, comes over to France, under pretence of procuring an accommodation between her brother and her hufband Edward II, but in reality to obtain fuccours againft Spencer, a favourite of Edward, who endeavoured to fet this princefs and her hufband at variance. It is faid that the queen was guilty of too familiar a commerce with Mortimer an Englifhman. Charles entertained his fifter in the beginning; but Edward having gained the French miniftry, preffed him hard to fend her back: upon which fhe withdrew from France, with the prince of Wales her fon, who was come to yield homage for Guienne, which had been ceded to him by his father. Charles being obliged to fend away his fifter, gave her fome fuccours underhand; fhe fled for refuge to the count of Hainault, who, after fettling the marriage between his daughter and the prince of Wales, fent Ifabella over to England, along with his brother John de Hainault. The kingdom revolted in favour of this princefs, Spencer was hanged, the king imprifoned, and obliged to confent to his own dethronement. This was the firft inftance of a king of England depofed by act of parliament. In the mean while Edward III. was crowned, and his father died in confinement, a red hot iron having been barbaroufly run through his fundament. Heaven avenged the cruel treatment of this unfortunate prince upon his guilty wife. Mortimer, who wanted to govern the kingdom under Ifabella's name, was executed in 1329; and the queen was confined to a caftle in 1331, where fhe died in 1358, after an imprifonment of eight and twenty years.

While

The THIRD RACE.

MINISTERS.	WARRIORS.	MAGISTRATES.	EMINENT and LEARNED MEN.
Peter Remy hanged in 1328. Macé de Maches, the king's receiver general, and René de Siran, underwent the same punishment.	*Constable.* Gaucher de Chatillon. 1329. *Marshals of France.* Renaud de Trie. 1324. John des Barres. 1324. Matthew de Trie. 1344.	*Chancellors.* John de Cherchemont. 1328. Peter Rodier, living in 1328. *Attorneys general.* Peter de Villebreme, living in 1325. Simon de Buci. 1369. *King's advocate.* Peter des Cugnieres, living in 1329.	Petrus Aureolus, towards 1323. Francis de Maironis. 1325. Hervé Noel. 1323. John of Paris towards 1322.

REMARKABLE EVENTS under CHARLES IV.

While providence was preparing the way for one of the longest and most memorable reigns that England ever beheld, by the succession of Edward III, France saw herself bereft of the last heir of Philip the Fair. This prince had left three sons, from whom he promised himself a numerous posterity; yet they all three died in less than fourteen years, and the crown devolved to their cousin-german. Charles the Fair, the youngest of the three brothers, being taken ill at Vincennes in the month of December, died on the first of February, 1328. His reign affords nothing remarkable, except the fruitless efforts of pope John XXII. to raise him to the imperial throne, which he would fain have wrested from Lewis of Bavaria. There was likewise some talk of a crusade, which was to begin with the conquest of Constantinople; and indeed the two Andronicus's, father and son, who reigned conjunctly, had conceived some uneasiness on that account: but Charles had none of the abilities requisite for so arduous an enterprize; and without having done any one thing, no more than his brothers, either for the advantage of his people or for his own glory, he left the state overburdened with debts.

The relicks of the holy chapel always attended the king's person, wherever he went to spend the four great annual festivals; and when he happened not to remove above four and twenty leagues from the capital, the Hotel Dieu at Paris was charged with the carriage of these relicks: for their trouble the king gave them a hundred loads of wood out of the forest of Cuise *(now Compiegne).*

The barony of Bourbon erected into a dutchy and peerage, in favour of Lewis I, eldest son of Robert of France, the sixth son of St. Lewis. In the letters of creation we find an expression worthy of remark, as it has the air of a prediction in regard to Henry IV. *I hope*, says the king, *that the descendants of the new duke will contribute by their valour to maintain the dignity of the crown.*

The Floral games instituted at Toulouse (1324); they may be reckoned the remains of ancient chivalry, when the knights errants roamed from castle to castle, chanting their songs, and making love to their Dulcineas.

1328.
Accession to the crown.

PHILIP VI, surnamed of VALOIS, *comes to the crown in* 1328. *He was surnamed the* FORTUNATE; *but this must have been before the battle of Cressy; and in all probability he had the above surname from his attaining to be king of France, though at so great a distance from the throne. He was grandson of Philip the Hardy, and son of Charles of Valois. He was crowned at Rheims the 29th of May the same year, by the archbishop, William of Trie.*

REMARKABLE EVENTS.

1328.

FRANCE was hardly ever more unfortunate, than during the period in which the branch of Valois sat upon the throne. Charles the Fair left his queen pregnant; and she was brought to bed of a daughter, named Blanche. The disputes which arose under Philip the Long, were revived once more in regard to the succession. Edward III. laid claim to the crown, in right of his mother Isabella, daughter of Philip the Fair; to whom he was consequently grandson, and therefore nearer akin, than Philip of Valois, who was only his nephew, as son of Charles of Valois, brother of Philip the Fair. Edward's claim did not appear to the twelve peers and the barons to be better founded, than that of Jane, the daughter of Lewis Hutin: he was a male indeed, but not descended from a male; which gave room for Loisel's maxim, borrowed from Alain Chartier, that in France, " whensoever a " female is deprived of her succession to a *noble* " *fief*, the males born of her body, and descending " from her, are also excluded." Robert, count of Artois, did very great service to the king upon this occasion. It cost a rich burgher of Compiegne his life, for being so rash as to declare himself in favour of Edward III; his name was Simon Pouillet. Philip restores the kingdom of Navarre to Jane, the daughter of Lewis Hutin, which kingdom had been forcibly detained from her by Philip the Long and Charles the Fair. In consequence hereof, her husband, Philip Eureux, became king of Navarre.

Edward III. was a great prince, as appeared by his conduct during this whole reign, in which he gave vast uneasiness to Philip of Valois. On the eve of St. Bartholomew, the king defeats the Flemings

WIVES.	CHILDREN.	1350. DEATH.	Cotemporary PRINCES.
Jane of Burgundy, daughter of Robert I, duke of Burgundy, and of Agnes of France, married in 1313, died in 1348. Blanche, daughter of Philip, count d'Evreux, and of Jane of Navarre, married in 1349, died in 1398.	JOHN LEWIS, died coming into the world. Lewis, died a little after he was born. John, died young. Philip, duke of Orleans, who married Blanche, daughter of king Charles the Fair. 1375. He was nominated dauphin by Humbert, in virtue of the first treaty for transferring the dauphiné in 1343. The king, his father, upon marrying him to the only daughter of Charles the Fair, settled the dutchy of Orleans upon him, to hold it in peerage, as an appanage, or younger brother's provision; but the peerage became extinct, and the country was annexed to the crown by this prince's decease without issue. Mary, wife of John of Brabant, duke of Limburg. 1333. Blanche. 1371. Thomas of Walsingham, an English historian, mentions his having had a natural son, named John, count d'Armagnac, who fought a duel, and was victorious over a knight of Ipres in Flanders, in 1350. (Simplician.)	PHILIP of VALOIS dies at Nogent-le-Roi, near Chartres in Beauce, (father Simplician says, Nogent-le-Rotrou) the 22d of August, 1350, aged fifty-seven years. He is interred at St. Denis. His heart was carried to the Carthusians of Bourgsontaines, and his entrails were removed to the Dominicans at Paris. Though he was no more than fifty-seven years of age, he died old and worn out, says Brantome: he took to his second wife, Blanche of Evreux, who was no more than seventeen years of age. She was the most beautiful princess of her time; and the king's fondness for her, hastened his days.	*Popes.* John XXII. 1334. Benedict XI, or XII. 1342. Clement VI. 1352. *Emperors of the East.* Andronicus II. 1332. Andronicus the younger. 1341. John Paleologus. 1384. John Cantacuzenus. 1357. *Emperors of the West.* Lewis V, duke of Bavaria. 1347. Charles IV. 1378. *Turkish emperor.* Orchan. 1357. *King of Spain.* Alfonso XI. 1350. *King of Portugal.* Alfonso IV. 1357. *King of England.* Edward III. 1377. *Kings of Scotland.* Robert Bruce. 1329. David II. 1370. *Kings of Denmark.* Christopher II. 1333. Waldemar III. 1375. *King of Sweden.* Magnus. 1365. *Kings of Poland.* Ladislaus. 1333. Casimir III. 1370. *Dukes of Russia.* George Danielowitz. 1330. Demetrius Michaelowitz. 1330. Iwan Danielowitz. } 1365. Iwan Iwanowitz.

mings at the battle of Caſſel, notwithſtanding their bravado in placing a cock with theſe words upon the top of their retrenchments, *When this cock will come to crow, the king will take Caſſel.* He obliges them to ſubmit to Lewis their ſovereign. The king performs wonders in this battle, and the conſtable Gaucher de Chatillon likewiſe behaves with the greateſt valour, though he was fourſcore years old. The trial of Peter Remy, receiver general, and of other financiers, who are condemned to death. The confiſcation of Peter Remy's effects is ſaid to have amounted to twelve hundred thouſand livres, which in our preſent ſpecie is about twenty millions; but this ſeems to be exaggerated. An ordinance in regard to the *free-fiefs*, laying a duty or fine upon churches, and upon roturiers or plebeians * that purchaſed freeholds. This was not the firſt regulation upon the ſubject; we have the like ordinance of Philip the Hardy in 1275, under the title of *the law of mortmain:* there is alſo another of Charles the Fair in 1326, which takes notice of one of a prior date in the reign of St. Lewis, *Beatiſſimi Ludovici proavi noſtri inhærendo veſtigiis (Bruſſel)*, ſo that St. Lewis may be deemed the firſt of our kings, who thought it incumbent upon him to derive ſome advantage from the aggrandizement of churchmen, and from the ambition of plebeians.

The emperor, Lewis of Bavaria, takes a moſt extraordinary ſtep, in depoſing pope John XXII, and ſubſtituting Peter de Corbiere, a friar minor, in his ſtead: Peter took the name of Nicholas V; but, being oppoſed by France, and by moſt of the catholic powers, he was at length taken priſoner by the pope. The emperor's reſentment againſt John XXII. was owing to this pontif's having declared in favour of Frederic, his competitor to the imperial throne.

1329. 30.

On the 6th of June, Edward, after ſtarting a great many difficulties, yields homage to the king for Guienne, in the

---

* This is what the French lawyers call the *droit des francs fiefs,* which is the fine due to the king upon the purchaſe of a fief by a burgher of an unprivileged town, a *roturier,* villain, or other ignoble perſon; this was ſix years value, if the land were held of the king; and three years, if of another lord; but now it is left to the regulation of the officers of the exchequer.

The Third Race. 239

Ministers.	Warriors.	Magistrates.	Eminent and Learned Men.
William Flotte, living in 1352. Matthew de Trie. 1344. Peter de Beaucour.	*Constables.* Gaucher de Chatillon. 1329. Raoul de Brienne, count d'Eu. 1344. Raoul II, count d'Eu his son, beheaded 1350. *Marshals of France.* This office was during pleasure; as appears by a letter from Philip of Valois to Bernard, lord of Moreuil, where he mentions, that by depriving him of the post of marshal, in order to make him governor to his eldest son, John duke of Normandy, he has done him no prejudice, neither as to his honour, nor to his estate. Matthew de Trie. 1344. Robert Briquebec. 1347. Ancel de Joinville, living in 1351. Charles lord of Montmorency. 1381. Robert Vaurin. 1360. Bernard de Moreuil, living in 1350.	*Chancellors.* Matthew Ferrand. 1329. John de Marigni, C. S. 1351. William de Sainte Maure. 1334. P. Rogier, C. S. He was pope by the name of Clement VI. 1352. Guy Baudet, towards 1337. Stephen de Vissac, towards 1350. William Flotte, living in 1352. Firmin de Coquerel. 1349. Peter de la Foret. 1361. *First president.* Simon de Buci, the first that bore this title (1344) died in 1369. *Attorneys general.* P. de Demiville practised in 1343. Gil. Haudri. 1349. James Dandrie, living in 1365. *King's advocates.* Peter des Cugnieres, living in 1329. Peter de la Foret. 1361. John de Fourci, practised in 1344. Robert le Cocq, provided in 1347. John Desmarés, living in 1365.	Alexander de Saint Elpide towards 1339. Alvarus Pelagius, living in 1340. Arnold of Villanova, towards 1340. Peter des Cugnieres, living in 1329 Durand of St. Porcian. 1333. Gerardus Odo. 1349. Guido Perpignanus, towards 1330. Holkot, towards 1349. Laura. 1348. Ludolfus, the Carthusian, living in 1350. Nicolaus de Lyra, 1340. Ocham 1347. Joannes Thalerus, living in 1350.

REMARKABLE EVENTS under PHILIP VI.

cathedral church of Amiens, as duke of Aquitaine, peer of France, count of Ponthieu and Montreuil, without specifying the nature of the homage, which king Philip pretended ought to be full: but Edward, at his return to England, hearing that the count d'Alençon had committed some hostilities in Guienne, sent letters patent to Philip, acknowledging that it ought to be a liege homage *(Rapin Thoyras)*.

A project for a new crusade is set on foot by John XXII. and the king, who had a conference for that purpose at Avignon; but it did not take place. The fashion of crusading was over: since the taking of the town of Acra by the sultan of Babylon in 1291, these expeditions to such distant climes were looked upon as schemes of knight-errantry, and it would have been well if they had been always considered in that light. The count of Clermont is made duke of Bourbon.

The beginning of the disputes concerning the limits of the civil and ecclesiastical jurisdiction. The latter was strongly attacked by Peter de Cugnieres, the king's advocate, who stood up in defence of the secular power. Bertrand, bishop of Autun, and Peter Roger, nominated to the archbishopric of Sens, maintained the rights of the clergy. Introduction of the form of appeal to a *future general council*, the principles of which are more ancient than the name. The king favours the clergy; but this quarrel is the source of all the contests that have arisen since that period, in regard to the civil and ecclesiastical authority; the effect of which has been to circumscribe the latter within narrower bounds. We might likewise assign another cause, namely, that the bishops began about this time to neglect convoking their provincial councils, where the body of the clergy being assembled every year, maintained their original authority; whereas the parliaments established their power, by becoming a sedentary court, or a perpetual assembly.

1331. 32. 33. 34. 35.

The condemnation of Robert of Artois, remarkable for the forms observed on the occasion, which shew us the manner of trying the peers of France in criminal causes. Robert had been cast twice already, in suing for the county of Artois, once under Philip the Fair, and the other time under Philip the Long, and he

REMARKABLE EVENTS under PHILIP VI.

he had lain still during the reign of Charles the Fair, though he was the chief favourite of that prince. But, thinking he had a much stronger interest under Philip of Valois, since he had the honour to be his brother-in-law, and had done him great service during his contest for the crown with Edward III, and the king had made his estate of Beaumont le Roger a dutchy and peerage, he revived the process a third time in 1329, in opposition to the sentences passed in favour of Maud, on a suggestion that he could produce new proofs or title-deeds. Maud disputes the genuineness of these deeds, and dies suddenly, together with her daughter Jane, widow of Philip the Long, not without suspicion of poison. Jane, dutchess of Burgundy, daughter of Philip the Long and of the above Jane, maintains the suit against Robert; and the deeds are found to have been forged by a woman, whose name was Divion: in consequence hereof Robert is summoned four times by the knights and counsellors, according to the practice of that time: in default of appearance, the king, in his bed of justice at the Louvre in 1331, pronounced an edict of banishment against him, with a confiscation of his whole estate. On this occasion it may be observed, that the king emancipated his eldest son John, duke of Burgundy, and raised him to the peerage, to the end that the court might be sufficiently furnished with peers.

By virtue of this sentence a female was seized of one of the great fiefs of the crown, contrary to the vulgar error, that, as those great fiefs could be served only by males, none but males ought to be invested with them; and indeed examples to the contrary are frequent in our history, founded no doubt on local customs. Thus Henry II, king of England, succeeded to the dukedom of Normandy in right of his mother Mathildis; and his issue inherited Guienne and Poitou, in consequence of his marriage with Eleanor: thus Charles of Anjou, brother of St. Lewis, took possession of Provence in right of his wife Beatrix; while Alphonsus, brother of that same king, acquired the county of Toulouse by his marriage with the only daughter of Raymond: thus Joan, the daughter of Henry, king of Navarre, brought the counties of Champagne and Brie in dower to Philip the Fair, upon the decease of her father: thus the counts d'Evreux, who

REMARKABLE EVENTS under PHILIP VI.

succeeded to the rights of Jane, daughter of Lewis Hutin, demanded those counties back again of Charles VI, and this prince gave them the town of Nemours as an equivalent, and made it a dutchy in their favour.

Robert, having withdrawn from France, made a short stay in Flanders, from whence he went over to England, and became a formidable enemy to Philip of Valois, by solliciting king Edward to declare war against this prince. He had tried before to assassinate the king and queen, together with their eldest son; but, seeing that his project had taken wind, he attempted to destroy the king by witchcraft, (a ridiculous practice, frequent in those ignorant times: this was to make a waxen image of the enemy they intended to kill, and to prick it to the heart) at length finding all his attempts unsuccessful, he went over to England in the disguise of a merchant, towards the beginning of the year 1334, in order to make preparations for invading his native country; and he died in 1342.

The death of John XXII, (1344) aged about ninety years. This pope added a third crown to the pontifical tiara: pope Hormisdas made use of the first, and Boniface VIII. invented the second.

1336. 37. 38. 39.

The beginning of the war between France and England, which, with very little interruption, lasted upwards of a hundred years. Edward III. is desirous to recover the towns in Guienne, which had been seized by the king: he is assisted by the Flemings, who, rebelling anew against their sovereign, declare in favour of Edward, notwithstanding the treaties concluded with France: they required only that Edward should take the title of king of France, with a view to assert his claim to that crown; for then, by espousing his cause, they should conform to the letter of their treaty. This revolt was managed by James d'Arteville, a brewer, and by the emperor Lewis of Bavaria, incensed against Philip of Valois for marrying his eldest son to Bonne of Luxemburg, daughter of the king of Bohemia, who was at variance with that emperor. The king ravages Flanders; and his son John duke of Normandy takes Thun-l'Evêque upon the Schelde,

REMARKABLE EVENTS under PHILIP VI.

after laying waste the county of Hainault: but these advantages did not make amends for the defeat at sea in the neighbourhood of Sluys, where the king's fleet, consisting of a hundred and twenty large ships, with forty thousand men on board, was defeated by the English squadron. It has been said, that the misunderstanding between the two admirals (for there were two on board the French fleet) was in part the cause of this disaster: to which we might add another, as the author of the *Essay on the navy and on commerce* observes, after cardinal d'Ossat, namely, *that our princes having taken no care to maintain the navy, though they had so fine and so extensive a kingdom, washed on one side by the ocean, on the other by the Mediterranean,* we were obliged to make use of foreign mariners, who seldom appeared ready and chearful in complying with orders.

The invention of fire-arms, as appears from the account given in by Bartholomew du Drach, pay-master of the army, in 1338. Yet there is no doubt but gunpowder was of an earlier date. There are great uncertainties in regard to the author of this fatal discovery: by some it is attributed to Roger Bacon an Englishman, who flourished in the 13th century; others will have it to be a more modern invention, and pretend that the original of it is owing to a monk, named Bernard Schwartz, a native of Fribourg in Brisgaw, who discovered it in 1380. A terrible famine. A decree, whereby the German princes declare, that the imperial dignity is held of God alone, and that the pope's approbation is not at all necessary.

1340.

Edward lays siege to Tournay. Jane of Valois, widow of the count of Hainault, mother-in-law to king Edward, and Philip's sister, prevails on those princes to agree to a suspension of arms; which Edward comes into the more readily, as the Scotch war required his presence in England.

A year's truce concluded the 20th of September.

1341. 42. 43.

The war with England breaks out a-new, in consequence of the troubles in Britany. John III. duke of Britany, having no issue, proposes a match between Jane the Lame, daughter of his younger brother, Guy of Penthievre, lately deceased, and

Charles,

REMARKABLE EVENTS under PHILIP VI.

Charles, count of Blois, nephew to Philip de Valois; and settles the dutchy of Britany upon her for her dower. After the death of John in 1341, his brother, the earl of Montfort, also named John, disputed his niece's succession; but, imagining she would be supported by king Philip, he enters into an alliance with the king of England, and does homage to him for Britany. Philip orders John IV, earl of Montfort, to be summoned to parliament, where the process is determined in favour of Janes's husband, the count of Blois. The king and the earl of Montfort go to war. The earl was taken prisoner, and died two years after: his wife Jane, daughter of Lewis of Flanders, count of Nevers, continues the alliance with Edward, and the war with France. A truce for three years. By the death of Robert, surnamed the *Sage*, king of Naples, his grand-daughter Jane ascends the throne. It appears from the register of the chamber of accounts in 1343, that *the clerks of the cabinet* bore at that time the title of *secretaries of the revenue*. Philip of Valois had several of them.

1344. 45. 46.

An ordinance of the 10th of April, incorporating the counsellor *judges*, with those who sum up the evidence; the former used to be taken from among the nobility, and the latter from among the citizens.

The truce is broke by the execution of Oliver de Clisson, and some other lords in Britany, who were beheaded by order of king Philip*, upon suspicion of their holding intelligence with the king of England. The origin of the gabelle, or tax upon salt is generally referred to this time; whence Edward III. took occasion to call Philip of Valois, by way of jest, *the author of the salic law*. Yet it appears, that Philip the Long was the first that laid a duty upon salt: indeed Philip of Valois raised this duty; but hitherto it had been a marketable commodity, as we find by regulation of the 13th of January, 1350, in regard to the conduct of the dealers in salt: and it was not till after the battle of Poitiers that the king engrossed the whole trade to himself, by erecting public magazines for all the salt of the country. The gabelle was

---

* They were put to death without any form of law; which gave great uneasiness to the nobility, whose blood had hitherto been sacred in France.

afterwards

REMARKABLE EVENTS under PHILIP VI.

afterwards farmed out by Henry II, as appears from a decree of council, dated the fourth of January, 1548, for the first lease of ten years. The northern countries have not a sufficient heat for the making of salt, and those situate beyond the forty-second degree, as Spain, produce a salt of too corrosive a nature, which eats and destroys the meat instead of preserving it. France alone is the proper climate for making of salt: hence it may be said, that this is one of its principal sources of wealth; and cardinal Richelieu, in his political testament, observes, that, by the accounts he had received from the most intelligent officers, the produce of the duty on salt throughout the realm, was equal to the revenue of the Spanish West-Indies. Edward, directed by Geoffrey de Harcourt, lands in Normandy. The battle of Cressy the 26th of August, 1346, where Philip is defeated by making an imprudent attack on Edward, who had forded the Somme. The prince of Wales, son of Edward III, though no more than fourteen years of age, contributed greatly to this victory, and, according to the expression of the king, his father, *merited his spurs* *. An ordinance by which it appears, that the king alone had the prerogative of coining money throughout his kingdom. The famous queen Joan of Naples causes her first husband, Andrew of Hungary, to be strangled.

1347.
The taking of Calais by Edward on the third of August, after a siege of eleven months and some days †: the English kept possession

---

* This battle was fought on a Saturday. The prince of Wales was sixteen years old, being born at Woodstock in the month of June, 1330. Among the slain on the side of the French were the king of Bohemia, the duke d'Alençon, the duke of Lorrain, the earl of Flanders, the earl of Blois, with fifteen other noblemen of the first distinction; they lost likewise 1200 knights, and upwards of 80 standards. The English are said to have first made use of cannon at this battle.

† The besieged were starved out; for, when they capitulated, the fortifications were as entire as the first day of the siege. The terms of the capitulation were very severe; six of the principal inhabitants were to be given up to Edward, who, full of resentment for their obstinate defence, declared his intention of putting them to death. The treaty would therefore have been ineffectual, if six of the chief burghers had not voluntarily offered themselves, and went out in their shirts, with halters about their necks, to throw themselves at Edward's feet, who sternly ordered their execution; from which they were with difficulty saved by the queen, upon condition they quitted the place. They were honourably received, and amply rewarded by king Philip. The person who first offered to sacrifice himself on this occasion

sion of this place till 1558, when it was retaken by Francis, duke of Guise. The king, in order to requite the inhabitants of Calais for the brave resistance they had made, granted them all the offices that should become vacant, whether in his own nomination, or in the gift of his sons, the dukes of Normandy and Orleans, *till they were sufficiently provided for*, and declares all other donations void, that should be made to their prejudice. A six years truce between France and England, renewed at different times.

1348.

A general plague, which sweeps away a vast multitude of people. This scourge awakened religion; but at the same time gave rise to the fanatic sect of flagellants or whippers, who from folly made a transition to sedition and violence.

Pope Clement VI. (Peter Rogier, who had been chancellor of France) purchases the city of Avignon of queen Joan, by a deed of the 19th of June, for the sum of fourscore thousand florins, and engages to assist this princess in the recovery of her dominions. The popes were already in possession of the county of Venaissin, by a donation from Philip the Hardy at an interview between him and Gregory X. in the city of Lyons.

1349. 50.

Our kings acquire the full sovereignty of Dauphiné and of the county of Viennois, in consequence of three treaties between Philip of Valois and the dauphin Humbert II, the last prince of the house of Tour du Pin, possessed of Dauphiné. This prince, being inconsolable for the loss of his only son, by Mary of Baux, thought of retiring from the world; in this disposition he resigned, and transferred his dominions to the king by a treaty, signed in 1343, confirmed in 1344, and at length completed in 1349. After the two first treaties he altered his mind, and entered into a marriage contract with Jane of Bourbon: Philip, finding that this marriage would deprive him of so valuable a possession, broke off the match, and procured this princess for his grandson Charles V; then it was that the treaty of 1349 was concluded.

occasion was the brave burgher Eustace de St. Pierre, whose example was soon followed by the other five. Rapin mentions that the queen ordered clothes to be brought them, gave them an entertainment in her own tent, and dismissed them with a present to each of six pieces of gold.

The

REMARKABLE EVENTS under PHILIP VI.

The dauphin became afterwards a member of the order of St. Dominic, on the 17th of July, according to the following expressions of the 287th article in the proofs of the history of Dauphiné, *item die craſtina (17 Julii) ordinem et habitum prædicatorum induit:* there he died in 1355. It is a vulgar error, that one of the conditions of the treaty was, that the eldeſt ſon of our kings ſhould bear the title of Dauphin; ſo far from it, the firſt dauphin, named by Humbert in the original agreement of 1343, was the ſecond ſon of Philip of Valois: we own indeed that this did not take place, and that the above title has been aſſumed ſince by the king's eldeſt ſon. We find that, in 1426, Charles VII. reſigned this province to the dauphin his ſon, then only three years old, and confirmed the ſaid renunciation in 1440. This was the laſt time the kings of France relinquiſhed Dauphiné to their eldeſt ſons; ever ſince they have only honoured them with the title. Notwithſtanding the reunion of this province to the crown, it has preſerved a particular ſeal, whereof the chancellor is keeper, to the contrary of other provinces, which were deprived of their court of chancery upon every reunion. *(Marillac treat. of Chanc.)* Philip purchaſed of the king of Majorca the barony of Montpellier in Languedoc, for which the houſe of Arragon did homage to the kings of France; and having likewiſe acquired the counties of Anjou and Maine, in right of his mother Margaret, daughter of Charles II. king of Naples, and count of Anjou and Maine, he annexed them to the crown. The univerſity of Perpignan founded. The inſtitution of the order of the garter by Edward III. An ordinance concerning the inalienability of the king's demeſnes.

1350.
Accession to the crown.

JOHN ascends the throne the 23d of August, 1340, aged thirty years. He was crowned at Rheims the 26th of September, together with Joan of Boulogne, his 2d wife. He had been baptized in the church of Mans, as appears by some letters of Charles V. in 1372.

REMARKABLE EVENTS.

1350. 51.

NO prince ever assembled the states general, or the particular states of the provinces, so often as king John; indeed he convened them every year till the battle of Poitiers. France was at that time divided into two parts; *Languedoyl*, and *Languedoc*, which were separated by the Loire; the former contained the northern provinces of the kingdom, and the latter the southern. Institution of the order of the star, in favour of the principal nobility; their motto was, *monstrant regibus astra viam*, alluding to the star of the wise men of the East: the seat of this order was at St. Ouen, in the neighbourhood of Paris; but, being afterwards debased by growing too common, it was left to the captain of the watch at Paris, and his archers. The constable Raoul, count of Eu and Guines, accused of holding a correspondence with the English, is beheaded without observing the forms of justice. This act of violence, in the beginning of the king's reign, alienated the minds of the people, and was in part the cause of all his misfortunes.

1352. 53. 54.

Charles de la Cerda of Spain, created constable after the execution of the count d'Eu, is assassinated by Charles, surnamed the *Bad*, king of Navarre; his motive for committing this crime was, that the county of Angouleme had been conferred upon that prince, when the king of Navarre expected it in dower with his wife, the daughter of king John. Letters patent (1353) by which the king declares the counsellors in parliament free from all tolls on provisions, to the end that they may apply themselves entirely to the discharge of their offices, *ferventius laborare pro republicâ*. An ordinance

(1353)

The THIRD RACE.   249

WIVES.	CHILDREN.	1364. DEATH.	Cotemporary PRINCES.
Bonne of Luxemburg, daughter of John, king of Bohemia, married in 1332, died in 1349. She was interred at Maubuisson.	CHARLES V. Lewis, founder of the dukes of Anjou, who formed the second branch of the kings of Naples. 1384. John, duke of Berry. Amadeus VIII, duke of Savoy, who had been pope in the time of the schism, by the name of Felix V, was this prince's grandson by Mary of Berry, his mother. Philip the Hardy, from whom the last dukes of Burgundy were descended. 1404. Jane, wife of Charles the Bad, king of Navarre. 1373. Mary, married to Robert I, duke of Bar, towards 1404. Agnes. 1349. Margaret. 1352.	JOHN died at London the year 1364, aged forty-four. He was interred at St. Denis.	*Popes.* Clement VI. 1352. Innocent VI. 1362. Urban V. 1370. *Emperors of the East.* John Paleologus. 1384. John Cantacurenus. 1357. *Emperor of the West.* Charles IV. 1378. *Ottoman family.* Amurath I. 1388. *King of Spain.* Peter the Cruel. 1369. *Kings of Portugal.* Alfonso IV. 1357. Peter the Just. 1367. *King of England.* Edward III. 1377. *King of Scotland.* David II. 1370. *King of Denmark.* Waldemar III. 1375. *Kings of Sweden.* Magnus. 1363. Albert, vanquished by Margaret in 1387. *King of Poland.* Casimir, 1370. *Dukes of Russia.* Iwan Danielowitz. } 1366. Iwan Iwanowitz.
Jane, wife of William XII, count of Boulogne, and of Margaret d'Evreux, who had been already mother of Philip de Rouvre, the last duke of the first branch of Burgundy, married in 1349, died in 1361.	Isabella, wife of John Galeas, first duke of Milan. 1372. " *King John being obliged to pay a very considerable sum for his ransom, was reduced, says Villani, to sell his own flesh and blood, as it were, by auction; having disposed of his daughter to Galeacius Visconti for 600,000 florins, in order to be married to John, the son of Galeacius, who was then but eleven years old.*"		

REMARKABLE EVENTS under JOHN.

(1353) for summoning the *ban,* and *rear-ban;* which we find mentioned in the capitularies of Charlemain. The difference between these two words was, either that the *ban* related to the fiefs, and the *rear-ban* to the rear-fiefs; or that the former was the usual service of each vassal according to the nature of his fief; and the latter an extraordinary summons of all the vassals. The king alone, or his son, could summon the ban; which was never done but in cases of the greatest emergency. The vassal might be excused from personal service, either by paying a sum of money, or by finding another to supply his place. The tragical end of Nicholas Rienzi, who had attempted to restore the tribunitian power at Rome, while the pope resided at Avignon in 1354. Some years before that (1328) Castruccio Castracani died at Lucca, after having made himself sovereign of that republic. This was the age of adventurers, when Italy was torn by the factions of Guelfs and Gibellines.

1355. 56.

Charles, son of king John, the first who bore the title of dauphin, is made duke of Normandy: he invites the king of Navarre, with whom he had entered into some connexion, to be present at his reception. The king of Navarre goes thither, and is arrested by king John the 5th of April. The states general held at Paris for raising the subsidies. The imprisonment of the king of Navarre occasions the revolt of his brother Philip, and of the relations of those lords, who had been massacred at Rouen at the time of his imprisonment. They invite Edward III. to their assistance; upon which the truce, concluded between France and England in 1347, and so often broke, and renewed, is changed into a bloody war in 1356. The king of England sends his son Edward, prince of Wales, celebrated for the victory of Cressy, to command his army: in consequence of which Auvergne, Limousin, and Poitou, are laid waste. John, having assembled his forces, came up with him at Maupertuis, within two leagues of Poitiers, in a post encumbered with vines and hedges, from whence it was impossible for the English to retreat. The prince of Wales makes proposals of peace to king John, offering to restore all that he had taken in France, and a truce for seven years.

The Third Race.

MINISTERS.	WARRIORS.	MAGISTRATES.	EMINENT and LEARNED MEN.
Peter de la Foret, cardinal. 1361. John, cardinal de Beauvais. 1373.	*Constables.* Raoul, count d'Eu, beheaded in 1350. Charles de la Cerda of Spain. 1354. James de Bourbon. 1361. Walter de Brienne. 1356. Robert de Fiennes, living in 1380. *Marshals of France.* Guy de Nesle. 1353. Edward, lord de Beaujeu. 1351. Rogues de Hangest. 1352. John de Clermont. 1356. Arnold d'Audeneham. 1370.	*Chancellors.* Peter de la Foret. 1361. Giles Aycelin de Montagu, cardinal, bishop of Therouane. 1378. John de Dormans, called the cardinal de Beauvais. 1373. *First president.* Simon de Bucy. 1369. *Attorney general.* James Dandrie. 1365. *King's advocates.* Gerard de Montaigu, provided in 1351. William de Dormans. 1373. Renaut de Aci, murdered in 1357.	Bartoli. 1355. The emperor Charles V.I. made him a member of his council, and permitted him to bear the arms of Bohemia, tho' he was of very mean extraction. Buridan, living in 1355.

REMARKABLE EVENTS under JOHN.

years. John refuses these conditions, attacks eight thousand men with fourscore thousand, and is defeated and taken prisoner at the well known battle of Poitiers, on Monday the 19th of September, 1356 *. The prince of Wales conducts him to Bourdeaux, from whence he was sent prisoner the next year to England. Peter of Bourbon was killed close by the king; he was very much in debt, and had been excommunicated at the suit of his creditors; his son Lewis of Bourbon procured an absolution for him after his decease, in order to have his soul prayed for; pope Innocent VI. would not take off the excommunication, but upon condition that the son would engage to pay his father's debts. An assembly of the states general: they grant an aid to the dauphin, who took the government into his hands, upon very hard terms; for they obliged him to consent to the deposition of the principal magistrates, such as the chancellor, the first president, &c. whose virtue rendered them obnoxious to those, who wanted to fish in troubled waters: they likewise insisted that the king of Navarre should be set at liberty; but the dauphin refused to comply. He was obliged however to let them appoint the receivers of the public money; as they had been nominated before, with king John's permission, by the assembly of the states general in 1355. These officers were to continue in employment no longer than while the subsidy was raising, and may be considered as the original of the courts of aids: that of Paris was set up in 1390, suppressed by the ordinances of Orleans in 1560, by those of Moulins in 1566, and restored at length by the edict of Charles IX. in 1569. The golden bull, an imperial law enacted by Charles IV. to regulate the election of an emperor; it contains forty articles, twenty-three of which were published at Nurenberg, and the other seventeen at Metz, where Charles the dauphin was present. This law was drawn up by the famous Bartoli: the last article enjoins

---

* There fell in the field of battle about six thousand French, and about fifteen thousand were taken prisoners, among whom were king John and Philip his fourth son, the duke of Bourbon, and the constable of France, with fifty of the principal nobility of the kingdom, and eight hundred gentlemen. King John lost the battle by his own obstinacy and indiscretion. On his arrival in England, he made a public entry into the city of London; he rode on a white courser, and the prince of Wales rode by his side on a little black horse.

the secular electors to get their children instructed in the learned languages. Henry VI. having published a constitution in 1196, in order to render the imperial crown hereditary in his family, even in favour of the females, for want of male issue; this constitution was received at Rome, and agreed to by fifty-two princes of the empire, although they were possessed of the right of election; but it had no effect after the decease of his son Frederic II, at the time of the long interregnum, which involved all Germany in confusion. Then the elective government was restored, and the conditions were settled by the golden bull, which is become a standing law of the empire.

1357.

The king of Navarre escapes out of prison, and forms a project of making himself king of France. With this view he takes up arms against the dauphin, who governed the realm as the king's lieutenant during the imprisonment of his father; and the same year, on the 19th of March, he took the title of Regent. From the king's captivity till his deliverance, the name of Charles the dauphin was prefixed to the king's *letters patent*.

1358.

The peasants rise up in arms against the *noblesse*: this insurrection was called the *Jacquerie* *. The Parisians, headed by Stephen Marcel, provost of the merchants, revolted against the dauphin: Marcel assassinates Robert de Clermont, marshal of Normandy, and John de Conflans, marshal of Champagne, in the dauphin's own apartment, clapping his *chaperon* or embroidered hood on that prince, as a signal of protection. The dauphin retires from Paris, where the king of Navarre commits all manner of violence, but at length is expelled that city. Marcel, afraid of being punished by the regent, whose army had invested Paris, fills up the measure of his iniquity, by attempting to betray the town to the English: but, as he was advancing to the

---

* The poor peasants in those days were called, by way of contempt, *Jacque bon homme*, that is, *good man James*, or, as we would say, *the poor Jacks shall pay for all*. Finding themselves in a starving condition, and oppressed by their lords, they wrought themselves to such a height of fury, that they resolved to extirpate the whole nobility. This mutinous rabble, from the circumstances before mentioned, were called *Jacquerie*.

gate

gate of St. Antony, the 1st of August about midnight, John Maillard, a trusty and resolute citizen, dispatched the traitor with a hatchet: his death put an end to the rebellion, and the dauphin returned to Paris the 4th of the same month.

Auxerre is taken by the English; who lost possession of it in 1360.

1359.

The king of Navarre declares war in form against the regent, who retakes several towns. Du Guesclin begins to distinguish himself.

The province of Languedoc expresses its zeal by granting a considerable subsidy. The regent concludes a peace with the king of Navarre. The war had for several years hindered the parliament from sitting, which occasioned great confusion in the state, with regard both to civil and criminal matters. The regent this year ordains, that the presidents of the parliament, *the said parliament not sitting,* may decide such causes as shall be brought before them till the court can be assembled. It is proper to observe the very words of the ordinance; " *As by means of the present long war, the parliament, which always was, and still is, when assembled, the chief and supreme court of judicature throughout the whole kingdom of France, immediately representing the person of my said sovereign Lord, and myself,* &c." He reduces the number of officers of parliament, with those of the courts of inquests, requests, accounts, &c. and directs that " they who, in " consequence of the reduction made by this ordinance, happen " to be no longer in employ, shall be restored upon the first " vacancy in those offices."

The treaty negotiated in England for the deliverance of king John, had been so disadvantageous to France, as to raise the indignation of the whole kingdom, and the states, having deliberated upon this subject, would not agree to it. Upon which the English, returning to France, fell upon Artois, Champagne, and Burgundy; and the king of England, after marching up to the walls of Paris, retired into the neighbourhood of Chartres, where a violent storm so terrified his army, that he considered it as an order from heaven to conclude a peace.

1360.

REMARKABLE EVENTS under JOHN.

1360.

The treaty of Bretigny, in the neighbourhood of Chartres, concluded on the 8th of May by Charles the regent, and the deputies of king Edward: by the 12th article it is stipulated, that king John shall renounce all sovereignty to Guienne, &c. the property of which shall remain to king Edward, who on the other hand shall relinquish his pretensions to the crown of France, to Normandy, &c. They agree to meet at Calais, in order to determine the place and time of making the renunciations. This treaty was ratified by the two kings at Calais the 29th of the ensuing October, except the 12th article only, which is left out: yet the two princes agree, by letters signed the same day, to send the renunciations to Bruges by St. Andrew's day, 1361, which by the treaty of Bretigny were designed to be made at Calais. But the latter convention did not take place; for John having sent a person with his renunciations to Bruges, in pursuance of his promise; and king Edward's deputies happening not to come to the place appointed, things remained, with respect to the sovereignty of Guienne, in the same condition as they stood before the treaty of Bretigny, and Edward was put into possession of Guienne, &c. *the king's commissioners reserving*, as *le Songe du Vergier* * says, *the sovereign jurisdiction over his subjects*, without any opposition from the English commissioners. In consequence of the treaty of Bretigny, king John was set at liberty, after four years imprisonment. An ordinance, permitting the Jews to continue in the kingdom during the space of twenty years: to this were added letters patent, by which the king appoints the count d'Estampes *(of the house of Evreux)* guardian and conservator of the privileges of those people. The king of Navarre was included in this treaty; but he had entered into an accommodation with the regent the preceding year. King Edward prohibits the use of the French tongue in all public acts in England, where it had been hitherto established †.

---

* *Somnium Viridarii*, a book so called. See the year 1371.

† He ordained that all pleadings and judgments in the courts of Westminster should for the future be in English, whereas before they were in French. As for other public acts, such as statutes, and the like, it does not appear they were written in French till about the time of Edward I. *See Tindal, note* 6, *on Rapin, Vol. I. p.* 43. *and Tyrrel's Introduction to Vol. II. p.* ci.

1361.

REMARKABLE EVENTS under JOHN.

1361. 62. 63.

Philip de Rouvre, the last duke of Burgundy, of the first house of that name, died at Rouvre in the neighbourhood of Dijon the 21st of September, at the age of fourteen. John reannexed this dukedom to the crown, by right of blood, as the next of kin, being son of Joan of Burgundy, sister to duke Eudes, who was grandfather of Philip de Rouvre. He gave it afterwards, viz. the 6th of September, 1363, to Philip the Hardy, his fourth son, by way of *appanage*, reversible to the crown in failure of *heirs male*; for thus are we to understand these words, *hærede succedente*, in the letters patent, which are agreeable to the law established by Philip the Fair in 1314. Philip was surnamed the Hardy, for fighting valiantly near his father at the battle of Poitiers; or rather from placing himself by main force, as dean of the peers, above Lewis, duke of Anjou, his elder brother, created peer in 1360, who had taken his seat next the king *.

This same Philip the Hardy reunited the county and peerage of Flanders to the branch of Burgundy, by his marriage with Margaret, heiress of the counts of Flanders, and widow of Philip de Rouvre; so that his children by this princess reaped the whole succession of Philip de Rouvre, and his widow: he is the founder of the second royal house of Burgundy. By the charter of king John he was instituted the first peer of France: hitherto the dukes of Aquitaine and Normandy had, on many occasions, taken place of the duke of Burgundy, whose precedency was not fully settled till the year 1380. This fact appears worthy of observation, as it regards the royal authority, which in some measure may alter the nature of things, by giving to a new institution a priority over those of a more ancient date; and no doubt but it was this example that authorized Henry III. to act as he did, in favour of the dukes de Joyeuse and d'Epernon.

The king reunites the dukedom of Normandy, and the counties of Champagne and Toulouse, to the crown. James of Bourbon, count de la Marche, is defeated and slain at the battle

---

* Some say, that king Edward gave this prince the surname of Hardy, for reprimanding a gentleman who served that monarch with wine before his father.

REMARKABLE EVENTS under JOHN.

Brignais, attempting to disperse what they called the *great* [com]panies, who had ravaged France, and afterwards marched into [It]aly. These companies consisted of disbanded soldiers, who [as]sembled themselves in a body, under a commander of their own [cho]using, without the authority of the prince. They began to [ap]pear in France, according to the continuator of Nangis, in [13]60; he calls them, *filii Belial, guerratores de variis nationibus, non habentes titulum:* they were likewise stiled *tard-venus,* the [lat]e-comers *, or *malandrins, disbanded soldiers.*

1364.

King John returns to England, in order to treat of the ransom of [his] son the duke of Anjou, who had made his escape while he was an [hos]tage: some attribute the father's return into that kingdom to an [am]our; however, there he died. The variation of the coin under [thi]s prince, is the strongest proof of the misfortunes of his reign; [the]re was hardly a man who, *from one day to another, could exactly [tell] what payment he was to make.* (Coll. of Ord.) This was [a] tax of those days, and doubtless the most prejudicial to com[me]rce; for which reason the people obtained, as a favour, that [the] *tailles* and the *aides* should be substituted in its stead. And, [wh]at is something extraordinary, never was luxury carried to a [hig]her pitch by the nobility, than in this prince's reign.

* They stiled themselves such, to signify that they had only the gleanings of the harvest that had been made in France.

1364.
Accession to the crown.

CHARLES V. *comes to the crown in the year 1364, at seven and twenty years of age; his great prudence obtained him the surname of* Wise. *He was the first of the sons of France, who took the title of dauphin. He was crowned at Rheims, with the queen his consort, by John de Craon, the archbishop of that city, on the 19th of May, 1364.*

REMARKABLE EVENTS.

1364.

CHARLES, surnamed the *Bad*, king [of] Navarre, only sought for a pretence to ha[ve] recourse once more to arms: with this view h[e] renewed the claim which he had formerly laid t[o] the dukedom of Burgundy, when the late kin[g] took possession of it, upon the decease of Phili[p] de Rouvres: to which he added his rights t[o] Champagne and Brie, and the war broke o[ut] again with greater fury than ever.

The battle of Cocherel on the 6th of Ma[y] near the village of that name, between Evreu[x] and Vernon, where the army of king Charles V[.] under the command of du Guesclin, defeated th[e] troops of the king of Navarre, commanded b[y] the *Captal* * de Buch, who was taken prisone[r.] The war in Britany continues between Charl[es] de Blois and the young count de Montfor[t] named John V. They conclude a treaty o[n] Beaumanoir heath, which Charles de Blois, b[y] the instigation of his wife, the countess [of] Penthievre, refuses to execute. The battle [of] Auray on Michaelmas-day, where Charles [is] killed, and du Guesclin is taken prisoner b[y] Sir John Chandos, an English commander [of] great renown. The count de Montfort conclude[s] a peace with the widow of Charles de Blois; an[d] by the treaty of Guerande in 1365, he is acknow[-] ledged duke of Britany, for which he does fealt[y] to the king. During this war, which had laste[d] ever since the year 1341, two princesses gave si[g-] nal marks of courage, the countess of Montfo[rt] and Joan the Lame, during the imprisonmen[t] and after the death, of their husbands.

A revocation of the demesnes that had bee[n] alienated since the decease of Philip the Fair.

* An old French name for a commander, or chief.

WIVES.	CHILDREN.	1380. DEATH.	Contemporary PRINCES.
...an, daugh-ter of Peter I, ... of Bour-... and of I-...la of Va-... married in ..., died in 1377.	CHARLES VI. Lewis duke of Orleans, grandfather of Lewis XII, and great grandfather of Francis I. 1407. He was also duke de Valois, by the erection of this county into a peerage made by Charles VI, in 1406. He was the father of Philip, count de Vertus, who left only an illegitimate son; and of the famous bastard of Orleans, otherwise called count de Dunois, who died, according to some, in 1470, to others in 1468. He had the latter by Mariette d'Enghien, wife of Aubert de Cani. The dukedom of Orleans, which had been granted him as an appanage, to be held in peerage, was re-united to the crown, upon the accession of his grandson, Lewis the Twelfth. John, died young. Joan, died young. Bonne, died young. Joan, died young. Mary. Isabella. Catharine, married to John de Berry, count de Montpensier. 1388.	CHARLES V. died the 16th of September, at the castle of Beauté, in the wood of Vincennes, in the forty-fourth year of his age. He was interred at St. Denis. Christian de Pisan, daughter of Thomas de Pisan, affirms, that the king died at the very hour her father had predicted; she gives him the title of the king's astronomer. We may judge of the great vogue of this officer, by the pensions he enjoyed. Thomas was paid monthly a hundred livres salary, and his board-wages did not amount to much less, a very considerable sum for those days: in such reputation was judiciary astrology, even among princes, the most sage, and the most religious.	*Popes.* Urban V. 1370. Gregory XI. 1378. Urban VI. 1389. *Emperor of the East.* John Paleologus. 1389 *Emperors of the West.* Charles IV. 1378. Wenceslaus. 1400. *Emperor of the Turks.* Amurat I. 1388. *Kings of Spain.* Peter the Cruel. 1369. Henry II. 1379. John I. 1390. *Kings of Portugal.* Peter the Just. 1367. Ferdinand I. 1383. *Kings of England.* Edward III. 1377. Richard II. 1399. *Kings of Scotland.* David II. 1370. Robert II. 1390. *Kings of Denmark.* Waldemar III. 1375. Olaus V. 1387. *King of Sweden.* Albert, vanquished by Margaret in 1387. *Kings of Poland.* Casimir III, stiled the Great. 1370. Lewis, king of Hungary, stiled the Great. 1382. Those two princes merited the title of Great, the former by his wife laws, and the latter by his valour. *Dukes of Russia.* John Danielowitz. } 1366. John Joannowitz. Demetrius Joannowitz. 1381.

REMARKABLE EVENTS under CHARLES V.

1365.

A treaty of peace betwixt Charles V. and the king of Navarre concluded the 6th of March. The latter continued in possession of the county of Evreux, which was his patrimonial estate; he had also a grant of Montpellier and its dependencies, with reserve of the sovereignty and jurisdiction, as an indemnity for Mante and Meulan, and for his pretensions to Burgundy, Champagne, and Brie.

The university of Orange founded by Raymond V.

1366.

Bertrand du Guesclin undertakes an expedition into Spain, and engages the *great companies* with him, by which means he clears France of those banditti. He dethrones Peter the Cruel, king of Castile: this prince, already stained with the murder of his brothers, made himself completely odious by poisoning his wife Blanche of Bourbon, sister-in-law to Charles V, in order to indulge his lawless passion with Mary de Padille. Bertrand raises Don Henry, count de Transtamare, a bastard brother of that king, to the throne; who, in return, made du Guesclin constable of Castile.

1367. 68.

Peter the Cruel having retired into Guienne, the prince of Wales marches to his assistance, and restores him to the crown. Peter quarrels with the prince of Wales, his benefactor. Henry returns to Castile, kills Peter with his own hand, and becomes peaceable possessor of the kingdom. It is said that Peter the Cruel, finding that Don Henry was come back to Castile, had turned mussulman with a view to obtain succours from the Moors; but this is a tale invented by ancient writers of Romances, "who "are ranked nevertheless among historians by the ignorant vulgar, because they relate some truths." (*Revol. of Spain*, father Orleans.)

The revolt of Guienne (1368) against Edward, prince of Wales, who oppressed that country with heavy taxes.

1369. 70.

The count d'Armagnac, and several other lords, appeal to the parliament of Paris: Edward is cited to appear in this court as vassal to the crown; and, upon his not complying, the lands he possess

The Third Race.

NISTERS.	WARRIORS.	MAGISTRATES.	EMINENT and LEARNED MEN.
, de la range, lled the rdinal of miens. 1402. p de Mai- res. taries of the evenue. rd de ontaigu, her of hn, lord ward of e king's ushold. tier de Bag- aux. olas de rres. Blanchet, ho signed edict of 74 for fet- ng the ig's majo- y at the e of four- n.	*Conflables.* Robert de Fiennes, called Moreau, living in 1380. Bertrand du Guef- clin. 1380. *Marshals of France.* Arnoul d'Auden- cham. 1370. John le Meingre, called Bouci- caut. 1367. John, Sire de Neu- ville, living in 1359. John de Mau- quenchy, lord of Blainville, died before 1391. Lewis de Sancerre. 1402.	*Chancellors.* John de Dormans, called the cardinal of Beauvais. 1373. William de Dormans. 1373. Peter d'Orgemont was elected by scrutiny in the king's pre- sence. 1389. *First presidents.* Simon de Bucy. 1369. Peter de Demeville, stiled first president in the letters patent of the 2d of August, 1370, which are in a parliament roll; commencing the 12th of November. 1369. William de Sens. 1373. Peter d'Orgemont. 1389. Arnaud de Corbie. 1413. *Attorney general.* William de St. Her- mant. 1384. *The king's advocates.* John Pastoral, living in 1367. Raoul de Présles, a na- tural son of the for- mer, died in 1382. John d'Ay. 1375. John Daillois, practis- ed in 1374. John Desmarés, who had given displea- sure to the dukes of Anjou and Berry, by his bold speech con- cerning the majority of the king, was be- headed in 1382. John Canart, living in 1387.	Hugh Aubriot, living in 1381. John Bocace. 1375. St. Bridget. 1373. St. Catharine of Sien- na. 1380. Master Gervais. William de Machant, living in 1370. Fr. Petrarch. 1374. Sufon. 1365. Alf. Vargas. 1366. The reign of Charles V. is a memorable æra in the republic of letters. *This prince,* says Christi- na de Pisan, *was a very good scholar.* About this time, ac- cording to Pasquier, the *chants royaux* * *ballads, rondeaus, and pastorals, were first introduced.* And in- deed, from this prince's reign we date the uninter- rupted succession of our French poets. Froissart wrote verses at this time. Charles of Orleans, father of Lewis XII. has left us a collection of his poems in MS. At the decease of this prince, Francis Villon was three and thirty years old; and John Marot, fa- ther of Clement, was born. (Memoirs of the Academy of Belles Lettres.)

* A kind of ancient poem, dedicated to the honour of Christ, or of the virgin Mary.

REMARKABLE EVENTS under CHARLES V.

possessed in France, are confiscated. The war is renewed between Charles V. and Edward III.

Du Guesclin, during this dispute, recovers almost all Guienne, Poitou, (where Chandos the brave English general was slain) Xaintonge, Rouvergue, Perigord, part of the Limousin, Ponthieu, &c. Aubriot, provost of Paris, lays the foundation of the Bastille in 1370. Du Guesclin is made constable of France upon the resignation of the lord of Fiennes.

An ordinance prohibiting games of hazard, and exciting the people to sports of agility and strength, such as the bow, the cross-bow, &c. proper for invigorating the body, and inuring it to the use of arms, &c. This ordinance shews the spirit of the times, when the French were altogether a military nation: but in the enumeration of prohibited games, we are surprized to find some that were not games of hazard, but of thought and judgment, or that contributed to render the bodies of young people more pliant and supple. *By these presents* we prohibit all games, *dice, draughts, tennis, nine-pins, quoits, billiards*, &c.

A new ordinance concerning the right of mortmain.

The crown of Scotland devolves to the house of Stuart by the death of David king of Scotland, whose heir was Robert Stuart his sister's son.

1371. 72. 73. 74. 75.

Charles V. grants the privilege of noblesse to the citizens of Paris, which was confirmed to them by Charles VI, Lewis X, Francis I, and Henry II. But Henry III. restrained this privilege in 1577 to the provost of the merchants, and the sheriff; it was suppressed in 1667, restored in 1707, suppressed again 1715, and at length restored in 1716 upon the present footing.

An ordinance forbidding private wars.

The king receives great assistance from the Jews, whom he obliges to wear a mark of distinction on their clothes.

John V. duke of Britany, who had sided with the English, was declared a rebel by an arret of parliament, and deprived of his dutchy, where he kept possession only of the harbour of Brest. The English are defeated by the Castilian fleet in a sea engagement near the harbour of Rochelle: thus Henry king of Castile repaid Charles V. for the succours granted him

REMARRKABLE EVENTS *under* CHARLES V.

him againſt Peter the Cruel. The captal de Buch, who had obtained his liberty upon the concluſion of the treaty between Charles V. and the king of Navarre, is taken priſoner again in the neighbourhood of Soubiſe, by Yvain, the only ſurvivor of the ancient family of the princes of Wales *. The taking of this general was more fatal to the Engliſh, than the loſs of a battle. Charles V. refuſing to releaſe him, he died a priſoner in the Temple at the expiration of five years, after having generouſly declined to engage in the ſervice of France.

A truce between France and England, by which the former preſerves all her conqueſts. In the reign of king John ſhe had loſt the provinces which Philip Auguſtus had taken from the Engliſh; and they were once more recovered by Charles V. In the courſe of this hiſtory we ſhall ſee Henry V. as victorious as Edward III; and Charles VII. as fortunate as Charles V. was cautious and prudent.

An ordinance of Charles V. in the month of Auguſt, 1374, whereby our kings are declared to be of age at fourteen, *donec decimum quartum ætatis annum attigerint*. This prince ordered the rector of the univerſity, the provoſt of the merchants, and the ſheriffs of the city of Paris, to aſſiſt at the regiſtering of the above edict in parliament. The chancellor de l'Hopital afterwards explained that ordinance in the reign of Charles IX, ſaying, that it was the ſpirit of the law, our kings ſhould be of age in their fourteenth year commenced, and not finiſhed, purſuant to the maxim, that, in favourable cauſes, *annus incœptus pro perfecto habetur*.

An ordinance concerning the regency, in the month of October, 1374, where Charles declares, that, if he ſhould happen to die before his ſon enters into his fourteenth year, the duke of Anjou, his brother, ſhall be regent till the young king is of age. At the ſame time he publiſhes another edict, mentioning that, in caſe he died before his eldeſt ſon enters into his fourteenth year, the queen ſhould have the tutelage of her ſons and daughters till the king comes of age; that the dukes of Burgundy and Bourbon ſhould be joint guardians with her; and that if, by death, marriage, or otherwiſe, ſhe becomes incapable of the

---

* According to the Engliſh hiſtorians, David, brother of Leoline, was the laſt of the family; Leoline was killed in battle, and David was taken and beheaded by Edward I.

REMARKABLE EVENTS under CHARLES V.

tutelage, the duke of Burgundy should be guardian, and, in failure of this prince, the duke of Bourbon.

It was high time to redress the abuse of regencies, which absorbed the royal authority: under the first and second race the king was not of age till two and twenty, and, during his minority, the regent's seal was fixed to all public instruments. This custom was founded on the vulgar opinion, that the king was not a sovereign till his coronation; and therefore that ceremony was deferred by the regent as long as possible: hence we find that, even under the third race, when the power of regents was greatly diminished, our kings caused their sons to be crowned in their life-time, with a view of settling the succession, which the authority of the regent might render precarious. This subject being too copious to be treated in its full extent, it will suffice to make a few remarks. 1°. The regency was distinct from the tutelage, so as not to be confounded in the same person: thus, for instance, Charles V. had granted the tutelage of his son to the queen, his wife; and the regency to the duke of Anjou; which did not take place, for the queen died before Charles V. Queen Blanche, the mother of St. Lewis, was the first that enjoyed both those titles, which used to imply distinct offices, though they were never separated after the reign of Charles V. 2°. Our kings have disposed of the regency by testament, and their disposition has been followed. 3°. Charles IX. was the first that made a solemn declaration of his majority. 4°. The first of our kings, that attempted to make any regulation concerning the regency, was Philip the Hardy: this prince published two ordinances, one at the time when he was in Africa, the other upon his return, by which he declared that his son should be of age at fourteen; but these ordinances were not carried into execution after his decease; and even those of Charles V. were broke through during the minority of Charles VI, who likewise published two ordinances conformable to those of his father, which at length are become a fundamental law of the kingdom.

The *Somnium Viridarii*, or *Dream of the Orchard*, is said to have been written in 1374. Among the several authors to whom it has been attributed, the honour, I think, is due to Raoul de Presles: it treats of the ecclesiastic and secular power.

1376.

REMARKABLE EVENTS under CHARLES V.

1376. 77.

The celebrated prince of Wales died the 17th of July, 1376, aged forty-six; the English commonly called him the *Black Prince*, becaufe his armour was of that colour. *He was poffeffed,* fays Rapin Thoyras, *of all the virtues in an eminent degree; a good foldier, and a great general, brave without fiercenefs, bold in battle, but very affable in converfation . . . . . ever fubmiffive and refpectful to the king his father.* The king of France ordered a folemn dirge to be celebrated for him at Notre Dame. The king of England died within a twelvemonth after his fon, and was fucceeded by Richard, fon of the prince of Wales, aged only eleven years. The Florentines, being connected in intereft with Gregory XI, fend Catharine of Sienna to this pontif, who is perfuaded by her arguments to re-eftablifh the papal court at Rome (1377), from whence it had been removed to Avignon fince the year 1308. (He was the laft of the French popes.) The motive of this ftep was the revolt of the inhabitants of Bologna, who wanted to fhake off the papal yoke, and could not be quelled at fo great a diftance,

1378.

The death of Edward III. enabled Charles V. to complete the conqueft of Guienne, which he intirely recovered from the Englifh, except the town of Bourdeaux. The emperor Charles of Luxemburg, and Wenceflaus his fon, are entertained at Paris the 4th of January. The emperor came to fulfil a vow of vifiting the abbey of St. Maur, in the neighbourhood of Paris. He died a few months after: it was faid of this prince, that he had ruined his family to attain the imperial dignity; and that he had ruined the empire to retrieve his family. The accomplices of the king of Navarre, in a fecond attempt to poifon Charles V, (for he had made one before) are put to death. The duke of Anjou wrefts the town of Montpellier from the king of Navarre.

1379.

Charles V. takes the opinion of Canart, his council, and condemns the count de Montfort for the crime of felony; in confequence of which he confifcates Britany, and reunites that province to the crown, faving the right of the children of Charles de Blois: but this reunion did not take place, for the duke knew how to defend himself, and the king died a short time after.

The beginning of the great schism upon the death of Gregory XI, which happened the 27th of March, 1378. Urban VI. was elected by all the cardinals then at Rome; but after several of them had withdrawn from that capital, they pretended that the violence of the people had hindered the freedom of election; in consequence of which they chose Clement VII. the 20th of September the same year, and this pope afterwards retired to Avignon. The schism lasted forty years, viz. till the holding of the council of Constance. It is said that the cardinals, who elected Clement, had first offered the pontificate to king Charles V, who was a widower; and that this prince refused the proposal, because, as he was lame of his left arm, he could not celebrate mass *(Martene).*

1380.

The constable du Guesclin falls sick, and dies the 13th of June, aged sixty-six years, before Chateauneuf de Rendon, to which he had laid siege: he was buried at St. Denis, near the tomb which Charles V. had erected for his own interment. In taking his last farewel of all the old officers, who had served under him during the space of forty years, he begged they would not forget what he had told them a thousand times, *that in whatever country they waged war, neither the clergy, nor the women, children, and poor people, were their enemies.*

The enemy paid him a very singular honour. The governor of Rendon had capitulated with the constable, and it was agreed that he should deliver up the town the 12th of July, in case no succours arrived in the mean time: upon being summoned to surrender the day following, on which du Guesclin happened to die, the governor said he would keep his word to that commander even after his decease; accordingly he marched out with the principal officers of the garrison, and came and laid the keys of the town on the constable's bier, paying the same honours to him as if he were still living. (Some historians pretend that he was alive when the keys were surrendered.) The famous captains, who had served under him, refused the constable's sword, not thinking themselves worthy to wear it after so great a man. Yet Oliver de Clisson was some time after obliged to accept of it.

REMARKABLE EVENTS under CHARLES V.

The king of Navarre had administered poison to Charles when he was only dauphin: a German physician suspended the effect of the poison by opening an issue in his arm, and told him that, whenever it stopped, death would be the consequence; and it stopped in 1380. This prince, the very day of his decease, published an ordinance, suppressing part of the taxes which he had laid on the people.

Charles V, among many good qualities, deserves to be celebrated for a particular virtue, which affords an excellent lesson to all kings. Never prince took so much pleasure in asking counsel, and yet never prince suffered himself less to be governed by his ministers. Edward III. used to say of him, *that no king whatever, with so little of the soldier, gave him so much trouble.* And du Tillet commends him by saying, *that he never put on any armour, or habiliment of war.* The truth is, that he did not appear at the head of his armies, but conferred the command on the constable du Guesclin; yet this extraordinary prudence repaired the losses, which France had sustained in the reign of king John: without stirring out of his cabinet, he recovered from the English almost all that his father and grandfather, after great instances of valour, and excessive fatigue, had been stripped of by the enemy; in short, the glory of this reign was to have the wisest prince, and the ablest general. We must not forget a bautiful saying of this king: some persons having complained of the respect he shewed to men of letters, who were then called *clerks*; he made answer, *Clerks cannot be too much cherished; for so long as we honour learning, this kingdom will continue to prosper; but, when we begin to despise it, the French monarchy will decline.* (Christina de Pisan.) According to Froissart, the public did not form a favourable judgment of Charles V. at the battle of Poictiers; which was owing to his governor, who, at the very beginning of the engagement, made this prince and his two brothers retire: *Charles, Lewis, and John,* says he, *sons of the king of France, were young of age and counsel, so that there was very little to be expected from them, and they would not undertake the government of the kingdom.* How comes it that Froissart, whose history is carried down to the year 1400, did not, for his own honour, recall a judgment so precipitate and unjust; and join in concert with the whole nation in acknowledging the extraordinary merit of this great prince? During the captivity of the king his father, he purchased the Hotel de St. Paul, which he called the *Hotel of high diversion*. It is impossible to account for his expending such immense sums on that place, in times so calamitous; however, he published letters patent in 1364 for re-uniting this hotel to the royal demesne.

The navy was almost forgotten in France, after the death of Charlemagne; from that prince's reign the great lords had what they called their *patrimonial* admirals. Our marine began to revive under St. Lewis, the first of our kings who had a principal officer, invested with the title of *admiral*. The war with England rendered the navy more considerable under Charles V, which was owing to the great care of his admiral John de Vienne, lord of Rollans. This commander used to say, that the English were no where so weak as at home. Under the following reigns our naval affairs were again neglected, and there is not the least mention of commerce; but they were both restored with eclat under the administration of cardinal Richelieu, and raised to the highest pitch by M. Colbert and his son M. de Seignelay, in the reign of Lewis XIV.

We may consider Charles V. as the real founder of the king's library: this prince was fond of reading, and would be greatly pleased with a present of books: he collected about nine hundred, a very large number for a time when the typographical art was not yet invented, and for a prince to whom his father, king John, had left no more than twenty volumes. The library of Charles V. consisted of books of devotion, astrology, physic, law, history, and romances; very few ancient authors of the pure ages; not a single copy of Cicero's works; of the Latin poets only Ovid, Lucan, and Boetius; with French translations of some authors, as of Livy, Valerius Maximus, the city of God, the Bible, &c. Charles ordered them to be placed in one of the towers of the Louvre, called the *tower of the library*. From such weak beginnings it could hardly be imagined, that the royal library should ever rise to the flourishing state, in which we now admire it. It was considerably augmented by the care of Lewis XII, and of Francis I, in proportion as the taste of polite literature and the

sciences

REMARKABLE EVENTS under CHARLES V.

sciences began to diffuse itself over France, by the protection of those princes. But chiefly under the auspices of Lewis XIV. and Lewis XV. it has been carried to that perfection, which renders it the most copious and most valuable library in the whole world.

The HISTORY of FRANCE.

1380.
Accession to the crown.

CHARLES VI. *succeeds to the crown in 1380, at the age of twelve years and nine months. He was crowned at Rheims on the 4th of November, by Richard Pique, archbishop of that city.*

Of all the lay peers, only Philip the Hardy, duke of Burgundy, assisted at this ceremony, Lewis count of Flanders being absent, and the other four peerages being re-annexed to the crown. He claimed and obtained his rank as first peer of France, in opposition to Lewis duke of Anjou, his elder brother, who had been created a peer so early as the year 1360, and whom he preceded on this occasion. Charles VI. was baptized in the church of St. Paul, by the cardinal de Beauvais; and was held at the font by Charles de Montmorency.

REMARKABLE EVENTS.

1380.

THE minority of Charles VI. occasioned the calamities of his reign, which were worked up to the highest pitch by his sudden phrenzy. The arms of France are reduced to three flower de luces; yet we may refer that reduction originally to Charles V. In the beginning of this reign there were some disputes relating to the regency, among the dukes of Anjou, Berry, Burgundy, and Bourbon, the king's uncles. A council was summoned in the palace, where the duke of Anjou declared his pretensions to act as guardian and regent: the dispute grew warm; and, in order to prevent any ill consequences, it was resolved to refer the matter to arbitrators, who declared that the duke of Anjou should be regent and president of the council; that the dukes of Burgundy and Bourbon should have the care of the king's education, and the superintendency of his houshold; and, that the age for the king's coronation should be anticipated. This was done accordingly; and on the 4th of November the duke of Anjou's administration expired. During the short time of his regency, he signed his own name to letters patent; but he was the last regent that had a particular seal. The king's four uncles break out into a fresh quarrel, which is followed by a second accommodation: among other articles, it was agreed, that the duke of Anjou should be president of the council; and the care of the king's person be committed to the dukes of Burgundy and Bourbon, who, with *the approbation* of the dukes of Anjou and Berry, were to nominate the officers of the king's houshold.

1381.

The THIRD RACE. 271

WIVES.	CHILDREN.	1422. DEATH.	Cotemporary PRINCES.
Isabella of Bavaria, married in 1385, died detested by all true Frenchmen in 1435. Such contempt was shewn to her body, that it was removed from her hotel, and put into a small boat on the Seine, without any other ceremony or pomp, and carried in that manner to her tomb at St. Denis, like the body of a private person. (*Brantome.*)	Charles, died young. Charles, duke de Guienne. 1400. Lewis died without any issue by Margaret of Burgundy in 1415. John, married to Jacquelina of Bavaria, by whom he had no children, interred at St. Corneille de Compeigne. CHARLES VII. Philip died the day of his birth. Joan, died young. Isabella, whose first husband was Richard II, king of England; her second, Charles duke of Orléans. 1409. Jane, married to John VI, duke of Britany. 1433. Mary. 1438. Michelle, married to Philip the Good, duke of Burgundy, by whom she had no issue. 1422. Catharine, married to Henry V, king of England, and afterwards to Owen Tudor, the grandfather of Henry VII, king of England. 1458. Charles VI. had by *Odette de Champdivers*, a natural daughter, named Margaret of Valois, demoiselle de Belleville, *who was married to John de Harpedene, lord of Belleville in Poitou*; she died before 1458.	CHARLES VI. died at Paris in the Hotel de St. Paul, the 20th of October, 1422, aged fifty-four years. He was interred at St. Denis. Bonincontri, in his annals, pretends that his madness was owing to a love potion, *potione amatoria*: he was deserted in such a manner, that not a single prince of the blood assisted at his funeral.	*Popes.* Urban VI. 1389. Boniface IX. 1404. Innocent VII. 1406. Gregory XII. 1409. Alexander V, 1410. John XXIII. abdicates 1415. Martin V. 1431. *Emperors of the East.* John Paleologus. 1384. Emmanuel II. 1418. John Paleologus. 1444. *Emperors of the West.* Wenceslaus. 1400. Robert. 1410. Sigismund. 1437 *Turkish emperors.* Amurat I. 1388. Bajazet I. 1401. Soliman. 1409. Moses. 1413. Mahomet I. 1421. *Kings of Spain.* John. 1390. Henry III. 1406. John. 1454. *Kings of Portugal.* Ferdinand I. 1383. John. 1433. *Kings of England.* Richard II. 1399. Henry IV. 1413. Henry V. 1422. *Kings of Scotland.* Robert II. 1390. Robert III. 1406. James II. 1437. *Kings of Denmark.* Olaus. 1387. Margaret. 1412. Eric IX. abdicates 1438. *Kings of Sweden.* Albert. 1396. Margaret. 1412. Eric IX. abdicates 1438. *Kings of Poland.* Lewis. 1382. Ladislaus Jagellon. 1434. *Dukes of Russia.* Basilius Demetrowitz. 1399. Gregory Demetrowitz. 1406. Basil Basilowitz. 1413.

REMARKABLE EVENTS under CHARLES VI.

1381.

The extortions of the duke of Anjou exasperate the people. The duke of Britany yields homage to the king. There had been some difficulty towards the end of the last reign with regard to the form of this submission. John, count of Montfort, succeeding to the dukedom of Britany, pretended the king ought to be satisfied with a simple fealty, which should affect his dukedom, but not his person; whereas, according to the use of fiefs, it ought to be liege, since the duke of Britany was considered in the same light as the other great vassals of the crown, who were capable of incurring the crime of felony. But as it was apprehended very much that he would offer himself to the king of England, and give that prince admittance into his harbours, recourse was had to the expedient of receiving his homage, *such as it ought to be according to law and ancient usage.*

1382.

Lewis, duke of Anjou, sets out for Naples, invited by the adoption of queen Joan. This princess, worthy of pity, if misfortunes were able to cancel the memory of her crimes, having lost all her children, and incapable of any more issue, (at the age of fifty-seven) by her fourth husband, Otho of Brunswick, married her niece to her cousin, Charles de Duras, stiled the *Peaceable*, from his having negotiated a treaty between the Hungarians and Venetians, but very undeserving of this title with reference to Joan his benefactress. Adopted by this princess, he grew impatient for her death; and the great schism favoured his ambition. Urban VI, out of hatred to pope Clement VII, who was supported by Joan, assisted Charles; and providence permitted that this princess should undergo the same kind of death, as Andrew her first husband had suffered by her order: Charles caused her to be strangled, while Lewis of Anjou, whom she had invited to her assistance, and who had carried away with him all the treasure of France to maintain his adoption, was unable to prevent this fatal catastrophe. Lewis, the founder of the second house of Anjou and Naples, perished in this expedition in the year 1384. Neither were his posterity more fortunate: they beheld the crown from afar; or, if they ascended it, they had but a momentary reign.

The Third Race.

MINISTERS.	WARRIORS.	MAGISTRATES.	EMINENT and LEARNED MEN.
John de Montaigu, superintendant of the finances, was beheaded in 1409. Peter des Efclats, fuperintendant of the finances, was beheaded in 1413. This man owed his rife to the duke of Burgundy, and poffeffed feven or eight of the chief offices of the state, is viz. those of provoft of Paris, mafter of the waters and forefts, great butler, great falconer, great general, and fovereign governor of the finances, captain of Paris, Cherburg, and Montargis. *Secretaries of the finances.* P. Blanchet. Yves d'Arian. John Tabary. J. Blanchet. Thibault Horie. J. de St. Louis. Hugh Blanchet. He was fucceffively mafter of the requefts in the room of Lewis of Orleans, (a natural fon of the duke of Orleans) bishop of Poitiers, treafurer of the holy chapel, and at length archbifhop of Sens. James Duval. Mace Ferou. J. de Crefpy. P. Conthan. P. Manchac. Lewis Blanchet deputed to treat with VOL. I.	*Constables.* Ol. de Cliffon. 1407. Philip d'Artois, count d'Eu. 1397. Lewis de Sancerre, of the house of Champagne. 1402. Charles d'Albert. 1415. Valeran de Luxemburg. 1413. Bernard d'Armagnac. 1418. Charles of Lorrain. 1430. *Marshals of France.* John de Mauquenchy, lord of Blainville, died before 1391 Lewis de Sancerre. 1402. Peter de Craon. It is dubious, whether he ever had this poft. (*Hift. de Sablé by Menage.*) John de Meingre, called Boucicaut II. 1421. J. de Rieux. 1417. Lewis de Loigny, living in 1413. James d'Heilly, called the marfhal of Guienne. 1415. Amaury de Severac. 1427. P. de Rieux. 1439. Cl. de Beauvoir. 1453. John de Villiers, de l'Ifle Adam. 1437. James de Montberon. 1422. Ant. de Vergy de Dampmartin. 1439. John de la Baume. 1435. Gilbert de la Fayette. 1463.	*Chancellors.* Peter d'Orgemont, who refigned in 1380, died in 1389. Miles Dormans. 1387. Peter de Giac. 1407. Arnaud de Corbie. 1413. In 1390 he Inftituted a notary royal, that is, a king's fecretary; and the king to render him worthy of fo high an employ, made him a knight of the Louvre. N. Dubofe. 1408. Montaigu. 1415. Euft. de Laiftre, elected in 1420. He was obliged to refign his poft of chancellor in 1417, and Henry de Marle, firft prefident, was chofen by fcrutiny to fill his place; Robert Madger was elected firft prefident, and the office of fourth prefident was alfo given by fcrutiny to John de Railly, purfuant to the new ordinances, by which the parliament was invefted with that power. Henry de Marle. 1418. J. le Clerc. 1438. R. le Maçon. 1442. He faved the dauphin's life, (afterwards Charles VII.) in 1418, when the duke of Burgundy made his entrance into Paris. Michael Gouge. 1444. *First prefidents.* Arnaud de Corbie. 1413. William de Sens II. 1399. John de Popincourt. 1403. Upon the death of John de Popincourt, the chancellor went to the parliament, and declared, that the king had given the vacant offices to Henry de Marle, third prefident; Peter Bo. T	Baldus. 1400. Honoré Bonnet, towards 1399. Nicholas Flamel, towards 1409. Naudé, who after having been librarian to the cardinals Bagni and Barberine, had the fame office under cardinal Mazarin, in which he died, makes no fort of doubt but Flamel was a knave, that held correfpondence with the Jews at the time they were driven out of France, and having robbed them of a vaft deal of their property, in order to conceal the fource of his wealth, pretended to have found out the philofopher's ftone. But ought not he to have concealed his difcovery, as well as his riches? And did not this expofe him to far greater danger, than his treafure, which after all was only taken from the Jews, about whom the government gave themfelves no concern? Yet as mankind are naturally fond of the marvellous, it is the received opinion that Flamel had found out the philofopher's ftone. This is the fentiment of the fieur Salomon, in his *Bibliotheca of Chemical Philofophers;* and one of his capital arguments, is the hieroglyphics in the church-yard of the Holy Innocents. Borel, in his *Treafure of Gallic Antiquities,* with-

REMARKABLE EVENTS under CHARLES VI.

The battle of Rosebecq, in which the Flemings were overcome by the French under the command of the duke of Burgundy. The king being present at this action, defeated 40000 Flemings; and their leader Arteville was slain: this man's Christian name was Philip; he was son of James, who had been murdered at Ghent. The duke of Burgundy, being heir, in right of his wife, to the count of Flanders, against whom the Flemings were armed, had a personal interest in this war: he carried the king with him, who, as lord paramount of the county of Flanders, was obliged to protect his vassal.

1383.

The king returns to Paris, which city had broke out into an insurrection in his absence: he punished the principal rebels, who were called *Maillotins* *. A year's truce betwixt the French and English; who resume their arms on account of the schism, the former holding with pope Clement, and the latter with Urban.

I find a very extraordinary fact in the letters patent of the 20th of June, in the 123d roll of the treasure of charters, piece 2. The king, being willing to reinstate John Mauclerc, an inhabitant of Senlis, whose hand had been cut off for striking a Fleming, named John le Brun, permits him to make another hand in its stead, of whatever stuff or matter he pleases.

1384.

The death of Lewis III. count of Flanders. Philip the Hardy, duke of Burgundy, who, in the year 1369, had married that prince's only daughter, the widow of Philip de Rouvre, by whom she had no issue, succeeds him in the counties of Flanders, Artois, Rethel, Nevers, &c.

1385.

The war continues between the duke of Burgundy and the Flemings.

An ordinance published in parliament, by which the bishops are left at liberty to dispose of their patrimonial, and acquired estates.

* From their having armed themselves with mallets.

1386.

The Third Race. 275

MINISTERS.	MAGISTRATES.	EMINENT and LEARNED MEN.
Secretaries of the finances. with the duke of Britany. John de Montaigu, bishop of Chartres, and afterwards archbishop of Sens. J. de Montreuil, provost of St. Peter de l'Isle, employed in different embassies, assassinated at Paris by the Burgundians. 1418. Gontier Col, deputed in the year 1395 to treat with pope Benedict, about settling the peace of the church. John de Behisac, a creature of the duke of Berry, burnt at Toulouse for his acts of oppression. John Hue. William d'Aunoy. William de la Fons. Stephen la Charité. William Barau. Jaudé des Bordes. Lawrence Callot. George d'Ostende. J. Seguirat.	Boschet, the second president, opposed it; upon which the chancellor left them to their liberty of proceeding to an election, which fell upon the person nominated by the king. Henry de Marle. 1418. Robert Mauger. 1418. Philip de Morvilliers. 1438. *Attorneys general.* William de St. Hermant, or St. Germain. 1384. J. Ancher, admitted in 1384. G. de Villaminou, practised in 1397. Peter le Cerf. 1409. Denis de Maurroy. 1412. John Aguenin. 1429. William le Tur, living in 1427. Gautier Jaye, deprived of this place in 1421. William Barthelemy, living in 1435. *King's advocates.* John Desmarés, beheaded in 1382. J. Canart, living in 1387. John de Cessieres, practised in 1389. Oudard Bethune. Peter le Fevre. 1411. John le Cocq, practised in 1393. John de Popincourt. 1403. Clement de Reilhac, practised in 1398. John Perrier. 1413. John Jouvenel, or Juvenal des Ursins, provost of the merchants, ce-	without pointing out the source of Flamel's fortune, only pretends to prove, that it was not owing to the Jews. "As for his great " riches, it is beyond " all doubt he had " them not from the " Jews, nor from the " English, nor from " the hospitals, nor " from the Templars; " for he never managed the estates of " any of those people: " nay, the contrary " appears from the " anachronisms committed by those, " who bring this " charge against him; " for he was not living at the time " when the Jews, or " the others above" mentioned, resided " in France; and so " far from having enriched himself by " the hospitals, he " left them his whole " fortune." John Froissart, towards 1400. John Huss. 1415. John de Montreuil. 1418. Nicholas Oresme. 1382. John Petit, towards 1413. Christina de Pisan, living in 1411. Jerome of Prague. 1416. St. Vincent of Ferrier. 1419. John Wicleff. 1384. Wicleff's doctrine was much the same as that of the Protestants, who appeared a hundred years after. John Huss, though not so guilty as Wicleff, adopted

T 2

REMARKABLE EVENTS under CHARLES VI.

1386.

An expedition againſt England, diſappointed by the jealouſy of the duke of Berry, who joined the army too late in the ſeaſon. An arret of parliament, ordering battle between Carrouge and le Gris. Carrouge's wife accuſed le Gris of an attempt to raviſh her; le Gris denied the fact: upon the complaint of Carrouge, the parliament commanded pledges of battle, and the affair to be tried by ſingle combat. Le Gris was killed, and afterwards proved to be innocent, by the teſtimony of the very accuſer, who declared it at her death.

1387. 88.

Charles the Bad, king of Navarre, and ſon-in-law to king John, dies by a very odd accident *: this deteſtable prince had poiſoned king Charles V, and attempted to poiſon Charles VI. He is ſucceeded by his ſon Charles. The duke of Britany ſeizes the conſtable de Cliſſon, and, notwithſtanding the ſtrong inſtances of the king of France, refuſes to ſet him at liberty, till he had extorted a ranſom from him, and obliged him to deliver up four or five fortreſſes in his territory.

The beginning of the diſpute between the Dominicans and Franciſcans, about the immaculate conception, which was attacked by the former. The council of Baſil decided in the 30th ſeſſion, that the opinion of the immaculate conception ought to be approved and embraced by all Catholics. The council of Trent has not paſſed judgment on this matter. Paul V, in the year 1617, forbid any one to ſtand up againſt this opinion, which was confirmed by Gregory XV, and by Alexander VII.

The king, by his declaration of the 15th of February, 1388, *for his honour, and for the advantage of himſelf and his people*, reduces the places in his court of parliament, and in thoſe of the inqueſts and requeſts; and moreover ordains, that, when a place becomes vacant, the parliament ſhall elect *the moſt capable to fill it up*.

---

* Having wrapped himſelf up in ſheets ſteep'd in brandy and ſulphur, in order to revive his natural heat, which had been greatly weakened by his debauchery; or, as ſome ſay, to relieve him under the leproſy; the fire laid hold of the ſheets, and burnt him to ſuch a degree, that he died three days after in exquiſite miſery on the 1ſt of January, 1387.

MAGISTRATES.	EMINENT and LEARNED MEN.
celebrated for his courage during the troubles of Paris; this city made him a present of the hotel *des Ursins*, whose name and arms he adopted. He was chancellor to the first dauphin, and father of the chancellor of France, and of the archbishop of Reims. 1431. William le Tur, living in 1427. Andrew Cottin, living in 1418. Peter de Marigny, living in 1420. Nicholas Rauolin, deputy in 1420.	adopted several of his principles, equally rash and injurious to religion and to the holy see. He came to the council, where his obstinacy in refusing to make a recantation, was the cause of his being condemned to the flames, notwithstanding the emperor's safe conduct. Jerome of Prague, his disciple, but greatly his superior in wit and eloquence, underwent the same punishment. These executions were the cause of those bloody wars, which the Hussites stirred up in Bohemia.

REMARKABLE EVENTS under CHARLES VI.

1389.

Lewis, duke of Orleans, brother of Charles VI, marries Valentina of Milan.

Isabella of Bavaria makes a magnificent entry into Paris. The king, upon a tour through his kingdom, pays a visit at Avignon to pope Clement VII, by whom Lewis, duke of Anjou, is crowned king of Naples.

The order of the *girdle of hope*, founded by the king at Toulouse.

1390.

An expedition of some Christian princes, to whom the Genoese had applied for succour against the corsairs of Tunis.

1391. 92. 93.

The ordinance of the month of January, 1392, regulating the tutelage of the children of France, in case the king should die before his eldest son comes to age: another ordinance of the same month, concerning the regency. Peter Craon, after squandering away the money with which he had been trusted for Lewis, duke of Anjou and king of Naples, incurred the displeasure of the duke of Orleans; attributing this disgrace to the constable de Clisson, he made an attempt on that officer's life (in 1393), but the constable recovered. John V, duke of Britany, protects the assassin. Upon the duke's refusing to give him up, Charles VI. undertakes an expedition into Britany. The king, who had already shewn some symptoms of madness, was seized with a sudden phrenzy upon his march. This indisposition was increased by an accident at a masquerade*. Yet, during the remainder of his days, he had lucid intervals. The dukes of Burgundy and Berry take upon them the administration, from which they exclude the duke of Orleans. The Jews are

---

* The king appeared at this masquerade in the disguise of a satyr, dragging four other satyrs in chains. They were all dressed in linen dawbed over with rosin, to which they had fastened some coarse flax and hemp. The duke of Orleans had the misfortune of running his torch against one of those habits, which took fire in an instant. The four lords were burnt, and with difficulty was the king's life preserved by the presence of mind of his sister-in-law, the dutchess of Berry, who wrapped him in her mantua.

expelled,

REMARKABLE EVENTS under CHARLES VI.

expelled, and ftripped of their property; a fcandalous but common fhift after a bad adminiftration.

Margaret of Waldemar, ftiled the *Semiramis of the North*, queen of Denmark in right of her father, and of Norway by Hacquin her hufband, affumed the government of both thofe kingdoms upon the death of Claus her fon: the fuccefsful war, which fhe had carried on againft Albert king of Sweden, made her alfo miftrefs of that crown; and, at an affembly of the ftates general of thofe countries, held at Calmar in 1393, fhe was declared fovereign of the three kingdoms.

1394. 95. 96.

Upon the marriage of Ifabella of France to Richard II. king of England, a truce is concluded between the two crowns for twenty years: one of the principal conditions was the redemption of Cherburg and Breft. The Englifh never forgave their king for this tranfaction. The fchifm continues. Sigifmund, king of Hungary, in right of Mary his wife, of the houfe of Anjou, and fon of the emperor Charles IV, (afterwards emperor himfelf) is defeated before Nicopolis, to which town he had laid fiege: Bajazet I. attacks him, and cuts his army in pieces; the count de Nevers, Enguerrand de Coucy, the laft of his branch, the count d'Eu, the marfhal de Boucicant, &c. are taken prifoners, after giving moft fignal marks of valour; but Tamerlane foon revenged their caufe: every body knows in what manner this prince treated Bajazet after his victory in Galatia, near Angoura*, in 1402.

1397. 98. 99. 1400.

The beginning of the contefts between the houfes of Burgundy and Orleans, about the adminiftration. Some monks and priefts, having falfely charged the duke of Orleans with bewitching his brother king Charles VI, are condemned to death; but permitted to confefs their fins to a clergyman before the time of execution: on this occafion was publifhed a declaration, allowing confeffors to criminals under fentence of death, contrary to the practice eftablifhed in France: the lord of Craon procures this declaration. (*Coll. of ordinances.*) A revolution in England:

---
* or Ancyra.

REMARKABLE EVENTS under CHARLES VI.

Richard II. is depofed; and his coufin-german, the duke of Lancafter, being proclaimed king by the name of Henry IV. caufes him to be put to death [*]. Archambault de Grailly, *captal* of Buch, having married Ifabella, fifter to the count de Foix, fucceeds to that county upon the death of his brother-in-law, by an arret of parliament; and is the founder of the fecond houfe of Foix, more illuftrious than the former, for it afcended the throne of Navarre. An affembly held in France in 1398, wherein it is refolved, that the induction to elective benefices fhall be made by election; that of the others by the collation of the ordinary; and as to thofe which were held by the adherents of the pretenders to the papacy, the ordinaries fhall difpofe of them in *commendam*. The ordinance of the 7th of January, (1400) declaring, " that " the prefidents and counfellors of the parliament fhall be elected " in court, in the prefence of the chancellor; that chiefly perfons " of noble families fhall be chofen, and from different parts of " the kingdom, becaufe of the difference of cuftoms." Upon the deceafe of John, duke of Britany, (1399) his three children were detained in France; *(du Tillet)* and his widow was married again to the king of England.

1401. 2. 3.

The republic of Genoa, having furrendered herfelf to Charles VI, defires to have Boucicaut for her governor, after the king had been obliged to recall the count de St. Paul, (of the houfe of Luxemburg) who was difagreeable to the Genoefe, by being too agreeable to their wives. The marfhal took upon him that government; but the natural inconftancy of the people, or, according to fome, the feverity with which he behaved on feveral occafions, was productive of a revolution, (1409) which placed the marquis of Montferrat at the head of the republic, and obliged Boucicaut to return to France.

---

[*] He was confined in Pontefract caftle in Yorkfhire. Henry fent eight men, headed by Sir Pyers Exton. Richard, refolving to fell his life dearly, wrung a pole-ax out of one of their hands, and flew four of them. But, happening at length to come near Sir Pyers, who was got upon a chair, the villain difcharged fuch a blow on his head, as put an end to his life, at thirty-three years of age, of which he had reigned twenty-two. This is the moft received account; but fome affirm he was ftarved to death.

REMARKABLE EVENTS under CHARLES. VI.

The duke of Orleans assumes the direction of the kingdom, in prejudice to the duke of Burgundy, who soon recovers the superiority. The church of France, which had withdrawn itself from Benedict XIII. till the schism was ended, is induced to renew her obedience to that pontif, by the interposition of the duke of Orleans. The ordinance of the month of April, 1403, declaring, *that, upon the king's accession to the throne, in whatever year of his minority, he shall be considered as king; and that the realm shall be governed by him, and, in his name, by the nearest in blood, and by the wisest of his council.*

A regulation of the month of December, 1402, by which the members of the confraternity of the Passion, settled in Paris, are permitted to exhibit a representation of theatrical pieces, known by the name of mysteries.

1404. 5. 6.

Philip the Hardy, duke of Burgundy, dies at Hall in Brabant: he is succeeded by his son John, stiled the *Fearless*, who seizes the regency of the kingdom, as his late father had done, excludes the queen and the duke of Orleans, and obliges them to retire from Paris. The abovementioned Philip, was the first duke of Burgundy, of the second house of that name; and, as we have already observed, by his marriage in 1369 with Margaret countess of Flanders, he became count of Flanders, Artois, Franche-Comté, &c. To these possessions his son John added the counties of Hainault, Holland, and Zealand, by espousing Margaret of Bavaria. Notwithstanding the death of the contenders for the papacy, the schism still continues. The dukes of Orleans and Burgundy feign a reconciliation. The famous battle between seven Frenchmen and seven Englishmen: the French were led on by Barbasan and the chevalier de l'Escale; the English were beaten.

1407.

The duke of Orleans is assassinated at Paris in the *rue Barbette*, on the 23d of November, by order of the duke of Burgundy. It has been said, that this murder was partly occasioned by the duke of Burgundy's being jealous of his wife, for which this princess

princess lost her life: he afterwards married the daughter of Lewis III. duke of Bourbon. The duke of Orleans left three legitimate sons behind him; Charles, father of Lewis XII; Philip, count de Vertus; and John, count d'Angouleme, grandfather of Francis I; besides one illegitimate son, the count de Dunois, founder of the house of Longueville. The ordinance of the 26th of December, confirming that of 1403, in relation to the majority of the kings of France.

1408. 9.

The court, instead of revenging the murder of the duke of Orleans, accepted of the duke of Burgundy's justification, who, upon withdrawing to Flanders, commissioned Dr. John Petit to undertake his apology: but it is not so easy to justify, as to commit, murder, said Papinian to Caracalla. A reconciliation between the two families in the town of Chartres; but it was only feigned. Valentina of Milan, widow of the duke of Orleans, dies with grief, to find the murder of her consort unpunished. Both the husband and wife had the good fortune of pleasing the king and queen. Between Valentina and Charles VI. there passed nothing but friendship; whereas Isabella of Bavaria was suspected of carrying her familiarity with the duke to a greater length. The council of Pisa, in which Gregory XII. and Benedict XIII. were deposed, and Alexander V. was proclaimed pope: but this council, not being generally acknowledged, was productive of one antipope the more, and the schism did not end till the time of the council of Constance.

1410. 11. 12. 13. 14.

The duke of Burgundy is possessed of the administration. The faction of the Burgundians and the Orleanois, called *Armagnacs*: the latter name was owing to the count d'Armagnac, who had joined his son-in-law the duke of Orleans. A peace is concluded between the two parties at the castle of Bicetre, near Paris. The troubles break out anew. The count de St. Paul, being appointed governor of Paris, with a view of expelling those who were not of the Burgundian party, endeavours to ingratiate himself with the populace: for this purpose he chose a number of butchers, and made them captains of a body of five

hundred

REMARKABLE EVENTS under CHARLES VI.

hundred desperate fellows, who were stiled *Cabochiens*, from Caboche, one of their chiefs, and committed all manner of violences. The duke of Orleans calls in the English; and the king marches against him by the advice of the duke of Burgundy. The peace of Auxerre. The disturbances are revived; the Parisians, inflamed by the duke of Burgundy, keep Lewis the dauphin (who was a friend of the duke of Orleans, and wanted to retire from Paris) confined to the Hotel de St. Paul. The king this once joins the duke of Orleans, and makes war against the Burgundians.

In the year 1413, Charles VI, being desirous to prevent the too great number of secretaries of the finances, ordained, that no man should be in that office who had not been been first admitted a notary; which regulation seems to subsist to this day, since the secretaries of state are obliged to have the qualification of king's secretaries: and, in the year 1633, the body of the king's secretaries having summoned M. de Chavigny, secretary of state, in order to give him notice, that he should be prohibited from signing the ordinary letters patent, for not being of their body, it was determined by an arret of council, that he should qualify himself as king's secretary in the space of six months.

Henry IV, king of England, breathes his last in 1413, not without remorse for having dethroned his sovereign; he was desirous of instilling these sentiments into his son, who nevertheless assumed the crown.

1415. 16. 17. 18.

The king, having laid a new tax upon the whole kingdom, appoints commissioners to receive the monies raised in Languedoc: this province pleads her privilege, by which it had been customary to assemble the states, in order to obtain their consent to the subsidies. Notwithstanding this claim, the subsidies were paid by order of the king, who made the dauphin write to the magistrates, that *it was only for this time, and without any prejudice to their privileges.*

The

REMARKABLE EVENTS under CHARLES VI.

The battle of Agincourt, in which Henry V. * gained a complete victory over the French, under much the same circumstances as that of Crecy had been obtained in the reign of Philip of Valois, and that of Poitiers in the reign of king John. At this action the Oriflamme appeared the last time, if we believe Tillet, Sponde, Don Felibien, and father Simplician; yet, according to a manuscript chronology, Lewis XI. also took the Oriflamme in 1465. The number of the nobility slain on this day cannot be ascertained: at the head of them were six princes of the blood, and the constable d'Albret, general of the army; after his death, the count d'Armagnac had the constable's sword. Could one imagine, that this same Henry V, conqueror of a great part of France, was obliged every year to pawn his jewels and his crown, to enable him to take the field? *(Rymer.)*

Lewis, the first dauphin, departs this life the 18th of December, 1415. The death of John, the second dauphin, who was poisoned the 5th of April, 1416. He was connected in interest with the duke of Burgundy, who was his uncle by his wife Jacquelina, and had taken care of his education. Lewis II. of Anjou, king of Naples, of which he had now no more than the empty title, and father-in-law of the last dauphin (Charles VII.) was suspected of that prince's death. The duke of Burgundy enters into an alliance with Henry V. The English, having gained a naval victory off Harfleur, take that town, possess themselves of Normandy, and over-run all France. The fatal revolution, which placed a foreign prince on the throne of our kings, was now drawing near. Isabella of Bavaria, the wife of Charles VI, enters into a treaty with the duke of Burgundy, the enemy of her husband, and of her son Charles, the third dauphin,

---

* Henry V. laid claim to Normandy, Anjou, Maine, and Poitou, and tried to obtain those provinces by negotiation; but this not succeeding, he declared war against France. He landed an army at Havre de Grace in Normandy, the 21st of August, 1415, and besieged Harfleur, which he took, after an obstinate defence. His army being greatly diminished by diseases and fatigue, he marched through Caux, crossed the Somme, and proceeded towards Calais, till he came near the castle of Agincourt, from whence this battle takes its name. It was fought on the 25th of October. The English were about 22000, and the French four times that number. The English lost about 1700 men, with the duke of York, the king's uncle; of the French 2000 were slain in battle, and 14000 taken prisoners, among whom were the dukes of Orleans and Bourbon.

This

REMARKABLE EVENTS under CHARLES VI.

This woman, actuated by the passions of avarice, ambition, and lust, determines to be revenged of the king for ordering Boisbourbon, one of her gallants, to be drowned; and of the Armagnacs, and the dauphin, for making her refund the treasure, of which she had plundered the state: with this design she delivers up Tours and Paris to the enemy, and obliges the dauphin to retire to Poitiers, whither he removes the parliament, and assumes the title of Regent. From thence he used to make a tour, till his father's decease, into the several provinces, in order to preserve the small remains of his authority. In 1420 he paid a visit to Languedoc, and, being well pleased with the fidelity of the inhabitants of Toulouse, he granted to the *Capitouls* * the privilege of possessing seignories, without paying any duty or acknowledgment: this is properly the original of the privilege of noblesse, now enjoyed by the magistrates of Toulouse.

The emperor Sigismund, king of Hungary, desirous of putting an end to the schism, and to the quarrel between France and England, arrived at Paris the 1st of March, 1415: the king received him with all possible honours, of which the emperor made an ill use. He was conducted to the court of parliament in the *palais*, where they placed him in the royal seat; and, upon the hearing of a cause, in which one of the parties was reproached with not being a knight, the emperor conferred that honour of his own authority: when he came to Lyons, he wanted to erect the county of Savoy into a dukedom; " but the king's " council gave him to understand, that this was an act of sove- " reignty; and that the king neither would nor ought to ac- " knowledge any other superior than God; which Sigismund " perceiving, departed from Lyons in great anger, and, passing " through Montluel, erected Savoy into a dukedom in the " year 1416." Before he proceeded to Lyons, he had paid a visit to London, where he entered into engagements against France with Henry V. and John duke of Burgundy.

The duke of Burgundy returns to Paris, where Villiers de l'Isle Adam arrived a month before him, and had committed all manner

* The name given to the principal magistrates of that city.

of outrages. The duke of Berry, and Lewis II. king of Sicily, the dauphin's father-in-law, who had enjoyed so great a share in the administration, both deceased. The count d'Armagnac is assassinated.

The close of the council of Constance, which began in 1414: it extinguished the schism, and Martin V. was elected pope. This assembly condemned the errors of Wicleff, John Huss, and Jerome of Prague: it is also the æra of the reformation of ecclesiastic discipline, with regard to the collation of benefices.

1419.

Henry V. makes himself master of Rouen, after a six months siege: thus France is rent in pieces by three enemies, the king of England, the duke of Burgundy, and the dauphin.

Disturbances in Britany, excited by Margaret de Clisson, the wife of John de Blois, count de Penthievre: knowing that her children might have been sovereigns of that country, she persuades her eldest son to seize the duke of Britany in a most perfidious manner, and to keep him prisoner. The Bretons fly to his assistance, and secure the countess de Penthievre, who is extremely fortunate to obtain her liberty in exchange for that of the duke. So extraordinary an adventure hinders the duke of Britany from interposing, as he had done before, between the dauphin his brother-in-law (who besides was suspected of favouring the Penthievres) and the duke of Burgundy. This prince, seeing Henry V. too powerful, listens to the proposals of accommodation made to him by the dauphin, who, on the other hand, was sensible of his inability to withstand the English by himself: they have an interview on the bridge of Montereau, where John the *Fearless* is murdered. Isabella enters into a treaty against the dauphin with Philip the Good, successor of John the Fearless; and concludes a truce with England, which was followed by a peace that proved fatal to France. This princess had established a supreme court of justice at Amiens, to serve instead of the parliament. The letters patent and mandates were issued out in the queen's name in this form: *Isabella, by the grace of God, queen of France, having the administration and government of the kingdom during the indisposition*

REMARRKABLE EVENTS under CHARLES VI.

indispofition of the king. All public employments at that time were double in France, the parliament, the great officers, &c.

René, duke of Lorrain, reannexes to Lorrain the dutchy of Bar, ceded to him by his uncle the cardinal of Bar.

1420.

The treaty of Troyes, signed the 21st of May, whereby it was stipulated, that Catharine of France should be espoused to Henry V; and, upon the demise of Charles VI, the crown should devolve to the king of England, who from that time assumed the title of regent and heir of the kingdom of France. This Catharine, after the decease of Henry V, was married to Owen Tudor, by whom she had Edmund earl of Richmond, father of Henry VII [*]. From the treaty of Troyes, till the decease of Charles VI, the chancellor de Clerc used to conclude the letters, issuing from the court of Chancery, with the following words; *By the king, and by the authority of the king of England, heir and regent in France.*

A bed of justice held the 23d of December, by judges sold to Henry V, where the persons concerned in the murder of John the *Fearless*, duke of Burgundy, are declared guilty of high-treason, and of course unworthy of any succession. In this arret, Charles VI, mentioning the king of England, stiles him his well-beloved *son and heir, and regent of the kingdom*; but, when he comes to speak of his own son, the only heir to the crown, he calls him, *Charles, who stiles himself dauphin*. We must also observe, in regard to the above declaration, that not one of the accomplices of the murder of John the Fearless is named in it; and, notwithstanding the awe inspired by the presence of the king of England, who without doubt was desirous that the dauphin should be declared guilty, no notice is taken of him in regard to the murder, except in ambiguous terms: and this is the more proper to remark, as none of our historians, who mention this arret, ever saw it, but are satisfied with transcribing Monstrelet, who, like an inconsiderate writer, imagined that the dauphin was summoned to the marble

---

[*] Edmund earl of Richmond married Margaret, daughter of John Beaufort, duke of Somerset, grandson of John of Gaunt, duke of Lancaster.

REMARKABLE EVENTS under CHARLES VI.

table, &c. and that, in default of appearance, he was outlawed, with all his accomplices, banished for ever, and declared incapable of succeeding to the crown; all which is absolutely contrary to truth. (*Rapin Thoyras, Rymer's Fœdera.*) The Benedictine fathers explain themselves in the same manner, (*The art of verifying dates.*) " This fact, though attested by Monstrelet, and by the gene-
" rality of historians, is not at all certain."

1421.

The battle of Beauge, where the marshal de la Fayette defeated the duke of Clarence, lieutenant general of Normandy, in the absence of his brother, Henry V. This success infuses fresh vigour into the dauphin. The earl of Douglas *, who brought seven thousand men over from Scotland, had a great share in this victory, and was made constable of France.

1422.

Henry V. dies at Vincennes the 31st of August, aged thirty-six †: he left the regency of France to his brother, the duke of Bedford; and that of England to his younger brother, the duke of Gloucester. Charles VI. followed him soon after; his death preserved France, as that of John Lackland had saved England. When we reflect on those calamitous days, we are surprized at the infatuation of the common people: at one time they abandon the fundamental laws of the state to the fury of a base queen, and to the imbecillity of a king, who had no will of his own; while at other times they violently oppose the most sage regulations, calculated to promote their happiness. They detest Anne of Austria; but repose a confidence in Isabella of Bavaria. They consent to become the subjects of a king of England; and yet they refuse to acknowledge Henry IV. They offer a reward for the head of cardinal Mazarin; but consider the coadjutor as their friend. The dead corpse of a minister, the great promoter of commerce and

---

* The Scotch were commanded by John Stuart, earl of Buchan, who killed the duke of Clarence with his own hand: he was made constable of France.

† Rapin says in the thirty-fourth year of his age; he expired on the 31st of August; some say he died of a dysentery, others of a fistula; but Peter Basset, his chamberlain, affirms he died of a pleurisy.

REMARKABLE EVENTS under CHARLES. VI.

he elegant arts, is in danger of being tore to pieces at his funeral; while a veneration is paid to the carcase of James Clement. Not but that there were men of sense at those different periods, who bewailed the public calamities; but as they are not the most numerous, so they are never the predominant party; neither are they so active and vigorous as those who break out into rebellion. Henry VI, son of Henry V, an infant only nine months old, was proclaimed king in both capitals; but was afterwards cast from both thrones; for Charles VII. recovered the crown of France, and Edward IV. stripped him of that of England. During this reign the parliament was rendered sedentary. Ever since Philip the Fair had made this a perpetual court, they met only twice a year, Easter and All-saints; and frequently but once a year: " nay, it sometimes happened, says Pasquier, that a whole twelvemonth passed without holding the court of parliament: each session lasted but two months; and, at every meeting, the king granted new letters patent in the form of a commission, with a list of those whom he desired to officiate; neither was it mentioned that the magistrate, appointed the preceding year, should sit the year following, unless he were included in the roll. In the reign of Charles VI, the parliament began to be held without discontinuance: now we have only a faint resemblance of that ancient practice, certain ceremonies being performed at Easter and All-saints, as if it were the opening of a parliament that had been discontinued."

Vol. I.   U   REMARK-

| 1422. Acceſſion to the crown. | REMARKABLE EVENTS. |

CHARLES VII. comes to the crown at the age of twenty. He was ſurnamed the Victorious, becauſe he reconquered almoſt his whole kingdom from the Engliſh. Yet this honour is diſputed with him, and attributed to the count de Dunois and to his other generals; in ſhort, there is no prince, in regard to whom hiſtorians are ſo little agreed. He was crowned at Poitiers in 1422, to which city he had removed the parliament; and he received the regal unction at Rheims from the archbiſhop of that city, Renaud de Chartres, on the 17th of July, 1429. He had enjoyed the title of count de Ponthieu.

1422.

THE Engliſh, commanded by the duke of Bedford, guardian of Henry VI. and regent of France, wage war againſt Charles VII, and are joined by Philip the Good, duke of Burgundy, who wanted to revenge the murder of his father.

1423.

The duke of Britany unites with the enemies of the ſtate. Charles is overpowered on all ſides. The battle of Crevant * in the neighbourhood of Auxerres, in which the Engliſh are victorious.

1424. 25.

The battle of Verneuil †, in which the king's army is defeated by the duke of Bedford; and the conſtable of France, John Stuart, earl of Douglas, is ſlain ‡. The beginning of the quarrel between the duke of Burgundy and the duke of Gloucester, in regard to Jacquelina of Bavaria, counteſs of Hainault and Holland, and widow to John the dauphin. This lady, refuſing to acknowledge the duke of Brabant for her huſband, was married afterwards to the duke of Gloucester: the match had been declared of no effect; but the death of the duke of Brabant rendering Jacquelina miſtreſs of her own perſon, ſhe did not think it beneath her to eſpouſe a private gentleman of Flanders.

---

* The Engliſh were commanded by the earls of Saliſbury and Suffolk: the earl of Buchan was defeated, and taken priſoner, but ſoon after exchanged. Crevant was a ſtrong place upon the Yonne, three leagues above Auxerre.

† A town in Perche.

‡ John Stuart, conſtable of France, was earl of Buchan, as hath been mentioned in a former note. Archibald, earl of Douglas, was this nobleman's ſon-in-law: he brought over an aid of five thouſand men to Charles VII, and was created duke of Touraine: he was ſlain in this battle.

The Third Race. 291

WIVES.	CHILDREN.	1461. DEATH.	Cotemporary PRINCES.
Mary of Anjou, daughter of Lewis II, king of Naples, betrothed in 1413, and married in 1416; she died in 1463; a princess of extraordinary merit, to whom her husband was in great measure indebted for the re-establishment of his affairs; and yet he did not meet with a suitable return.	LEWIS XI. James of France, died young. Philip of France, died young. Ch. of France, successively duke of Berry, Normandy, and Guienne. 1472. Radegonde of France, promised to Sigismund, duke of Austria. 1444. Catharine of France, wife of the count de Charolois. 1446. Joland of France, wife of Amadeus IX. duke of Savoy. 1478. Joan of France, married to John of Bourbon. 1482. Margaret of France, died young. Joan of France. 1446. Mary of France, died young. Magdalen of France, married to Gaston, count de Foix. 1486. *Natural children.* Charles VII. had by Agnes Sorel, who died in 1450. Charlotte, *married to James de Brezé, count de Maulevrier, and poniarded by her husband, upon being caught in the act of adultery.* Margaret, *married to Oliver de Coetivy.* Joan, *married to Antony de Bueil, count de Sancerre.*	CHARLES VII. *died at Mewn in Berry the 22d of July, aged fifty-eight years. He died through want of sustenance, for fear of being poisoned. He was interred at St. Denis.*	*Popes.* Martin V. 1431. Eugene IV. 1447. Nicholas V. 1455. Calixtus III. 1458. Pius II. 1464. *Emperors of the East.* John Paleologus. 1444. Constantine Paleologus. 1453. *Emperors of the West.* Sigismund. 1437. Albert of Austria. 1439. Frederic III. 1493. *Turkish emperors.* Amurath II. 1451. Mahomet II. 1481. *Kings of Spain.* John II. 1454. Henry IV. 1474. *Kings of Portugal.* John. 1433. Edward. 1438. Alfonsus V. 1481. *King of England.* Henry VI. dethroned 1461. *Kings of Scotland.* James I. 1437. James II. 1460. James III. 1488. *Kings of Denmark and Sweden.* Eric IX. abdicates. 1438. Christopher III. 1448. Charles Canutson. 1471. *Kings of Poland.* Ladislaus Jagelon. 1434. Ladislaus, king of Hungary. 1444. Casimir IV. 1492. *Czar of Muscovy.* John Basilowitz. 1505.

REMARKABLE EVENTS under CHARLES VII.

The duke of Burgundy having caused this gentleman to be arrested, Jacquelina ransomed him by resigning, in favour of Philip the Good, the provinces of Holland, Zealand, and Friseland; so that this prince acquired the sovereignty of almost all the seventeen provinces, and no notice was taken of the duke of Gloucester, who, notwithstanding the dissolution of his marriage, would fain have retained a part of his wife's portion. The king is obliged to sacrifice the president Louvet to the count de Richemont, brother of the duke of Britany, whom he creates constable of France: the president was accused of having been concerned in the murder of John duke of Burgundy, and in the conspiracy of the Penthievres. The duke of Britany is reconciled to the king, whose party still continues the weakest.

1426. 27.

The constable of Richemont, without any form of trial, causes the sieur de Giac, whom the president Louvet had substituted in his place, to be beheaded for embezzling the king's money. He likewise orders Camus de Beaulieu to be stabbed, and promotes the king's service against that prince's will, ridding him, indeed in a very audacious manner, of bad subjects, by whom he was surrounded. The public troubles still continue.

The count de Dunois (bastard of Orleans, afterwards duke de Longueville, and founder of that family, which expired with the abbé d'Orleans) distinguishes himself the first time before Montargis, and obliges the English to raise the siege of that place.

1428. 29.

A quarrel breaks out between the constable and the sieur de la Trimouille; the latter, unmindful that he owed his preferment to the former, promotes a misunderstanding between that officer and the king, and thereby throws a damp upon the French successes.

The English lay siege to Orleans. The battle of herrings (1429) in which the duke of Bourbon, attempting to intercept a convoy * on the road to the English camp before Orleans, was beaten. This siege lasted seven months; and the garrison offered to surrender, after the count de Dunois had done all that was

* It was a convoy of salt-fish, from whence the battle took its name.

The Third Race.   293

MINISTERS.	WARRIORS.	MAGISTRATES.	EMINENT and LEARNED MEN.
;eorge de la Trimouille. 1446. The prefient Louvet, fmiffed in 1425. he lord de Giac. 1426. mes Cœur. 1456. :cretaries of the finances. lain Chartier. obert de Thuery. Stephen Chelier, compoller of the ances, mar of the counts, and :afurer of ance, ambafdor to Italy d England, minated by gnes Sorel e of the exetors to her lf.	*Conftables.* Charles of Lorrain. 1430. James Stuart, earl of Douglas *. 1424. Arthur of Britany, count de Richemont. 1458. He was duke of Britany after his brother, and thought it an honour to retain the title of conftable. *Marfhals of France.* Amaury de Severac. 1427. Peter de Rieux. 1439. Cl. de Beauvoir. 1453. John de Villiers de l'Ifle Adam. 1437. James de Montberon. 1422. Antony de Vergy de Dampmartin. 1439. John de la Beaume. 1435. Gilbert de la Fayette. 1463. John de la Broffe. Giles de Laval, lord of Rets. 1440. Andrew de Laval, lord of Loheac. 1486. Ph. de Culant, lord of Jalagnes. 1453. * Earl of Buchan; fee note, p. 290.	*Chancellors.* Lewis of Luxemburg. 1443. T. Hoo, living in 1455. Thofe two chancellors were nominated by the king of England. Renaud de Chartres, card.nal and abp. of Rheims. 1443. William Juvenal des Urfins. 1472. *Firft prefidents.* P. de Morvilliers. 1438. Ad. de Cambray. 1456. Yves de Scepeaux. 1461. *Attorneys general.* P. Coufinot, living in 1444. John Simon, deputy in 1439. John Dauvet. 1471. *King's advocates.* J. Rapiout, preferred in 1421. John Rabateau, living in 1435. J. Jouvenel, or Juvenal des Urfins, brother of the chancellor, wrote the Hiftory of Charles VI. He was abp of Rheims 1473. J. Morand, admitted in 1433. John Barbin, practifed in 1451. James Jouvenel. 1456. J. Simon, practifed in 1442. J. Lullier. 1468. J. Rapiout, practifed in 1444. N. Thieffart, practifed in 1442. Henry Boileau. 1451. P. Simon, practifed in 1445. Nic. Jocy, practifed in 1415. John Dauvet. 1471. John Simon. 147 . N. Calepeau, practifed in 1464.	Peter d'Ailly. 1426. Leonard Aretin. 1444. Bureau Boucher, deputy keeper of the feals, living in 1451. Alain Chartier, towards 1458. Nicholas de Clemangis. 1440. Ferdinand of Corduba. John Gerfon. 1429. J. Fr. Poggio. 1459. Alphenfus Toftatus. 1454. Laurentius Valla. 1457.

U 3

possible towards defending the town. A misunderstanding * between the English and Burgundian generals prevented the surrender of the place. Joan d'Arc, stiled the *pucelle* or *maid of Orleans*, a native of the village of Domremy, in the neighbourhood of Vaucouleurs †, repairs to Charles VII. at Chinon, and informs his majesty, that she had received a commission from heaven to deliver his city of Orleans, and to see him crowned at Rheims: these were the only two points of her mission. Du Bellay Langey was the first who attempted to call in question the miraculous part of the history of the maid of Orleans; and he has had many followers. Le Clerc relates this event in such a manner, as needs neither fraud nor miracle to explain it. A young woman waits on the king, imagining herself to be inspired: her enthusiasm animates the troops; the generals take advantage of this impression; and, without engaging in any rash measure, at the very time she acts under their direction, they appear to be led by her example; she has no command, and yet every thing seems to be conducted by her order: the intrepidity of this amazon, being artfully encouraged, diffuses itself through the whole army, and produces an entire change in the face of affairs. (*Bibl. anc. & moderne.*) She begins with throwing herself into Orleans, and obliges the English to raise the siege on the 8th of May. The affairs of Charles VII. begin to wear a better aspect. The earl of Richemont defeats the English at the battle of Patay, where the famous general Talbot was taken prisoner. Lewis III, king of Sicily, celebrated for his courage, and for his patience under the frowns of fortune, came and joined the king his brother-in-law. Auxerre, Troyes, Chalons, Soissons, Compiegne, &c. surrender to the king; and Rheims opening her gates, he is crowned in that city the 17th of July.

1430.

The maid of Orleans applies for leave to retire, but is prevailed on to continue in the king's service: having thrown herself into Compiegne, at that time besieged by the English, she is

---

* The garrison offered to surrender to the duke of Burgundy, which the English generals rejected.
† In Lorrain.

REMARKABLE EVENTS under CHARLES VII.

made prisoner in a sally. Philip the Good marries Elizabeth of Portugal, his third wife, at Bruges, and institutes the order of the Golden Fleece.

1431.

Joan d'Arc is carried to Rouen, where she is tried, and burnt the 30th of May, in the old market, as a sorceress. *(See the abbé Langlet's history of the maid of Orleans.)*

René d'Anjou, brother of Lewis III. king of Sicily, and husband to Isabella, the daughter of Charles II. duke of Lorrain, attempts to succeed his father-in-law. Antony de Vaudemont, Charles's brother, disputes the succession, on account of its being a masculine fief, and defeats René at the battle of Bullegneville. Arnaud de Barbazan, who commanded the troops which the king sent to the assistance of his brother-in-law, died of the wounds he received in this engagement. René being made prisoner by the duke of Burgundy, an ally of Antony de Vaudemont, was confined by this prince till the year 1437, when he obtained his liberty; and Vaudemont marrying his daughter, acknowledged him as duke of Lorrain.

Henry VI, to animate his adherents in France, comes over from England, and is crowned in the church of Notre Dame at Paris on the 17th of December. The constable causes la Trimouille to be arrested in the castle of Chinon, though Charles VII. was there at the same time; the king was so tired of that minister; as not to punish this insult to his authority.

The council of Basil convoked by Martin V. The university of Poitiers founded.

1432. 33. 34.

During the space of four years the war continues without any remarkable event. In the council of Basil it is regulated, that the ambassadors of Castile shall take place next to those of the *most serene* king of France. It was also settled, that the ambassadors of the duke of Burgundy, with whom the electors of Germany disputed the precedency, should be seated in the very same place which was due to the abovementioned duke of Burgundy, as the first duke in Christendom, and next to crowned heads.

REMARKABLE EVENTS under CHARLES VII.

1435.

Philip the Good is drawn off from the English, and a peace * is concluded at Arras on the 22d of September, in one of the most august assemblies that had been seen a long time; all the princes in Europe had their ambassadors in that town, the pope and the council of Basil had also their legates: the conditions of this treaty were dictated by Philip the Good, and Charles VII. thought himself happy in obtaining them at any rate. The treaty of Arras was confirmed by the council of Basil. We may observe, on this occasion, that Philip the Good, after requiring the guaranty of the princes and great lords of the blood, demanded further, that those lords should bind themselves to espouse his cause, if ever the king violated his word. The death of the duke of Bedford, which made a considerable change in the affairs of Henry VI; he was succeeded in the regency by Richard duke of York.

1436. 37.

Paris surrenders to the constable on Low-sunday. The dauphin marries Margaret of Scotland; the same who, happening to find Alain Chartier asleep, the most learned and the most deformed man of his time, gave him a kiss †. The parliament returns to Paris in 1437, and the war continues between the English and the Burgundians.

1438.

The council of Basil, being continued under Eugene IV, confirms the decree of that of Constance, in regard to the superiority of a general council. The pragmatic sanction is settled at Bourges: it consists of various decrees of the council of Basil, in which the elections are established, but reserves, expectatives, and annates, are abolished. Charles VII. favoured the pragmatic sanction so much the more, as it was partly the work of a council which he had taken under his protection, seeing the fathers at

---

* This was a separate peace between Charles VII. and the duke of Burgundy, who was at the congress in person. King Charles's ambassadors offered to the king of England, Normandy and Guienne, the usual homage reserved, which the English ministers rejected, and withdrew.

† Observing the people about her to stand in amaze, she said, *it was not the man she had kissed, but the mouth that had uttered such fine discourses.*

Basil

REMARKABLE EVENTS under CHARLES VII.

Basil had espoused his cause, and constantly refused to acknowledge the treaty of Troyes, by which he had been disinherited. It is to be observed that, in 1441, the king issued a declaration relative to the pragmatic sanction, mentioning it to have been his intention, as well as that of the assembly at Bourges, that the agreement between Eugene IV. and his ambassadors, should take effect from the date of the pragmatic sanction, without any regard to the date of the decree passed before at Basil; and hence it was concluded, that the decrees of general councils, in matters concerning discipline, are of no force in France, till they have been confirmed by the edicts of our kings. The pope, dissatisfied with the council, removes it to Ferrara, and from thence to Florence; yet many of the prelates continued at Basil.

1439.

The council of Basil deposes pope Eugene IV, and chuses Amadeus, duke of Savoy, who was retired to the solitude of Ripaille, after resigning the dukedom to his son. It is said that this prince would not have abdicated, after the loss of his wife, had not he given credit to fortune-tellers, that he should one day attain the papal dignity. This antipope took the name of Felix V, and the schism lasted till the death of Eugene IV. At the accession of Nicholas V, the church recovered her tranquility by the abdication of Felix V. In consequence of this step, Felix, who died in 1450, obtained of Nicholas V. a bull or indult, whereby that pope engages not to nominate to any consistorial benefice throughout his dominions, without the consent of the duke his son. This bull, having been confirmed by several pontifs, and extended to all that prince's descendants, has occasioned great disputes between the court of Rome and the dukes of Savoy. The council of Basil concluded in 1443; *(Lenfant)* and that of Florence, which completed the union of the Greek and Latin churches, determined in 1442. Æneas Sylvius Piccolomini, who had been secretary to the council of Basil, disavowed its maxims when raised to the pontificate by the name of Pius II. At Rome, and in the countries directed by the principles of that court, they pretend that the council of Basil was not a legitimate assembly any longer than the twenty-sixth session;

session; some extend it to the translation of that council to Florence, and others to the deposition of Eugene.

1440.

The dauphin is inveigled by the dukes of Alençon and Bourbon to join the malecontents in a rebellion against his father, and forms a party, called the *Praguerie:* his father pursues, disarms, and forgives him. These were not the last vexations this king suffered from that quarter; which made him say, that he had been very ill used both by his father and by his son. The duke of Orleans, who had been a prisoner in England ever since the battle of Agincourt, obtains his liberty, and is reconciled to the duke of Burgundy, who contributes towards his ransom.

1441. 42.

The siege of Pontoise: the king recovers this place from the English, and acquires great glory: from thence he marches into Poitou, and scours the countries of Angoumois, Limousin, and Gascony; but the English continue to obtain some advantage in those provinces. An ordinance regulating the purchase of annuities at the rate of twelve per cent.; it was afterwards reduced by Henry IV. to six and two thirds per cent. to five and a ninth per cent. by the edict of 1634, and at length to five per cent. as it now stands, by the edict of 1667.

The king possesses himself of the county of Comminge. The dauphin obliges the gallant Talbot * to raise the siege of Dieppe. A truce of eighteen months begun in 1444, and continued till 1448, when the war broke out again.

René d'Anjou, stiled *René the Good,* who had laid aside all notion of conquering the kingdom of Naples, and was restored to his dukedom of Lorrain, (see the year 1431) engages the king to lay siege to Metz, which pretended to be independent of the dukes of Lorrain, in virtue of a privilege enjoyed by that place since the time of Godfrey of Bullion: the event was, that the city of Metz remained possessed of her rights and pretensions, upon paying two hundred thousand crowns to the king for the

---

* Talbot was now Earl of Shrewsbury: his patent of creation bears date March 20, 1442.

expences

REMARKABLE EVENTS under CHARLES VII.

expences of the siege, and giving a discharge to René for a hundred thousand florins, which she had lent to that prince.

The king had been induced to lay siege to that town, with a view of employing his troops during the truce with the English. The like motive determined him to succour Sigismund, duke of Austria, in the war against the Swiss, who were defeated within half a league of Basil: but, as Æneas Sylvius observes, this defeat was owing to the smallness of their numbers; for they had been quite exhausted in repelling the enemy: the bravery with which they behaved on this occasion made the dauphin (Lewis XI.) say, that he should avoid going to war with that nation; and accordingly he concluded a treaty of peace with them in 1444.

1445. 46.

Margaret of Scotland dies of grief, for the scandalous suspicions that had been raised against her virtue. *(Duclos.)* But the dauphin's tears were a sufficient proof of her innocence.

The *taille* became perpetual: according to several authors, the people began to pay this tax in the reign of St. Lewis, in order to be exempt from quartering the troops; but it had not been always continued: it was substituted in the room of the king's profits in altering the coin. The institution of regular troops of *gens d'armes*, or a reduction of the gendarmery to fifteen troops, each of which consisted of a hundred men at arms; every trooper was obliged to serve with six horses, which made the cavalry nine thousand. The like regulation for the infantry, under the title of *franc-archers*, or free archers, so called from their being free of all subsidies or taxes; one part of them fought on foot, and the other served as light horse. The counties of Valentinois and Diois, purchased by Charles VI, in 1404, of Lewis de Poitiers, and united to Dauphiné by a late treaty between Lewis of Savoy, who had some pretensions to that country, and Charles VII. The dauphin gives fresh uneasiness, in 1446, to the king his father, who resigns himself entirely to his passion for Agnes Sorel. This lady had great elevation of mind, and was particularly desirous of promoting the king's glory: Monstrelet pretends, that his majesty's affection for her did not exceed the bounds of virtue; which might pass very well, if she had not had three children by him:

REMARKABLE EVENTS under CHARLES VII.

him: but we may conclude, that she must have behaved herself extremely well at court, since she was in so great respect and esteem. Hence her memory was celebrated by the French poets, long after her decease, and even by Francis I; for St. Gelais has given us a stanza of that prince to her honour: it was said that she died by poison, (which is not true) and that James le Cœur had been the instrument of her death; Agnes gave no credit to it, since she made him one of her executors. She was stiled *madame de Beauté*, (a name she richly deserved) from a castle in the neighbourhood of Vincennes, of which the king had made her a present: she was soon succeeded by madam de Villequiers, her cousin-german, who, after the king's decease, resigned her person to Francis II, duke of Britany, by whom she had four children.

On the 17th of April, Palm-sunday, the dykes of Dordrecht were broke down by an inundation, which swept away above a hundred thousand persons, with a prodigious number of cattle.

1447.

Genoa surrenders herself to France, but it was only for a short time, till Fregosa could get rid of his rival; and then this inconstant republic, which, according as she was swayed by different factions, had chosen almost all the princes of Italy for her masters, refuses to admit of the French troops; yet we kept possession of Final, which had been surrendered to king Charles as a cautionary town.

The government of the viscounts of Milan ended in duke Philip Mary. He was the grandson of Isabella, daughter of king John, and of Galeas Visconti, who had made himself lord of Milan; and he was son of John Visconti, on whom the emperor had conferred the title of duke. This John was the terror of Rome, of the empire, and of all Italy, most of whose seignories he had usurped: upon his decease in 1403, there was a general revolt; and his son Philip Mary preserved but a small part of his dominions. Philip dying without legitimate issue, several princes pretended to the succession, and, among the rest, the duke of Orleans, in right of Valentina his mother, sister to Philip Mary; but, after a contest of some years, Francis Sforza, the bastard

of

REMARKABLE EVENTS under CHARLES VII.

of James Sforza, and a foldier of fortune, who had efpoufed Philip's natural daughter, poffeffes himfelf of that dukedom.

By the concordate between Nicholas V. and Frederic III, confirming the agreement between Calixtus II. and Henry V, the clergy of Germany enjoy the right of electing their bifhops.

1448. 49. 50.

The Englifh break the truce; and providence is pleafed to put an end to the calamities of France.

Charles VII, either by himfelf or by his generals, gradually recovers all the ftrong places in Normandy; fo that this province, which had belonged to England in 1066, in right of William the Conqueror; which had afterwards been reannexed to France in 1203, in the reign of John Lackland; which had been taken again from us by Henry V. in 1418, in the reign of Charles VI, was at length reunited for ever to the crown of France by Charles VII. in 1450. This revolution was completed by the battle of Fourmigny*, in which the Englifh were defeated.

Peter II. does liege homage to the king for *the dukedom of Britany, the peerage of France, and the county of Montfort.*

1451. 52. 53.

The counts de Dunois, de Penthievre, de Fois, and d'Armagnac, Charles's generals, retake Guienne and Bourdeaux. This city revolts anew, but is recovered by the king, notwithftanding the gallant refiftance of general Talbot †, who was defeated and flain at the battle of Caftillon: the king caufed the caftles of *Trompette* and *Ha* to be erected there; thus the Englifh were driven out of France, except the town of Calais, which had been taken by Edward III. in 1347, and was recovered by the duke de Guife in 1558.

---

* The French were commanded by the conftable Richemont, the Englifh by Sir Thomas Kiriel, who was taken prifoner, with the lofs of about 5000 men.

† He was then earl of Shrewfbury: on the 17th of July, contrary to his own opinion, and merely to oblige the people of Bourdeaux, this illuftrious commander attacked the French army before Caftillon, in their entrenchments: though at firft he was fuccefsful, yet, his horfe being killed by a cannon-fhot, and himfelf immediately after by a wound in the throat, his forces were defeated.

REMARKABLE EVENTS under CHARLES VII.

The reunion of the ancient lay peerages to the crown: thefe peerages, be their origin what it will, exifted at the time of Hugh Capet, *(fee the year* 992); they appeared in all their fplendor under the reign of Philip Auguftus; and fucceffively reverted to the royal demefne, from which they had been difmembered. The ancient peerages, which became extinct at length in the reign of Charles VII, were Normandy, reconquered by Philip Auguftus, and reannexed to the crown by Charles VII; the county of Touloufe alfo reannexed under St. Lewis; Champagne under Philip the Fair; Guienne, confifcated by Lewis the Young, and reunited under Charles VII. (I omit the dutchy of Burgundy, which, after the reign of king Robert, belonged to the houfe of France; as likewife the county and peerage of Flanders, reunited, upon the death of Lewis III, to the fecond houfe of Burgundy, by the marriage of Philip the Hardy to the heirefs of Flanders in 1369.) And this is, in fome meafure, the firft age of the peerage, which may be confidered under four different periods: the firft, that we have been mentioning: the fecond was not of the fame nature; our kings, in order to preferve fo great a dignity, (which, though productive of independency, had long adorned and fometimes fupported the crown) created new peerages upon the plan of the ancient; but with this effential difference, of being conferred by letters patent, which were granted only to princes of the blood; John, duke of Britany, was the firft invefted with this dignity in the year 1297, at a time when there were ftill fome of the ancient peerages exifting. The third age of the peerage was, when it came to be confered by our kings on foreign princes; the duke de Nevers was the firft who enjoyed this honour, by the erection of the county of Nevers into a dukedom and peerage in 1505. The fourth and laftage, which fubfifts to this day, was when our kings erected the eftates of the principal lords of their court into a dutchy and peerage; of thefe the firft was the baron de Montmorency, who, by the erection of that barony into a dutchy and peerage in the year 1551, attained this high dignity, which afterwards became fo common. But we are to obferve, according to what is mentioned in a manufcript belonging to the king's library, and quoted by father

Simplician,

REMARRKABLE EVENTS under CHARLES VII.

Simplician, *that the king's peers are not so called, from their being peers in regard to him (that is his equals) but in respect to one another.*

The taking of Constantinople by Mahomet II, (1453) put an end to the Eastern empire, which had lasted eleven hundred and eighty-three years. Such is the revolution of states. The empire of Rome was changed into that of Constantinople, which became afterwards divided into the Eastern and Western empires: to the empire of the East succeeded that of the Greeks, or the lower empire, which, being seized by the Latins, was recovered again by the Greeks, and at length intirely subdued by the Turks. *(See the year* 800.)

The dauphin, persisting in his revolt, promises to marry the duke of Savoy's daughter, then only nine years old; by which means he skreens himself from the king's resentment, and from the general hatred which he had incurred by his exactions in Dauphiné. The king is under such circumstances *, as oblige him to approve of this match; and even to give his daughter Ioland, or Violante, in marriage to the prince of Piedmont. The condemnation of James Cœur †; part of his estate, which had been confiscated, was restored to his children. This man had done as great service to the king, in the administration of the revenue, as the Dunois's, the la Hires, or the Xaintrailles, performed by their arms; yet he gave him up to his enemies, or rather to the rapacity of his courtiers, who wanted to share the plunder. It is pity that so great a prince, possessed of so many amiable qualities, should have suffered himself thus to be governed. How could he be a tame spectator of the punishment of the maid of Orleans? How came he not to hinder the infamous design of the Penthievres against the duke of Britany? or not to oppose the murder of the duke of Burgundy? The report

---

* The landing of five thousand English in Guienne, who were admitted by the inhabitants into Bourdeaux, and surprized the French garrison.

† James Cœur, the son of a merchant of Bourges, was brought up to trade from his infancy, acquired prodigious wealth, came early to court, was made steward of the king's coin, and master of the mint. He was reckoned the richest subject in Europe. His credit was of great use to the state. It was he who put the king's affairs in order, and enabled him to execute his project for disciplining the army. It was he who furnished the sums necessary for the conquest of Normandy.

of James Cœur's making a large fortune a second time, is fabulous; for he survived his sentence only three years. (*Mem. of the academy of belles lettres.*)

The first treaty of France with the Swiss: it is true there had been one concluded already with that nation in 1444; but it was only between them and the dauphin.

The parliament of Grenoble instituted by Lewis XI, then only dauphin; but it was confirmed two years after by his father.

1454. 55.

The memory of the maid of Orleans restored. John, king of Arragon, the widower of Blanche, heiress of Navarre, marries again, and unjustly withholds that kingdom from his son Charles, prince of Vianne.

1456.

The dauphin, after residing fifteen years in Dauphiné, retires into the territories of the duke of Burgundy, to avoid his father's resentment. "Lewis XI, says Philip de Comines, was main-
"tained and supported six years by the duke of Burgundy, who
"allowed him money for his subsistence." After Lewis's retreat from Dauphiné, we meet with letters patent from the king his father, ordering that province to be administered in his own name.

1457. 58. 59. 60. 61.

The trial of the duke d'Alençon, for encouraging the dauphin's revolt. This affair gave rise to several questions, which the king caused to be proposed to his parliament, by master John Tudert, his council and master of requests to his hotel: Whether the king can sit in person upon the trial of a peer of France? This had been disputed, in regard to Charles VI, by the duke of Bourbon, in the year 1386, at the time of the trial of the king of Navarre; and even in regard to Charles V, upon the trial of the duke of Britany. Whether any but the twelve ancient peers have a right to assist at the trial? Whether peers may appoint deputies in their room? To which the parliament, after examining the records, made answer, that

REMARKABLE EVENTS under CHARLES VII.

he king had not only a right to assist at the criminal prosecution of peers, but that his presence was even necessary on the occasion; that all the peers indiscriminately have a right to be present; but that they cannot appoint deputies in their place. (*Du Tillet, collection of ranks.*)

The duke d'Alençon, a prince of the blood, being descended from Charles of Valois, was condemned to death, and this sentence changed to imprisonment: he was released by Lewis XI, who confined him once more, upon his being convicted of treating underhand with the English. The civil war in England between the houses of York and Lancaster, by the name of the *white* and *red roses*. Richard, duke of York, descended from the heiress of the duke of Clarence, dethrones Henry VI, of the house of Lancaster, and makes him prisoner*. Margaret, the daughter of René, king of Naples, duke of Anjou, and wife of Henry VI, gives battle to Richard †, who is routed and slain. Edward, the son of Richard, supported by the earl of Warwick, gives battle to Henry VI; and, having taken him prisoner ‡, is proclaimed king of England by the name of Edward IV.

In the reign of Charles VII, towards the year 1440, the art of printing was invented in Germany. John Guttemberg, assisted by John Faustus, and Peter Sschoeffer, after repeated attempts, compassed, at length, about the year 1450, the entire impression of their works. Strange, that this discovery should have been so long making its way! Is there so great a distance from the engraving of letters, from medals and inscriptions, (inventions of the highest antiquity) to the typographical art?

This prince created the company of Scotch guards, the first captain of which was general Patilloc.

Charles VII. was but in some measure a spectator of the wonders of his reign; one would have been tempted to say, that fortune, in spite of the indolence of this monarch, and merely out of wantonness and sport, had raised formidable enemies to attack

---

* At the battle of St. Albans, May 23, 1454.
† At the battle of Wakefield, December 31, 1460.
‡ At the battle of Towton, March 29, 1462. King Edward was crowned the 20th of June that same year; and king Henry was not taken till the year 1464.

him, and gallant commanders to support his cause, without his concerning himself at all in its defence; not that he wanted courage; but, if he appeared at the head of his armies, it was as a soldier, and not as a general. His life was spent in gallantry, in sports, and feasts. One day that la Hire came to give him an account of some very important affair, the king, very busy about an entertainment, shewed him the preparations, and asked him what he thought of them. *I think*, said la Hire, *it is impossible to lose a kingdom with more gaiety.* Yet some historians, deceived by the wonders of his reign, could not be persuaded that he had no hand in them; and therefore they gave him the title of *victorious.*

REMARKABLE EVENTS.

1461.

1461. Accession to the crown.

Lewis XI. *comes to the crown at thirty-nine years of age, in the year 1461. He was at Genep in Brabant, when he received the news of the death of his father. He was crowned at Rheims the 15th of August, by John Juvenal des Ursins, archbishop of that city.*

LEWIS XI. pursued a quite different pl[an] of government from that of his father; [he] changed some of the officers and magistrat[es] whom that prince had preferred; he impr[i]soned several lords, among others Antony [of] Chabanes, which was a just judgment upon t[he] latter for being so unjustly concerned in confisca[t]ing the estate of James Cœur, when he sat up[on] his trial; and lastly, he suppressed the pragma[tic] sanction, which was not however totally ab[o]lished, till the signing of the concordate betwi[xt] Leo X. and Francis I.

The title of most Christian king, bestowed upon this prince in 1469, has been ever since appropriated to his successors.

1462.

John, king of Arragon, having espoused Ja[ne,] daughter of the admiral of Castile, by whom [he] had the celebrated Ferdinand the Catholic, wit[h]held the kingdom of Navarre from his own s[on] the prince of Viana, heir to that crown, and s[up]ported his injustice by arms. The inhabita[nts] of Navarre, having joined the king of Cast[ile,] after endeavouring in vain to support the prin[ce] of Viana, who was poisoned by his step-moth[er,] continue the war to revenge his death. J[ohn] of Arragon, in order to defend himself against [his] enemies, borrows three hundred thousand crow[ns] of Lewis XI, and grants him the counties [of] Cerdaigne and Roussillon, as a mortgage for [the] money.

The king lends twenty thousand crowns [to] Margaret of Anjou, whose husband, Henry [V,] king of England, is a prisoner in the Tower [of] London; and she promises to deposit the t[own] of Calais in his hands, as soon as her husba[nd's] affairs are re-established.

The Third Race.

WIVES.	CHILDREN.	1483. DEATH.	Cotemporary PRINCES.
Margaret of Scotland; she died in 1445, before her husband came to the crown. She is called ma-la Dauphine. Charlotte of Savoy, daughter of Lewis II, duke of Savoy, and of Anne of Cyprus, married in the year 1451, died in 1483.	Lewis, died young. 1448. Neither father Anselm, nor le Gendre, make mention of him, and he is known only by a piece extant in the archives of our Lady of Clery. Joachim, died young. CHARLES VIII. Francis duke of Berry, died young. Louisa, died young. Anne, married to Peter de Bourbon, lord of Beaujeu, governed under Charles VIII. 1522. Joan, married to Lewis of Orleans, afterwards Lewis XII, who was divorced from her, to marry Anne of Britany. 1504. *Natural children.* Lewis XI. had by *Phelise Regnard.* Guyette. By *Marg. de Saffenage.* Joan, *married to Lewis, bastard of Bourbon.* And Mary, *married to Aymar de Poitiers, lord of St. Vallier. She was grandmother to Diana of Poitiers.* He had also another natural daughter, named *Isabeau,* married to Lewis de Saint Priest.	LEWIS XI. died at Plessis les Tours, on Saturday the 30th of August, 1483, aged sixty years. He was interred at Notre Dame de Clery, where his tomb was opened, and insulted by the Huguenots in 1562. There are but three of our kings of the third race, that were not buried at St. Denis. Philip I. who was interred at St. Benoit sur la Loire. Lewis the Young, at the abbey of Barbeaux; and Lewis XI. He sent for St. Francis of Paul, in hopes of recovering his health by that holy man's prayers; he likewise sent for a number of relics.	Pope. Pius II. 1464. Paul II. 1471. Sixtus IV. 1484. *Turkish emperors.* Mahomet II. 1481. Bajazet II. abdicates 1512. *Emperor of Germany.* Frederic III. 1498. *Kings of Spain.* Henry IV. 1474. Ferdinand. } 1516. Isabella. } 1504. *Kings of Portugal.* Alphonsus V. 1481. John II. 1495. *King of England.* Edward IV. 1483. *King of Scotland.* James III. 1488. *King of Denmark.* Charles Canutson. 1471. Interregnum till 1483. *Kings of Sweden.* Christiern. 1481. John. 1513. *King of Poland.* Casimir IV. 1492. *Czar of Muscovy.* John Basilowitz. 1505.

REMARKABLE EVENTS under LEWIS XI.

The creation of the parliament of Bourdeaux, difmembered from that of Touloufe, whofe jurifdiction extended over Languedoc and Guienne: the Garonne formed the boundary of thofe two provinces. The inhabitants of Bourdeaux had already obtained this favour, upon their capitulation with the count de Dunois in the reign of Charles VII; but their fubfequent revolt prevented it from being carried into execution.

1463.

The univerfity of Bourges erected.

The king recovers poffeffion of the towns in Picardy, ceded to Philip the Good, duke of Burgundy, by the treaty of Arras, upon paying him four hundred thoufand crowns.

1464.

The count de Charolois * difpleafed with the reftitution of thofe places, enters into a treaty with the duke of Britany, and feizes the baftard de Rubempré †, upon fufpicion of his having been fent by Lewis XI. to fecure his perfon. An alliance formed by Charles, duke of Berry, the king's only brother, with the count de Charolois, the duke of Britany, the duke of Bourbon, the count de Dunois, and feveral other lords, who were offended with Lewis XI. for depriving them of their places at the commencement of his reign. John of Anjou, duke of Calabria, fon of René, king of Naples, came and joined thofe princes, and brought with him the firft body of Swifs that ever appeared in our armies; their number was five hundred. The pretext of the war, which arofe from this confederacy, was the eafe of the people, and from thence took the name of the *Public Good*. The count de Charolois draws near to Paris, and in vain attempts to make himfelf mafter of this city.

1465.

Paul II. grants the purple robe to cardinals. He fucceeded Pius II, who in his youthful days had been crowned *Poet Laureat* at Frankfort, by the emperor Frederic III, and who, towards the decline of life, not difcouraged by the ill fuccefs of former

---
* The duke of Burgundy's fon, named afterwards Charles the Bold.
† A determined bravo.

crufades,

The Third Race.

MINISTERS.	WARRIORS.	MAGISTRATES.	EMINENT and LEARNED MEN.
Philip de Comines. He quitted the service of the duke of Burgundy, whose subject he was, to enter into that of the king, in 1472. The real motive of his change was never justly known, he died 1509. Oliver le Daim. This man was of base original; from being barber to Lewis XI, he rose by his intrigues to the highest degree of favour, but ended his days unhappily in the following reign, for he was hanged in 1484. *Secretaries of the finances.* Stephen Chevalier. John, cardinal de la Balue. This man emerged from the meanest original to the first dignities in the church: he had been only a valet-de-chambre to M. de Beauveau, bishop of Angers; yet had the presumption and cun-	*Constables.* Lewis de Luxemburg, count de St. Paul. 1475. *Marshals of France.* John bastard of Armagnac, surnamed de Lescun. 1473. Joachim Ronault de Gamaches. 1478. Wolfart de Borselle. 1487. Peter de Rohan de Gié, living in 1505.	*Chancellors.* Will. Juvenal des Ursins. 1472. P. de Morvilliers, 1476. Peter de Oriole. 1485. He was *discharged* from his office in 1483, *Rex exoneravit eum*; and it is observable, that it was not owing to the king's being dissatisfied with his services, since he gave him the post of first president of the chamber of accounts; but it was intended as a reward to William de Rochefort, who had changed the service of Burgundy for that of France. Will. de Rochefort. 1492. *First president.* Yves de Scepeaux. 1461. Helie de Torrettes. 1461. Matthew de Nanterre. 1487. J. Dauvet. 1471. John le Boulanger. 1481. J. de la Vacquerie. 1497. He had been pensionary council to the town of Arras.	Æneas Sylvius. 1464. John Argyropulus towards 1474. Bessarion. 1473. Angelo Cattha, physician and astrologer to Lewis XI, the king's almoner, and afterwards archbishop of Vienna. It was he that engaged Philip de Comines to write his commentaries. Nic. de Cusa. 1464. Enguerrand de Monstrelet, towards 1468. J. Faustus, towards 1467. Theodore Gaza. 1475. George of Trebisond. 1486. J. Guttemberg, living in 1466. Baptista Mantuanus. 1472. Antony of Palermo (called *Panormitanus.*) 1471. *He sold his house to purchase a manuscript of Livy.* Nic. Perrot. 1480. Fr. Philelphus. 1481. Baptista Platina. 1481. P. Schoeffer, still living in the next reign. Thomas à Kempis. 1471. J. de Turrecremata. 1468. Franc. Villon (Corbeil) living in 1495. John Juvenal des Ursins. 1473.

X 4

crusades, was ready to make another attempt, and to conduct the expedition himself; but his death defeated the design.

The battle of Montlhery * on the 16th of July, in which neither the king nor the count de Charolois, who commanded the respective armies, had a stomach for fighting. The loss on both sides was equal; and the Burgundians kept possession of the field.

The treaties of Conflans and St. Maur put an end to the war of the *Public Good*: it was agreed, that six and thirty persons out of the three orders of the kingdom should be appointed to reform the abuses of the government. John Dauvet, first president of the parliament of Toulouse, had a great share in procuring this peace, and was rewarded with the post of first president of the parliament of Paris, possessed at that time by Matthew de Nanterne, who was substituted in his place at Toulouse, and afterwards came back to exercise the office of second president of the parliament of Paris. The count de Charolois reduces the inhabitants of Liege, who had made a diversion in favour of the king.

1466.

Lewis XI. had agreed to this peace, in hopes of recovering, by policy and intrigues, all that he had been forced to yield by treaty. After he had gained over the duke of Bourbon, foreseeing that the dukes of Berry and Britany would soon quarrel †, he took advantage of this conjuncture to resume the dukedom of Normandy, which he had granted as an appanage to his brother, in virtue of the above convention; the next thing he did, was to reduce most of the strong towns in that dukedom, which had been seized by the duke of Britany, though a few of them still remained in this prince's possession. And thus all that he executed, in virtue of the treaty of Conflans, was the cession of a few towns on the Somme to the count de Charolois, in whose hands they continued. Before the treaty of Conflans, the king had given the

---

* A castle about eight leagues from Paris.
† He made a treaty at Caen with the duke of Britany, who had got possession of some places in Normandy, which he foresaw would set him at variance with his brother.

sword

MINISTERS.

cunning, after causing his master to be declared incapable of his employment, to get it settled upon himself; he betrayed his benefactor, Charles de Melun, lord high steward of France, who lost his head in 1468: and he betrayed the king himself on several occasions, who is said to have confined him at last to an iron cage. After he had recovered his liberty, he was legate in France, and died in 1491.
John Bourré Dupleſſis.
Peter Parent.

MINISTERS.

Attorneys general.
J. de Saint Romain, practiſed in 1483.
Michael de Ponts, practiſed with the latter in 1479.

King's advocates.
Will. de Ganay, 1483.
Renaud de Dormans. 1472. We find in a manuſcript of Blanchard, that he was preſent, as maſter of the requeſts, at the declaration of 1470, by which the duke of Burgundy is declared guilty of high treaſon.
Francis Hallé, practiſed in 1576.
Peter Luillier. 1492.
John le Maitre. 1510.
Robert Thibouſt, living in 1487.

sword of constable to the count de St. Paul, a favourite of the count de Charolois, intending to hurt him in the opinion of that prince.

1467.

Philip the Good, duke of Burgundy, dies, and is succeeded by his son Charles, surnamed the *Bold*, or the *Hardy*. The inhabitants of Liege, having revolted again, are defeated.

A declaration, that *no office shall be granted, except it be vacant by death, resignation, or forfeiture.*

1468.

The assembly of the states at Tours, where it was determined that Normandy could not be dismembered any more from the crown, to be settled on the king's brother; it was likewise decreed, that the duke of Britany should restore the towns he had taken in Normandy, and that a number of persons should be appointed to reform the state.

The conference of Peronne, to prevent the war, which was likely to arise from the non-performance of the treaty of Conflans on the part of Lewis XI. This prince, at the same time that he abetted the insurrection of the inhabitants of Liege, was so imprudent as to trust himself into the hands of the duke of Burgundy at Peronne. Charles, apprized of the correspondence which the king held with the town of Liege, detained him prisoner at the very foot of the tower where Charles the Simple ended his days[*]; nay, he hesitated whether he should not carry his resentment further: at length he obliged him to conclude a treaty, greatly to the advantage of the house of Burgundy, and to march with him to the siege of Liege, against the very people whom he had excited to take up arms; accordingly the king assisted in the reduction of the town. Before this treaty, Lewis XI. had promised Champagne and Brié as an appanage to his brother, Charles duke of Berry; at the same time he never intended to keep his word, apprehending that those provinces, being so near to Burgundy, would prove a fresh source of broils and disputes.

[*] When confined by the count of Vermandois.

1469.

REMARKABLE EVENTS under LEWIS XI.

1469.

The duke of Berry, to the great concern of the duke of Burgundy, is perfuaded to accept of Guienne for his fetlement, inftead of Champagne and Brié. The king, to compafs this point, had gained the favourite of that prince, Odée d'Aidie, whom he afterwards made count de Comminge. At the fame time he punifhed the cardinal de la Balue, who was convicted of having encouraged the duke of Berry in his revolt, in order to render himfelf neceffary to the king; and of having held a correfpondence with the duke of Burgundy. The cardinal was imprifoned at Loches, where he remained eleven years; but was never brought to a trial, becaufe of the difputes between the king and the pope, in regard to the form of proceeding. Lewis XI. inftitutes the order of St. Michael; that of the Star being funk into contempt.

1470.

The earl of Warwick, diffatisfied with Edward IV*, joins in a confpiracy with the duke of Clarence, Edward's brother, and goes over to France; having entered into a treaty with Lewis XI, he returns to England, defeats Edward's army †, and takes him prifoner. Edward efcapes out of prifon, and obtains a victory over the forces under the earl of Warwick. The earl beats Edward a fecond time, who flies for fhelter to the duke of Burgundy. Henry VI. is releafed from prifon, and re-afcends the throne.

The duke of Guienne, without confulting the king, and in order to make head againft him, preffes the duke of Burgundy to grant him his only daughter in marriage: in this requeft he is feconded by the conftable of St. Paul, to whom the war

---

* Guy earl of Warwick had been deputed by Edward IV. to demand Bona of Savoy, fifter-in-law to Lewis XI, in marriage; but the king married the lady Elizabeth Grey, widow of Sir John Grey, while the earl of Warwick was upon his embaffy; and this provoked the earl to defert the king's intereft.

† The earl of Warwick did not defeat Edward's army, but furprized the king in his camp. King Edward, after his efcape, attacked the troops under young Wells, fon of lord Wells, at Stamford, before they could be joined by the earl of Warwick; and obtained a complete victory. The earl of Warwick was obliged to fly to France, but returned very foon to England, raifed an army, and compelled Edward to retire to Holland, without fighting a blow: upon this Henry VI. was releafed as above.

was necessary, in order to support his credit and influence, as well as to the duke of Britany, who plainly saw, that the king only sought for an opportunity to demolish them, as soon as he had done with the duke of Burgundy. The king takes St. Quintin, Amiens, Roye, and Montdidier. John count d'Armagnac, who had made his escape to Fontarabia, is condemned to death by an arret of parliament, for the crime of rebellion; he was murdered afterwards in 1473, at the siege of Leictoure. The art of printing is introduced into Paris.

1471.

The duke of Burgundy has recourse to arms *, and raises a suspicion in the king's breast concerning those who had advised the present war; in consequence of which a year's truce is concluded between the two princes. The constable carries on the treaty of marriage between the duke of Guienne and the duke of Burgundy's daughter. The last revolution in England, which renders the white rose triumphant, and restores Edward IV. to the throne. In an engagement between the two competitors, the earl of Warwick is defeated and slain †: Margaret of Anjou, the wife of Henry VI, loses a second battle ‡, where the prince of Wales is taken prisoner, and murdered by Edward's order, at the age of eighteen. This unfortunate princess, having been imprisoned by king Edward, was ransomed by Lewis XI, and died at length in 1482, after repeated proofs of the most unshaken constancy, under the greatest misfortunes. Who could imagine that this Margaret was the daughter of good

---

* By the advice of an assembly of the nobles at Tours, the king declares war against the duke of Burgundy; the duke, finding himself pushed hard, demands a peace, and writes a very humble letter to the king, ending with these words; *If you had known the inside of things, you would not have declared war against me.* By which he alluded to the treachery of the duke of Guienne, the constable, and the duke of Britany, who had signified to the duke of Burgundy, that he had nothing to do but to give his daughter to the duke of Guienne, and the best part of the troops would go over to his side.

† The battle of Barnet, fought on the 14th of April, being Easter day.

‡ The queen was just arrived, with her son, from France, when she received the news of the fatal battle of Barnet. However she levied a fresh army, and on the 9th of May was fought the battle of Tewksbury, where the queen and the prince of Wales were taken prisoners.

REMARKABLE EVENTS under LEWIS XI.

king René, duke of Anjou, who employed himself in colouring pictures, during a life spent in confinement? Edward caused Henry VI. to be murdered, and aftewards put the duke of Clarence to death in 1478. Henry VII. was desirous that Henry VI. should be canonized, in order to raise a greater horror against the usurpation of Edward; but this did not take place. Edward, being now in peaceful possession of the throne, is under the same apprehension as Lewis XI. of the match between the duke of Guienne and the heiress of Burgundy.

1472.

The duke of Guienne is poisoned, together with his mistress, madam de Montsoreau, by a peach divided betwixt them *, not without suspicion that the king himself was concerned in it. This prince was betrothed to John, the daughter of Henry IV, called the *Impotent*, king of Castile, in prejudice to whom, Isabella, Henry's sister, and wife of Ferdinand king of Arragon, seized the kingdom of Castile. The negotiations between the king and duke Charles are one continued series of fraud and imposture. The duke takes up arms, enters Picardy, and lays waste the country with fire and sword; but he is obliged to raise the siege of Beauvais, this place being bravely defended by some women, who joined the garrison, with one *Joan Hachette* at their head: from thence he proceeded to Normandy, and having ravaged that province, he marched back to Flanders. After his retreat, the king recovered some of the places he had taken. Lewis XI. brings over the duke of Britany to his interest. Philip de Comines quits the service of the duke of Burgundy, and enters into that of the king.

Foundation of the university of Bourdeaux.

1473.

The king, being highly incensed at the repeated acts of infidelity of John V, count d'Armagnac, whom he had pardoned more than once, and who still continued his intrigues with the dukes of Burgundy and Guienne, resolves to punish him; and for that end lays siege to Leictoure, which was defended by the

---

* The peach was said to have been given them by the duke's own chaplain, the abbot of St. John de Angeli.

count, who was killed, as we have already observed, after the capitulation: he left no issue; and his estate, which had been confiscated, was restored to his brother Charles d'Armagnac.

Lewis XI, having quarrelled with John king of Arragon, and espoused the cause of René king of Naples against him, lays siege to Perpignan, defended by the king of Arragon in person. The siege is raised, and those princes come to an accommodation.

The duke of Burgundy, being instituted heir by Arnold duke of Geldres, in prejudice to his own son, takes possession of that province, and forms a scheme of erecting his dominions into one independent sovereignty, under the title of the kingdom of Burgundy.

1474.

The treaty of Bovines, between the king and duke Charles, where the destruction of the constable is resolved upon; but it was deferred for the present.

The trial of René, duke d'Alençon; he was accused of entering into a conspiracy with the duke of Britany, and received sentence of death, which was changed into perpetual imprisonment. An interview between the king and the constable, who came attended with troops, and had the insolence to insist upon a barrier between him and his sovereign. The war in Catalonia, in relation to the interests of the duke of Calabria. A league, offensive and defensive, entered into by Edward IV, Charles duke of Burgundy, and the duke of Britany, against the king. The constable, being in possession of the town of St. Quintin, makes all parties court him: the league proved ineffectual, through Charles's ambition. This prince, impatient to establish a kingdom of Burgundy, had formed a scheme of making himself master of all the holds on the Rhine as far as Basil: intoxicated with these ideas, he declares for Robert of Bavaria, archbishop of Cologne, lays siege to Nuitz, and raises the jealousy of the emperor and the princes of Germany, as well as of René duke of Lorrain, whom Lewis XI. assisted under hand.

1475.

The king wages war against the duke of Burgundy: the preceding year his majesty had concluded a treaty with the Swiss, who began to make a considerable figure in Europe. These new allies

REMARRKABLE EVENTS under LEWIS XI.

were the more to be depended upon, as they had reason to complain of the duke of Burgundy, who, being possessed of the county of Ferette, by an engagement with the duke of Austria, had authorized the governor to commit several outrages against the neighbouring cantons. Edward IV, having made great preparations for the war against France, is gained by Lewis XI, who held a correspondence with the principal ministers in England; for which it cost him, says Comines, sixteen thousand crowns a year in pensions. The two kings conclude a treaty at Amiens the 29th of August, which they ratify at Picquigny: a truce of seven years is agreed upon; the marriage of the dauphin with Elizabeth, the daughter of king Edward, is also settled; and Lewis moreover engages to pay annually to Edward, during the joint life of the two kings, the sum of fifty thousand crowns. The duke of Britany was likewise included in the treaty; it being greatly the interest of Edward to keep fair with that prince; for he had in his custody the earl of Richemont, the only survivor of the house of Lancaster, who might have given him great uneasiness, had he been set at liberty; he afterwards ascended the English throne by the name of Henry VII. The duke of Burgundy, seeing himself deserted by the king of England, and betrayed by the constable, whose treachery the king laid open to him, signed a nine years truce at Vervins with Lewis XI, and agreed to abandon the constable: the latter, being apprized of this resolution, waits upon the duke to make him alter his resolution; but the duke delivers him up to the king, who causes him to be beheaded in the place de Greve, the 19th of December. His grand-daughter, Mary of Luxemburg, afterwards married Francis count de Vendome, and was great grandmother to Henry IV. The king gives all the constable's spoils to duke Charles, to whom he restores St. Quintin, with several other towns in Picardy. The duke of Burgundy makes himself master of Nancy.

1476.

Charles the Bold takes the town of Granson from the Swiss; where he is attacked by the troops of that nation, and his army defeated; he sets another army on foot, and, laying siege to Morat, is beaten a second time by the Swiss, headed by René II,

duke

REMARKABLE EVENTS under LEWIS XI.

duke of Lorrain, who afterwards retook Nancy. René was son of Ioland of Anjou, and of Ferri count de Vaudemont: he succeeded to the dukedom of Lorrain, which had been separated from his branch, in spite of all the endeavours of the count de Vaudemont, by the match between Isabella of Lorrain, daughter of Charles II, who died without male issue, and René of Anjou. The posterity of Charles being extinct with duke Nicholas, the last descendant of this branch of Anjou, all the rights centered in René II. by his father and mother.

1477, 78.

Charles lays siege to Nancy, and obstinately persists in his enterprize, notwithstanding the severity of the season, which had almost ruined his army. The duke of Lorrain, with a body of Swiss troops, marches to the relief of the place, and, on the 5th of January, attacks and defeats Charles duke of Burgundy, who lost his life in the engagement, having been betrayed by Campobasso, a Neapolitan *. He left an only daughter, princess Mary, who was heiress to his dominions. With him ended the second house of Burgundy, which had lasted near a hundred and twenty years under four princes. The king, who was the first that established the use of post-horses, hitherto unknown to France, by an edict in 1464, became quickly acquainted with this event, and laid hold of the opportunity to retake several towns in Picardy, Artois, and Burgundy. The trial of James d'Armagnac, duke de Nemours, and count de la Marche, who was convicted of high treason, and lost his head †: he was cousin-german to John d'Armagnac of the younger branch.

The institution of the parliament of Burgundy at Dijon; the date thereof is the 18th of March, 1476. The court of aids fixed at Montpelier; to which a chamber of accounts was added by Francis I.

---

* He was a soldier of fortune, who commanded a corps of Italians in the duke's army; he had long entertained a design of compassing Charles's destruction, in revenge of a blow on the ear given him by that prince.

† He was brought on horseback to a scaffold, where he was beheaded, and his blood, running through, fell upon his children, by an unparalleled scene of barbarity.

REMARKABLE EVENTS under LEWIS XI.

The king, from an ill-judged policy, neglects two great matches for the dauphin, viz. Mary of Burgundy, and Joan, the daughter of Ferdinand and Isabella. With regard to the dutchy of Burgundy, Comines observes, that Lewis XI. had such an aversion to all great lords, that he would not even suffer the count l'Angoulême to espouse the heiress of Burgundy, who would have been very well pleased with a prince of the house of France; and if this had taken place, the house of Austria would not have acquired the Netherlands. A most unaccountable jealousy! He chose to let this wealthy inheritance devolve to foreigners, rather than aggrandize a prince of his own blood. He seized the county of Artois, which, according to the law of appanages, ought to have been reannexed to the crown, for want of heirs male: but this reunion was not completed till the Pyrenean treaty. The states of Flanders take possession of the government, and of the person of Mary of Burgundy, who beheld the execution of two of her most faithful ministers, Hugonet her chancellor, and Imbercourt; neither her intreaties nor her tears could avail to save their lives: they were accused of having delivered the town of Arras to Lewis XI. She was afterwards married to Maximilian of Austria, son of the emperor Frederic III. This match proved the source of all those quarrels, which cost France and the house of Austria so much blood. I must not omit mentioning, on this occasion, that Lewis XV, happening to see the tombs of Charles the Bold and Mary of Burgundy at Bruges in 1745, expressed himself in these words; *there is the first cause of all our wars.* The emperor erects Austria into an archdukedom in favour of his son.

Establishment of the hundred gentlemen pensioners, called *becs de corbin, or ravens beaks* *.

A truce between Lewis XI. and king Edward IV, during their lives, and between their successors for the space of a hundred years, concluded at London the 13th of February: Lewis XI. promises, for himself and his successors, to pay fifty thousand crowns to the king of England, for the space of a hundred years, to commence from the death of the survivor. This treaty is looked upon as a master-piece in politics: in the

---

* They took this name from the falcions they carry in their hands.

first place, it prevented Edward from joining with Maximilian secondly, by leaving the rights of both nations undecided, th English were not disturbed in their idle pretensions to Normandy and to the provinces on the other side of the Loire: yet i gave time to the inhabitants of those provinces to resume th habit of their natural subjection; and to our kings an opportunit of strengthening themselves, till they should be able, as it hap pened under Henry II, to recover from the English all that ha been usurped by that nation from the kingdom of France *(Parallel of the Romans and French.)*

1479.

Maximilian breaks the truce with France: the king possesse himself of Franche Comté, by the valour and good conduct o Chaumont d'Amboise.

The siege of Terouene raised by Maximilian, after the battle o Guinegate between him and the French, in which the advantage was equal on both sides. Vice-admiral Coulon took a Dutch fleet of eighty sail, and carried them into Normandy. The beginning of the empire of the Czars.

1480. 81.

The Swiss were taken into the king's pay, after the death of the duke of Burgundy, in order to be joined to the *francarchers*, or *free-archers*, established by Charles VII; six thousand of them had been employed at the siege of Dole in 1478. Lewis, having suppressed the *free-archers*, strengthened the Swiss corps with an addition of ten thousand French foot, who were not maintained as in the preceding reign, by the boroughs and villages, but received a regular pay from the king.

The cardinal de la Balue is released from his confinement, at the intercession of the cardinal de la Rovere. A truce concluded with Maximilian. Charles of Anjou, count du Maine, to whom René of Anjou, his uncle, had given Provence, makes the king his heir to that country, and to his rights to Naples and Sicily. Lewis XI. is said to have been indebted for this favour to John Cossa, seneschal of Provence, and to Palamede de Forbin, whom he appointed governor of Provence and Dauphiné.

1482.

REMARKABLE EVENTS under LEWIS XI.

1482.

Mary of Burgundy dies of a fall she received from hunting. The treaty of Arras, in which the marriage of the dauphin to Margaret, the daughter of Mary, is settled. Mary left also a son, who married Joan, the daughter of Ferdinand and Isabella, from whence sprung the emperor Charles V. There is one thing worthy of notice in this treaty, viz. that Maximilian demands, as a security for the performance of this engagement of Lewis XI, the guaranty of the princes of the blood royal, *substituted in the place of the peers*.

1483.

Edward IV, whose daughter was to have been married to the dauphin, by virtue of the treaty of Pequigny, took offence at the treaty of Arras; but Lewis XI. prevented the effects of his resentment, by kindling a war between that prince and James III, king of Scotland. Edward died shortly after, poisoned, as it is said, by his brother Richard III, who, to reap the fruit of his iniquity, murdered Edward's two sons, (the eldest of whom he had suffered to reign but two months) and mounted the English throne. The eldest son's name was Edward V; and the shortness of his reign is the reason of his not being ranked in the list of the kings of England.

Lewis XI, says Comines, *was humble in his speech and apparel . . . he was naturally fond of people in a middling state; and spoke very freely of most persons, except those he feared, for he was of a sonorous disposition* . . . . To those who reproached him with not keeping up to his dignity, he would answer, *When pride precedes, shame and distress must follow*. It was likewise a saying of his, *that his whole council was in his head*, for indeed he consulted nobody; which occasioned a jest of the admiral de Brezé, upon seeing him mounted on a very slender nag, that surely the horse must be a great deal stronger than he appeared, since he was able to carry the king and his whole council. He was jealous of his authority to such a degree, that, after recovering from a fit of illness, in which he had been bereft of his senses, hearing that some of his officers had hindered him from going near the window, probably for fear he should do himself a mischief, he dismissed them from their

their employments. He was avaricious in his nature, but politically profuse; regardless of decency, and incapable of affection: he had a high notion of policy and cunning, so as to prefer them to every kind of virtue, and considered them not only as the means of obtaining his end, but even as the end itself; in short, he was less dexterous in avoiding, than in extricating himself out of, danger: yet he possessed great natural abilities; and, what is very extraordinary, he raised the royal authority to a very high pitch, while his manner of life, his character, and external deportment, seemed to debase it.

Lewis XI. had increased the *tailles*, to the amount of three millions; and, in the space of twenty years, he raised four millions seven hundred thousand livres annually, which makes about three and twenty millions of our present specie; whereas Charles VII. never levied above eighteen hundred thousand livres a year.

He had a ridiculous superstition, of suffering no business to be mentioned to him on holy Innocents day; neither would he take an oath upon the cross of St. Lo (for the custom of swearing upon relics still subsisted): this cross of St. Lo was in higher esteem than all other relics, even than those of St. Martin, so revered and so tremendous under our princes of the first race. His pretext was, that it would be shewing a disrespect to the instrument of our salvation; but one of his historians informs us, that his repugnance to this oath proceeded from a received opinion in those days, viz. that whosoever perjured himself in swearing by that relic, would die miserably within a twelvemonth; and the good king was a little more attached to life than to his word. It was he that honoured the coat of arms of the house of Medicis with the scutcheon of France. At first he had a mind to make himself head of the order of the Golden Fleece, upon the death of Charles the Bold, as heir to the rights of the house of Burgundy; but he changed his mind, says Brantome, thinking it beneath him to become the head of an order instituted by his vassal.

1483.
Acceſſion to the crown.

Charles VIII. comes to the crown in the year 1483, aged thirteen years and two months. He was crowned at Rheims by the archbiſhop Peter de Laval.

Du Haillan has the preſumption to mention a very abſurd anecdote, merely from hear-ſay, viz. that it was the opinion of a great many, that Charles VIII. was a ſuppoſitious ſon: and others ſay, that he was indeed the ſon of Lewis XI, but not by the queen his wife, Charlotte of Savoy, for whom the king had but very little affection.

REMARKABLE EVENTS.

1483.

ANNE of France, lady of Beaujeu, and ſiſter of Charles, has the government of the king's perſon, purſuant to the will of Lewis XI, without being regent of France.

1484.

This government is confirmed to her by the ſtates general, aſſembled at Tours, notwithſtanding the oppoſition of the duke of Orleans, who, as firſt prince of the blood, wanted to have the chief management of affairs. The ſaid aſſembly eſtabliſhed a council of ten perſons, compoſed chiefly of the princes of the blood, namely, the duke of Orleans preſident, the conſtable of Bourbon, the elder brother of Peter de Beaujeu, Peter de Beaujeu, and the count de Dunois. The ordinance publiſhed at the deſire of that aſſembly, was the firſt that permitted all ſorts of perſons to appear in court by their attorney.

The king begins his reign with an act of clemency: he releaſed Charles d'Armagnac, brother of John, killed at Leictoure; he likewiſe reſtored the children of James d'Armagnac to a part of their father's eſtate, which had been confiſcated at the time of his execution; and he recalled John d'Armagnac, biſhop of Caſtres, brother of James, from exile. This illuſtrious houſe was drawing to its final period; for we ſhall ſee it extinct in the reign of Lewis XII.

1485.

Anne de Beaujeu, having eſtabliſhed her authority, concluded a treaty at Montargis with the rebels of Britany. Differences between Anne de Beaujeu and the duke of Orleans, who retires to Britany, with the count de Dunois, ſon of the

famous

The Third Race. 327

Wives.	Children.	1498. Death.	Cotemporary Princes.
Margaret of Austria the daughter of Maximilian, who had been educated at the court of France, and bore the title of *Madam the Dauphiness*, was to have been married to Charles VIII; but she was sent back, and the king espoused Anne of Britany, the 13th of December, 1491, deceased 1513.	... Charles Orland, died young. Charles, died soon after he was born. Francis, died soon after he was born. Anne, died young. Charles VIII. had a natural daughter, named, Camilla Palvoisin.	CHARLES VIII. *died at the castle of Amboise the 7th of April, 1498, near twenty seven years of age. He reigned fifteen.*	*Popes.* Sixtus IV. 1484. He is believed to have been the first pope, that had his bust stamped upon the coin. Innocent VIII. 1492. Alexander VI. 1503. *Turkish emperor.* Bajazet II. abdicates. 1512. *Emperors of Germany.* Frederic III. 1493. Maximilian 1519. *King of Spain.* Ferdinand. } 1516. Isabella. } 1504. *Kings of Portugal.* John II. 1495. Emmanuel the Great. 1521. *Kings of England.* Richard III. 1485. Henry VII. 1509. *Kings of Scotland.* James III. 1488. James IV. 1513. *King of Denmark, and Sweden.* John. 1513. *Kings of Poland.* Casimir IV. 1492. Albert. 1501. *Czar of Muscovy.* John Basilowitz. 1505.

Y 4

REMARKABLE EVENTS under CHARLES VIII.

famous count of that name. He had already made a tour to that province, at the invitation of Landois, a favourite of Francis II, duke of Britany: this man, being desirous of assistance against the nobility of Britany, who were greatly incensed at his influence over their sovereign, had flattered the duke of Orleans with the hopes of procuring Anne of Britany for him in marriage. But, upon the return of the duke of Orleans to France, the malecontents gained the upper hand in Britany, and Landois was hanged. The death of this favourite restored the tranquillity of that province. The duke concludes a treaty with Maximilian and the duke of Orleans. Anne de Beaujeu marches an army into Guienne, and the king seizes the county of Comminge, to punish the count for giving bad counsel to the duke of Britany.

Richard III, the murderer of his brother and of his two nephews, did not long enjoy the fruit of his villainy; for this year he was defeated and slain by Henry earl of Richmond, of the house of Lancaster by the mother's side, who ascended the throne by the name of Henry VII. Thus the house of Lancaster, which had begun to wield the sceptre in the reign of Henry IV, recovered the crown, of which it had been deprived by Edward IV, of the house of York. With Richard III. ended the race of Angevine kings, surnamed Plantagenets. France assisted Henry VII. in this important expedition. What seems very extraordinary, this same Henry VII, whose accomplishments rendered him so worthy of the crown, and justly stiled the Solomon of England, perhaps was scarce a gentleman[*]: for he was not descended from Henry VI; but, like that prince, he

---

[*] It is said that Owen Tudor was descended from the ancient kings of Wales; but Rapin doubts whether the descent be well proved. Some say he was the son of a brewer. It is likewise to be observed, that, though Henry VII. was descended from John of Gaunt, it was by a bastard branch. For, whilst John of Gaunt's second wife, Constantia of Castile, was living, he had several children by his concubine, Catharine Roet, widow of sir Otho de Swineford. After his wife's death he married his concubine, and the children were legitimated by act of parliament, but not declared capable of succeeding to the crown: and they did not bear the name of Lancaster, but of Beaufort, the castle where they were born. The eldest was created earl of Somerset by Richard II. Margaret, the mother of Henry VII, was sole daughter of John duke of Somerset, the son of John earl of Somerset, who was son of John of Gaunt by Catharine Roet.

deduced

The Third Race. 329

Ministers.	Warriors.	Magistrates.	Eminent and Learned Men.
William Brissonet, cardinal. 1514. *Secretaries of the finances.* John Bourré du Plessis. Florimond Robertet, by whom this office was raised to its full splendor and authority.	*Constable.* John of Bourbon. 1488. *Marshals of France.* Peter de Rohan de Gié, living in 1505. Phil. de Crevecœur Descordes. 1494. John de Baudricourt. 1499.	*Chancellors.* Will. de Rochefort. 1492. Adam Fumé, keeper of the seals. 1494. Stephen Bertrand. 1483. Robert Brissonet. 1497. Guy de Rochefort. 1507. *First presidents.* John de la Vacquerie. 1497. Peter de Courtardy. 1505. *Attorneys general.* John de Nanterre, admitted in 1484. Christopher de Carmone, living in 1499. J. Luillier. 1496. J. Burdelot. 1507. *The King's advocates.* John de Nanterre, living in 1488. Peter de Courtardy. 1505. John de Montmirail, admitted in 1491. William Volant, admitted in 1497.	Rod. Agricola. 1486. Annius of Viterbo. 1492. Herm. Barbarus. 1493. Gabriel Biel. 1495. M. Boiardo, towards 1490. Oliv. le Daim. 1484. Martial of Paris, towards 1490. John Michel, first physician to Charles VIII. 1495. J. Picus of Mirandola. 1494. Angelus Politianus. 1494. Jerome Savonarola. 1498.

REMARKABLE EVENTS under CHARLES VIII.

deduced his original, by the female line, from the great king Edward III. This Edward, among other children, had a son, named John of Gaunt, duke of Somerset*, who founded the branch of Lancaster: John of Gaunt had a great grand-daughter, named Margaret of Somerset, who was married to Edmund, earl of Richmond, father of Henry VII. This Edmund was the son of Owen Tudor, an obscure person, who had no other recommendation than that of a handsome figure, which procured him the honour of marrying Catharine of France, widow of Henry V, and mother of Henry VI. Such was the grandfather of Henry VII; consequently, he had no other right to the crown, than that of being the son of Margaret, great grand-daughter of Edward III. Yet, as the rights of the house of York might be made use of by his enemies, he thought proper to unite them with those of Lancaster, (which he represented) by marrying Elizabeth of York; but taking care, at the same time, not to perform that ceremony till after his coronation, lest he should be said to hold the crown in right of his wife.

1486. 87.

The king goes to war with the duke of Britany. The duke of Angouleme and the constable of Bourbon are detached from the league. Philip de Comines, dissatisfied with having fallen from the degree of favour which he had enjoyed in the preceding reign, entered into connexions with the rebels; and was put under arrest. In the year 1487 the king makes himself master of several towns, but raises the siege of Nantes: he likewise obtains considerable advantages over the archduke on the side of Artois.

1488. 89.

The battle of St. Aubin, where the duke of Orleans is taken prisoner. If this prince could but have flattered the passion of Anne de Beaujeu, he might have enjoyed a considerable share in the government, for *she was a little smitten with him.* (Brantome.) The king's army was commanded by Lewis II, lord of Trimouille,

---

* This is a mistake: John of Gaunt was duke of Lancaster; his eldest son, by Catharine Roet, was earl of Somerset; and the son of this earl was created duke of Somerset.

REMARKABLE EVENTS under CHARLES VIII.

whom Guicciardin ſtiles the ableſt captain in the world. He had lately eſpouſed Gabrielle de Bourbon, daughter of the count de Montpenſier, the greateſt match in the kingdom, both for birth and fortune: he was ſlain at the battle of Pavia. The death of the duke of Britany, who left none but daughters behind him. The town of Ghent revolts againſt Maximilian, who, in 1489, marries Anne of Britany by proxy.

1490. 91.

The king, without conſulting his ſiſter, Anne de Beaujeu, ſets the duke of Orleans at liberty. The duke's friends at the court of Britany, and the duke himſelf, endeavour to break off the match between the dutcheſs of Britany and Maximilian. In 1491 Charles VIII. eſpouſes Anne of Britany, notwithſtanding her being engaged to Maximilian; and puts away Margaret, daughter of Maximilian, although he had been contracted to that princeſs: this is ſhe whoſe firſt huſband was the infant of Spain, her ſecond the duke of Savoy, and who, in her widowhood, was appointed governeſs of the Netherlands. Charles and Anne make a mutual ceſſion of their rights to Britany. The firſt money in France, with a buſt, is that which the city of Lyons cauſed to be minted for Charles VIII. and Anne of Britany. *(Bizot.)* The city of Aquila fabricated a coin in honour of that prince, with a French legend.

1492.

Henry VII, jealous of the power which Charles VIII. derived from his marriage with Anne, and pretending to revenge the affront done to Maximilian, lays ſiege to Boulogne; but matters are accommodated. This prince was called back to England by Perkins[*], who pretended to be the duke of York, ſon of

---

[*] Perkin Warbeck: he was the ſon of a converted Jew of Tournay, but born in England; he poſſeſſed his native language very well, was handſome, well ſhaped, and had a noble engaging air, which occaſioned the dutcheſs of Burgundy to put him upon acting this part. There had been another rebellion before in Henry VII's reign, ſet on foot by Lambert Simnel, a young ſtudent of Oxford, and ſon to a baker, who pretended to be the young earl of Warwick, whom he exactly reſembled. He was taken priſoner, but Henry ſpared his life. Perkin was alſo taken priſoner, and ſent to the Tower; but, endeavouring to eſcape, he was hanged at Tyburn.

Edward

REMARKABLE EVENTS under CHARLES VIII.

Edward IV, murdered by his uncle, Richard III. This imposture of Perkin was abetted by the dutchess dowager of Burgundy, sister to Edward IV, who desired to revenge the cause of the house of York upon that of Lancaster. The extinction of the Moorish government in Spain, by the taking of Granada. Christopher Columbus, supported by Ferdinand and Isabella, discovers the islands of Cuba, and Hispaniola. A few years after (1498) Americus Vespasius found out the continent of America, which received its name from this adventurer. How different the times! In the eighth and ninth centuries barbarians invaded civilized nations; but now civilized nations undertake to subdue barbarians. *(Voltaire's Universal History.)* Towards the year 1402, John de Bethencourt, a Norman gentleman, chamberlain to Charles VI, and cousin to the admiral of France, had made a voyage to the Canaries, and declared himself the sovereign of those islands.

1493.

Charles VIII, pleased with the idea of conquering the kingdom of Naples, exchanges the substance for the shadow, and concludes a peace with the king of the Romans, relinquishing the advantages he had obtained in that war; he likewise comes to an agreement with the king of Arragon, to whom he restores the provinces of Cerdaigne and Roussillon, without even so much as demanding back the three hundred thousand crowns, which Lewis XI. had lent that prince: this is said to have been the work of Oliver Maillard, a Cordelier *. From that time the province of Roussillon remained in the possession of Spain, till Lewis XIII. made a conquest of it in 1640. The kingdom of Naples was still a scene of amazing revolutions. (See the years 1265 and 1292.) The first house of Anjou expired with Joan in 1435. The second house was less fortunate than the

---

* This man was the king's confessor, and is said to have been influenced by presents of Spanish wine, of a very rich flavour, (that is, considerable sums of money put up in casks) from the Spanish agent at the court of France, who was also a Cordelier: he persuaded the king, that nothing troubled his father Lewis so much, in his last illness, as the injustice he had committed in retaining the counties of Cerdaigne and Roussillon.

REMARKABLE EVENTS under CHARLES VIII.

first: it had been invited thither in 1382, to revenge the cruelties which the different branches of the former house were committing against one another; so that these two houses, towards the latter end were cotemporary; the one possessed of the throne, the other aspiring to the sovereignty. The first house being extinct, at the death of Joan; the descendants of Lewis, founder of the second house, were not able to support their right to the Neapolitan throne, against the kings of Arragon. (See the years 1255, 1292, and 1382.) The last of those kings was Alphonso, who died in 1458, and procured his bastard son Ferdinand to be acknowledged his heir to the kingdom of Naples. Ferdinand was not even Alphonso's bastard, but a child imposed upon him by a favourite mistress: hence the pope, says Giannone, considered the crown of Naples as devolved to the holy see, for want of issue. This Ferdinand was king of Naples at the time of the expedition of Charles VIII, whose right was founded on the renunciation of Charles of Anjou in favour of Lewis XI; and Charles had been appointed heir to that kingdom by his uncle René. (See the year 1480.)

The differences between Ferdinand the Catholic and John II, king of Portugal, concerning their conquests, induced pope Alexander VI. to fix the boundaries by a meridian, called the line of *limitation*; but neither the Spaniards nor the Portuguese having agreed to the meridian marked by the pope, they fixed another, which was stiled *declination*, because it declines from that of Alexander VI.

The death of the emperor Frederic III. He had taken for his device the five vowels, A, E, I, O, U, which he thus explained; *Austriæ est imperare orbi universo*. Surely never was there a prince less deserving of so pompous a device: he died despised by the whole empire, at the age of seventy-eight, and was the only emperor since Augustus, that filled the throne upwards of fifty years: he married Eleonora of Portugal, whose exquisite beauty turned the brain of the unfortunate Don John de Silva, so as to make him an hermit. Frederic was succeeded in the Imperial dignity by Maximilian.

1494.

REMARKABLE EVENTS under CHARLES VIII.

1494.

The king sets out upon his expedition to Naples: de Vesc and William Briſſonnet, ſtiled the cardinal of St. Maloes, brother to the chancellor, were the chief promoters of this enterprize, which was not at all approved of by the cardinal de Graville; it was founded on the rights of the houſe of Anjou, which had been ceded to Lewis XI. All the princes of Italy took part in the quarrel, according as their ſeveral intereſts directed them; the Venetians, with the hopes of aggrandizing their ſtate in the midſt of public troubles; Alexander VI, to procure different eſtabliſhments for his family; but, above all, Lewis Sforza, the adminiſtrator of Milan: this man had formed a deſign to uſurp that dukedom from his nephew Galeas, whom he intended to poiſon; but he wanted, at the ſame time, to cut out employment for Ferdinand king of Naples, (whoſe grand-daughter had been married to Galeas) to prevent that prince from oppoſing his deſign. Ferdinand was frightened, and died of an apoplectic fit, leaving his kingdom to his ſon Alphonſo. John Galeas, the lawful heir to the dukedom of Milan, dies by poiſon: although he left a ſon, Lewis Sforza was made duke of Milan, and obtained the inveſtiture from the emperor. The king is received at Florence the 17th of November, and makes his entry into Rome, as a conqueror, by torch-light, the 31ſt of December. That ſame year, on the 6th of September, Andrew Paleologus, deſpot of Romania, the only heir to the empire of Conſtantinople, after the deceaſe of his uncle Conſtantine Paleologus, dethroned by Mahomet II, renounces all his rights to the Eaſtern empire, in favour of king Charles VIII. and his ſucceſſors: this donation was made at Rome, before the cardinal de Gurce, who accepted it in the name of the moſt Chriſtian king, though he had no power from his majeſty. Paleologus's renunciation was no great matter; beſides, he had rendered himſelf contemptible by his infamous marriage with a Greek courtezan.

The king delivers the city of Piſa from the Florentine yoke; but it was ſoon reduced to its former ſervitude.

1495.

REMARKABLE EVENTS under CHARLES VIII.

1495.

Charles VIII. performs acts of sovereignty in Rome. Alexander VI. capitulates with his majesty, and, among other conditions, delivers up Zizim, the brother of Bajazet, who might have been of service to the king in his intended war against the Turks; but it is said the poor prince had been previously poisoned.

Alphonso, king of Naples, seeing his subjects intimidated at the approach of the French army, and knowing how odious he had rendered himself by his ill conduct, resigns his crown to his son Ferdinand, a young prince of great courage, and beloved by the people; but the terror of the French name was too great, to oppose the progress of their arms. Ferdinand retires, and Charles VIII. clad in imperial robes, makes a triumphant entry into Naples on the 21st of February. Was he acting as emperor of Constantinople, according to the inscription of a medal struck at that time? or was it a consequence of the renunciation of Andrew Paleologus? Father Daniel does not seem to surmise any such thing, but says, that this triumphal pomp made *the emperor* (Maximilian) *suspect, that he intended to divest him of the imperial dignity*. All these conquests were made in less than six months. During this war the Italians were surprized at the French artillery.

A league concluded at Venice, by the pope, by the emperor Maximilian, by his son, the archduke Philip, surnamed the *Fair*, with Ferdinand, king of Arragon, Henry VII, king of England, Lewis Sforza, and the Venetians, to drive Charles VIII. out of Italy. This prince finds great difficulty in getting back to France. The battle of Fornova, where Charles displayed the most signal proofs of valour, on the 6th of July, against the confederate army, commanded by the marquis of Mantua. The gaining of this battle facilitated the king's return, and enabled him to march to the assistance of the duke of Orleans, who was besieged in Novara by Lewis Sforza: but we were obliged to surrender Novara, as well as the port of Spezzia, to Lewis, who advanced a large sum of money to the king, and to the duke of Orleans, besides a promise, which he never intended to keep, of sending succours to the French in the kingdom of Naples. Notwithstanding the battle of Seminara, gained by Aubigny, the kingdom of

REMARKABLE EVENTS under CHARLES VIII.

Naples was recovered with the same rapidity as it had been conquered: Ferdinand is recalled by his subjects, and supported by Gonsalvo of Cordova, that famous general of Ferdinand the Catholic, king of Spain.

1496.

Ferdinand, king of Naples, did not long enjoy this return of prosperous fortune; he died soon after, without issue, and was succeeded by Frederic his uncle. Guicciardin observes, that, in the space of three years, the kingdom of Naples had five kings, Ferdinand, Alphonso, Ferdinand II, Charles VIII, and Frederic. The count de Montpensier, whom Charles VIII. had appointed viceroy of Naples, dies of the plague at Pozzuolo.

Establishment of the company of a hundred Swifs, whose first captain-colonel was Lewis de Menton.

1497.

Notwithstanding the fatal consequence of the Neapolitan expedition, there were some who would persuade the king to resume it, or at least to send the duke of Orleans against the Genoese. But this prince, perceiving that his majesty's health declined, and being now presumptive heir to the crown, since the death of the dauphin at three years of age, did not think proper to remove to any distance, nor to suffer the king to repass the mountains: and indeed Charles had no inclination for it himself, being employed in an amour at Tours with one of the *queen's maids of honour*, (for this was the name given to young ladies of quality, whom Anne of Britany began first to keep about her person). The establishment of the grand council as a sovereign court, with the chancellor at their head. Francis I. created a first president, (who was afterwards suppressed) and empowered this court to take cognizance of all causes relating to confistorial benefices. In 1690, Lewis XIV. created a first president, with eight presidents, who were suppressed in 1738, when Lewis XV. substituted, in their stead, a counsellor of state, and eight masters of requests. Charles VIII, as well as his predecessor, had Swifs troops in his armies; to whom he added the Lansquenets, that is, a body of German foot. The French infantry,

REMARKABLE EVENTS under CHARLES. VIII.

infantry, consisting of the scum of the nation, was at that time in no esteem.

Charles VIII, says Comines, *was but a little man, both in body and understanding; but so good-natured, that it was impossible to meet with a better creature.*

Upon his decease, Anne of Britany put a black knotted lace * round her coat of arms, a custom which has been preserved ever since.

* The French call it a *cordelier*, from its being made in imitation of the cord, wore by the order of St. Francis, and out of respect to that saint.

REMARKABLE EVENTS.

1498.
Accession to the crown.

Lewis XII, surnamed the father of his people, grandson of Lewis, duke of Orleans, and Valentina of Milan, son of Charles, duke of Orleans, and Mary of Cleves, came to the crown in the year 1498, aged thirty-six years. He was crowned at Rheims, by William Brissonnet, archbishop of that city: his device was a porcupine, with these words, COMINUS ET EMINUS.

Where could Machiavel learn, that, after the decease of Charles VIII, it was positively affirmed, that Lewis, duke of Orleans, was incapable of the succession, and had forfeited his right to the crown, for having served under the duke of Britany, when at war with France?

1498.

IT was in regard to Lewis de la Trimouille, who had defeated Lewis XII, and taken him prisoner at the battle of St. Aubin, that this monarch made use of a memorable expression, at his coming to the crown, *it did not become the king of France to revenge the quarrels of the duke of Orleans*. Equally beautiful is that saying of the emperor Adrian, upon his accession to the empire, under similar circumstances, to a man whom he hated, *now thou hast escaped*.

It was not at all expected, that the duke of Orleans, who had opposed the second expedition to the kingdom of Naples, would march into Italy as soon as he ascended the throne. But the conjunctures determined him. Alexander VI. wanted to procure a settlement in France, for his son, cardinal Cæsar Borgia, who had taken a dislike to the church, and, in consequence thereof, was created duke de Valentinois by Lewis XII. The Venetians had quarrelled with the duke of Milan. Both these powers courted Lewis XII, who, beside the rights of the house of Anjou to the kingdom of Naples, had his own claim to the dukedom of Milan. His grandmother, Valentina of Milan, only sister to the last duke of the family of Visconti, was heiress to that dutchy; Galeas, Valentina's father, had declared her title in the marriage-contract with Lewis, duke of Orleans, brother of Charles VI. This contract had been confirmed by the pope, so far as on him depended, during the vacancy of the imperial throne; and the emperor afterwards granted the investiture of that dutchy to Lewis XII. in the year 1501. But Francis Sforza, having married the bastard daughter of the duke of Milan,

seized

The Third Race.   339

WIVES.	CHILDREN.	1515. DEATH.	Cotemporary PRINCES.
Joan, daughter of Lewis XI. married in 1476. Lewis XII. caused his marriage to be annulled, and Joan retired to Bourges, where she founded the order of the *Annonciades*, in 1501, and died in 1504. Anne of Britany, married the eighth of Jan. 1499, died the 9th of Jan. 1513. She founded some convents of *bons hommes**. Mary of England, sister to Henry VIII. married in 1514: three months after her first husband's death, she espoused the duke of Suffolk, and died in 1534. She had been contracted to Charles the Fifth, before he was emperor. * The order of Minims, or of St. Francis of Paula, called *bons hommes* in France, from the usual appellation of *bon homme*, which Lewis XI. used to give to St. Francis their founder.	Two princes, who died in their cradle. Claude, who was married to Francis I, king of France. Renée, who was married to the duke of Ferrara, died in France in 1575: her daughter married Francis, duke de Guise. *A natural son.* Michael de Bucy, archbishop of Bourges. 1511.	LEWIS XII. died *in his hotel des Tournelles at Paris, on the 1st of Jan. 1515, aged fifty-three years, and reigned seventeen. He was interred at St. Denis.* At his decease, the bellmen went about ringing their bells, and crying along the streets, *the good king Lewis, father of his people, is dead.*	*Popes.* Alexander VI. 1503. Pius III. 1503. Julius II. 1513. Leo X. 1521. *Turkish emperors.* Bajazet II. abdicates. 1512. Selim I. 1520. *Emperor of Germany.* Maximilian I. 1519. *Kings of Spain.* Ferdinand. ⎱ 1516. Isabella. ⎰ 1504. Philip I. 1506. *King of Portugal.* Emmanuel the Great. 1521. *Kings of England.* Henry VII. 1509. Henry VIII. 1547. *Kings of Scotland.* James IV. 1513. James V. 1542. *Kings of Denmark and Sweden.* John. 1513. Christiern II. deposed 1523. *Kings of Poland.* Albert. 1501. Alexander. 1506. Sigismund I. 1548. *Czars of Muscovy.* John Basilowitz. 1505. Basil Joannowitz. 1533. *Maximilian gave him the title of emperor.*

REMARKABLE EVENTS under LEWIS XII.

seized that dutchy. Lewis Sforza, furnamed the Moor, a defcendant of Francis, was then poffeffed of the fovereignty, after poifoning his nephew, and had received the inveftiture from the fame emperor in 1495.

An edict, ordaining, that henceforward the bailiffs and feneſchals fhall be graduates.

1499.

Lewis XII. marries Anne of Britany. The fate of this princefs was very extraordinary. She became the wife of Charles VIII by a kind of divorce from Maximilian, to whom fhe had been married by proxy; and fhe efpoufed Lewis XII, by means of another divorce of that prince from his firſt wife Joan, to whom he had been forced to plight his faith by Lewis XI; after the death of Charles VIII, he applied to the pope for a declaration of the nullity of his marriage, and, upon making an affeveration that he had had no carnal knowledge of Joan, the fentence of nullity was pronounced. John Standons, having been banifhed from France, for fpeaking too freely of this affair, was recalled foon after, and died at Paris in the year 1501: he was interred in the chapel of Montaigu. It is faid, that the marriage of Lewis XII. with Anne of Britany was owing to his regard for that princefs; but Varillas, whofe authority is not always to be rejected, thinks it might have proceeded from reafons of ftate as well as from love. By the treaty, concluded with the ftate of Britany, it was exprefsly mentioned, that, if Charles VIII happened to die without iffue, before the dutchefs, fhe fhould efpoufe his fucceffor.

The fupreme court of judicature in Normandy, ftiled the Exchequer, is erected into a parliament, and rendered perpetual. The king, difpenfing with Philip, fon of Maximilian, archduke of Auftria, and lord of the Netherlands, from a perſonal attendance in France, to do homage for the counties of Flanders and Artois, fends his chancellor, Guy de Rochefort, to receive this homage at Arras.

The conqueft of the Milanefe, performed in the fpace of twenty days, by the king's army, under the command of Lewis of Luxemburg count de Ligny, of Robert Stuart lord of Aubigny

The THIRD RACE.

MINISTERS.	WARRIORS.	MAGISTRATES.	EMINENT and LEARNED MEN.
George, cardinal d'Amboise. 1510. This minister, says Mezeray, was justly beloved by France, and by his master, because he was equally fond of them both. Francis le Roy Chavigny, great almoner. 1515. *Secretaries of the finances.* Florimond Robertet. Robert Gedoin. B. Bochetel.	*Marshals of France.* John James Trivulce. 1518. Charles d'Amboise de Chaumont. 1511. James de Chabanes de la Palice. 1524. Robert Stuart d'Aubigny. 1543.	*Chancellors.* Guy de Rochfort. 1507. John de Ganay. 1512. Stephen Poncher. 1524. *First presidents.* John de Ganay. 1512. Antony du Prat. 1535. *Attorney general.* William Rogier. 1523. *King's advocates.* John Olivier, living in 1517. Roger Barme, living in 1517. John le Lievre. 1521.	Americus Vespusius. 1508. Phil. Beroald. 1505. Amb. Calepin. 1510. Demet. Chalcondylas. 1513. Ant. Urceus Codrus. 1500. Christ. Columbus. 1506. Phil. de Comines. 1509. John Despauter, after 1514. Jerome Donat, towards 1499. Marsilius Ficinus. 1499. St. Francis of Paula. 1507. Robert Gaguin. 1502. Octav. de St. Gelais. 1502. Nicholas Gilles. 1503. John le Maire, towards 1510. Oliver de la Marche. 1501. Ludovicus Vives, towards 1500.

REMARKABLE EVENTS *under* LEWIS XII.

and of John James Trivulce, a Milanese lord. The king makes his entry into Milan the 6th of October, and leaves the government to Trivulce. Genoa submits to his majesty.

1500.

By a sudden change of fortune, which frequently happens in the wars of Italy, Sforza, after having been expelled from the dukedom of Milan, was returned to that province, and had retaken several towns. The king sends a reinforcement of troops, under the command of Lewis de la Trimouille, who, holding a correspondence with the Swifs in Sforza's army, makes that duke a prisoner: Sforza is carried into France, and confined to the castle of Loches, where he died in 1510. He was surnamed the Moor, not from his complexion, for he was rather fair than swarthy, but from an allusion to the Italian word *moro*, which signifies a mulberry-tree, and which he had taken for his device, considering this tree as the symbol of prudence. (*Mem. of the Acad. of belles lettres, tom.* 16.) In consequence of this event, the king once more becomes master of Milan; and Charles d'Amboise, the cardinal's brother, is appointed governor of that dukedom.

Lewis XII. and Ferdinand the Catholic, king of Spain, agree to share the kingdom of Naples betwixt them.

The birth of Charles V, on the feast of St. Matthias, which proved a fortunate day to him, during the whole course of his life. Maximilian divides the empire into ten circles, six of which he instituted in 1500, and four in 1512. There had been already a former division of the empire into four circles, made by the emperor Albert II. at the diet of Nurenberg in 1438.

1501.

Lewis XII. and Ferdinand the Catholic complete the conquest of the kingdom of Naples in less than four months. Lewis d'Armagnac, duke de Nemours, and Stuart d'Aubigny, commanded the French army; Gonsalvo of Cordova, surnamed the *Great Captain*, had the direction of that of his Catholic majesty: it is said, that this general was so strongly attached to queen Isabella, as to give displeasure to her husband king Ferdinand.

Frederic,

REMARKABLE EVENTS under LEWIS XII.

Frederic, king of Naples, retires to France, and resigns, in favour of Lewis XII, all his right to that portion of his dominions, which had been adjudged to him by the partition treaty of 1500. This resignation is made with a proviso, that Frederic shall receive the county of Maine, &c. in exchange for himself and his heirs, *male and female:* he died at Tours in 1504. Anne de Laval, his grand-daughter, was married, in 1521, to Francis de la Trimouille, prince of Talmond; from whence are derived the claims of this family to the kingdom of Naples. The Venetians begin to take umbrage at the conquests of Lewis XII, with whom Maximilian concludes a truce.

The creation of the parliament of Aix.

An arret of parliament, which deprives the provost of Paris of the right of presiding at the Chatelet, and confers it on the lieutenant-civil, or one of the counsellors, in his absence.

1502.

The French and Spaniards quarrel about the spoils of the kingdom of Naples: and at first the French have the advantage. An insurrection in Florence, with a view of restoring Peter de Medicis, who had been expelled from thence, when Charles VIII. took that city in his way to the kingdom of Naples. Lewis XII. maintains the liberty of that republic. The perpetual peace, signed this year between Henry VII. and James III, king of Scotland: a remarkable article of this treaty was the marriage of Margaret, the daughter of Henry, to James Stuart; in consequence of which the crown of England devolved, some time after, to the house of Stuart.

1503.

A treaty between Lewis XII. and Ferdinand the Catholic, concluded at Lyons by the archduke Philip, son-in-law of Ferdinand: it was stipulated, that, in virtue of the marriage agreed to between Claude of France and Charles of Luxemburg, (afterwards Charles V.) the kings of France and Spain should resign, the former the kingdom of Naples, the latter the dutchies of Calabria and Apulia, in favour of the bride and bridegroom. In consequence of this agreement, Lewis XII. sent an order to his general to suspend hostilities. Ferdinand, less faithful to his engagement,

engagement, enjoins Gonsalvo to pay no regard to it. Gonsalvo therefore continues the war; and receives reinforcements from Hugh de Cardonne and Antony de Leve. D'Aubigny is defeated at the battle of Seminara, on Friday the 12th of April, by Antony de Leve, on the very same spot where he had gained a victory eight years before: on the 28th of the same month of April, and on the same day, was fought the battle of Cerignola, where Gonsalvo gained a victory over the duke de Nemours, who was slain in the beginning of the action, (with him expired the branch of Armagnac, descended from Charibert, the son of Clotharius II.) which occasioned the loss of the kingdom of Naples. It is said, that those two fatal days gave rise to the superstitious notion of the common people, who consider Friday as unfortunate.

The death of Alexander VI. on the 18th of August. He was master of profound policy and addicted to cruelty, qualities which seldom unite in the same person. Providence permitted that all his crimes should redound to the advantage of the church: and indeed it is chiefly since the reign of Alexander VI, that the popes have begun to make a figure as temporal princes. Francis Piccolomini, his successor, who took the name of Pius III, died in five and twenty days. The cardinal de la Rovere is elected pope, by the name of Julius II, after amusing the cardinal d'Amboise, who might have been raised to the pontificate, if he had not dismissed the French troops. These revolutions of the court of Rome did infinite prejudice to Lewis XII, whose army, having been successively commanded by la Trimouille, by the marquis of Mantua, who was defeated in passing the Garigliano, and by the marquis of Saluzzo, who was beaten on the same spot, mouldered away through sickness and want of pay.

1504.

The king marches three armies against Ferdinand, in revenge of that prince's treacherous behaviour: these armies were very expensive, but did him very little service.

Cæsar Borgia is seized by Gonsalvo, and sent to Spain, where he died three years after. The king of the Romans grants the investiture of the dukedom of Milan to Lewis XII. The
death

REMARKABLE EVENTS under LEWIS XII.

death of Isabella of Castile. This princess, sister of Henry IV, surnamed the *impotent*, succeeded her brother, to the prejudice of Joan her sister, whom she caused to be declared a bastard, and whom the queen is really said to have had by Bertrand de la Cueva, with her husband's consent, who was grieved that he had no heir. Isabella, though two and thirty years of age, married Ferdinand, who was but sixteen; among other children they had Joan, called the *foolish*, wife of Philip, surnamed the *handsome*, son of the emperor Maximilian. From this marriage sprung Charles V. The archduke Philip succeeds Isabella his mother-in-law, in the kingdom of Castile, the administration of which had been reserved for Ferdinand, by Isabella's will, which is supposed to have been forged; but Ferdinand was obliged to relinquish his pretensions, when Philip his son-in-law arrived in Spain.

1505. 6. 7.

Ferdinand, in order to wrest Castile from Philip his son-in-law, endeavours to marry that very same Joan, the daughter of Henry IV, whom he had procured to be declared a bastard; but, not being able to succeed, he espouses Germaine de Foix, the daughter of Mary, sister of Lewis XII, who gives, in portion with his niece, his rights to the kingdom of Naples.

The county of Nevers is the first peerage erected in favour of a foreign prince. By a treaty, concluded at Blois, the king had confirmed his promise of marrying his daughter Claude to Charles the son of Philip; but he found the conditions too onerous to observe them: it was determined, by the assemblies of the states, held at Tours, that the marriage should not take place, and that the princess Claude should be affianced to Francis, count d'Angouleme. The order observed at this assembly is remarkable; the king had upon his right hand the cardinal d'Amboise, the cardinal de Narbonne, the chancellor, and a great many prelates; on the left, the duke de Valois, the princes of the blood, the lords and barons, the first president of the parliament, and several counsellors. It was before this assembly that the states of the kingdom had their audience; whence it appears, that the persons accompanying the king are distinct from the states-general. The

death

REMARKABLE EVENTS under LEWIS XII.

death of Philip, king of Castile. The Genoese revolt against Lewis XII, who repasses the Alps, defeats the rebels, enters their city with a victorious army, and shews them mercy. He had, for his coat of arms, a royal bee, surrounded by a swarm, with this motto, *Non utitur aculeo rex cui paremus*, *The monarch we obey uses no sting.* An interview at Savona between the king and Ferdinand.

Lewis XII, in pursuance of Philip's will, is declared guardian to Charles, archduke of Austria, by the states of Flanders; he confirms the choice which this prince had made of Philip de Crouy, lord of Chievres, for his governor. It may seem extraordinary, that the king of France should be nominated to the guardianship of Charles, and accept of it. But if Philip, who, in other respects, had a great esteem and affection for Lewis XII, thought to engage his honour by this act of confidence; the king of France, on the other hand, by accepting the guardianship, was freed from any restraint on the side of the Netherlands, and found himself at full liberty to act in Italy.

The county of Nemours erected into a dutchy and peerage, in favour of Gaston de Foix, son of Mary de Foix, sister of Lewis XII.

A process being instituted against the marshal de Gié, the parliament of Toulouse suspends him from his functions of marshal of France the space of five years: this was the effect of Anne of Britany's resentment, who, looking upon the king as past all hopes of recovery, had loaded three or four boats with her most valuable effects, to convey them to the town of Nantes in Britany, which was to revert to that princess upon the king's decease. The marshal de Gié stopped the boats between Saumur and Nantes: the king recovered; and the queen would never forgive the marshal.

1508.

The league of Cambray against the Venetians, concluded by pope Julius II, and the emperor Maximilian, with the king of France, Ferdinand king of Spain, the cardinal d'Amboise, and Margaret of Austria, governess of the Netherlands. This princess was daughter of Maximilian and Mary of Burgundy: she had been contracted to Charles VIII, who sent her back to her father;

she

REMARKABLE EVENTS under LEWIS XII.

she was afterwards married to John, infant of Spain, who soon left her a widow; and at length she espoused Philibert II, duke of Savoy, who died in 1504. She wrote divers pieces in prose and verse.

The league of Cambray connected several powers that were jealous of each other, but especially of France; their view was by united efforts to recover the possessions of which they had been stripped by the Venetians; so that they all intended to quit the alliance, as soon as they recovered their respective rights. A league undertaken on that footing can never be durable: Lewis XII, of whom all the Italian princes had taken umbrage, fell the first victim to their suspicions; the Venetians, by dividing the confederates, found themselves the strongest in the end, and recovered all their dominions. The Turks proposed to march to their assistance: but the sage republic, knowing it was more dangerous to be protected by the Turks than attacked by Christian powers, contented herself with accepting of some salt-petre, corn, and ammunition. (*Fra. Paolo.*)

1509.

The battle of Aignadel, gained by Lewis XII. in person, against the Venetians the 14th of May: he had under him the marshals de Chaumont and de Trivulce, the duke of Burgundy, la Trimouille, &c. L'Alviane commanded the Venetians. The pope, and the king of the Romans, as well as Lewis XII, reaped the fruits of this victory, by stripping that republic of all she had acquired in Italy these fifty years. Who would not have thought the Venetians undone? But so true it is, *that great powers weaken themselves by alliances.* The king of the Romans had sent but a very small number of troops to the confederate army. Ferdinand was suspected from having had some towns in Apulia restored to him by the Venetians. The pope began to be jealous of the king of France. This combination of circumstances determined Lewis XII, whose health was upon the decline, to repass the Alps. The Venetians retake some of the places they had lost, and oblige Maximilian to raise the siege of Padua.

REMARKABLE EVENTS under LEWIS XII.

The death of Henry VII, king of England.. Rapin Thoyras, who has constantly recourse to Rymer's Fœdera, draws a very different portrait of this prince from that which has been left us by my lord Bacon, who has transmitted him to posterity as the Solomon of England. The former writer, on the contrary, represents him as a person, whose distinguishing characteristic was, that he lived intirely for himself, considering things only with respect to his own private interest; averse to war, yet making as if he intended to engage in it, only to squeeze money out of his parliament, and to maintain himself on a throne to which he had but a very dubious right; yet ready to accommodate matters with his enemies for the sake of money: so that, as father d'Orleans says, he sold war to his subjects, and peace to foreigners. Rapin finds fault with him especially for not opposing Lewis XII, in his design upon Britany, since it was so greatly the interest of England to prevent the reunion of that province to the crown of France.

1510.

Julius II, who, by the league of Cambray, had obtained very near all he wanted, was possessed now with no other fear than that of seeing the French settled in Italy. He therefore enters into a league against them, with Ferdinand, Henry VIII, king of England, Ferdinand's son-in-law, who had lately succeeded his father, Henry VII, and with the Swiss, who were dissatisfied that the king had too haughtily refused to increase their subsidy. This pontif pushes on the war against the duke of Ferrara with great vehemence, and is twice very near being taken; the first time in Bologna, by Chaumont*; the second in the little town of St. Felice, by the chevalier Bayard. In the mean time the king, being greatly displeased with the pope, assembles a national council at Tours, where was present the cardinal de Gurce, deputed by the emperor: and it was agreed to convene a general council at Pisa.

* The marshal de Chaumont, one of the ablest officers of his age.

REMARKABLE EVENTS under LEWIS XII.

1511.

Julius II. takes Mirandola in person. Chaumont dies, and is succeeded by Trivulce. The pope, being summoned to the council of Pisa, by Lewis XII, and by the king of the Romans, convokes a council of his own in the Lateran palace. The battle of Bastide, where Bayard defeats the troops of the confederates. Trivulce makes himself master of Bologna, and routs the papal and Venetian forces. The pope, alarmed at these successes, endeavours to make up matters; but, had he known the scruples which Anne of Britany raised in the breast of Lewis XII, for waging war against the holy see, he might have made himself perfectly easy. The council of Pisa met the 30th of October, and was transferred to Milan. The Swifs march into the Milanese, from whence the French troops were withdrawn. Gaston de Foix, duke de Nemours, the king's nephew, (his mother Mary being sister to Lewis XII.) and the marshal de Trivulce, retire into Milan, which would have been in great danger of surrendering, if the Swifs, for reasons unknown, had not taken it into their heads all of a sudden to return to their own country. Some authors pretend they were bribed by French money.

1512.

The duke de Nemours, having obliged Peter Navarre, the Spanish general, to raise the siege of Bologna, flies to the relief of Brescia, which he retakes from the Venetians, and lays siege to Ravenna. The battle of Ravenna, fought on Easter-sunday, the 11th of April, where the confederate army is cut in pieces. The duke de Nemours performed prodigies of valour, in which he was seconded by the chevalier Bayard, Lewis d'Ars, de Lautrec, &c. but, being too eager in the pursuit of a body of Spaniards, who were retiring in good order, he was slain at the age of twenty-three: his death was attended with the loss of the Milanese, notwithstanding the vigorous efforts of la Palice, (Chabannes) who had taken upon him the command of the army. The emperor concluded a truce with the Venetians. Lewis XII, seeing all Europe combined against him, especially the Swifs, who were on their march towards the dutchy of Milan, recalls

his

his troops, and, of all his possessions in Italy, retains no more than the castles of Milan, Novara, Cremona, with a few other places. Genoa rebels, and chuses John Fregosa for her duke. The council of Pisa is removed to Milan, and from thence to Lyons. The pope interdicts the kingdom of France, and particularly the city of Lyons. The king of the Romans detaches himself from the council of Pisa, and adheres to that of the Lateran.

Ferdinand wrests the kingdom of Navarre from John d'Albret, who was the lawful king, in right of his wife, the last heiress of Charles, count d'Evreux. The pope supports him in this enterprize; under colour that this prince had entered into a confederacy with Lewis XII, and was an encourager of the council of Pisa. Lewis XII. succours John d'Albret; but the activity of the duke of Alba rendered this expedition ineffectual, and obliged the king of Navarre and la Palice to raise the siege of Pampelona. Catharine de Foix said to the king her husband, after they had been dispossessed of that kingdom; *Don John, if you had been Catharine, and I Don John, we should never have lost Navarre.*

Maximilian Sforza, the son of Lewis, is restored to the dukedom of Milan; and the family of Medicis recovers the sovereignty of Florence.

The emperor Maximilian aims at the papal dignity. This appears from what he wrote to his daughter Margaret (tome iv. p. 1. of the Collection of Letters of Lewis XII.) " We can see " no sufficient reason for marrying again; but are resolved to " send the bishop de Gurce to-morrow to Rome, in order to " settle with the pope the proper measures for making me his " coadjutor, to the end that, after his decease, I may be sure " of succeeding him in the papal dignity." &c.

1513.

The death of queen Anne of Britany the 9th of January.

Julius II. dies on the 21st of February, and is succeeded by John, cardinal de Medicis, who took the name of Leo X. Maximilian, having been reconciled to Julius II, continues united to his successor. The king concludes a year's truce with Ferdinand, and enters into an alliance with the Venetians; his army, under

REMARKABLE EVENTS under LEWIS XII.

under the command of Lewis de la Trimouille, retakes the Milanese the third time. Genoa submits once more; but, after the battle of Novara on the 6th of June, in which the Swiss defeated la Trimouille, the French were at length dispossessed of the Milanese; and Genoa entered into a new rebellion. Lewis XII, says Machiavel, committed five capital blunders in Italy: " he " ruined the weaker governments; he increased the power of a " particular state; he introduced a foreign prince, who was already " too powerful; and he neglected to reside there himself; nor did " he send any new colonies."

Maximilian, Henry VIII, and the Swiss, enter into an offensive alliance against France. The English lay siege to Terouene, which is obliged to surrender after the affair of Guinegate, otherwise called the battle of *the Spurs*, where the French were routed *: The Swiss also lay siege to Dijon, which Lewis de la Trimouille preserved by a treaty highly advantageous to that nation, which he reckoned the king would refuse to ratify. The Venetians, on the other hand, did not meet with better success, but were defeated by the Spaniards; and Sforza retook all the towns which Lewis XII. had conquered for that republic.

1514.

The death of queen Anne of Britany, the preceding year, facilitated the marriage between her daughter, the princess Claude, and the count d'Angouleme, the queen having a great aversion to that prince's mother. I find one thing extraordinary in regard to Lewis XII. and Anne of Britany. She had an affection for Lewis XII, which she plainly shewed by giving him her hand after the death of her husband; and yet so greatly was she affected with the loss of Charles VIII, that she mourned in black,

---

* Henry VIII. landed in the month of July at Calais, and soon formed an army of thirty thousand men. He was joined by the emperor with a good corps of horse, and some foot; the emperor was so mean as to act as a mercenary to the king of England, who allowed him a hundred ducats a day for his table. They invested Terouene with an army of fifty thousand men; the duke de Longueville marched to its relief, and was defeated. The action was called the battle of the *Spurs*, because the French used their spurs more than they did their swords: it happened on the 18th of August; the place surrendered the 24th, and the allies, not agreeing who should keep it, razed it to the ground. Henry then laid siege to Tournay, which surrendered in a few days.

though

REMARKABLE EVENTS under LEWIS XII.

though hitherto it had been the custom on such occasions to wear only white: on the other hand, Lewis XII, her second husband, who mourned in black upon her decease, contrary to custom, within a year after espoused Mary of England; and his passion for that princess cost him his life.

Lewis XII, being reduced to extremity, has recourse to treaties: first of all he treats with Leo X, renounces the council of Pisa, and submits to that of the Lateran; secondly, he enters into a treaty with Ferdinand, and continues the truce with that prince, promising to give his daughter Renée in marriage to one of his grandsons, Charles or Ferdinand, and to resign his rights to the Milanese; thirdly, he treats with Henry VIII, and espouses that king's sister Mary, though she had been betrothed to the archduke Charles (afterwards Charles V.) The latter treaty was conducted by Lewis, duke de Longueville, who became sovereign of Neufchatel, by marrying the heiress of that principality: he was grandson of the famous count de Dunois, and had a bastard, from whom messieurs de Rothelin are descended.

The count d'Angouleme conceived a passion for the young queen; but was made sensible of the danger of encouraging it, since it might be a means of excluding him from the crown. Grignaux was the author of this prudent advice, according to some; others give the honour of it to Gouffier, and others to du Prat.

1515.

Lewis XII. was meditating another expedition into Italy, for the recovery of the dukedom of Milan, when death put an end to the reign of this good prince. He was fifty-three years old when he married princess Mary, and his health upon the decline; but he forgot his age to please his wife, and met with death in her arms, after he had been married only two months and a half. *The good king, for the sake of his wife, had intirely altered his manner of living; for before he used to dine at eight o'clock, and now he was obliged to dine at noon; it had been likewise his hour of going to bed at six, and now he frequently sat up till midnight.* (History of Bayard.)

The

REMARKABLE EVENTS under LEWIS XII.

The device of the porcupine, assumed by Lewis XII, with these words, *cominus & eminus*, alluded to an order of knighthood which had been founded by his grandfather, the duke of Orleans.

The memory of Lewis XII. will be always revered by the French nation: *we had never such good times*, says St. Gelais, *under any other king, as during his reign!* Yet this prince is blamed for having favoured and enriched the family of a pope, (Alexander VI.) who was the greatest villain that ever existed; in order to procure a divorce from a princess, to whom he was indebted for his liberty in the preceding reign: but this separation was a sacrifice he owed to the welfare of the state. We could have wished he had never quarrelled with his allies the Swifs, nor resigned himself implicitly into the hands of Ferdinand, the most treacherous prince in that age, who boasted of having often deceived him: besides, he may deserve censure for engaging in rash enterprizes, and for having sometimes prejudiced his affairs by an injudicious parsimony*. But he diminished half the taxes, and never created new ones; he loved his subjects; and his most passionate desire was to make them happy; for which he deserved to be called their *father*: so true it is, that the chief virtue of a king is to love his people.

* In the beginning of his reign, his subjects took the liberty to ridicule his saving; the king knew it well, and it gave him no offence; *for*, said he, *I had much rather my subjects should laugh at my parsimony, than weep at their own oppression.*

1515.
Accession to the crown.

REMARKABLE EVENTS.

FRANCIS I, *surnamed the* PATRON OF LEARNING, *count d'Angouleme, and duke de Valois, great grandson of Lewis, duke of Orleans, and Valentina of Milan, born at Cognac the 12th of September,* 1494, *ascends the throne on the 1st of January,* 1515, *aged twenty-ons years, and was crowned at Rheims the 25th by the archbishop Robert de Lenoncourt.*

His device was a salamander in the fire, with these words, *nutrisco & extinguo**; which was an instruction given him in his youth, and not an allusion either to his conquests or to his amours; for the first medal, with this device, is of the year 1504.

* *I am nourished, and I extinguish.*

1515.

THE alliance betwixt France and England is renewed during the joint lives of the two kings. The archduke Charles, being come to age, concludes a treaty of peace and perpetual amity with the king, without consulting either the emperor or Ferdinand. Claude, who had been promised to this prince, having married Francis I, it is agreed that he shall have Renée, the youngest daughter of Lewis XII; though at the same time the king of France, says Guicciardin, had no intention to accomplish the marriage, because it would have rendered the archduke Charles too powerful. For, when the dutchess Anne espoused Lewis XII, the Bretons, desirous to have a prince of their own, had expressly stipulated, that, if the eldest child of that princess came to the crown, the youngest should have the dukedom of Britany; and the case actually happened, since the eldest daughter was queen of France.

Francis I. marches an army into Italy, where he had no other ally but the Venetians: he was obliged to pass through Savoy; but the dukes of that country were attached to our kings, who, during the last minority, had even disposed of the government; besides, those princes having neither money, trade, nor forces, and not being possessed of the Montferrat, or the marquisate of Saluzzo, or even of any strong town, would have found it difficult to dispute the passage of the Alps, unless they had been supported, as they afterwards were, by other powers. Before he set out upon this expedition, he appointed madam d'Angouleme, his mother, regent of the kingdom; and, all things being ready, he began his march, in

order

The Third Race. 355

Wives.	Children.	1547. Death.	Cotemporary Princes.
Claude of France, daughter of Lewis XII, and Anne of Britany, married in 1514, died in 1524.	Francis, the dauphin, poisoned in 1536. Henry II. Charles, duke of Orleans. 1545. Louisa. 1514. Charlotte. 1524. Magdalen, married to James V, king of Scotland. 1537. Margaret, married to Emmanuel Philibert, duke of Savoy. 1574.	Francis I. died at the castle of Rambouillet the last day of March, 1547, aged fifty-two years, of which he had reigned thirty-two. He was interred at St. Denis. It is said, that this prince died of a distemper, which did not begin to shew itself at Paris, according to the parliament-rolls, till towards 1494. And it may be observed, that this is the very year in which he was born.	*Popes.* Leo X. 1521. Adrian VI. 1523. Clement VII. 1534. Paul III. 1549. *Turkish emperors.* Selim I. 1520. Solyman II. 1566. *Emperors of Germany.* Maximilian. 1519. Charles V. 1558. *Kings of Portugal.* Emmanuel the Great. 1521. John III. 1557. *King of England.* Henry VIII. 1547. *Kings of Scotland.* James V. 1542. Mary Stuart. 1587. *Kings of Denmark.* Christiern II. deposed. 1523. Frederic I. 1534. Christiern III. 1559. *Kings of Sweden.* Christiern II. deposed. 1523. Gustavus Vasa, descended from the ancient kings of Sweden, and founder of the present race. 1560. *King of Poland.* Sigismund I. 1548. *Czars of Muscovy.* Basil Joannowitz. 1533. John Basilowitz. 1584.
Eleonora of Austria, sister to Charles V, and widow of Emmanuel, king of Portugal, married in 1530, died in 1558.	Francis I. had a *natural son* named Vilcouvin. He had no children by his two mistresses. *Frances de Foix, countess of Chateaubriant, died in* 1537. And *Anne de Pisseleu, dutchess d'Etampes,* commonly called Mademoiselle d'Helli, whom the regent chose for her maid of honour; she was married to John of Britany, whose mother was the daughter of Philip de Comines, and who was made duke d'Etampes.		

REMARKABLE EVENTS under FRANCIS I.

order to make a conquest of the Milanese, which was defended only by the Swiss. The battle of Marignano: it lasted two days, viz. the 13th and 14th of September; the Swiss were defeated; and Francis I. behaved with distinguished bravery. The marshal de Trivulce, who had been present at eighteen engagements, said that this was the battle of the giants, and all the rest were but children's play. In consequence of this victory, the king becomes master of the Milanese. Maximilian Sforza cedes that dutchy to him, and retires to France, where he ended his days, as his father Lewis had done before him. The Genoese declare in favour of the king. The pope, intimidated by the successes of Francis I, concludes a peace with that prince, and has an interview with him at Bologna; here they lay the foundation of the Concordate, which was confirmed the next year by the council of Lateran. The king returns to France, and leaves the constable de Bourbon governor-general of the Milanese. A parliament established at Milan, in imitation of that of Paris; John de Salve was the first president. His majesty gains over part of the Swiss cantons. Henry VIII, at the instigation of cardinal Wolsey, an enemy to Francis I, prevails on the emperor Maximilian to march an army into Italy: this prince accordingly makes an attempt of that kind the year following, but without success. A decree of the senate of Venice, by which Francis I, and all the princes of the house of Valois, are declared noble Venetians. It was to support the expence of the Italian war, that the sale of offices began to be introduced, rather by custom than otherwise; for we know of no law to this purpose; and even a long while after the reign of Francis I, it was still the practice for officers to make oath in parliament, that they had not purchased their places; but this was wisely abolished by an arret of parliament in 1597. (*See the particular remarks.*)

Erection of the county of Angouleme into a dutchy and peerage, subject to the jurisdiction of the parliament of Paris.

1516.

The death of Ferdinand king of Castile, on the 23d of January. This prince was justly stiled king of Spain, since he had reunited

The Third Race.   357

Ministers.	Warriors.	Magistrates.	Eminent and Learned Men.
Anne de Montmorency. 1567.	*Constables.* Charles de Bourbon. 1527.	*Chancellors.* Antony du Prat. 1535.	Corn. Agrippa. 1534. Lewis Ariosto. 1533.
Claude d'Annebaut. 1552.	Anne de Montmorency. 1567.	Antony du Bourg. 1538.	Lazarus Baif. 1544. Will. du Bellay. 1543.
James de Baune Semblansay, superintendant of the finances, hanged in 1527.	*Marshals of France.* Till this prince's reign, they held this post only by commission, and there were but two of them at a time: Francis I. created them for life; and the great wars, which he was obliged to maintain, induced him to establish four of those officers. The number afterwards ceased to be fixed; and each of them had his own department. Yet it is observable, that there were four at one time in the reign of Charles VII. James de Chabanes de la Palice. 1514. Robert Stuart d'Aubigny. 1543. He was made a marshal of France, in exchange for the office of lord steward of the houshold, which had been given him by Lewis XII, and which Francis	Matth. de Longuejoue, keeper of the seals. 1558. William Poyet. 1548. Francis de Montholon, keeper of the seals. 1543. Francis Errault, keeper of the seals. 1544. Francis Olivier de Leuville. 1560. He had a natural son, named Seraphin Olivier, a person of extraordinary merit, who was made cardinal in 1604. *First presidents.* P. Mondot de la Marthonie. 1517. J. Oliver de Leuville. 1519. J. de Selve. 1529. Peter Lizet. 1554. It was he that treated with Charles the Fifth, about the ransom of Francis I. *Attorneys general.* William Rogier. 1523. Francis Rogier. 1532. N. Thibault. 1541. Noel Brulart. 1557.	Peter Bembo. 1547. Will. Budé. 1540. Barth. Cassanée. 1541. Nic. Copernicus. 1543. Stephen Dolet. 1546. John Eckius. 1543. Desiderius Erasmus. 1536. Ferdinando Cortez. 1547. Fr. Guicciardini. 1540. J. A. Lascaris. 1535. Martin Luther. 1546. Nic. Machiavel. 1529. Ferdinand Magellan. 1520. Baptista Mantuanus. 1516. Aldus Manutius. 1516. Clem. Marot. 1544. John Marot. 1523. Sir Tho. More. 1533. Theophr. Paracelsus. 1541. Paulus Æmilius. 1529. Steph. Poncher. 1524. Raphael. 1520. James Sadolet. 1547. James Sanazar. 1534. Cl. de Seissel. 1520. Benedictus Theodoretus, preceptor to the children of Francis I, a Genoese, bishop of Grasse, and a lyric poet. 1536. J. Trithemius. 1516. Fr. Vatablus. 1547. Polyd. Virgil. 1540. Card. Wolsey. 1530. Francis, cardinal de Ximenez. 1517.
Fr. de Tournon, cardinal of Ostia. 1562.			
Secretaries of the finances. Florimond Robertet. William Bochetel. 1558. Bayard, lord de la Font. He was sent to prison in the next reign, for joking on the age and beauty of the dutchess de Valentinois. Breton de Villandry. Bourgeois, son to the first physician of Francis I. Nicholas de Neufville. Claude de Laubespine. William Prudhomme.			

the several parts of that monarchy; Arragon in his own right, Castile in right of his wife Isabella, the kingdom of Granada by the conquest of the Moors, and lastly the kingdom of Navarre by usurpation. But it is very extraordinary, that, out of so many crowns possessed by Ferdinand, three of them should be derived from bastards. He was king of Castile in virtue of Isabella, a descendant of Henry de Transtamare, the bastard of Alphonso XI, by whom Peter the cruel was dethroned: he assumed the title of king of Sicily, as being descended from Manfred, an illegitimate son of the emperor Frederic II: and lastly, as king of Arragon, he sprung from Ramire, a natural son of Sancho, king of Spain. John d'Albert makes some fruitless attempts to recover the kingdom of Navarre.

The treaty of Noyon betwixt Charles V. and Francis I: one of the principal articles is the restitution of Navarre; it was likewise stipulated, that Charles should espouse the princess Louisa, the king's daughter, then only a year old: it is amazing to what a number of princesses Charles V. was promised. Maximilian accedes to the treaty of Noyon, and, in pursuance thereof, surrenders Verona to the king of Spain, by whom it was to be yielded to Francis I, who restored it to the Venetians: so that this republic saw herself reinstated in the condition she was in before the league of Cambray. At the time of concluding this treaty, the two sovereigns, Charles and Francis, invested each other, one with the order of the Golden Fleece, and the other with that of St. Michael.

The treaty of Friburg with the Swiss, to which was given the name of *perpetual peace*; and indeed ever since those people have been steady to our alliance.

1517.

A treaty with Leo X. The king promotes a match between Lawrence de Medicis and Magdalen of Boulogne, heiress of that family, and niece to Francis de Bourbon, duke de Vendome: from this marriage sprung an only daughter, Catharine de Medicis, who was afterwards queen of France.

This year began the Lutheran controversy in Germany; it took its rise from the indulgences published in that country, by

WARRIORS.	MAGISTRATES.
Francis I. desired he would resign to de Boisy, his governor. Odet de Foix de Lautrec. 1528. Gaspard de Coligny. 1522. Anne de Montmorency. 1567. Thomas de Foix de Lescun. 1524. Theodore Trivulce. 1531. Rob. de la Marck. 1537. René de Montejean. 1538. Cl. d'Annebaut, who was also admiral. 1552. Oudard du Biez. 1553. Ant. de Lettes de Montpesat. 1544. John Carraccioli, prince of Melphi. 1550.	*King's advocates.* J. le Lievre. 1521. Peter Lizet. 1554. John Ruzé. 1529. Will. Poyet. 1548. Oliver Alligret. 1532. Fr. de Montholon. 1543. Peter Raymond, living in 1545. James Cappel. 1541. John Ruzé practised in 1536. Giles le Maitre. 1562. Gabriel Marlhac. 1551.

REMARKABLE EVENTS under FRANCIS I.

order of Leo X, with a view of opposing the Turkish emperor, Selim, whose successes in Egypt, against the Mammelukes, gave reason to apprehend he would turn his arms against the Christian powers.

1518.

The alliance with England, renewed by means of cardinal Wolsey, whom Francis I. had gained over to his interest, in consequence of which he obtained the restitution of Tournay. The king had likewise entered into a negotiation for the recovery of Calais; but Charles V. having had notice thereof, prevented the bargain, and repurchased Wolsey's favour.

1519.

The death of the emperor Maximilian. Julius II. used to say, that the cardinals and electors were mistaken in their choice; for the papal dignity ought to have been conferred on Maximilian by the former, and the imperial crown on Julius by the latter.

Charles V. is elected emperor, after the decease of Maximilian, though the king of France had been a candidate for the same dignity; he was so piqued at that disappointment, as never to forgive his rival. On this occasion was introduced the custom of a capitulation, by which the emperor submits to the conditions imposed upon him by the electors.

1520.

The interview of Francis I. and Henry VIII. between Ardres and Guines, called the *camp of the cloth of gold*. The emperor, apprehending the consequence of this meeting, thought to prevent its doing him any prejudice, since he could not break it off. Having taken his way by sea to Germany, in order for his coronation, he put into Dover, and there had assurances given him, that Henry would enter into no engagement with the king of France, contrary to the Austrian interest. And indeed the interview was spent in feasts and rejoicings, where politics had but very little share.

1521.

The absence of Charles V. occasions some disturbances in Spain, from the remaining princes of the house of Arragon, who
disputed

REMARKABLE EVENTS under FRANCIS I.

disputed the crown with him. Henry d'Albret, king of Navarre, takes advantage of these troubles to recover all Navarre, by means of his general Andrew de Foix, surnamed de l'Esparre, brother of Lautrec de Lescun, and of the countess de Chauteaubriant; but he loses this country again with the same rapidity as he had conquered it. During the course of this war, Ignatius de Loyola, a Spanish gentleman, thirty years of age, having been wounded in the castle of Pampelona, to which we had laid siege, was reserved to be the founder of a society*, which is become so celebrated from its struggles and successes. Charles V, upon his return to Spain, created the dignity of grandee, as it subsists to this day. Fernando Cortez completes the conquest of Mexico.

The beginning of the long wars between Francis I. and Charles V, occasioned by Robert de la Marck, duke of Bouillon: the pretext or cause was, that the duke had declared war against the emperor, who made no doubt but he was encouraged by Francis I. The emperor takes Mouzon, which the king recovers soon after. Charles, being afraid to dispute the passage of the Schelde with the French troops, thinks proper to retire: Francis might have obtained considerable advantages, had he followed the advice of the constable of Bourbon, who was backed by la Trimouille and the marshal de Chabannes; but he preferred the opinion of the marshal de Chatillon, who had joined with the dutchess of Angouleme in her opposition to the constable.

The admiral Bonivet makes himself master of Fontarabia, which he might have dismantled, but was prevented by his vanity; and this gave time to the Spaniards to retake it: he was a younger brother of Gouffier de Boisy, governor of Francis I. The ill conduct of Lautrec; the intrigues of Leo X; the succours sent by Charles V, who wanted to restore Francis Sforza, brother of Maximilian, to the dukedom of Milan; the artifices of the cardinal of Sion, to hinder the Swiss in the king's army from acting; want of money; and the great extravagance of the king, as well as of the dutchess of Angouleme; all these circumstances combined to dispossess the French once more of the Milanese.

* The Jesuits.

REMARKABLE EVENTS under FRANCIS I.

The last action in this war was the bloody battle of Bicoque *, fought the ensuing year, when Francis I. had nothing left but the castle of Milan, Novara, and Pizzighittone. Pope Leo is said to have died of joy, at hearing of our misfortunes. This pontif had published a bull, which declared, that the cardinals should henceforwards share the benefices of the pope elect; Clement VII, who possessed a great many, and in all probability had been aimed at by this bull, was raised to the pontificate; but not till after Adrian, who succeeded Leo X.

This year the French began to wear short hair and long beards, the very reverse of the ancient custom. This fashion was introduced by the king, who, having been unluckily hurt with a firebrand † by captain de Lorges, lord of Montgomery, had his head shaved: in the reign of Lewis XIII, the old mode was restored, and still continues.

The king makes himself master of Hesdin, which compensates the loss of Tournay, taken by the Imperialists.

1522.

Cardinal Wolfey, whom Charles V. had flattered with the hopes of the papal dignity, quarrels with this prince, when his preceptor, Adrian VI, was chosen successor to Leo X. It is strange that this Adrian, who rose by his learning, should have paid so little regard to men of letters.

De Baune Semblansay ‡ is charged with embezzling the sums designed for Lautrec in Italy: he lays the blame upon the dutchess of Angouleme, who had received the money, and given him acquittances, but diverted it to other purposes, with a view of ruining Lautrec, and making room for her brother, the bastard of Savoy. Semblansay is arrested: but the process did not end till the year 1527, when he was condemned to be hanged, and the sentence was accordingly executed. He was betrayed by Gentil his clerk, who, being in love with one of the dutchess's maids of honour, delivered up to this lady her mistress's receipts.

---

* An old country seat, with a park, and gardens, well walled, and fenced, in the dutchy of Milan.
† It was by tossing a firebrand at a tournament, or some diversion of that kind.
‡ He had the direction of the finances.

Gentil

REMARKABLE EVENTS under FRANCIS I.

Gentil was made prefident of the parliament, but met with the gallows fome years after. Henry VIII. declares war againft Francis I; and the war alfo continues towards the Pyrenees.

In order to conciliate the minds of the people, Charles V. reinftates Francis Sforza in the dukedom of Milan. A league againft Francis I, for the prefervation of Italy, entered into by the pope, the emperor, the king of England, Ferdinand, arch-duke of Auftria, the duke of Milan, the Venetians, the Florentines, and the Genoefe.

The knights of St. John of Jerufalem are difpoffeffed of the ifle of Rhodes by Solyman II. Viterbo ferved for a retreat to thofe knights, till Charles V. granted them the ifland of Malta, to cover the kingdom of Sicily. This order muft have been very rich at that time, fince the grand mafter l'Ifle Adam propofed to the grand fignior, to reimburfe him all the expences of the war, if he would but raife the fiege of Rhodes. Indeed that ifland was extremely well fituated for a piratical trade on the coaft of Turky and Syria; and its harbour was highly convenient for European merchants trading to the Levant. Some thought it very extraordinary, that Leo X. and Charles V. fhould fuffer a place of fuch importance to be taken; but their animofity againft Francis I. prevailed over the general intereft of Chriftendom.

1523.

The conftable of Bourbon, incenfed at the perfecution of the dutchefs of Angouleme, whofe paffion he is faid to have flighted, quits his country*, and retires into the emperor's fervice. After his departure, the king, we are told, " fent and demanded back " the conftable's fword and his order: he made anfwer, as for " the fword, he took it from me in the march to Valenciennes, " by giving the command of the vanguard to M d'Alenfon, which " belonged to me; and my *order* I left under my pillow at Chan- " telles; but as to the emperor's order, he never would accept " of it." (*Brantome.*)

* After drawing on him continual mortifications, fhe had changed her battery, and commenced a fuit againft him for his whole eftate, the largeft any fubject poffeffed in France.

REMARKABLE EVENTS under FRANCIS I.

The emperor gives him the command of his armies, and promises to let him have his sister Eleonora, widow of the king of Portugal. A Spanish nobleman, named the marquis de Villane, refused to lend his palace to the constable of Bourbon. Guicciardin, who commends him for so noble a way of thinking, thus recounts the fact: "I can refuse your majesty nothing, says the " nobleman to Charles V; but I declare, that, if the duke of " Bourbon comes to lodge in my house, I shall set fire to it " when he is gone, as a place infected with treason, and unfit " for men of honour." The revolt of the constable of Bourbon prevented the king from marching into Italy, and threw the command into the hands of admiral Bonivet. The Germans penetrate into Champagne, but are repulsed by the duke de Guise. The English, having made an incursion into Picardy, are opposed by the duke de Vendome and the sire de la Trimouille, who obliged them to retire, and confine themselves to the taking of Bouchain*. The league is strengthened by the election of the cardinal de Medicis to the pontificate: he succeeded Adrian VI, and took the name of Clement VII.

1524.

Bonivet, supported by the dutchess of Angouleme, prosecuted the war he had begun the preceding year in Italy. Being abandoned by the Swiss, he makes his retreat to Rebec, where the constable of Bourbon defeats his rear, and recovers all that the other had conquered: *thus it fares with generals elected by court favour.* (Memoires de Tavannes.) The chevalier Bayard having been killed in this engagement, the enemy sent his body to France in a most honourable manner: he left a natural daughter, the mother of Chastelard, whom the queen of Scots caused to be beheaded. The French are intirely dispossessed of the Milanese.

The constable of Bourbon is obliged to raise the siege of Marseilles.

---

* An army of about fifteen thousand English, under the command of the duke of Suffolk, landed at Calais, and was joined by the count de Bure with a body of imperial troops. They made themselves masters of Bray sur Somme, took Mondidier, burnt Roye, and advanced within eleven leagues of Paris; but, upon the approach of the duke de Vendome, they were obliged to retire.

REMARKABLE EVENTS under FRANCIS I.

The king recovers the dutchy of Milan. The alternate succession of good and bad fortune during this reign is very extraordinary.

1525.

The king, whom no disappointments could deter from his favourite design against the dukedom of Milan, had undertaken a new expedition the preceding year into Italy, and laid siege to Pavia. The writers on the military art have observed, that, in this war, Francis I. had four thousand horse for his park of artillery. Among other mistakes with which this prince is charged, the most considerable, without doubt, was his having weakened his army by two detachments, one to Naples, and the other to Savona, after he had undertaken the siege of Pavia. On the 24th of February, the feast of St. Matthias, he lost the battle of Pavia, by the imprudent advice of Bonivet, and was taken prisoner. He received several wounds; one near the eye-brow, another in the arm, and a third in his right hand; he had likewise received some musket-shot in his cuirass. The Spaniards removed the royal prisoner into Spain. *The misfortune of the French in this battle,* says the duke of Parma, *is an instruction to all generals, never to divide their forces within sight of the enemy.* The king of England, grown jealous of Charles's successes, listens to the proposals of the regent of France*, by the advice of his minister, cardinal Wolsey. Before the battle of Pavia, the emperor used to write to Wolsey with his own hand, and subscribe himself, *Your son and cousin Charles.* But, after this victory, he discontinued writing with his own hand, and altered his stile. *(Guicciardin.)* Wolsey was offended with this behaviour, and, according to the usual practice of persons in his station, he sought an opportunity of being revenged. As Italy was equally alarmed, the pope, Sforza, and the Venetians, entered into a league, to wrest the crown of Naples from Charles V, and to confer it on his general, the marquis of Pescara, who had reason to complain, that Francis I. had been committed to the custody of Lannoy, viceroy of Naples; but, whether Pescara was afraid of being detected, or he continued true to his allegiance, he

---

* The dutchess of Angouleme, the king's mother.

disclosed

disclosed the whole affair to Charles V. In order to punish Sforza for his treachery, Charles orders Pescara to seize the principal fortresses in the Milanese. This general died soon after, not without suspicion of poison either from the Spaniards or from the Italians.

The duke d'Alençon, husband of Margaret, afterwards queen of Navarre, dies of grief for the mistakes he was conscious of having committed at the battle of Pavia: he was the last of the branch of Alençon, descended from Charles of Valois, brother of king Philip the Fair. There were other princes of this name, who died without issue.

The county of Dunois is erected into a dutchy and peerage. Charles IX. granted afterwards, by letters patent in 1571, to messieurs de Longueville, the rank of princes of the blood, which was confirmed to them in 1653, by Lewis XIV. Notwithstanding what Varillas and Baudot de Juilly have written, the privileges of this illustrious family went no further.

Margaret, dutchess of Alençon, sister of Francis I, takes a journey to Madrid, in order to facilitate the deliverance of her brother; but, finding her endeavours ineffectual, she returned to France: after a great many difficulties, the treaty was signed the 14th of January following. Charles V. knew not how to make a right use of his victory: he should have either penetrated into France with sword in hand; or acted upon a generous footing, by discharging his prisoner without any conditions: but he did neither. (This question is accurately discussed by Guicciardin, and worthy of the reader's curiosity.)

Albert, margrave of Brandenburg, grand master of the Teutonic order, having embraced the errors of Luther, undertook to seize the sovereignty of provinces which belonged to that order: he was nephew to Sigismund, king of Poland, with whom he concluded a treaty for sharing Prussia, on condition of yielding homage to that crown. Hence this province happened to be divided into Prussia royal and ducal; the former was ceded to the king of Poland; the latter remained subject to the prince of Brandenburg, whose descendants are since become kings of Prussia.

1526.

REMARKABLE EVENTS under FRANCIS I.

1526.

The king returns to France, and delivers up his two sons in pledge. The dutchess of Angouleme behaved with great policy on this occasion: Charles V. insisted upon having either the king's two sons, or a certain number of our best generals, for hostages: the regent did not hesitate a moment; but chose to send the two princes, rather than leave France defenceless.

The viceroy of Naples waits upon the king, in the name of Charles V, to demand the ratification of the treaty of Madrid. For answer, he was desired to be present at the remonstrance of the deputies of Burgundy, who declared to his majesty, that they would never consent to the article of the last treaty, containing the cession of their country: but what surprized the viceroy most of all, was the publication of the holy league. This was concluded by pope Clement VII, the king of France, and all the princes of Italy; the king of England was declared protector of the confederacy. The intent of the contracting parties was to hinder the emperor from possessing himself of the dutchy of Milan, and to stop his progress in Italy: it was called holy, from the pope's being at the head of it.

Ferdinand I, brother of Charles V, having, in 1521, married Anne Jagellon, sister of Lewis, king of Bohemia and Hungary, becomes master of both those kingdoms, upon the demise of Lewis, who perished at the battle of Mohats, without leaving any issue by Mary his wife, sister of Charles and Ferdinand. He maintained himself in possession of Hungary, though disputed by John de Zapol, Waywod of Transilvania, who was beaten at Tokay; and by Stephen his son, who was left under the guardianship of his mother Isabella, (daughter of the king of Poland,) and of cardinal Martinuzzi. Ferdinand obliged Stephen to submit, and it cost Martinuzzi his life.

The constable of Bourbon, having been promised the investiture of the Milanese, completes the conquest of that dutchy. Duke Sforza is obliged to make his escape. Guicciardin pretends, that, if the duke of Urbino, who commanded the papal and Venetian troops, had made a proper use of his advantages, he was so superior in force to the constable, that he might have easily dis-
lodged

REMARKABLE EVENTS under FRANCIS I.

lodged him from the Milanese; but this duke betrayed the common cause, apprehending left, if the pope succeeded in his scheme of expelling the emperor out of Italy, he should afterwards deprive him (the duke) of the territory of Urbino, which he had recovered upon the decease of Leo X.

1527.

The constable, distressed for want of money, marches towards Rome, in hopes of plundering that city: he takes it by assault the 6th of May, and is slain at the age of eight and thirty. The revolt of the constable, which proved so fatal to France; and the disturbances of the Guises, whose ambition aimed at the crown; are a lesson to princes, that it is equally dangerous to persecute men of signal merit, as to leave them possessed of too great authority.

The Imperialists, intimidated by the arrival of Lautrec in Italy, conclude a treaty in the utmost hurry for the pope's ransom, and quit the ecclesiastic state. Genoa surrenders to Lautrec.

Francis I. and Henry VIII. offer two millions of crowns to the emperor, for the ransom of the young princes, and in lieu of the articles of the treaty of Madrid, on condition that Charles shall discharge the sum he owes the king of England, viz. fifty thousand crowns, for which Henry had the *rich jewel, called the flower-de-luce*, that had been pawned many years before. (Rymer.) The emperor rejects these proposals. The constable of Montmorency carries the order of St. Michael to Henry VIII.

The estate of Guise erected into a dukedom and peerage, after repeated orders to the parliament, in favour of Claude de Lorrain. In former times, as at present, the peers could be tried by no other jurisdiction than that of the parliament of Paris; consequently, the decision of all matters relative to the peerage belonged to this court: thence it came to pass, that appeals from the jurisdiction of the peers, though no way relative to the peerage, were made to those magistrates; which occasioned a prodigious expence to the parties. In order to remedy this abuse, Francis I. ordained, that appeals from the jurisdiction of the peers, in matters not relating to the peerage, should be lodged before

REMARKABLE EVENTS under FRANCIS I.

the respective parliaments, within whose jurisdiction those peerages were situated.

1528.

Lautrec marches to Naples, and, laying siege to that city, falls sick, and dies. The death of this general, together with the defection of Andrew Doria, obliged the French to raise the siege; during which their army was almost intirely destroyed by diseases. The war is carried on but faintly in the dutchy of Milan. Genoa and Savona follow the torrent, and surrender to the emperor. Charles and Francis I. send each other a challenge. Philip of Savoy, the dutchess of Angouleme's uncle by her father's side, is created duke de Nemours: this is the father of that prince, who distinguished himself so greatly during the league under Henry III.

1529.

The last action in this war was the defeat of the count de St. Paul, of the branch of Vendome, who was surprized at Landriana, in the neighbourhood of Milan, by Antonio de Leva.

The treaty of Cambray, concluded between Margaret of Austria and the regent, deviating but very little from the proposals already made by the king. His majesty renounces all his rights to the Milanese, to the county of Asti, and to the counties of Flanders, Artois, &c. One of the articles was the marriage of the king to Eleonora, widow of the king of Portugal, and the emperor's sister. How destructive was the ambition of those two princes to Europe! "They inherited, says Montluc, a jealousy "of each other's greatness, which has been the ruin of a million "of families." Henry VIII. had entered now into a strict union with Francis, knowing he should want that prince's assistance, in obtaining a divorce from Catharine, the emperor's aunt. The pope had already made his peace with the emperor on very disadvantageous conditions, by the treaty of Barcelona; and, in a succeeding interview with this prince at Bologna, he obtained the restoration of Sforza to the dutchy of Milan. The Venetians likewise come to an accommodation with Charles V.

The Lutherans acquire the denomination of Protestants, from their protesting against a decree of the diet of Spire in favour of the Roman religion; the Calvinists afterwards assumed the same name. Solyman II, under pretence of avenging the caufe of John Waywood of Tranfylvania, from whom Ferdinand had wrefted the crown of Hungary, lays fiege to Vienna, but is obliged to rife from before that capital in the fpace of a month.

1530.

The Florentines are at length compelled to acknowledge Alexander de Medicis, the pope's nephew, for their fovereign: this prince had efpoufed a natural daughter of Charles V. The tranquillity of Italy is reftored. Don John Vitrian, in his Spanifh commentary, fays, that Charles V. committed a very great blunder, in preferring his natural daughter to Philip his legitimate fon, to whom the dukedom of Tufcany would have been of vaft importance, for the prefervation of his other territories in Italy.

The *confeffion* of Augfburg, fo called from the Proteftants having prefented it to the emperor at a diet held in that city.

Charles V. grants the ifland of Malta to the knights of St. John of Jerufalem.

The death of Margaret of Auftria, daughter of the emperor Maximilian and Mary of Burgundy. This princefs never forgot the indignity done her by Charles VIII, in fending her back to her father; and therefore fhe fomented the averfion between the houfes of France and Auftria, which had its firft rife from her mother's marriage, and was afterwards tranfmitted to fucceeding generations. She had been married to John, the only fon of Ferdinand and Ifabella; and, after the death of that prince, fhe efpoufed Philibert II, duke of Savoy, by whom fhe had no iffue. This princefs was afterwards governefs of the Netherlands.

1531.

The death of Louifa of Savoy, mother of Francis I. The foundation of the royal college.

1532. 33.

The dukedom of Britany annexed to the crown of France: the reafon of taking this ftep was, that, before the ordinance relating to the démefnes of the crown in 1566, the patrimonial eftate

REMARKABLE EVENTS under FRANCIS I.

of our kings was in their own power to difpofe of as they pleafed, and did not become part of the royal demefne without an exprefs reunion, which rendered them inalienable. Such is our common law under the third race. The emperor, apprehenfive that the kings of France and England would enter into the league concluded at Smalcald in 1530 by the proteftant princes, and likewife dreading the approach of the Turkifh army, is induced to fign a treaty at Nurenberg, allowing liberty of confcience to the Lutherans, till the meeting of a general council. In return they grant him fuccours againft Solyman, who at that time menaced Hungary.

The ftrength of our armies, under the firft, and great part of the fecond, race, that is, before the inftitution of fiefs, confifted in infantry, to the contrary of the ancient Gauls, who depended chiefly on their horfe; hence it is *(Mem. of the acad. of belles lettres)* that the flower of the Roman cavalry was draughted from Gaul; and Cæfar, having fubdued thofe provinces as much by their inteftine divifions as by his own valour, ever after made ufe of the Gallic horfe, which he commends in feveral parts of his commentaries. This eftablifhment was revived upon the introducing of feudal tenures; and, before the third race of our kings, the cavalry began to be in chief efteem. But Charles VII. grew fenfible of the neceffity of a well difciplined infantry, without being obliged to foreigners; fo that, after he had inftituted a body of horfe, by the name of *companies of ordonnance,* or regular companies, he eftablifhed the *franc-archers,* or free-archers. Thefe were fuppreffed by Lewis XI, who took Swifs troops into his pay, and ftrengthened this corps with the addition of French infantry: but Lewis XII, finding thefe forces infufficient, hired German foot. At his requeft, the duke of Gelders raifed a body of fix thoufand men, all choice troops, who went by the name of the *black bands,* from the colour of their enfigns. This corps was deftroyed at the battle of Pavia, and from that time we had none but French infantry, commanded by the chief nobility, who were ftiled captains of the bands. Francis I. then refolved to eftablifh a body of infantry upon the fame plan as that of the Roman legions, and to diftinguifh it by the fame name; but this eftablifhment was not of long duration, fo that we were obliged to have recourse again to the bands, which consisted only of five or six hundred men, whereas a legion amounted to six thousand. Henry, the younger brother of Francis the dauphin, is married to Catharine de Medicis at Marseilles, where the pope and the king have an interview.

1534.

The English schism, occasioned by the divorce of Henry VIII, to marry Anne Bullen. This prince had been honoured with the title of defender of the faith by Leo X, and was desirous of being thought the author of a book, which he had caused to be written against Luther*. But, what is more singular, it appears, by one of Luther's letters, that, at the very time the king of England was writing against that reformer, he encouraged him underhand to proceed in his undertaking, and congratulated him upon his success. Wolsey, who had advised the divorce out of hatred to Charles V, did not approve of the match with Anne Bullen; but, in concert with Francis I, had endeavoured to persuade the king his master to espouse Margaret, sister of Francis I, and widow of the duke d'Alençon, who was afterwards married to the king of Navarre. This intrigue occasioned his disgrace, and he died in the year 1530, after he had been deprived of the greatest part of his estate. Sir Thomas More, lord chancellor of England, who was executed the 6th of July, 1535, made a more honourable exit: he had declared against the king's divorce, against his marriage with Anne Bullen, and against his making himself supreme head of the church of England.

Anne Bullen came over to France very young, with queen Mary, in order to be bred up among her maids of honour: after the return of that princess to England, she continued with queen Claude, who resigned her to the dutchess of Alençon, afterwards queen of Navarre. At length her propitious or unlucky star brought her back to England, whither she carried the new mode of religion, with the gallantry of the court of France; and she concluded the scene with the loss of her head on a scaffold, charged with several acts of infidelity to her husband. Strange fatality of passion! Henry VIII. could not

---
* Upon the seven sacraments; it was said to have been written by bishop Fisher.

REMARKABLE EVENTS under FRANCIS I.

gain the affection of a woman, who was indebted to him for so great an elevation, and for whom he had put away the aunt of Charles V, made a schism in the church, and thrown his whole kingdom into confusion.

It was on the occasion of this schism, that Francis I. complaining one day of the pope to the nuncio in France, and threatening him with the example of Henry VIII, the nuncio made answer, "Indeed, Sir, you would be the first to repent it; the spreading of a new religion among the common people, is soon attended with a revolution in government." And the admiral de Coligny happening to converse with Strozzi about the new doctrine, the latter said to him; " if the king wants to destroy the monarchy, he cannot take a better way than to change the religion of the country." Monsieur d'Aillé, in the exordium of one of his sermons, makes a very just remark, that never was there a new religion promulged, but a great many prophets started up, who followed one another in propagating their reveries. This declaration from a protestant is very ingenuous.

Francis Sforza, being restored to the dutchy of Milan by the treaty of Cambray, causes M. Merveille, the French agent, to be beheaded.

The king, being determined to take satisfaction for this affront, and finding Charles V. ready to embark upon his African expedition, prepares once more for the conquest of Milan. Calvin begins to broach his new doctrine: he was protected by Margaret, queen of Navarre, sister of Francis I. This reformer, having been obliged to retire from Paris in 1533, took shelter at Angouleme, from whence he proceeded to Poitiers, where he spread his opinions; and after the year 1538 he appeared no more in France. The society of Jesuits founded by Ignatius de Loyola, who was afterwards canonized.

1535.

The duke of Savoy, refusing to grant a passage through his territories, the king sends the admiral de Brion, who possesses himself of Savoy, and the greatest part of Piedmont. During the life of the dutchess of Angouleme, the duke of Savoy's sister, there was a good understanding between that prince and the king her son; but, upon her decease, the duke, having married the emperor's sister-in-law, was governed by that princess, so as to devote himself intirely to the imperial interest.

The death of Francis Sforza, owing, as it is said, to the terror of the king's arms, revived this monarch's pretensions to the Milanese; since by the treaty of Cambray he had resigned it only in favour of Sforza: he demands the investiture of that dutchy.

Francis I. growing infirm, applies himself more carefully to the administration of his kingdom. " Alexander made love, says " M. de Tavannes, when he had nothing else to do; but king " Francis gave his attention to business, when he was no longer " capable of making love."

1536.

Charles V, upon his return from the African expedition, in which he had defeated Barbarossa, and restored the king of Tunis, imagines that nothing is able to withstand his power: elated with the idea of universal monarchy, and with the defection of the marquis de Saluzzo, who had lately withdrawn from France to enter into his service, he rejects the king's demands with disdain; and, after retaking several places in Piedmont, he marches an army into Provence, against the advice of the most experienced members of his council: but he had reason to repent his temerity. His miscarriage did not deter the house of Austria from following the same example more than once, and more than once they have met with the same fate. Charles V. is repulsed on every side; and, having in vain laid siege to Marseilles, he is obliged to retire with the loss of almost his whole army: in consequence of this event, the king's troops recover several places in Piedmont. When the emperor undertook this expedition, he desired Paul Jovius, his historian, to lay in a good stock of pen, ink, and paper, for he would furnish him with abundance of matter: but it would have been better, had he waited for the issue. During the irruption into Provence, the Flemings invaded Picardy, but met with the same fate, being obliged to raise the siege of Peronne. Francis, the king's eldest son, is poisoned, not without suspicion of the emperor's being concerned in it. The edict of Cremieu, to regulate the inferior courts of judicature.

The

REMARKABLE EVENTS under FRANCIS I.

The see of the bishops of Maguellone is transferred to Montpelier, with the consent of Paul III.

The reign of the anabaptists concluded with the execution of Jack of Leyden at Munster, where he had been declared king by his followers.

1537.

Charles V. is summoned before the court of peers. The war continues on every side. The emperor is induced to accept a truce for three months, intimidated by Solyman's army, under the command of Barbarossa, with whom Francis I. had signed a treaty.

1538.

The pope prevails on the emperor and the king to have an interview at Nice: they came, but did not see one another; neither could they conclude a peace; so that they only agreed to a ten year's truce, called the *truce of Nice*.

The two princes met afterwards at Aigues-mortes. The bull of indult*. This privilege, in favour of the chancellors of France, and of the parliament of Paris, seems to have begun in the reign of Charles VII: it was granted by pope Eugene IV, to the intent, says Pasquier, "that such indulgence might prevent the court of
" parliament from being such strenuous opposers of the annates:
" it was neglected for some time, till the reign of Francis I,
" (towards the year 1538) when M. Jammes Spifame, a counsel-
" lor of parliament, having examined into the rolls, obtained the
" revival of it from pope Paul III; and these magistrates have
" enjoyed it ever since."

1539.

The inhabitants of Ghent having revolted, the emperor applies to Francis I. for leave to pass through France, promising the investiture of the Milanese for one of his sons. Charles was received in France the beginning of the next year with the greatest honours; but, as soon as he arrived in Flanders, and was reminded of his promise, he declared he had made none. Cardinal de Tournon was of opinion, that the king should have obliged the emperor, in his passage, to enter into an

---
* A special grant from the pope for conferring of benefices.

REMARKABLE EVENTS under FRANCIS I.

engagement in writing; but the conftable de Montmorency, on the other hand, being gained by the queen Eleonora, the emperor's fifter, advifed the king to rely on his word. Francis had reafon ever after to repent this ftep; and it was the caufe of the conftable's difgrace, who retired to Chantilly. Among the manufcripts of the cardinal de Granvelle, which are preferved in the library of St. Vincent in Franche Comté, we meet with an original letter, dated in the year 1539, wherein Francis I. invites Charles V, in the moft affectionate manner, to make France his way to the Netherlands. Triboulet, the king's fool, wrote in his pocket-book, that Charles V. was a greater fool than himfelf, in venturing to travel through France. *But,* faid the king to him, *if I fuffer him to pafs unmolefted, what wilt thou fay? That is an eafy matter,* replied Triboulet, *I will ftrike his name out, and put in yours.* The ordinance of Villiers Cotterets in the month of Auguft, for the reforming of the law, and fhortening of proceffes; the ecclefiaftic tribunals were alfo reftrained from incroaching on the ordinary courts of juftice; and all public inftruments were ordered to be written in French. So fage a regulation had been long expected. There cannot be a ftronger proof of the abufe of the ecclefiaftic courts, than what Loifeau mentions in his treatife of feignories, that, before the ordinance of 1539, there were five or fix and thirty proctors in the epifcopal court of Sens, whereas there were but five or fix in the bailiwick; and, fince the above ordinance, there have been only five or fix proctors in the bifhop's court, and upwards of thirty in the bailiwick. The reafon is, that the ordinance of Villiers Cotterets reftored things to their natural ftate, by removing the feveral pretences of the ecclefiaftics, to draw caufes to their jurifdiction. So early as the year 1281, the emperor Rodolphus ordained, in an affembly at Nurenberg, that the public inftruments fhould no longer be written in Latin, but in the German language.

1540.

The difgrace of admiral Brion, who had been fo greatly in favour with Francis I. as to excite the jealoufy of the conftable, and of the cardinal of Lorrain. The king, having ordered him to be brought to his trial, he is ftripped of all his employments,

REMARKABLE EVENTS under FRANCIS I.

his estate is confiscated, and he is condemned to banishment: at the head of the commissioners appointed to try him, was the chancellor Poyet, a tool of the court. But the dutchess of Etampes, mistress to Francis I, having a regard for Brion, prevailed with the king to let him have a second trial before the parliament of Paris, who declared him innocent, and restored him to his estate; upon which the king reinstated him in all his employments. The charge against the admiral Brion, (otherwise *Chabot*) was his having been too precipitate in following the advice of the cardinal Lorrain; for having, in the midst of his conquests, agreed, without orders, to a cessation of arms in Piedmont, where that prelate was negotiating a peace.

1541.

A dispute betwixt the duke de Montpensier and the duke de Nevers, in regard to precedency. The parliament determined in favour of the duke de Montpensier, as a prince of the blood, though the duke de Nevers was a more ancient peer: the edict of Henry III, which regulates the precedency, was not published till 1576. But Tillet informs us, that this determination in favour of the duke de Montpensier was not owing to his title of prince of the blood, but to his enjoying the two qualifications of prince and peer.

The chancellor Poyet, still persecuted by the dutchess of Estampes, and guilty indeed of misconduct, is committed to prison. He was brought soon after to his trial, and condemned in 1545 to lose his office, &c. Francis de Montholon was made keeper of the seals: on which occasion we may make two remarks; one, that the oath was administered to this magistrate by the cardinal de Tournon, in the king's absence; the other, that the dauphin also appointed him keeper of the seals to Britany, as sovereign of that dutchy.

An Irish act of parliament, declaring, that Henry VIII. and his successors shall be stiled kings of Ireland. This island had been under the English government ever since the reign of Henry II. Solyman seizes Hungary; in order to make a diversion, Charles V. undertakes an expedition to Algiers, where his fleet was almost intirely destroyed.

1542.

REMARKABLE EVENTS under FRANCIS I.

1542.

The war breaks out anew between Francis I. and Charles V, in consequence of the murder of Rinſon and Fregoſa, the king's ambaſſadors, (the one to Venice, and the other to the Ottoman porte) committed by order of Dugaſt, governor of Milan for the emperor after the death of Sforza. The firſt alliance between the French and the kings of the north; this was with Guſtavus Vaſa, king of Sweden, to whom the king ſends an ambaſſador, named Richard, with the mark of confraternity, as they expreſſed themſelves at that time, and the order of St. Michael. Sweden, as we have already obſerved, (1391) after having had kings of its own, became ſubject to Margaret of Waldemar, queen of Norway and Denmark. After that princeſs's death, the Swedes, though expoſed to the flames of civil wars, recovered their liberty, but were again enſlaved by the Daniſh tyrant, Chriſtiern the Cruel. Canutſon, great general of that kingdom, reſcued his country from thraldom, and aſcended the throne: his iſſue however aſſumed only the title of adminiſtrators, till a ſecond Chriſtiern, ſtill more cruel than his grandfather, obliged the Swedes to ſubmit once more to the Daniſh yoke. Then it was that Guſtavus appeared on the ſtage: this prince, deſcended from the royal line, emerged of a ſudden from the foreſts of Dalecarlia, in a manner the moſt extraordinary, and worthy of a hero; then, triumphing over Denmark, and over his own country, which was fighting for Chriſtiern, he mounted the throne of his anceſtors: happy, if he had not changed the religion of Sweden, to humble the pride of the clergy, who indeed were worthy of the ſevereſt chaſtiſements. That kingdom ever ſince has adhered to the Lutheran perſuaſion. The dauphin lays ſiege to Perpignan, defended by the duke of Alba. The duke of Orleans, the king's ſecond ſon, imprudently diſcontinues his conqueſts in Flanders, (where he had under him Claude de Guiſe) to ſhare the glory of taking Perpignan, the ſiege of which was raiſed. The war is carried on remiſsly in Piedmont. The king forgives the rebellion of the Rochellers, upon their making a proper ſubmiſſion.

1543.

REMARKABLE EVENTS under FRANCIS I.

1543.

Henry VIII, having already had some bickerings with Francis I, broke out into a war with this prince, for hindering the match between his son Edward and Mary queen of Scots, who was yet in her cradle. (It is she that was afterwards married to Francis II.) He then enters into a close alliance with Charles V, of whom he had received, and (what is still less pardonable) to whom he had offered, the greatest affronts. Francis, on the other hand, has recourse once more to Barbarossa, and concludes a treaty with him by means of his envoy at Constantinople, the baron de la Garde, formerly called captain Paulin. Barbarossa, in conjunction with the captain d'Anguien, lays siege to Nice; but the castle made so gallant a defence, that they were obliged to desist. The war is prosecuted on every side, in the dutchy of Luxemburg, in Brabant, Picardy, and Piedmont. The Imperialists are defeated by the troops under the command of the duke of Cleves, who was obliged soon after to make his peace with the emperor. The duke of Orleans, having under him the admiral d'Annebaut, subdues the dutchy of Luxemburg. Du Bellay possessed himself of Landrecy, which Gonzaga of Mantua attempted to retake; but the king obliged him to raise the siege.

1554.

A severe winter. The battle of Cerisolles*, gained by Francis count d'Anguien. "This prince, seized with despair, upon seeing the unprosperous turn of fortune on the side where he commanded, made two attempts to kill himself; so that by his impatience he had like to have lost the enjoyment of so glorious a victory." (*Montagne.*) The battle of Cerisolles was followed by the conquest of Montferrat, without any other advantage; the king being obliged to weaken this army, in order to make a stand against the emperor and the king of England. Charles V. penetrated into Champagne, and Henry VIII. into Picardy. The emperor obtained great advantages, which were further heightened by the animosity between the dutchess of Estampes and Diana de

---

* A small village of Piedmont, situated on a hill in the neighbourhood of Carmagnola. The battle was fought on the 14th of April. The Spaniards were commanded by Alfonso d'Avalos, marquis du Guast.

REMARKABLE EVENTS under FRANCIS I.

Poitiers, the former miſtreſs to the king, the latter to the dauphin. The dutcheſs encouraged the marriage of the duke of Orleans to the emperor's daughter; and Diana oppoſed it, as contrary to the dauphin's intereſt. A peace is concluded with Charles V. at Crepy, and publiſhed in Piedmont; whereby it was agreed, that things ſhould continue on the ſame footing as before the truce of Nice. Henry VIII. makes himſelf maſter of Boulogne, ill defended by Vervin, who was afterwards beheaded. About this time the poſt of colonel-general of infantry began to be known. Le Laboureur (or Caſtelnau) is of opinion, that the baron de la Garde was the firſt that had been inveſted with the office of general of the gallies; and he produces letters patent to that purpoſe, of this year's date: but Ruffi makes it of a longer ſtanding by fifty years, and mentions Pregent de Bidoux as the firſt general of the gallies.

1545.

The king's troops commit the moſt horrid cruelties in the Huguenot towns of Cabrieres and Merindol, under the colour of religion. This affair was afterwards inquired into: the authors of the maſſacre, and, among the reſt, the preſident d'Oppede and the baron de la Garde, were confined; but they found means to clear themſelves, and, in 1552 and 1553, were ſet at liberty: Guerin, the king's advocate in the parliament of Aix, being concerned in this affair, and likewiſe charged with other crimes, was hanged in 1554. Admiral d'Annebaut makes an unſucceſsful deſcent upon England. Marſhal de Biez lays ſiege to Boulogne, but is obliged to raiſe it. The death of the duke of Orleans. The opening of the council of Trent.

1546.

The death of Francis count d'Anguien, who was killed at Rocheguyon, by a cheſt thrown out of a window upon his head. Signor Cornelio Bentivoglio fell under the ſuſpicion of having committed this murder, as there had been a quarrel between him and the count. The king would not ſuffer him to be proſecuted, leſt Henry the dauphin, and the marquis d'Aumale of the houſe of Lorrain, ſhould appear to have been concerned in the affair. This count d'Anguien was brother to the king of Navarre and the

prince

REMARKABLE EVENTS under FRANCIS I.

prince of Condé, and had a younger brother, who was slain at the battle of St. Quentin. A peace is concluded with Henry VIII, by virtue of which Boulogne is to be restored in the space of eight years, upon paying eight thousand crowns. The death of Luther, at sixty-three years of age. Two days before he died, he wrote the following remarkable words with his own hand; preserved by John Aurifabert, who was present, and took a copy of them: " 1°. No body can understand Virgil's Bucolics, un-
" less he has been a shepherd five years. 2°. No man is capable
" of understanding the Georgics thoroughly, except he has fol-
" lowed the business of a husbandman the space of five years.
" 3°. There is no possibility of understanding Cicero's epistles,
" I say and maintain it, unless he has been in the administration
" of some republic for twenty years. (The abbé Mongault has
" proved the contrary.) 4°. Let no man therefore imagine he
" has acquired a sufficient relish for the reading of the Holy
" Scriptures, so as to think he understands them, except he has
" governed the church a hundred years, in conjunction with such
" prophets as Elias, Elijah, St. John Baptist, Christ, and his
" apostles." With such principles it is very droll to see him reject the assistance of tradition, explanatory of those sacred writings, which no man, he says, can live long enough to understand. He wore his religious garment a long time after he deserted the church of Rome, and did not put on a lay habit till 1523.

1547.

The death of Henry VIII, in the night between the 28th and 29th of January. He had espoused six wives; Catharine of Arragon, whom he repudiated; Anne Bullen, whom he beheaded; Jane Seymour, who died in childbed; Anne of Cleves, whom he put away; Catharine Howard, who was beheaded; and Catharine Parr, who, soon after the king's decease, was married to Thomas Seymour, lord high-admiral. Henry was succeeded by king Edward VI, the son of Jane Seymour. Francis I. caused a funeral service to be performed for him, in the church of Notre Dame, according to the established custom of our kings, as M. de Thou observes, though, at the time of his decease, he was separated from the Roman communion. His daughter Mary

forbad

REMARKABLE EVENTS under FRANCIS I.

forbad the offering up of prayers for his soul, because he died out of the pale of the church. Francis I, after having declared himself a persecutor of the Protestants of his own kingdom, entered into an alliance with those of Germany against the emperor. Shocked at the death of the king of England, he survived that prince but two months. In this reign the tailles were increased above nine millions. The conspiracy of Fiefchi against Genoa miscarries by that nobleman's happening to be drowned. The death of Barbarossa, who had raised himself to be king of Algiers. The first instance of marshals de camp was under Francis I; and even those were by commission: they did not begin to have this title, with commissions for life, till the reign of Henry IV. The marshals de camp, created by commission, were the chief officers next to the general; for there were no lieutenants-general till the time of Lewis XIII.

Francis I. is so well known from different elogiums, and from the parallels between him and Charles V, that we shall add only a few words to his character.

He wanted nothing but success to render him the first prince of his time: it is not however in the power of fortune to degrade kings, by involving them in difficulties. *Every thing is lost, except my honour*, said he, in a letter to the dutchess of Angouleme, after the battle of Pavia. Adversity only served the better to discover the greatness of his mind; and the shining qualities of this monarch had perhaps no less an effect on the writers of his age, than the protection with which he honoured them. He found himself placed in the very time of the revival of letters; he collected what had escaped the ravages of Greece, and shared, with Leo X, the glory of making the arts and sciences flourish in Europe. His openly favouring them, procured him the just elogiums he merited; and it ought to be remarked, as what did equal honour to this prince and to learning, that he assumed the glorious title of being its protector.

We see, in a letter from Erasmus, dated in 1516, that, Francis I. having told William Petit, his confessor, that he would draw into France as many learned men as possible, William Petit desired Budeus, and Cope the king's physician, to write to him, in order to prevail on him to come and settle there; that Stephen Poncher

REMARKABLE EVENTS under FRANCIS I.

Poncher (and not Ponchery, as le Clerc fays) who was the king's ambaffador at Bruffels, had preffed him on this fubject; but that Erafmus excufed himfelf by alledging, that his Catholic majefty, Charles V, detained him in the Netherlands.

Anne of Britany had begun to draw the ladies to court; but, as Lewis XII. gave himfelf little concern about them, it was only under Francis I. that they made a brilliant appearance: he alfo invited thither the moft diftinguifhed cardinals and prelates of his kingdom, thinking by this means to render his court more fplendid, and to polifh the manners of his courtiers, who had contracted the ruft of war, by fhewing them the abilities and examples of this firft order of the ftate. (Brantome.) His mother, the dutchefs of Angouleme, who lodged at the palace of Tournelles, having found the air unwholefome, came, in 1519, to live at the houfe of the chevalier Nicholas de Neuville, fecretary of the finances, and audiencer * of France: this houfe was between the Seine and the gate of St. Honoré, and ftood near the place where the Thuilleries are now fituated. The king bought the houfe; and afterwards Chatharine de Medicis converted it into a palace.

Nothing can be more furprizing than the fimplicity, which had prevailed in France for above a thoufand years, with refpect to edifices and gardens. The revival of learning, by enlarging the mind, made it perceive its wants. The arts became improved by culture; and their cultivation furnifhed new ideas. People began to think themfelves too much limited and confined; in proportion as they thought more, they grew afhamed of the former objects of their contentment; but, having once opened their minds, and given a loofe to imagination, they foon regained the time in which they had been involved in ignorance and darknefs. The epocha of this great revolution in Europe was the fixteenth century; when the deftruction of the Greek empire, by Mahomet, made all the arts and fciences flourifh in the Weft. The Medicis at Florence, Leo X. at Rome, and Francis I. in France, revived the polite arts; and thus it was twice the fate of Greece to inftruct and embellifh the weftern world.

* An officer in the Chancery, that examines all letters patent before they pafs the feal, receives the fees of the feal, and pays all wages affigned unto the offices.

The HISTORY of FRANCE.

1547.
Accession to the crown.

HENRY II, *born at St. Germain en laye the 31st of March, 1518, ascends the throne the 31st of March, 1547, at twenty-nine years of age. He was crowned at Rheims the 25th of July by Charles of Lorrain, archbishop of that city.*

The dukes de Guise and Nevers took place of the duke de Montpensier, and other princes of the blood, at this ceremony; but we find, in the parliament rolls, that, in 1547, 1551, 1561, and 1563, the duke de Montpensier, and the rest of the princes of the blood, had the precedency of those noblemen.

This prince, upon coming to the crown, gave, for his device, a crescent, in favour of Diana of Poitiers, with these words, *donec totum impleat orbem*, till her orb shall become full.

REMARKABLE EVENTS.

1547.

IT has been observed, that this reign began and concluded with a single combat, though of a different kind: the first was, that between Jarnac and Chataigneraye *, where the latter, who was the king's favourite, lost his life; he was gentleman of the bed-chamber to his majesty, and had been *child of honour*, which was something more than page of the bed-chamber: the former was brother-in-law to the dutchess of Etampes, mistress to Francis I. The second combat was the fatal tournament, in which the king was mortally wounded by Montgomery.

The persons most in credit during this reign, were, the constable de Montmorency, (who was invited again to court upon the death of Francis I) Francis duke de Guise, Charles cardinal of Lorrain his brother, the marshal de St. André, and the dutchess de Valentinois, who having already made a figure at court in the reign of Francis I, of whom she had obtained her father's pardon, possessed herself intirely of the affections of Henry II, although she was at that time forty-seven years of age.

An arret of parliament, limiting the authority of the cardinal legate of St. George, conformable to the decrees which had been published on the like

* This was a duel, on a private quarrel about their amours, between Guy Chabot, lord of Jarnac, and Francis de Vivonne, lord of Chataigneraye. The court was present; Vivonne, being borne to the ground by Jarnac, grew so enraged at his disgrace, that he refused to have his wounds dressed, and died in despair. The duel was fought in the park of St. Germain en laye. Jarnac behaved so modestly, and spoke so well after his victory, that the king called him up to the scaffold, where he stood himself, and told him, *that he had fought like Cæsar, and spoke like Cicero.*

occasion,

The THIRD RACE.

WIVES.	CHILDREN.	1559. DEATH.	Cotemporary PRINCES.
Catharine de Medicis, only daughter and heiress of Lawrence de Medicis, duke of Urbino, and of Magdalen de la Tour d'Auvergne, niece to Clement VII. She was married in 1533, and died in 1589. *Fœmina vasti animi, & superbi luxus (de Thou)*, a woman of vast capacity, and excessive magnificence. She was great granddaughter, by the mother's side, of John, count de Vendome. The princess of *Roche sur Yon*, being maid of honour to this queen, was upbraided by the prince of Condé with demeaning herself as a servant: *and why should not I?* answered the princess, *was not you a colonel of foot under Bonivet and the Vidame de Chartres?* (Brantome.)	FRANCIS II. Lewis died young. CHARLES IX. HENRY III. Francis, duke d'Alençon, d'Anjou and Brabant. 1584. Elizabeth, married to Philip II. 1568. Claude, married to Charles II, duke of Lorrain. 1575. *She was held at the font by the Swiss ambassadors.* Marg. the first wife of Henry IV. 1615. Victoria } died young Jane } *Natural children.* Henry II. had *by a Scotch lady of the family of Leviston, named Fleming*, Hen. of Angouleme, *grand prior of France, governor of Provence, and admiral of the seas.* 1586. *By Philippa Duc, a young lady of Piedmont, who became a nun, after she was brought to-bed.* Diana of Angouleme, *married to Horatio Farnese, and afterwards to Francis de Montmorency.* 1619. It was she that reconciled Hen. III. to Hen. IV. king of Navarre. *By Nichole de Savigny*, Hen. de Saint Remy. Hen. II. had no issue *by Diana of Poitiers, the widow of Lewis de Brezé, whom he created dutchess of Valentinois, and who died in 1566. By her husband she left two daughters, the first of whom was married to the marshal de Bouillon la Marck, and the second to the duke d'Aumale.*	HENRY II. *died at Paris the 20th of July, 1559, of a wound he received in tilting with the count of Montgomery, a splinter of whose lance flew into the king's right eye. He was one and forty years of age, and had reigned twelve. His body was interred at St. Denis.*	*Popes.* Paul III. 1549. Julius III. 1555. Marcellus II. 1555. Paul IV. 1559. *Turkish emperor.* Solyman II. 1566. *Emperors of Germany.* Charles V. abdicates in 1556. dies in 1558. Ferdinand. 1564. *Kings of Spain.* Charles V. 1558. Philip II. 1598. *Kings of Portugal.* John III. 1557. Sebastian. 1578. *Kings of England.* Edward VI. 1553. Mary. 1558. Elizabeth. 1603. *Queen of Scotland.* Mary Stuart, beheaded. 1587. *King of Denmark.* Christiern III. 1559. *King of Sweden.* Gustavus. 1560. *Kings of Poland.* Sigismund I. 1548. Sigismund II. 1572. *Czar of Muscovy.* John Basilowitz. 1584.

REMARKABLE EVENTS under HENRY II.

occasion, in regard to the cardinals, Alexander Farnese and James Sadolet.

The battle of Mulberg, where the emperor Charles V. took John Frederic, elector of Saxony, prisoner. He gave the electorate afterwards to prince Maurice, of the same family, though a Lutheran; to convince the public it was not a religious war, but that his design, in having recourse to arms, was to quiet the disturbances of the empire. He likewise imprisoned the landgrave of Hesse-Cassel, Maurice's father-in-law, who had waited upon him in confidence of a promise of security to his person.

The divorce of Henry VIII, who declared himself supreme head of the church of England, produced only a schism: but Thomas Cranmer, archbishop of Canterbury, changed the established worship, and introduced the protestant religion.

1548.

Fresh troubles break out between England and Scotland. The English wanted to marry the young king Edward VI. to Mary queen of Scots, and, by means of that match, to unite Scotland to England. Henry II. warded off the blow, and sent for queen Mary to France, where she was married to Francis II.

Jane d'Albret, only daughter and heiress of Henry king of Navarre, and of Margaret, sister to Francis I, was espoused to Antony of Bourbon, whom she made king of Navarre; but the English would never call him by any other name than that of the duke de Vendome. (Charles V. had some thoughts of a match between her and his son Philip II, with a view of putting an end to the disputes about Navarre.) From this marriage sprung Henry, afterwards Henry IV, king of Navarre.

The *interim* of Charles V. in favour of the Lutherans: it was a provisional agreement, touching the articles of faith that were to be believed, till the determination of a general council. Julius Pflug, counsellor to George, duke of Saxony, was one of those that had a principal hand in it. Upon the demise of Gabriel, the last possessor of the marquisate of Saluzzo, Henry II. reunited this country to the crown, as a fief depending on Dauphiné. Disturbances in Guyenne, in regard to the *Gabel* *; the rioters

---
* The impost on salt.

were

The THIRD RACE.

MINISTERS.	WARRIORS.	MAGISTRATES.	EMINENT and LEARNED MEN.
Secretaries of state. The first that bore this title, was M. de l'Aubespine, who is stiled *secretary of state* in the treaty of Cateau Cambresis, since which time the *secretaries of the finances* have been called secretaries of state. In this reign they also began to take the oath of fealty to the king himself in person, whereas before they used to take it between the hands of the chancellor. Will. Bochetel. 1558. Cl. de l'Aubespine. 1567. . du Thier, also comptroller of the finances.1559. Come Clausse. 1558. James Bourdin. 1567. Flor. Robertet. lord of Frene. 1567. John d'Avanson, superintendant of the finances.	*Constable.* Anne de Montmorency. 1567. *Marshals of France.* Ever since Hen. II. (the first of our kings, that honoured the marshals of France with the title of *ceusic,*) not one who possessed this dignity, was commanded by any other person than by a constable, or by a prince of the blood. Cl. d'Annebaut. 1552. Oudart du Biez 1553. Henry II. had been made a knight by this marshal; yet he was removed from court upon the accession of this prince, who even deprived him of his post of marshal of France; but he was afterwards restored. John Caraccioli, prince of Melphi. 1550. Rob. de la Marck. 1556. John d'Albon de St. André. 1562. Ch. de Cossé de Brissac. 1563. P. Strozzi. 1558. P. de la Barthe de Termes. 1562.	*Chancellors.* Francis Olivier de Leuville. 1560. J. Bertrandi, cardinal, the first keeper of the seals in France, by way of office. 1560. At first he had the seals in commission. *First presidents.* Peter Lizet. 1554. J. Bertrandi. 1560. Gilles le Maistre. 1562. *Attorneys general.* Noel Brulart. 1557. Giles Bourdin. 1570. *The king's advocates.* Gab. Marlhac. 1551. Peter Seguier. 1580. Den. Riant. 1557. Giles Bourdin. 1570. Baptist du Menil. 1569. Aimon Boucherat. 1564.	And. Alciat. 1548. P. Aretin. 1556. Martin du Bellay. 1559. P. Chastelain, great almoner. 1552. Robert Stephen. 1559. John Fernel. 1558. Jer. Fracastor. 1553. *It is said, that he found out the use of the telescope before Galileo, to whom this invention is attributed.* (Maffei.) St. Francis Xavier. 1552. Luke Gauric. 1559. Mellin de St. Gelais. 1558. St. Ignatius. 1556. Paul Jovius. 1552. John Maynier, baron d'Oppede. 1558. Margaret, queen of Navarre. 1549. John Pena. 1558. Fr. Rabelais. 1553. Jul Cæs. Scaliger. 1558. Michael Servetus. 1553. James Silvius. 1554. John Sleidanus. 1556. Andrew Tiraquean. 1558. Le Trissin. 1550.

were severely punished. Francis duke d'Aumale, afterwards duke de Guise, stiles himself duke d'Anjou, in the marriage contract between Anne, daughter of the duke of Ferrara, and Renée of France; and the cardinal of Lorrain, then at Rome, assumed the title of cardinal Anjou; they both grounded those titles on the claims of their family, which was descended from Ioland, the daughter of Renée of Anjou. *(De Thou.)*

Foundation of the university of Rheims.

1549.

A renewal of the alliance with the Swifs cantons and their confederates, except Zurich and Berne, which refused to sign it, by reason of the great severities exercised against the Protestants throughout the kingdom. Henry lays siege to Boulogne. The death of Margaret, queen of Navarre: this princess, blessed with all the endowments of nature, was sister of Francis I, widow of the duke d'Alençon, and at length queen of Navarre: she was the chief cause of the rapid progress of Calvinism, which she afterwards renounced.

The wars having augmented the tailles, a great many of the provincial inhabitants, to avoid paying this tax, came and settled at Paris: this occasioned the suburbs to increase to such a degree, that the government apprehended the capital would grow so large, as to prejudice the rest of the kingdom. The king therefore issued out an edict, dated the month of November, 1549, which is the first regulation for fixing the boundaries of Paris. This apprehension was but too well founded, as appears by the letters patent of Lewis XIV. in 1672, where he renews the same prohibitions, so often repeated, not to extend the limits of Paris, which by this time was enlarged one half; his words are remarkable; " that it was to be feared the capital of France, by " swelling to an enormous bulk, would meet with the same fate " as the most powerful cities of antiquity, which had the seeds " of destruction within themselves, it being very difficult for order " and good policy to be conveniently distributed through the " several parts of so vast a body." This is the very town, which, at the time the Normans laid siege to it, was inclosed between the two branches of the Seine, and is now called the city.

1550.

REMARKABLE EVENTS under HENRY II.

1550.

A peace is concluded with England: Henry II. recovers possession of Boulogne, upon paying four hundred thousand crowns at two different terms. An edict against the abuses of the court of Rome in the presentation of benefices. The death of Claude duke de Guise, the second son of René duke of Lorrain: he came and settled in France, after he had endeavoured in vain to exclude his elder brother Antony from his paternal succession: his son Francis, who was killed before Orleans, founded the branch of Mayenne, which became extinct in 1621, and was father of Henry, whom Henry III. caused to be massacred at Blois. Charles, son of the latter, was father of Henry duke of Guise, who distinguished himself in the insurrection of Naples, and died without issue. The male line of the dukes of Guise ended in his nephew in 1675; but Claude's posterity still subsists in the house of Elboeuf, which has founded three other branches, namely, that of Harcourt, extinct, and those of Arnagnac and Marsan.

1551.

A league for supporting the liberty of Germany, entered into by Henry II. on the one hand, and, on the other, by Maurice, elector of Saxony, and Albert, marquis of Brandenburg, who had quitted their connexions with the emperor. The king publishes a declaration, ordaining, that every third month there shall be sittings in his court of parliament, (stiled *Mercuriales*, from *dies Mercurii*, or Wednesday, the day appointed for those meetings) in which the king's council are obliged to examine into the conduct of any of the members of that assembly, who misbehave in their office: there had been already two edicts to the same purpose, one by Charles VIII. in 1493, and the other by Lewis XII. five years after.

The king issues out an edict, to prohibit the sending of money to Rome for the expediting of pontifical bulls, in consequence of a personal quarrel betwixt him and the pope concerning the duke of Parma*:

---

* Pope Julius III, wanting to dispossess Octavio Farnese of the city of Parma, under pretence of its being a fief that belonged to the church, demanded the assistance of the emperor; but Henry II. was determined to support him, and his assistance proved effectual.

REMARKABLE EVENTS under HENRY II.

he likewife enters his proteft at the council of Trent, by means of Amiot; but at the fame time he publifhes a new edict at Chauteaubriant againft the Lutherans.

The peers begin to take their feats in parliament with their fwords on, notwithftanding the remonftrances of thofe magiftrates, who reprefented to the king, *that, from time immemorial, this was a privilege belonging to the king only, as a mark of his royal dignity;* and that, when Francis the dauphin, fon of the late king Francis I, and Charles of Bourbon, came into court, they left their fwords at the door. The barony of Montmorency erected into a dutchy and peerage, in favour of Ann, conftable of that name: in regard to which we are to obferve, that, in the erection of the county of Beaufort into a dutchy and peerage, in favour of Cæfar, the natural fon of Henry IV, the precedency was ftill continued to the dutchy of Montmorency, while that of Beaufort took place of every other peerage, though of a more ancient ftanding.

The eftablifhment of the prefidial courts: the chamber of moneys or coinage erected into a fovereign tribunal.

The king and the emperor had already begun hoftilities in Italy, without a declaration of war; on account of the dutchies of Parma and Placentia.

1552.

Maurice, elector of Saxony, is very near furprizing Charles V. at Infpruck. The taking of Metz, Toul, and Verdun, by Henry II, who was upon his march to join the princes of the proteftant league. He was obliged to return, in order to ftop the incurfions of the enemy on the frontiers of Picardy, under the direction of Mary of Auftria, queen of Hungary, fifter of Charles V, and governefs of the Netherlands: another motive of his return was his having received intelligence of the pacification of Paffau, by which the Lutherans were made eafy in regard to their religion. The landgrave of Heffe-Caffel is fet at liberty: and Henry II. is the only member of the league that continues to oppofe the emperor. In order to fupport fo expenfive a war, he alienates part of his demefne, lays a tax of five and twenty livres upon every fteeple, and another upon the church plate.

An

REMARKABLE EVENTS under HENRY II.

An arret of parliament of the 6th of August, forbidding the *écoles buissonieres:* these were schools which the Lutherans kept in the country, for fear of being discovered by the chanter of the cathedral of Paris, who had the direction or superintendency of the like institutions. This is the original of that French expression.

1553.

Charles V. raises the siege of Metz, which was gallantly defended by Francis duke de Guise, and by the chief nobility of France. To wipe off this disgrace, he takes Therouene, and razes it to the ground; he likewise makes himself master of the town of Hesdin. Emmanuel Philibert of Savoy, prince of Piedmont, served under him this campaign: he was a very experienced general, and strongly attached to the emperor; still he had some hopes of recovering his dominions, forcibly withheld by Henry II, and restored to him towards the latter end of this reign. The French, for want of supplies, make no great progress in Piedmont, where their army was commanded by the marshal de Brissac, a general celebrated for his military abilities, and for the impression he is said to have made on the dutchess of Valentinois. The king's jealousy was the cause of his being employed as lieutenant-general beyond the mountains.

M. de Termes possesses himself of part of the island of Corsica.

Edward VI, king of England, dies at sixteen years of age, that is, during his minority; for, pursuant to his father's will, it seems he was not to be of age till eighteen, which is the term fixed for the majority of the kings of England. He is succeeded by Mary, his eldest sister, daughter of Catharine of Arragon. In order to remove all doubt concerning her legitimacy, this princess procures an act of parliament, annulling the sentence of divorce between Henry and Catharine, and of course rendering the marriage of Anne Bullen and the legitimacy of Elizabeth very suspicious. She put the duke of Northumberland to death, with his daughter-in-law, the lady Jane Gray, whom that nobleman had caused to be proclaimed queen. Jane was descended from that same duke of Suffolk, who had espoused Mary, the widow of Lewis XII; and on her mother's side she was the

great

great niece of Henry VIII. But she was not executed till the year following. Queen Mary restored the Roman catholic religion in England.

Michael Servetus*, a heretic, is burnt at Geneva twenty years after that city had renounced the Roman religion. This execution was at the instigation of Calvin, who by that single act refuted his own doctrine with regard to the severities against heretics.

The edict of Henry II. concerning the collation of benefices; it confirms the partition of months established in Britany, where the pope has eight months, and, according to the council of Lateran, is obliged to nominate within six months after the benefice is become vacant. The agreement, by which this partition was first established, is said to have been concluded at the council of Constance; but there is not the least vestige of any such agreement; and there is a greater probability of its having been made in consequence of a bull of Eugene IV. It is observable, that, at the time of signing the concordate, both Britany and Provence, though subject to Francis I, were not included in that treaty; because the concordate was made only with a view to abolish the *pragmatic sanction*, at the settling of which, in the reign of Charles VII, those two provinces did not belong to the king: hence it is, that Francis I. obtained an indult for nominating to the benefices of both those provinces, which indult has been continued to his successors. The same may be observed of the provinces annexed to France since the concordate.

The institution of the parliament of Britany.

1554.

Philip, the son of Charles V, espouses Mary queen of England, to the great dissatisfaction of the English and French. The king, having ravaged Brabant, Hainault, and Cambresis, defeats the Imperialists at the battle of Renty, yet is obliged to raise the siege of that place: in this engagement he fought for an opportunity of encountering Charles V. in person, but Charles avoided it. The duke of Guise distinguished himself on this memorable day. Strozzi, general of the French troops, is beaten at the battle of

---

* His right name was Michael Reves; he was a Spaniard, and had undertaken to impugn the mystery of the Trinity.

Marcian

REMARKABLE EVENTS under HENRY II.

Marcian in Tuscany, by the marquis of Marignan, who marches to Sienna: this city being gallantly defended by Montluc, does not surrender till after a siege of ten months. M. de Termes maintains his ground in the island of Corsica; and the marshal de Brissac makes himself master of Yvrée.

1555.

The war is carried on but faintly in the Netherlands, both parties, the emperor and the king, being exhausted. The marshal de Brissac meets with success in Piedmont. Charles V. resigns the crown of Spain in favour of his son Philip, at an assembly of the states in Brussels: he had already given him the kingdoms of Naples and Sicily, upon his marriage with queen Mary: soon after this he granted him the investiture of the dutchy of Milan; and, two months before the convening of this assembly, he put him into possession of the Netherlands and Burgundy, and made him head of the order of the Golden Fleece. This same prince had caused his brother Ferdinand, who succeeded him in the imperial dignity, to be elected king of the Romans; but he soon repented his having taken a step so prejudicial to the interest of his son Philip, and therefore used all his endeavours to make Ferdinand forego his right; but he found himself disappointed. Hence sprung the two Austrian branches in Europe.

The popes of the house of Medicis had made their relations dukes of Tuscany. Paul III. had raised his son Octavio Farnese to the sovereignty of Parma and Placentia. The Caraffas wanted in like manner to try their fortune under the pontificate of Paul IV. Hence this pope proposed a league to Henry II, with a design of making a joint conquest of the kingdom of Naples. The king accepted the proposal, notwithstanding the prudent remonstrances of the constable de Montmorency and the cardinal de Tournon: but he followed chiefly the advice of the cardinal of Lorrain, who was said to have aimed at the triple crown; and of the cardinal's brother, the duke de Guise, who was to have the command of the army, and whose head was full of the pretensions of his family to the kingdom of Naples.

1556.

REMARKABLE EVENTS under HENRY II.

1556.

A five year's truce between the emperor and the king, concluded at Vaucelles the 5th of February. Charles V. resigns the imperial dignity in favour of his brother Ferdinand, king of the Romans. The electors and princes of the empire had objected greatly against the election of a king of the Romans, from a notion that this was subjecting them to two masters, *(grave imperium futurum duos habere eodem tempore dominos,* Struvius) an innovation in the empire, and a direct violation of the golden bull. But they were mistaken as to the fact; for, long before that time, there had been an election of a king of the Romans, even in the emperor's lifetime, as in the year 1056, (see that year) when Henry III. procured his son to be elected to that dignity: with regard to the golden bull, it takes no notice of the matter; besides, did not Charles IV, the author of that bull, who of course must be supposed to have understood it, did not he procure his son Wenceslaus to be elected king of the Romans? It is true, he met with an opposition; yet he carried his point, by promising to each elector a hundred thousand florins, in lieu of which he granted them some lands.

Charles V, having resigned the empire, retired to a monastery in the province of Estramadura. He was accompanied in his retreat by his sister, Mary of Austria, widow of Lewis of Hungary, who succeeded Margaret, her aunt, in the government of the Netherlands, where she acted so vigorously against France; and by his sister Eleonora, the widow of Francis I, neither of whom survived him long, for they both died in 1558. Mary of Austria has not escaped the shafts of calumny; for several pretend that Don John of Austria was not the son of Barbara Blomberg; and she never would forgive Henry II. for some songs that had been made in France upon her and Barbanson *(d'Aremberg)*. Balzac, mentioning this retreat of Charles V, quotes a writing he had received from Rome, which begins with these words: *When Charles, disgusted with the world, wanted to take his leave of it, during the reign of his brother over the empire of Germany, and that of his son over the kingdom of Spain,* &c. And indeed these were a good many masters for so vain a man. Cardinal Caraffa, the

pope's

REMARKABLE EVENTS under HENRY II.

pope's legate in France, determines the king to break the truce, and to send two armies, the one into Italy, under the duke de Guise, the other into Flanders, commanded by the duke de Montmorency. An edict concerning clandestine marriages. What gave rise to it, was a promise of marriage from the duke de Montmorency to mademoiselle de Pienne, without the constable's consent. Pope Paul IV, to whom both the king and the constable applied for a dispensation, to release the duke from his promise, that he might espouse madam de Farnese, a natural daughter of Henry II, shewed himself very tardy in granting this dispensation; wherein he seemed to be desirous of gratifying the duke de Guise, who was jealous of the new influence which the house of Montmorency would naturally derive from that match: under these circumstances was published the edict concerning clandestine marriages. And it is observable, that the king gave it a retroacting force.

A severe ordinance, making it capital for young women to procure abortion.

1557.

Philip II. brings over the princes of Farnese again to his interest by restoring Placentia; as likewise the duke of Tuscany, by putting him once more into possession of Sienna. The duke de Guise is unsuccessful in Italy, where he was ill supported by the pope, and had the duke of Alva to oppose him. Queen Mary of England declares war against France. Emmanuel Philibert, duke of Savoy, having laid siege to St. Quintin, this place is gallantly defended by the admiral de Coligny: the constable de Montmorency, with an army greatly inferior to the enemy, attempts to throw succours into the town, contrary to the opinion of the marshal de St. André: a few troops forced their passage; but the constable, being attacked in his retreat, was routed and taken prisoner, together with the marshal de St. André: the count d'Anguien, brother to the prince of Condé, lost his life, and the duke de Montpensier his liberty: St. Quintin was obliged to surrender, and the admiral was taken prisoner. This was the *battle of St. Quintin*, which spread great consternation throughout France. The duke de Guise is immediately recalled from Italy

REMARKABLE EVENTS under HENRY II.

with his army. The marſhal de Briſſac maintains his ground in Piedmont with the few remaining troops. The enemy had like to have ſurprized the city of Lyons.

1558.

A meeting of the ſtates in one of the chambers of the parliament: here the body of magiſtrates took their ſeat the firſt time, and conſtituted the fourth order, for they were not admitted before to thoſe aſſemblies; and it is a miſtake to confound them with the third eſtate: but this was their firſt and laſt appearance; ſince they neither aſſiſted at the ſtates of Blois, nor at thoſe of Paris. The duke de Guiſe is made lieutenant-general of the kingdom, and revives the ſpirits of the people by taking the important town of Calais, which had been in the hands of the Engliſh ever ſince the year 1347, when it was wreſted from Philip of Valois by Edward III. The Engliſh are driven intirely out of France. The duke de Guiſe makes himſelf maſter of Guines and Thionville, where Strozzi * was ſlain. While the duke de Nevers is employed in taking Charlemont, M. de Termes, who ſucceeded Strozzi as marſhal of France, makes himſelf maſter of Dunkirk and St. Vinox, but is defeated at Graveline by count Egmont: the latter is the ſame nobleman who won the battle of St. Quintin, and who had his head ſtruck off ten years afterwards upon a ſcaffold, leaving his wife, Sabina of Bavaria, with three ſons, and eight daughters, in great diſtreſs.

Mary queen of Scots is married to Francis the dauphin, (afterwards Francis II.) in conſequence of which he had the title of the dauphin king in his father's life-time, this princeſs having brought him the kingdom of Scotland for her portion. The belligerant powers begin to talk of a peace: Philip II. was become more indifferent, in regard to the loſſes of the Engliſh,

---

* Peter Strozzi, of a noble family of Florence, was marſhal of France, and general of the gallies: he fell by a muſket-ſhot, reconnoitring a proper place to erect a battery againſt the town of Thionville. His father, John Baptiſt, endeavoured to reſcue his country from the oppreſſion of the Medicis, after the death of Clement VII; but was taken priſoner by Coſmo, after the loſs of the battle of Maronne, and ſtabbed himſelf in priſon, where he wrote theſe words of Virgil on the chimney-piece:

Exoriare aliquis noſtris ex oſſibus ultor.

REMARKABLE EVENTS under HENRY II.

since the death of queen Mary; and besides, he had affairs upon his hands which required his presence in Spain. To queen Mary succeeded her sister Elizabeth, whose life had been saved by Philip II, when Mary resolved her death: this action does him honour, as it bears the appearance of humanity; but Cabrera, his historian, frankly acknowledges, that it was the effect of policy; for, having no issue by Mary, he was willing to save Elizabeth, lest the queen of Scots, who was likely to be also queen of France, should join the crown of England to her other dominions, and become too formidable to the Netherlands. Philip II. also offered to marry queen Elizabeth. *(Mem. de Nevers.)* The duke de Guise declines in the king's favour, by incurring the displeasure of the dutchess de Valentinois. The constable is employed in the negotiations of peace, and prevails with the duke of Savoy to lend a hand, in hopes of recovering his lost dominions. Francis de Noailles, bishop of Acqs, one of the ablest statesmen that France ever produced, obtains the precedency at Venice over Vargas the Spanish ambassador. Queen Elizabeth succeeds her sister queen Mary. The king makes his son and daughter-in-law take the title and arms of king and queen of Scotland, England, and Ireland.

1559.

The king's edict published at Escouan in the month of June, inflicting death on those who professed the Lutheran religion; it was registered in all the parliaments without restriction, with a strict order to the judges not to mitigate the punishment, as had been hitherto the practice. Some of the counsellors of the parliament of Paris having declared, at one of their *Mercurial* or extraordinary sittings, that it would be right to connive at the escape of an obstinate Lutheran, *contrary to the edict of Romorentin*, the king came in person to the parliament, which was then sitting at Austin friars, and ordered five of those magistrates to be taken into custody. *(Mem. of Castelnau, book i. ch. 3.)* The parliament then consisted of a hundred and thirty judges; and there were seven of those courts throughout the kingdom.

REMARKABLE EVENTS under HENRY II.

The peace of Cateau-Cambresis, the conditions of which were disapproved of by the Guises, from their enmity to the constable, who concluded the treaty, and was then in high esteem by the marriage of Damville his son to Henrietta de la Marck, granddaughter of the dutchess of Valentinois. The Guises were in the right, and the treaty was contrary to the opinion of the whole council; for, just as the king began to gain the ascendant of Spain, he resigned what that crown would not have been able to wrest from him in a successful war of thirty years. The French were left in possession of Calais, only for a term of eight years, at the expiration of which it was to be restored to the English, on condition that, during the aforesaid space, queen Elizabeth entered into no engagement contrary to the interest of France or Scotland; but, as she broke through this condition, by assisting the admiral, and the Protestants in Scotland, Calais remained in our hands. Part of the dominions of the duke of Savoy was restored to that prince, till the rights of the dutchess of Angouleme, the king's grandmother, were settled: all the other conquests on both sides, whether in Italy or in France, were given back, except the three important towns of Metz, Toul, and Verdun, which remained in the hands of the French. In consequence of this very treaty was concluded the marriage of Elizabeth, the king's daughter, with Philip II, and that of his sister Margaret with the duke of Savoy. In the midst of the entertainments, occasioned by these second nuptials, the unfortunate king Henry met with his untimely fate. We read in M. de Thou, who was somewhat credulous in regard to judiciary astrology, that Luke Gauric, the famous astrologer, had predicted the time and manner in which king Henry II. was to resign his last breath. The celebrated Gassendi gives us this prediction of Gauric at full length; the purport of it was, that, if this prince could surmount the dangers with which he was threatened in his sixty-third, and sixty-fourth year, he would live very happy till he attained the age of sixty-nine years and ten months; whereas he died at forty.

The diversions of those days were single combats, tournaments, tilts, and trials of strength. Brantome relates in what manner the duke de Nemours mounted on a strong horse, called the *Real*, galloped

galloped down the steps of the holy chapel at Paris, to the surprize of all the world. This exertion of agility and strength, in which the gentlemen of the army so greatly prided themselves, was a part of the discipline that obtained before the invention of fire-arms. As they often fought man to man, it was of use to inure themselves to those exercises, which rendered their bodies supple and robust; and therefore we find, that, when such athletic diversions were grown less serviceable, they fell into disuse; and, if they sometimes revived, it was only to exhibit a representation of the ancient customs. It was shrewdly observed by a Turkish ambassador, who came to France in the reign of Charles VII, and had often assisted at those spectacles, where generally some misfortune happened; *that, if they were in earnest, it was too little; if in jest, it was too much.*

REMARKABLE EVENTS.

1559.

1559. Accession to the crown.

FRANCIS II. ascended the throne the 10th of July, 1559, at sixteen years of age. He was crowned at Rheims the 10th of September the same year, by the archbishop, Charles, cardinal of Lorrain, without any great pomp, because he was still in mourning. (Brulart's journal.)

There was no money coined in France with this prince's name; but in Scotland were coined testoons, with the names of Francis II, and Mary, queen of Scots.

WE are apt to complain of the dearth of great men, and to regret those times, when a cluster of illustrious names adorned our annals. And indeed history affords us high entertainment, when it exhibits to our view a series of heroic atchievements: but are the people the happier for all this? I freely acknowledge, that a number of great men, living in subordination to the supreme authority, and exerting their abilities in the service of the public, may and must perform mighty atchievements: but, as such a combination of circumstances is extremely rare, a heavier calamity cannot befal a country, than a concurrence of men of high abilities and power, who, claiming an equal share in the administration, begin with weakening, and conclude with subverting, the supreme authority.

Such was the reign of Francis II, that short-lived reign, for it lasted only seventeen months, big with all those mischiefs which afterwards ravaged France, and principally owing to the number of great men who appeared at that time upon the public stage. The Guises, abusing the authority with which they had been entrusted by the king, were able to maintain themselves against the princes of the blood, who claimed a right to the administration, on account of the minority of the sovereign. Against the Guises the king of Navarre and the prince of Condé had interest enough to form a party; and the grandees were so ambitious as to foment those divisions, with a view of profiting by the public calamities. Religion was too specious a pretence not to be used by both parties. The Guises, pretending a zeal for the ancient and true worship, to which the body of the nation

still

WIVES.		1560. DEATH.	Cotemporary PRINCES.
Mary Stuart, daughter of James V, king of Scotland, and of Mary of Lorrain, daughter of Claude I, duke de Guise, married to Francis II. in 1558, and beheaded the 18th of Feb. 1587.		FRANCIS II. died at *Orleans the 5th of December,* 1560, *in his eighteenth year. He was interred at St. Denis.* It is said, that a Scotch valet de chambre, belonging to the king, was so blinded by his zeal for the new religion of the Huguenots, as to poison the king's nightcap, on the side he wore next the ear, which was troubled with a fistula. *(Le Laboureur on Castelneau.)*	*Popes.* Paul IV. 1559. Pius IV. 1565. *Turkish emperor.* Solyman II. 1566. *Emperor of Germany.* Ferdinand I. 1564. *King of Spain.* Philip II. 1598. *King of Portugal.* Sebastian. 1578. *Queen of England.* Elizabeth. 1603. *Queen of Scotland.* Mary Stuart. 1587. *King of Denmark.* Frederic II. 1588. *Kings of Sweden.* Gustavus. 1560. Eric, deposed 1568. *King of Poland.* Sigismund II. 1572. *Czar of Muscovy.* John Basilowitz. 1584.

REMARKABLE EVENTS under FRANCIS II.

still adhered, found means to maintain their authority among the populace; while the princes of the blood endeavoured by the love of novelty to supply the want of power, which was in the hands of the Guises.

Francis duke de Guise and the cardinal of Lorrain, the queen's uncles, are placed at the head of the administration: it was on this occasion that du Tillet, the register, wrote his book of the *majority of kings*, to prove that a sovereign, when he is come to age, may, notwithstanding his youth, chuse what council he pleases. The constable de Montmorency and the dutchess de Valentinois are disgraced. The queen could not forgive the former for saying, that, except a natural daughter, there was not one of the king's children like his majesty. His place of high steward was given to the duke de Guise; and, as an indemnity, his eldest son was created a *supernumerary* marshal of France.

The seals are taken from Bertrandy, a creature of the dutchess de Valentinois, and restored to the chancellor Olivier, a person remarkable, says M. de Thou, for his politeness and wit, as well as for his integrity, and knowledge in the law: but this magistrate quickly perceived, that he had been recalled to servitude, rather than to a free discharge of the first employment in the state; and that their design was only to screen their iniquity under the sanction of his name. Bertrandy was sent to Rome. The Guises, however, to give a lustre to their administration, publish some excellent edicts; one prohibiting the use of fire-arms; another revoking all grants of alienation of the royal demesnes; and a third ordaining, that, whenever there happened to be a vacancy in the courts of justice, the judges should present three proper candidates for his majesty's nomination. They likewise persuade the king to make a promotion of eighteen knights of St. Michael; so that the reputation of this order, which was to consist only of six and thirty members, was greatly reduced: hence le Laboureur took an opportunity of reflecting on the increase of honours in France. " The prince is mistaken, who imagines that the
" multiplication of honours is conducive to his interest; they
" are so many debts with which he encumbers his crown; they
" are so many new interests in support of future parties and
" factions; for, as fortune raises new favourites, she leaves
                                              " them

MINISTERS.	WARRIORS.	MAGISTRATES.	EMINENT and LEARNED MEN.
Francis, duke de Guife. 1563. Charles, cardinal of Lorrain. 1574. *Secretaries of ſtate.* Cl. de l'Aubeſpine. 1567. James Bourdin. 1567. Flor. Robertet. 1567. Flor. Robertet d'Alluie. 1569.	*Conſtables.* Anne de Montmorency. 1567. *Marſhals of France.* James d'Albon de St. André. 1562. Charles de Coſſé de Briſſac. 1563. Paul de la Barthe des Termes. 1562. Francis de Montmorency. 1579.	*Chancellors.* John Bertrandy, cardinal, keeper of the ſeals. 1560. Francis Olivier de Leuville. 1560. Michael de l'Hopital. 1573. *Firſt preſident.* Gilles le Maitre. 1562. *Attorney general.* Gilles Bourdin. 1570. *The king's advocates.* Bapt. du Meſnil. 1569. Aimon Boucherat. 1564.	John, cardinal du Bellay. 1560. Joachim du Bellay. 1560. Charles de Marillac, archbiſhop of Vienne. 1560. Philip Melancthon. 1560. Emard Ranſonnet. 1559.

"them for the public to maintain." (*Le Laboureur on Caſtelnau.*) "Marks of honour, ſays M. de St. Palaye, are the public coin, which it is equally dangerous either to raiſe or to debaſe." Antony of Bourbon, king of Navarre, by deferring to come to court, ſerves the ambitious views of the Guiſes; and, upon his arrival, finds their power eſtabliſhed: he is ſent back, with his brother, the cardinal de Bourbon, and the prince de la Roche-ſur-Yon, under colour of conducting the princeſs Elizabeth of France to Philip II, her huſband, and of preſenting him with the order of St. Michael. Antony Minard, preſident of the parliament, a magiſtrate firmly attached to the true religion, was killed with a piſtol-ſhot on the 12th of December, between five and ſix in the evening, as he was returning from the *Palais* upon his mule: he had been entruſted with the care of Mary queen of Scots. On this occaſion was publiſhed an edict, ordaining, *that the court ſhall riſe henceforward at four in the afternoon from Martinmas to Eaſter.* A Scotchman, named James Stuart, was ſuſpected of this murder. Anne du Bourg, a counſellor in parliament, and in deacon's orders, is firſt degraded, and then hanged and burnt * at the Greve for profeſſing the proteſtant religion. As the murder of the preſident haſtened the execution of du Bourg; ſo the ſeverity of this ſentence gave riſe to the conſpiracy of Amboiſe, and to the civil wars that enſued.

1560.

The conſpiracy of Amboiſe againſt the Guiſes breaks out in the month of March: the difference in beginning the year, whether from the month of January or from Eaſter, has occaſioned a diverſity in the dates; ſome placing this conſpiracy, for inſtance, in 1559, and others in 1560. The prince of Condé was ſaid to be the *ſilent* or *concealed chief* of this plot, while Renaudie was the avowed conductor. The latter owed his life to the duke de Guiſe, by whoſe aſſiſtance he had made his eſcape out of the town gaol at Dijon, where he was ſaid to have been confined for forging the hand of the regiſter du Tillet, to obtain the living of Champigners in Angoumois. (*Brantome.*) The pretence for the conſpiracy of Amboiſe was religion, *though it was reported to be more owing to diſaffection than to Calviniſm.* (Brulart's journal.)

* He had been condemned in the late reign.

REMARKABLE EVENTS under FRANCIS II.

The Guifes get intelligence of it from Avennelles the advocate. The court removes from Blois to Amboife. The duke de Guife is declared lieutenant-general of the kingdom. The greateft part of the confpirators are feized, and put to death. The chancellor Olivier dies of grief at the breaking out of thefe troubles, and is fucceeded by Michael de l'Hopital. The prince of Condé, who was then at court, is accufed of being concerned in the plot, and proves his innocence. The duke de Guife was for diffembling with the prince, left defperation fhould hurry him into the arms of the Proteftants; but the cardinal of Lorrain was of a different opinion. The dutchefs of Ferrara, a zealous Proteftant, and fifter to queen Claude, being then returned to France, and imagining that the duke de Guife, her fon-in-law, acted in concert with the cardinal, told him, "that he had behaved very ill; "for that it was no trifling matter to treat a prince of the blood "in that manner." (*Brantome.*) Marot was fecretary to this princefs, and Calvin had been to pay her a vifit to Ferrara. The confpirators, having an opinion of the admiral's attachment to the king, were afraid to truft him with their defign; fo that he was not let into the fecret.

The edict of Romorentin, which debars the parliament from meddling with the crime of herefy, and leaves the cognizance thereof to the bifhops: this edict was regiftered, but not without great difficulty, and with limitations in regard to the laity, whom the court permits to bring their caufe before the royal tribunal. It is faid, that the chancellor de l'Hopital fet his hand to this edict, only to avoid a greater evil, that of the inquifition.

An edict touching fecond marriages. The king calls an extraordinary council at Fontainebleau, where the admiral de Coligny prefented a petition in favour of the Calvinifts. The refult hereof was, that the ftates of the kingdom fhould be convened at Orleans, that the Calvinifts in the mean time fhould remain unmolefted, and that a national fynod fhould be called, if the pope refufed to convoke a general council: this refolution haftened the meeting of that affembly. The king of Navarre and the prince of Condé are invited to the ftates of Orleans, where the king affifted in perfon. The prince of Condé

REMARKABLE EVENTS under FRANCIS II.

is arrested immediately upon his arrival, on pretence of a new conspiracy, discovered by James de la Sague, that prince's agent; and is condemned to lose his head: the king dying in the mean time, the prince was saved. In regard to this sentence, le Laboureur informs us, that Lewis de Beuil, count de Sancerre, generously refused to sign it; and that the prisoner owed his life to this delay. Others pretend that the chancellor, and the president Guillard du Mortier, refused to set their hand to it, for the very same reason; but M. de Thou thinks the sentence of death was not signed.

Though the kingdom fell under a minority by the death of Francis II, yet this prince was not regretted, the people preferring a real minority to an imaginary majority.

The Protestants at this time were distinguished by the name of Huguenots *.

* There are various accounts of the origin of this word. Some derive it from John Hus; as much as to say, *les guenons de Hus*, the *apes of Hus*. Others from Hugh Capet; the Huguenots defending the right of his descendants to the crown, against the house of Guise, who pretended to be descended from Charlemagne. There are some who deduce it from Hugh the Sacramentarian, who taught the same doctrine as Calvin, in the reign of Charles IV. Others derive it from the harangue of a German, who, being taken and interrogated by the cardinal of Lorrain concerning the conspiracy of Amboise, stopped short in his harangue, which began with these words, *huc nos venimus*, we are come hither; and the courtiers, not understanding Latin, said to one another, these fellows are come from *Huc nos*. Pasquier relates, that the common people at Tours were persuaded that a hobgoblin or night spirit, called king *Hugo*, ran about the town at night; and, as the Reformed assembled in the night to perform their devotions, from thence they were called *Huguenots*; as much as to say, the *disciples of king Hugo*: and this opinion appears the most plausible. Others affirm it was owing to their meeting near the gate called *Hugon*. Others, in fine, and, among the rest, M. Voltaire, derive it from the *Eidgnossen* of Geneva. There had been two parties for some time in that city; one of the Protestants, and the other of the Roman catholics. The former were called *Egnots*, from the German word *Eidgnossen*, allied by oath; and at length triumphed over the latter. Hence the French Protestants who were before stiled Lutherans, began to be distinguished by the name of *Egnots*, which, by corruption, was changed into that of *Huguenots*.

REMARKABLE EVENTS.

1560.
Accession to the crown.

CHARLES IX, born at St. Germain en Laye the 27th of June, 1550, comes to the crown the 5th of December, 1560, at about ten years of age. He was crowned at Rheims the 15th of May, 1561, by Charles, cardinal of Lorrain.

M. de Cipierre had been his governor when he was only duke of Orleans; but, upon his accession to the crown, the prince de la Roche-sur-yon was joined with M. de Cipierre. James Amiot was his preceptor. His father-in-law, Maximilian, archduke of Austria, and afterwards emperor, was sponsor for him at baptism, and gave him the name of Maximilian, which he changed for that of Charles.

The chancellor de l'Hopital was the author of his device, which was two columns, with these words, *pietate & justitia*.

1560.

THE states-general are held at Orleans, and afterwards adjourned to Pontoise: the deputies of the three states having represented, that their powers were expired upon the demise of the king, and therefore required to be renewed, it was determined that the deputies should continue to act, by virtue of their commission, upon this principle, that, pursuant to the laws of the kingdom, the royal authority never dies, but is uninterruptedly transmitted from the deceased king to his lawful successor.

The government at that time was forty-two millions in debt, although Henry II, upon his accession, found seventeen hundred thousand crowns in the treasury; so that this debt must have been contracted in the space of fourteen years. The states of Orleans did no manner of good; we shall only take notice of the famous ordinance relating to ecclesiastical matters, and to the administration of justice. The eighth article forbids the abuse of monitories, except in criminal cases, and those of public scandal: in one of the articles, substitutions, or intails, are reduced to two degrees: it is also enacted, that henceforward all bailiffs and seneschals shall be swordsmen. Lewis XII. had ordained, that those officers should be graduated, because of the inconveniency in having justice administered by swordsmen, who understood nothing of the law; but, as their degrees did not render them in the least the wiser, the chancellor de l'Hopital thought the shortest way would be to deprive them of the judiciary power, by ordaining that they should be all swordsmen; in consequence of which the administration of justice

The THIRD RACE. 409

WIVES.	CHILDREN.	1574. DEATH.	Cotemporary PRINCES.
Elizabeth of Austria, daughter of the emperor Maximilian II, married in 1570, died in 1592. Philip II, after the decease of Anne of Austria, his wife, employed a very learned Jesuit to make proposals of marriage between him and queen Elizabeth, widow of Charles IX, and sister to queen Anne. Her father and mother, the emperor, and the empress, sister to Philip II, used their endeavours to persuade her to this match, but all in vain. (Brantome.) *Prisci moris vel juvenili ætate fœmina.* (De Thou.) *A princess, who even in her younger days, followed the manners of ancient times.*	Mary Elizabeth, died at five years of age. *Natural children.* Charles IX. had by Mary Touchet, daughter of a private lieutenant in the presidial of Orleans, N . . . . a son, died young. Charles of Valois, who was successively grand prior of France, count d'Auvergne, and duke d'Angouleme, *which forms the last branch of the dukes of that name.* 1650. Mary Touchet, married afterwards to Francis de Balzac, lord d'Antragues, father of Henrietta de Balzac, one of Henry IVth's mistresses.	CHARLES IX. *died in the castle of Vincennes the 30th of May, 1574, on Whitsunday, betwixt three and four in the afternoon, at twenty-four years of age; of which he had reigned thirteen and a half. His heart was carried to the Celestine monks at Paris, and he was interred at St. Denis.* At the public dinner after his funeral at St. Denis, the parliament having Christopher de Thou for their president, sent orders to M. Amiot, the great almoner, to come and say grace to them, as representing the monarchy; which he refused to do, and even kept out of the way. The same difficulty arose at the interment of Lewis XIV, when M. de Mesmes was first president. Muretus pronounced Charles IXth's funeral oration at Rome.	*Popes.* Pius IV. 1565. Pius V. 1572. Gregory XIII. 1585. *Turkish emperors.* Solyman II. 1566. Selim II. 1574. *Emperors of Germany.* Ferdinand I. 1564. Maximilian II. 1576. *King of Spain.* Philip II. 1598. *King of Portugal.* Sebastian. 1578. *Queen of England.* Elizabeth. 1603. *Queen of Scotland.* Mary Stuart. 1587. *King of Denmark.* Frederic II. 1588. *Kings of Sweden.* Eric, deposed 1568. John, brother of Eric. 1592. *Kings of Poland.* Sigismund II. 1572. Henry, afterwards king of France. *Czar of Muscovy.* John Basilowitz. 1584.

REMARKABLE EVENTS under CHARLES IX.

justice was left in the hands of their deputies or lieutenants, which produced two distinct states, those of the long robe, and the sword. By the article L of the same ordinance, when there happen to be two courts of justice, not within the precinct of a royal seignory, the king reduces them to one, by which means the parties at law, in cases of appeal, avoid a degree of jurisdiction. But, what is more extraordinary, by the article LXXXIV, the king decrees, that the minutes of the instruments shall be signed by the parties; and it is amazing, that, for the security of contracts, and the conveniency of dispatch, this remedy was not thought of sooner. The first article renewed the pragmatic sanction with regard to elections: and the reason for taking this step was, that the pope had annulled the concordate, as too favourable to the king, (that very concordate, so greatly disliked in France) and wanted to restore the collation of benefices, after the manner practised in Italy and Spain, and make the French submit to the rules of the Roman chancery. Charles IX, in order to oppose the court of Rome, revived the pragmatic sanction, under colour that the concordate ought to have expired with Francis I. The pope, finding himself hereby deprived of the profit of the bulls, without having the advantage of the collation of benefices, desired the concordate to be restored; and cardinal d'Este, upon his coming to France, obtained this favour of the king. By a declaration, published at Chartres in 1562, Charles IX. revoked the first article of the ordinance of Orleans, and restored the concordate, which was afterwards confirmed by Henry III. in the first article of the ordinance of Blois. This is the law now in force.

On the 8th of December the king sends a letter to the parliament of Paris, wherein he acquaints them with the death of Francis II, and mentions that, by reason of his tender age, *confiding in the virtue and prudence of the queen his mother, he has begged that she would undertake the administration of the kingdom, supported by the sage counsel and advice of the king of Navarre, and of the other noble personages of his late majesty's council.* The parliament, in their letter of the 12th of the same month, write, in answer to the king, that *they thank God for having inspired his majesty with the thoughts of committing the administration to the queen his mother,*

The THIRD RACE.

MINISTERS.	WARRIORS.	MAGISTRATES.	EMINENT and LEARNED MEN.
Charles, cardinal of Lorrain. 1574. Arth. de Coſſé, lord of Gonnor, maſter of the pantry to his majeſty, ſuperintendant of the finances, and afterwards marſhal of France.1582. *Secretaries of ſtate.* Cl. de l'Aubepine. 1567. James Bourdin. 1567. Flor. Robertet. 1567. Flor. Robertet d'Alluie. 1569. Cl. de l'Aubeſpine de Hauterive. 1570. Sim. Fizes de Sauves.1579. Nic. de Neuville de Villeroy. 1617. Peter Brulart. 1608. Cl. Pinart. 1605.	*Conſtable.* Anne de Montmorency. 1567. *Marſhals of France.* John d'Albon de St. André. 1562. Charles de Coſſé de Briſſac.1563. Paul de la Barthe de Termes. 1562. Francis de Montmorency. 1579. Imbert de la Platiere de Bourdillon. 1567. Francis de Scepeaux. 1571. Henry de Montmorency, duke de Damville. 1614. Arthur de Coſſé. 1582. Honorat. de Savoie. 1580. Gaſpar de Saux de Tavannes. 1573.	*Chancellors.* Michael de l'Hopital. 1573. J. de Morvilliers, keeper of the ſeals. 1577. *Firſt preſidents.* Giles le Maitre. 1562. Chriſt. de Thou. 1582. *Attorneys general.* Giles Bourdin. 1570. John de la Gueſle. 1589. *The king's advocates.* Baptiſt du Meſnil. 1569. Aimon Boucherat. 1564. Guy du Faur de Pibrac. 1584. Auguſtin de Thou. 1595. *At this time there was alſo a king's advocate, who was a clergyman, and had the precedency of the king's lay-advocate; and to remove from the latter office to the former, it was neceſſary to take a new oath. But in 1570, Charles IX. aboliſhed this formality, and ordained that when the former office came to be vacant, the ſecond advocate ſhould ſucceed without any further ceremony.*	Beauvais, governor of Henry IV, killed at the maſſacre of St. Bartholomew. 1572. John Calvin. 1564. Hannibal Caro. 1566. Cl. d'Eſpenſe. 1571. Ch. Stephen. 1564. St. Francis de Borgia. 1572. Cl. Gudimel. 1572. He ſet Marot's pſalms to muſic. Stephen Jodelle. 1573. Denis Lambin. 1572. Paul Manutius. 1514. Ch. du Moulin, 1566. Michael Angelo.1564. Michael Noſtradamus. 1566. Bernard Ochin. 1564. Henry d'Oyſel. 1566. William Peliſſier, the firſt biſhop of Montpellier, upon the tranſlation of that ſee from Maguelonne, was one of the earlieſt contributors towards enriching the king's library with Greek, Syriac, and Hebrew manuſcripts. 1568. Peter Ramus. 1572. Odet de Selves. 1564. Lel. Socinus. 1562. John du Tillet. 1570. Adr. Turnebus. 1565. Hieronymus Vida. 1568.

REMARKABLE EVENTS under CHARLES IX.

in conjunction with the king of Navarre. The 30th of March the king wrote to the parliament, that *the queen his mother and the king of Navarre had signed an instrument, or agreement, concerning the administration of the kingdom, as he had declared already by his letters of commission, issued out the 25th of the same month, for convening an assembly of the states general.* In this commission the king of Navarre is stiled lieutenant-general of the kingdom. The states of the provostship and viscounty of Paris were come to a resolution, that the regency should be conferred on this prince; but it did not take effect. Neither had Catharine de Medicis the title of regent during the minority of Charles IX; but it is well known what share she had in the government, both in this and the following reign. It is astonishing, that the whole torrent of historians, beginning with M. de Thou, Mezeray, Daniel, le Gendre, &c. should all concur in bestowing this title on Catharine de Medicis: perhaps they were led into this mistake, by her having been appointed to the regency till the king's return from Poland, in virtue of the letters patent which Charles IX. signed just before his death, and which were registered four days after.

Upon the very entrance of this king's reign the prince of Condé is set at liberty. A triumvirate is formed by the duke de Guise, the constable de Montmorency, and the marshal de St. André. They all three died of a violent death, as well as the king of Navarre, who joined in the confederacy.

1561.

The edict of July, published at St. Germain, for regulating the point of religion, and preserving peace among the people.

The colloquy or conference of Poissy, granted by the queen at the request of the Huguenot leaders: the cardinal de Tournon had the prudence to oppose this meeting; but the cardinal of Lorrain, expecting to make a figure on that occasion, had the vanity to accept of it. Theodore Beza was the spokesman for the Huguenots. Francis II. had sent letters patent in 1560, to oblige the chapter of the cathedral church of Paris, to grant him a loan: and Charles IX. published fresh letters patent in 1561, to compel all the beneficed clergy

clergy in the kingdom to give in an estimate of the income of their livings; but these letters were revoked.

A solemn arret of the parliament, acquitting the prince of Condé of being concerned in the conspiracy of Amboise. These magistrates issue out another arret against John Tanquerel, who had publickly maintained the following proposition: *Papa potest reges et imperatores hæreticos deponere**.

Mary queen of Scots, who neither loved nor was beloved by Catharine de Medicis, returns to Scotland by the advice of her uncle the cardinal of Lorrain, which she reluctantly complied with, after laying aside the arms and title of queen of England: she was very near being taken at sea by some English men of war; queen Elizabeth having denied her a passport, upon Mary's refusing to make a solemn renunciation of her right to the crown of England.

1562.

The edict of January, granting public exercise of the Protestant religion, (this is the first.) The queen's motive was through fear, lest the junction of the king of Navarre to the triumvirate should render that party too formidable. The parliament refuse to register it, *his verbis, non possumus nec debemus* †. Yet it was registered at last, after two express orders from the king. In this edict there was a very remarkable article, viz. a kind of regulation concerning the manner in which the Protestants ought to conduct themselves; and it is mentioned, " that they shall advance nothing contrary to the council of Nice, to the apostles creed, and to the book of the Old and New Testament." The first civil war, occasioned by the massacre of Vassy†, where Francis duke de Guise was wounded. The prince of Condé, being declared the head of the Protestants, surprizes Orleans,

---

* *The pope may depose heretical kings and emperors.*
† *In these words, we neither can nor ought to do it.*
‡ The duke de Guise, having had an interview with the duke of Wirtemberg at Saverne, in his return to Paris, passed through the little town of Vassy in Champagne. Here his retinue insulting the Huguenots, who were at their devotions in a barn, from words proceeded to blows, and there were about sixty of the Huguenots killed. The duke is said to have used all his endeavours to put an end to the fray, and was wounded in the face with a stone.

which

which becomes the bulwark of that religion. The Huguenots, led by his example, poffefs themfelves of feveral towns; and, among others, of Rouen. The king of Navarre is wounded in the trenches the 19th of October at the fiege of this laft city: he died the 19th of November following of his wound, and the place was taken by ftorm. "The queen, his wife, fays Bran-
"tome, was very uneafy in the beginning, at his turning Hugue-
"not; telling him, that he wanted to ruin himfelf, and to have
"his whole eftate confifcated; but, for her part, fhe was not
"willing to lofe what little fhe had left .... yet both fhe and
"her hufband foon after changed their minds, the latter turning
"Catholic, and the former becoming a rigid Proteftant."

At the opening of this war, the moft diftinguifhed captains, under the prince of Condé, were, the count de Gramont, who commanded the Gafcons; John de Rohan, who had the conduct of the troops of Dauphiné and Languedoc; and d'Andelot, general of the infantry, who had the command of the troops of the ifle of France.

The battle of Dreux *, where the Huguenots were defeated, and the generals of both armies, the prince of Condé and the conftable, taken prifoners: the marfhal de St. André was killed by Bobigny †. The duke de Guife gained the victory, though he had not the chief command. A modern writer has obferved, as fomewhat very extraordinary, that Francis duke de Guife, feveral times general of the king's armies, and twice lieutenant-general of the kingdom (which gave him a fuperiority over the conftable himfelf) had no other military rank than that of captain of gendarmes, and was obliged to obey even the marfhals de camp: it is true, no body ever attempted to give him orders, and he had in fome meafure an authority over his generals. No man ever fo greatly refembled Pompey, who commanded armies, and had triumphal honours, when he was only a Roman knight.

The prince of Conde and the duke de Guife lay in the fame bed the night after the battle: the next morning the former declared, that he could not clofe his eyes all night; but that the duke de

* In Latin *Drocum*, a fmall town in the government of the ifle of France, and diocefe of Chartres, fixteen leagues from Paris.
† The fon of a perfon whofe confifcation he had begged.

Guife

REMARKABLE EVENTS under CHARLES IX.

Guife flept as foundly, as if they had been the beft friends in the world.

The duke of Savoy, by a convention with the court, recovers poffeffion of Turin, Chivas, &c. which had been withheld from him on account of the claims of the dutchefs of Angouleme, mother of Françis I. The marfhal de Bourdillon, the king's lieutenant in Piedmont, endeavoured, in vain, to hinder this reftitution.

The univerfity of Doway founded.

1563.

The fiege of Orleans, where Francis duke de Guife is affaffinated by Poltrot. The power of this prince was arrived to fuch a height, that the conftable Anne de Montmorency ufed to write to him in this ftile; *My lord, your moft humble and moft obedient fervant:* whereas M. de Guife ufed thus to begin his letters to the conftable, *Monf. le connetable;* and at the bottom he figned himfelf, *your very good friend.* He died two hundred thoufand crowns in debt.

The edict of pacification on the 19th of March, extremely favourable to the Proteftant party. But the Englifh being then in poffeffion of Havre de Grace, which had been delivered up to them by the Huguenots, this accommodation was become neceffary. The prince of Condé was fincere on his fide; and, if the queen had kept her promife, which was to let him have the fame rank in council, and the fame degree of confidence, as had been granted to his brother the king of Navarre, the Proteftants would have been foon weakened; but he was neglected, when they had no longer any occafion for his fervice. Charles IX. is declared of age at thirteen years and a half, in the parliament of Rouen, after recovering Havre from the Englifh, who had fent fuccours to the Calvinifts: the king was prefent at this fiege. The parliament of Paris did not regifter this declaration till after repeated remonftrances; for they claimed a right to verify the royal edicts before any other court in the kingdom. Charles IX. is the firft of our kings who was declared of age in parliament: it was the intereft of Catharine de Medicis to obtain this declaration; for, by anticipating the age of majority, which by Charles V. was

fettled

REMARKABLE EVENTS under CHARLES IX.

settled at fourteen years complete, she made her son publickly affirm, that he continued to entrust her with the administration of the realm, and by that means she kept every other pretender at a distance. Mary of Medicis and Anne of Austria were actuated by the same motives, when they caused their sons, Lewis XIII. and Lewis XIV, to be declared of age: but the impatience which Catharine shewed to put an end to the minority, is a further proof of what we have already advanced, that she was not regent. Conferences held at Troyes for settling the peace with England. The closing of the council of Trent, which began in 1545. Du Ferrier, the king's ambassador, entered his protests against every thing that had been transacted in that assembly. We find, by a letter of John de Morvilliers to his nephew the bishop of Rennes, ambassador to the court of Vienna, dated from Fontainebleau the 3d of March, that, " as soon as the cardinal
" was returned from the council, the presidents of the parliament
" and the king's council were summoned to court, to see the
" decrees and acts of that assembly; and, the matter being de-
" bated, the attorney-general said, that, with regard to the doc-
" trine, the parliament did not intend to meddle with it, but
" held every thing for sound and orthodox, that was determined
" in a general and lawful council; but as for the decrees of dis-
" cipline and reformation, they had found them in several things
" derogatory to the rights and privileges of the Gallican church,
" which were an objection against their being received in
" France. Du Moulin was ordered to write against the council
" of Trent." The count de Luna, ambassador from the court of Spain, having attempted to dispute the article of precedency with the king's ambassadors at this assembly, the latter kept their place; so that the Spanish minister was obliged to remove, and to seat himself between the last cardinal priest and the first cardinal deacon, to avoid sitting below the French ambassador. An edict for the establishing of *consignments* *.

* In French *consignation*; it signifies the depositing money, or writings, in the hands of a trusty person, till a law-suit is decided. The receivers of the *consignments* of the parliament, or of the chatelet, are public depositaries, appointed by the authority of the king, and by the courts of justice.

The THIRD RACE. 417

REMARKABLE EVENTS *under* CHARLES IX.

1564.

The king makes a tour through part of his dominions. A peace concluded with England. There was no mention of the restitution of Calais, which, according to the treaty of Cateau-Cambresis, ought to be made in eight years; and no doubt the reason was, that Elizabeth had violated the essential condition, under which the town of Calais was to be restored to England, namely, that of undertaking nothing in prejudice to France. Only, by way of indemnity, she received a hundred and twenty thousand crowns, instead of five hundred thousand, the sum agreed to be given to England, in case we kept possession of that town: and the French hostages were set at liberty. My lord Hunsdon[*], cousin-german to queen Elizabeth, waited on the king at Lyons, to see the peace sworn to, and to present him with the order of the Garter. The king quitted this city, on account of the plague which raged at that time in several parts of the kingdom; and he came to reside at the castle of Roussillon in Dauphiné. Here he published the famous edict of Roussillon, which fixes the beginning of the year to the first of January, instead of Easter. The parliament did not agree to this regulation till towards the year 1567. On this occasion we shall observe, that the Romans began their year the first of January, on which day they presented their *strenæ, or new year's gifts:* and M. Ducange observes, that, in France, even when the new year commenced at Easter, they still made their presents on the first of January, because they considered it as the beginning of the year, from the retrogressive motion of the sun. By the XXIVth article of the edict of Roussillon, double jurisdictions, except in royal courts of justice, are reduced to one; which was of great advantage to individuals: this article is agreeable to that of the ordinance of Orleans in 1560; and Philip of Valois had made a law to the same purpose in 1328. Charles IX. published an edict in the same place, revoking some of the advantages which he had granted to the Huguenots by the treaty of pacification. Catharine de Medicis, having conceived a dislike to the palace of Tournelles, since the demise of Henry II, orders it to be pulled down, and takes up her residence in the Louvre with the king. This same princess begins to build the palace

[*] Henry Carey; his mother was Mary Bullen, sister of Anna Bullen.

Vol. I. E e of

of the Thuilleries, which was joined to the old Louvre by a gallery finished in the reign of Henry IV. The edict for establishing the jurisdiction of consuls verified.

The university of Besançon founded.

1565.

The king, and queen Catharine de Medicis, have an interview with Isabella of France, consort of Philip II, and with the duke of Alva, at Bayonne. The queen, affecting to take umbrage at the duke of Alva's march towards the Netherlands, ordered a body of troops to be raised, with a view, as she pretended, of watching the motions of that general. The Protestants of France and of the Low Countries being alarmed at these military preparations, their jealousy gave rise to the second civil war in France, and the troubles in the Netherlands. Catharine occasioned the first civil war by favouring the Huguenots, and the second by provoking them.

Margaret of Austria, a natural daughter of Charles V, was assisted by the cardinal de Granvelle in the government of the Netherlands. William of Nassau, prince of Orange, and count d'Egmont, displeased to see the whole authority engrossed by that minister, were the first to blow the coals of sedition; and, as it generally happens in weak governments, the king of Spain, thinking to quiet their minds by complying with their demands, resolved to sacrifice Granvelle, who was recalled before the conference of Bayonne. Philip II. soon perceived his error, and appointed the duke of Alva to succeed him.

The Turks are obliged to raise the siege of Malta, which was defended by John de la Valette the grand master. Many of the French nobility assisted as volunteers in the defence of that place. When the chevalier de la Roche came to impart this news, in the name of the grand master, to the king, and to the queen mother; the chancellor de l'Hopital, addressing himself to her majesty, made this observation, that the knights of St. John of Jerusalem having maintained three important sieges, their grand masters each time happened to be Frenchmen; the first was d'Aubusson, who defended Rhodes; the second l'Isle Adam, who indeed was obliged to quit that island, but not till he had performed prodigies of valour,

REMARKABLE EVENTS under CHARLES IX.

and been the cause of destroying a hundred and eighty thousand Turks; the third was Parisot de la Valette.

1566.

An ordinance published at Moulins in the month of February, known by the name of the *Demesne:* by the 2d and 13th articles it puts the ancient and new demesnes on the same footing; and particularly by the second article it declares the king's patrimonial lands to be annexed to the crown, after the farmer-general has administered the revenue thereof the space of ten years. Another ordinance of the same month: this is the famous edict of Moulins for the reformation of justice; wherein, among other articles, is regulated the right of *committimus* *: our last law upon this head is the declaration of 1669. By the same ordinance, interpreting that of Orleans, substitutions or intails, antcedent to the latter, are reduced to four degrees only; and it ordains, that delinquents shall be punished on the spot where they have committed the crime.

A declaration published at Paris in the month of July, concerning the erection of dukedoms, &c. which henceforward shall be reunited to the crown for want of heirs male: this edict is still in force; so that, to avoid the effect, there must be a particular exception.

The death of the dutchess de Valentinois. She had erected a tomb to her husband in the cathedral of Rouen, with an inscription in Latin verse, still extant, wherein she promises to be as faithful a companion to him in his grave, as she had been in the nuptial bed. Little did she dream that this promise would be so exactly fulfilled; for she separated from him in her life-time, and was interred at Anet. Her grandmother was Mary, a natural daughter of Lewis XI. and of Margaret de Sassenage. A like instance was afterwards seen in the marchioness de Verneuil, daughter of Mary Touchet and of Charles IX, who became the mistress of Henry IV. by a kind of hereditary lewdness.

The beginning of the troubles in the Netherlands, occasioned by the religionists, under the name of *Gueaux*, or *beggars*, whose

* Special commissions directed in the behalf of privileged persons unto their peculiar judges.

chief view was to prevent the establishing of the Inquisition. The king of Spain makes preparations for calling them to an account: the prince of Orange, foreseeing the storm, retires to Germany, and leaves the counts d'Egmont and de Horn in Flanders, after endeavouring in vain to render those noblemen sensible of their danger.

From the memoirs of Nevers it appears, that the chief view of Philip II, in raising disturbances under this and the following reign, was to disable Charles IX. and Henry III. from assisting his rebellious subjects in the Netherlands.

1567.

The duke of Alva, upon his arrival in the Low Countries, arrests the counts d'Egmont and de Horn, who were executed the year following. The Huguenots, led on by the prince of Condé and the admiral, attempt to surprize Charles IX. at *Monceaux*. The queen has timely notice of their design, and retires to Meaux, from whence the Swifs, commanded by their colonel Lewis Siffer of Lucerne, conduct the king back to Paris. The duke de Nemours marched in the van, with the horseguards; and the constable in the rear, with the whole retinue belonging to the court. (*Davila.*) "The prince of Condé was arrived to so high a degree of power, that he caused money to be coined, with this inscription, *Lewis XIII. king of France.*" (Brantome.) The battle of St. Denis on the 10th of November, where the constable Anne de Montmorency was mortally wounded: this engagement lasted but three quarters of an hour; the success so dubious, that both sides claimed the advantage; yet la Noue gives the victory to the Royalists. The constable had maintained himself in the first employment of the state, under four tempestuous reigns: at seventy-four years of age he fought so manfully, as to receive eight mortal wounds; (this was also the eighth battle in which he had been engaged) yet he had so much strength left as to make up to the person who wounded him last, and to beat out three of his teeth with the pommel of his sword. This was a Scotchman, named James Stuart, who, happening to be taken prisoner two years after at the battle of Jarnac, was put to death, to appease the manes of the deceased constable. Le Laboureur doubts, whether

REMARKABLE EVENTS under CHARLES IX.

whether this James Stuart was of the royal house of Scotland. The Scotch, as well as the Romans, took their names from the families to whose service they were attached: this the latter called *clientela*; and it greatly resembles the *aggregations* so common in Italy. This is the same man who was suspected of the murder of the president Minard in the reign of Francis II. The constable had five children; Francis, marshal duke de Montmorency; Henry, who was a peer, marshal, and constable of France; Charles, created duke d'Anville, and admiral of France; Montbron, and Thoré. He was buried with royal honours; and his effigy was carried before him at the public funeral. Charles d'Ailly de Picquigny, vidame of Amiens, and his son, happening to be both killed at the battle of St. Denis, their succession gave rise to a law-suit: as the point was to know which of the two died first, the parliament, not being able to come at the truth, were of opinion that it was not right to invert the order of nature, and therefore determined that the succession had been transmitted from father to son.

The city of Orleans, having been delivered up to the king after the edict of pacification in 1563, is surprized by the Huguenots. The duke d'Anjou is made lieutenant-general of the kingdom: marshal de Tavannes was to assist him, by order of the queen; and to this officer he owed the reputation he enjoyed under the present reign. This same general and the marshal de Retz were privy to the intended massacre of St. Bartholomew's, which was attributed chiefly to their contrivance.

Creation of the post of colonel-general of horse, which was split at first into two branches; one intitled *on this side the mountains*, and given to Charles of Savoy, duke de Nemours; the other *beyond the mountains*, in favour of Henry de Montmorency, duke d'Anville: but this distinction was afterwards suppressed.

The edict of St. Maur, known by the name of *the mothers*, to hinder them from inheriting their *children's paternal estates*: it was published at the request of John de Montluc, to prevent his nephew's widow from running away with the estate of the family.

Letters patent, ordaining, that no person shall be admitted to a judicial office, without inquiring into his life and character, and whether he be of the Roman catholic religion. Stobæus mentions a law at Athens, by which no citizen could be admitted to a public office, before he made the following oath in regard to his religion; *I will defend the altars, I will conform to the national worship.*

1568.

The war continues throughout the kingdom. The second peace signed at Longjumeau, called the *short peace*, because it lasted but six months: the edict of pacification was renewed, free from all the restrictions of that of Roussillon.

The third civil war, more furious than the two preceding, the Protestant princes of Germany being concerned in it. This was owing to the queen's design of seizing the prince of Condé and the admiral, who were retired to their estates, and had intelligence thereof from the marshal de Tavannes.

The death of Don Carlos and of his mother-in-law Elizabeth of France. Pius V. publishes the bull *in cœna Domini*, excommunicating all princes and others, who shall demand any contribution whatever of the clergy: this bull is read publickly in Rome every Maundy Thursday. The parliament issued an arret against it in 1580. Queen Elizabeth imprisons Mary queen of Scots, who had fled to England, with a view of obtaining succours against her rebellious subjects.

The chancellor de l'Hopital, being suspected by the queen, chose to retire from court. We can no where better place, than at this article of the chancellor de l'Hopital, (one of the greatest magistrates and civilians in France) some reflections on the progress of the laws from the beginning of the monarchy to that age.

All societies have laws; but, though these laws appear to be invariable, it is however true, that they partake of the inconstancy of man, and that they have been changed in proportion to the alterations which have happened in manners and customs. It is certain, that those who composed the *Salic law*, did not foresee what has been added to it in the capitularies, because that law was for the guide of men whose sole employment was war; on the other hand, the capitularies related to men formed into a more regular society, and to citizens assembled together, whose passions shewed themselves under a different shape. The introduction of fiefs produced a much greater change: France, in the time of Charles the Simple, had not the least resemblance to the same country

REMARKABLE EVENTS under CHARLES IX.

country in the time of Charlemagne; and new evils required new remedies: for the laws are only remedies, and men of sense have no great need of them. The character of the French made it necessary for their happiness, that they should be governed by a single person; it was therefore proper to bring them back insensibly to those happy times, in which they had but one master; and not to suffer them to destroy themselves by a love of independence, the consequences of which they could not foresee: had the private wars lasted one century longer, there would have been an end of the French monarchy. It was requisite then to form laws on that fantastic kind of possession, which the prudence of our kings endeavoured to regulate, till it gave them no manner of umbrage: from thence arose that uninterrupted train of wise precautions, transmitted, as by a kind of miracle, from reign to reign; by which our kings, without suffering the secret to be disclosed, at length recovered the authority so necessary to the happiness of the people: the enfranchising of villains, the establishing of corporations, royal cases, ennoblements, &c. were all so many mortal blows given to the licentiousness and rebellion authorized by the feudal laws.

But there were still greater evils behind, to which we were yet strangers; these were the religious wars, that rent the kingdom under the unhappy reigns of Francis II, Charles IX, and Henry III. Had the grandees and the people abandoned themselves to their fanaticism, France would soon have fallen, if not into her ancient barbarism, from which luxury and the love of pleasure would perhaps have defended her for some time; at least into anarchy, the consequence of a contempt of the laws, and an ignorance of literature. Who would not then have believed every thing lost? But the chancellor de l'Hopital watched over the safety of his country: that great man, in the midst of civil commotions, made the laws be heard, which are commonly silent in those tempestuous times: it never once entered into his thoughts to doubt of their power; he did honour to reason and justice, in thinking them stronger than even the force of arms; and that their venerable majesty had inalienable rights over the heart of man, when properly enforced. Hence arose those laws, whose noble simplicity rivals that of the laws of Rome; those edicts, which, from a wife forefight, comprehend the future as well as the prefent time, and are fince become a fruitful fource, in which has been found the decifion of cafes that were not even forefeen; thofe ordinances, where ftrength and wifdom, combined, make us forget the weaknefs of the reign in which they were publifhed: immortal works of a magiftrate above all praife, who knew the duties, power, and high dignity of his employment, yet could refign it, as foon as he perceived that the court refolved to limit the functions of his office; and by a comparifon with whom all thofe are condemned, who have dared to fit on the fame tribunal, without having either his courage or his abilities.

1569.

The battle of Jarnac*, on the 13th of March, in which the duke of Anjou defeated Lewis I, prince of Condé, who was killed in cold blood by Montefquieu. The prince was then only nine and thirty years old: he had his arm in a fling; and, a moment before the action, his leg was broke by a kick from a horfe belonging to his brother-in-law, the count de la Rochefoucaud. When firft he appeared in life, he had but fix thoufand livres a year: the marfhal de St. André's lady made him a prefent of her eftate of Valery; but it is not true that it was on condition he and his defcendants fhould be buried there. He is faid to have been flain by order of the duke d'Anjou. The battle lafted feven hours without great effufion of blood: the Catholics gained the victory. The queen intended to govern the prince of Condé by means of his miftreffes, who all expected to be married to him: mademoifelle de Limeuil proved with child, and was difmiffed from court; the marfhal de St. André's lady fpent her fortune; and the Guifes had no other way to gain him, than by flattering him with the hopes of marrying the queen of Scotland. After the deceafe of Eleonora de Roy, he efpoufed the duke de Longueville's fifter.

* A little village in the province of Angouleme. The prince endeavoured to decline the action, on account of the misfortune of his leg; but, being once engaged, he fought like a hero. After he had received feveral wounds, he was taken prifoner; but fo weak, through lofs of blood, that two gentlemen lifted him up in their arms from his horfe, and carried him to a bufh, where the baron de Montefquieu, captain of the guards to the duke of Anjou, came behind and fhot him through the head.

REMARKABLE EVENTS under CHARLES IX.

The admiral de Coligny revives the courage of the Huguenots: Jane d'Albret, queen of Navarre, repairs to the army with her son Henry, prince of Bearn, afterwards Henry IV, and with the prince of Condé's son, who was also named Henry. The young prince of Bearn is declared head of the party: although his father was dead, he did not take the title of king of Navarre till after the death of his mother, Jane d'Albret.

A considerable skirmish on the 25th of June, in the neighbourhood of Roche-la-belle in the Limousin: the duke of Anjou was encamped on this spot, to hinder the admiral, who had been reinforced by the Germans, from penetrating into the upper Poitou. The admiral had the advantage, being seconded by William prince of Orange. Here the prince of Bearn, at sixteen years of age, made his first campaign. De Coligny raises the siege of Poitiers, which was gallantly defended by Henry the young duke de Guise.

On the 3d of October was fought the battle of Moncontour, the 4th of this reign: the first was that of Dreux in 1562; the second that of St. Denis in 1567; then followed those of Jarnac and Montcontour. The Huguenots lost them all four. This was a bloody engagement: the duke of Anjou obtained the victory, but did not make a right use of it; for, instead of pursuing the admiral, he laid siege to St. John d'Angeli, where he lost a great number of men, but took the town.

1570.

The war is continued on the other side of the Loire with equal fury. The admiral, being under the command of the prince of Bearn, and his cousin the prince of Condé, the former sixteen years old, the latter seventeen, undertakes to conduct the army across the kingdom, in order to join the German succours: he succeeds in this enterprize, and at Arnay le Duc defeats the marshal de Cossé, who attempted to obstruct his march. The third peace, which proved favourable to the Huguenots, signed at St. Germains in the month of August: it was called the *lame* and *ill-set* peace; having been concluded by the sieurs de Biron and de Mesmes, the former of whom was lame, and the latter bore the name of the seignory of *Mal assisse*, which signifies *ill-set*. The duke of of Anjou goes to meet the princess Elizabeth of Austria, who had been just married to the king, and was conducted by the elector of Mentz. There arose some difficulty in the ceremonial between the duke and the elector; but the affair was settled, and the latter yielded the precedency to the former. *(Mem. de Cheverny.)*

1571.

The advantages granted to the Huguenots by the peace of St. Germains, raise a suspicion in the breasts of the Protestant leaders: this the court of France attempts to remove by a proposal of marriage between princess Margaret, Charles IXth's sister, and Henry prince of Bearn, making a feint at the same time as if they were preparing for war against Spain. A marriage is also proposed between the duke of Anjou and queen Elizabeth. If ever that princess entertained any serious thoughts of matrimony, it was with this prince, who was afterwards Henry III. It is said that Mary queen of Scots had the same view in regard to the duke of Anjou; and that, during her confinement, she resigned her right to the crown of Scotland in his favour, from an expectation of their future nuptials. *(Bibl. Britan.)*

The battle of Lepanto, where Don John of Austria, a natural son of Charles V, gained a complete victory over the Turks. This young prince died in 1578, at the age of thirty-two: his brother Philip II. suspected him of aiming at the sovereignty of the Netherlands, where he had appointed him governor; and his connections with queen Elizabeth, who loved neither the king of Spain nor the Spaniards, seemed to justify his suspicions: his death, following soon after, was not looked upon as natural; and the generality of historians, except Cabrera, say he was poisoned. Strada affirms, that Philip II. had conceived a jealousy against Don John, by the artifices of the prince of Orange; and, as this jealousy retarded the succours from Spain, it must needs have contributed as much as the resolution and good conduct of the Dutch, to the establishment of their liberty. There is another curious anecdote on this subject: Philip II. meeting, amongst Don John's papers, with a treaty of alliance between him and Henry duke de Guise, which would have been equally fatal to France and Spain, laid hold of the discovery to make the same proposals to the

duke

REMARKABLE EVENTS under CHARLES IX.

duke de Guife: fo that he converted to his advantage what had been defigned to do him prejudice; and Don John was indirectly the caufe of that famous league, which afterwards produced fuch an infinite deal of mifchief.

1572.

The queen of Navarre is drawn to Paris by the marriage of her fon; and the admiral, by the great preparations for war; the king pretending to have a defign of invading the Netherlands, and of employing the admiral on that expedition. The death of the queen of Navarre. D'Aubigné, who makes no doubt but fhe was poifoned, gives a fine elogium of this princefs: "She had nothing of the woman about her, except her "fex; her mind was bent on manly undertakings; her capacity "equal to the weightieft affairs; and her heart unfhaken in the "greateft adverfity." The king of Navarre efpoufes princefs Margaret. The admiral is wounded with a mufket-fhot by Maurevert, and attributes this affaffination to the duke de Guife: there feems to have been the more grounds for this fufpicion, as the duke had fworn, that he would never be at repofe till he revenged the murder of his father, which was attributed to the admiral, and happened when the fon was only thirteen years old. *(Brantome.)* The maffacre of the Huguenots at Paris on the feaft of St. Bartholomew: "an execrable action, which "never had, and God grant never more may have, its paral- "lel." *(Perefixe.)* Coligny was affaffinated by one Befme, and fell the firft victim on that fatal day; his poft was given to Honorat de Savoie, marquis de Villars. Among other papers belonging to the admiral, there was found a journal, where he advifes his majefty not to grant too generous an allowance to his brothers, for fear of rendering them independent of his authority: the queen fhewed this article to the duke d'Alençon, knowing that he was greatly afflicted at Coligny's death: there, "faid fhe, is your good friend; fee what counfel he gives the "king. I know not, anfwered the duke d'Alençon, whether "he had a regard for me, or not; this I am confident of, that fuch "an advice could come from no man, that was not zealoufly "attached to his majefty and to the ftate." The maffacre of St.

Bartho-

REMARKABLE EVENTS under CHARLES IX.

Bartholomew's was extended throughout the kingdom, except a few provinces, where the governors had too much probity and courage to obey such execrable orders; their names, though mentioned in the memoirs of the times, cannot be too often repeated; these were the counts de Tendes and de Charny, messieurs de St. Heraut, Taneguy le Veneur, de Gordes, de Mandelot, d'Ortes, &c. The king of Navarre and the prince of Condé made their recantation to save their lives. Charles IX, after throwing the whole blame of those horrid executions on the duke de Guise, took it upon himself; in consequence of which the parliament instituted a process against the admiral and his accomplices, and sentenced him to be hanged in effigy upon the gibbet of Montfaucon. The feast of St. Bartholomew fell this year upon a Sunday, and the massacre was perpetrated in the evening. Ambrose Paré and the king's nurse, both of the Protestant religion, were the only persons excepted out of this abominable proscription. *Ever since that day,* says Brantome, *this prince seemed to be entirely altered; and it was said, that he had no longer that sweetness in his countenance, for which he had been so remarkable before.* Francis de Noailles, bishop of Acqs, ambassador to the Porte, negotiates a peace betwixt the Turks and Venetians, and preserves a part of the island of Candia, to which the Turks had laid siege.

The dutchy of Uzés, created in 1565, is erected into a peerage.

1573.

Who would not have thought that the Huguenots were intirely crushed? But the time was not yet come. Montauban gives the signal for a new revolt, which occasions the fourth civil war, the Huguenots refusing to deliver up the cautionary towns. In order to shew how greatly the royal authority was weakened, it will suffice to give the following extract of a letter to the duke d'Alençon, dated Perigueux, the 13th of March, 1574, from Andrew de Bourdeille, seneschal of Perigord, whom Charles IX. had charged to inquire privately into the state of the province. *If the king, the queen, and yourself, do not provide better than you have done hitherto,* (against the public disturbances) *I am afraid I shall see you reduced as low as myself.* The duke of Anjou, having laid siege to Rochelle, loses the greatest part of his army, and

REMARKABLE EVENTS under CHARLES IX.

and at length grants favourable terms to the inhabitants, who, upon surrendering, remain the predominant party in that town. The fourth peace, which shewed the weakness of the government, and the strength of the Huguenots after all the endeavours to crush them.

The duke of Anjou is elected king of Poland, upon the demise of Sigismund II. This was originally an hereditary kingdom; neither did the Poles proceed to an election till towards the year 1386, after the death of Lewis, king of Hungary and Poland. Lewis, though surnamed the Great, did not appear in that light to this nation, who could not forgive his partiality to the Hungarians; and, though he had nominated his son-in-law to succeed him, yet they elected Jagellon, great duke of Lithuania, who purchased their suffrages, by reuniting Lithuania and his other principalities to the crown: then this throne became elective, and has continued so ever since.

The duke of Anjou, having been apprized of his election to the crown of Poland during the siege of Rochelle, by the care of John de Montluc, bishop of Valence, sets out upon his journey to take possession of that kingdom. Charles IX. at this time was in a bad state of health; and the queen mother, at taking leave of the duke, gave him hopes of a speedy return. His only uneasiness was not that of leaving his native country, where he had so near a prospect of ascending the throne; it is well known how strong a passion he had for the marchioness d'Isle (Mary of Cleves), the first wife of Henry I, prince of Condé

1574.

A new faction appeared this year, known by the name of the *Politicians*, headed by the duke d'Alençon and the Montmorencies, and strengthened by the accession of the Huguenots. The queen mother, being informed of this confederacy, orders the duke d'Alençon and the king of Navarre to be arrested: but the prince of Condé made his escape into Germany. The marshals de Montmorency and de Cossé are sent to the Bastile on the same account. La Mole and Coconnas, favourites of the duke d'Alençon, are executed. The former was upon very good terms with queen Margaret; and the latter with madame de Nevers (Henrietta

rietta of Cleves). The court raises three armies, which obtain considerable advantages against the Huguenots.

The Jesuits begin to keep a public school in the college of Clermont.

The death of Charles IX. All the princes and great lords belonging to the court quitted the funeral procession at the church of St. Lazarus in the suburb of Paris; so that there remained no more than Brantome, and four other gentlemen of the bedchamber, with some of the archers of the guard, to attend the corpse to St. Denis.

During this reign the kingdom was torn with civil broils, and the royal authority was considerably impaired. And yet this period is remarkable for the enacting of our best laws, and for regulations most conducive to the public welfare, the greatest part of which are to this day in full force. For these we are indebted to the chancellor de l'Hopital, whose name will be ever revered by such as have a regard for justice. But, what is very extraordinary, this same prince, who is represented by all historians to have been so violent and cruel in his disposition, and who avowed the massacre of St. Bartholomew's, was an encourager of learning, and took a particular delight in the softer arts which humanize the soul; he has even left us some proofs of his taste for poetry. Indeed he had a great inequality of temper: *it was the marshal de Retz, a Florentine,* as Brantome says, *that spoiled him, and made him soon forget all the fine things he had learnt of the brave Cipierre.*

It is observable, that, in the reign of Charles IX, the secretaries of state began to sign the king's orders and letters patent. This prince was very impetuous in his temper; and Villeroy, having waited upon him several times with dispatches to sign, just as he was going to play at tennis; *sign, father,* said he, *sign for me. Well then, sire,* replied Villeroy, *since your majesty commands me, I will sign.* Brantome, speaking of ancient times, says, that formerly the young men were willing to learn the military art, and therefore remained subalterns a considerable while: " but " now, continues he, this custom is laid aside; they are not so " easily satisfied; but as soon as a youth begins to bear arms, he " must have a command, either in the light horse, or in the

" gen-

REMARKABLE EVENTS under CHARLES IX.

" gendarmes, or in some regiment of foot, without having learnt
" to obey." Le Laboureur on Castelnau enlarges upon this
subject: " At that time they did not mount so quick to military
" preferments; ambition had its bounds; valour had none; but
" reputation was its choicest reward. By means of this mode-
" ration, the greatest and most experienced captains continued
" to serve the state in the same employment; whereas at present
" there is no post left for a gentleman of any credit, that has
" served five or six campaigns. In those days, the utmost extent
" of the ambition of princes, of the greatest and bravest men at
" court, was to command fifty or a hundred men at arms: in the
" day of battle, the silver beards were seen waving on the cuirasses
" of most of the officers, as a mark of their long services; but
" now they would conceal this badge of honour, either by dying
" their hair, or by wearing a peruke; and they blush at not
" having gone through an office, before they have attained the
" proper age, or done the due service to merit it." The reason
of this is, that gentlemen desire only to learn the common track,
but have no ambition to be eminent.

1574.
Accession to the crown.

HENRY III, who was already king of Poland, ascends the throne in the year 1574, aged about three and twenty years. He was crowned at Rheims the 13th of February, 1575, by Lewis, cardinal de Guise, a twelvemonth after his coronation in Poland.

His governor was Francis de Carnavalet, a brave and valiant lord, *says Brantome*, who knew all Cæsar's commentaries in Latin by heart.

When they came to put on the crown he complained of its hurting him; and it rolled twice about his head, as if it was going to fall off, which was interpreted as a very unfavourable omen.

REMARKABLE EVENTS.

1574.

THIS was stiled the reign of favourites. Montgomery, who had been taken prisoner at Domfront in the preceding reign, is condemned to death for high-treason. "Fifteen years before he had the misfortune of killing Henry II. at a tournament: this accident brought him to the scaffold, loaded with all the mischiefs which that death occasioned to the state, rather than with his own crimes. For, in regard to the high-treason with which he was charged, he could not be prosecuted for it after the publishing of so many edicts, and especially after the last act of indemnity: but it was necessary to offer up this sacrifice to the queen regent, who thirsted after the blood of a man that had slain her royal spouse. A memorable example to posterity, that a meer accidental blow against a crowned head is deemed criminal, even when there has been no malice prepense." (De Thou, tom. 7.) By the same arret, his children were declared *roturiers* or plebeians, which drew from him this beautiful expression at his execution; "If they have not virtue enough to recover their birthright, I consent to the arret." This is an unfortunate name: we have mentioned already, that, in 1521, captain de Lorges, sieur de Montgomery, being at some diversion with Francis I, burnt that prince's hair, by tossing a firebrand.

The late king, on his death-bed, had declared Catharine de Medicis regent, till his successor returned to France.

Henry III. makes his escape out of Poland, with thirteen more in company. Great honours are paid him at Vienna and Venice. The reception he met with in Piedmont from the duke and

dutchess

The Third Race. 433

WIVES.	CHILDREN.	1589. DEATH.	Cotemporary PRINCES.
Louisa of Lorrain, daughter of Nicholas, count de Vaudemont, a younger brother of the duke of Lorrain; she was married in 1575, died in 1601, and was interred in the church of the Capuchin nuns (at present the Conception) founded by herself. The famous count d'Egmond, beheaded in 1568, was her uncle by her mother's side. Henry III. had been fond of Renée de Rieux, whom he wanted to marry to Francis de Luxemburg, and who was afterwards espoused to Philip de Castellane. (Memoirs of Castelnau.)		HENRY III. was assassinated at St. Cloud the 1st of August, 1589, at eight o'clock in the morning, by James Clement, a Dominican friar, only twenty-two years old, who was born in the village of Sorbonne, near Sens, and had been educated in the convent of Dominicans, belonging to that town. The king died the day following, aged about thirty eight; he had reigned fifteen years and two months. His body was deposited in the abbey of Compiegne till the year 1610, when it was removed to St. Denis.	*Popes.* Gregory XIII. 1585. Sixtus V. 1590. *Turkish emperor.* Amurath III. 1595. *Emperors of Germany.* Maximilian II. 1576. Rodolphus II. 1612. *King of Spain.* Philip II. 1598. *Kings of Portugal.* Sebastian. 1578. Don Henry, cardinal. 1580. Philip II. 1598. *Queen of England.* Elizabeth. 1603. *Kings of Scotland.* Mary Stuart. 1587. James VI. 1625. *Kings of Denmark.* Frederick II. 1588. Christian IV. 1648. *King of Sweden.* John. 1592. *Kings of Poland.* Stephen Battori. 1587. Maximilian of Austria. 1587. Sigismund III. 1632. *Czars of Muscovy.* John Basilowitz. 1584. Fœdor Joannowitz. 1597.

Vol. I.   F f

REMARKABLE EVENTS under HENRY III.

dutchefs of Savoy, daughter of Francis I, coft the king very dear, when he confented to reftore Pignerol, Savillan, and Peroufe, by the advice of the marfhal de Bellegarde, who fold himfelf to the duke of Savoy: thefe were the only ftrong holds that France had kept poffeffion of beyond the mountains. The duke de Nevers, governor of thofe fortreffes, oppofed the agreement; and the chancellor de Birague having refufed to fign the letters patent for this reftitution, the king figned them himfelf. Birague was afterwards difgraced.

A famous affembly, where a confultation is held what part to act againft the Huguenots. The emperor Maximilian and the Venetians had, from different motives, advifed the king, when he paffed through their territories, in his way from Poland to France, not to make ufe of force: the Venetians gave their opinion *bona fide*, and agreeably to his real interefts; but the emperor was fufpected of being inclined towards the new religion. Paul de Foix is ftrongly for peace; M. de Villequier openly declares for war; and this opinion is embraced by the king, who equally hated the Huguenots and the duke de Guife. The prince of Condé and marfhal d'Anville are at the head of the Huguenots. The war is carried on with indifferent fuccefs on both fides. The Rochellers recommence hoftilities. The duke de Montpenfier makes himfelf mafter of Lufignan. The death of the cardinal of Lorrain.

1575.

Montbrun, commander of the Huguenots in Dauphiné, is put to death: he had the audacioufnefs to plunder the king's baggage, in coming out of Pont de Beauvoifin, upon his majefty's return from Poland; and he added this infolent fpeech, that the fword and gaming put all mankind upon a level. Lefdiguieres is fubftituted in his place. The duke d'Alençon, whom Henry III. had lately forgiven a confpiracy againft his life, undertakes to head the rebels. Queen Elizabeth fends him fuccours; and the king, having been defirous of a match between her and this prince, begins to be afraid that this alliance will encourage the difturbances of his kingdom. The queen mother releafes the marfhals de Montmorency and de Coffée out of the Baftile, to place them

The THIRD RACE. 435

MINISTERS.	WARRIORS.	MAGISTRATES.	EMINENT and LEARNED MEN.
Philip Hurault de Cheverny, who was chancellor, 1599. Pomponne de Bellievre, superintendant. 1607. Francis d'O, superintendant of the finances. 1594. Marcel, comptroller of the finances; he had been provost of the merchants. *Secretaries of state.* Sim. Fizes de Sauves. 1579. Nic. de Neuville de Villeroy. 1617. Peter Brulart. 1608. Cl. Pinart. 1605. Lewis Revol. 1594. Martin Ruzé. 1613. Lewis Potier de Gevres. 1630. P. Forget de Frene. 1610. *It was Forget that drew up the edict of Nantes.*	*Marshals of France.* Francis de Montmorency. 1579. Henry de Montmorency, duke d'Anville. 1614. They were both sons of the constable Anne de Montmorency; and Henry the youngest was constable in the next reign. Charles de Montmorency, their youngest brother, bore for a long time the name of Meru, and was made duke and peer by Lewis XIII, by the name of Anville, was admiral of France, and the first that had the title of colonel general of the Swifs. Arthur de Coffé, lord of Gonhor. 1582. Honorat de Savoie. 1580. Albert de Gondy de Retz. 1602. Roger de St. Lary de Bellegarde. 1579. Blaife de Montluc. 1577. He has given us the commentaries of his life. Armand de Gontaut de Biron. 1592.	*Chancellors.* René de Birague. 1583. Philip Hurault de Cheverny. 1599. Francis de Montholon, keeper of the feals. 1590. Son of the keeper of the feals, named also Francis. *First presidents.* Christ. de Thou. 1582. Achilles de Harlay. 1616. *Attorneys general.* John de la Guefle. 1589. James de la Guefle. 1612. *King's advocates.* Guy du Faur de Pibrac. 1584. Auguft. de Thou. 1595. Barnaby Briffon. 1591. James Faye d'Efpeiffes. 1590. *Loifel obferves, that the firft fale of the offices of attorney general and king's advocate, was, when Bellievre, president of the parliament of Paris, having refigned his employment in the month of Auguft, 1580, in favour of Barnaby Briffon, who paid him sixty*	Michael Baius. 1589. Remy Belleau. 1577. Fr. de Belleforets. 1583. George Buchanan. 1582. Joach. Camerarius. 1574. Lewis de Camoens. 1579. Jerome Cardanus. 1576. St. Charles Borromæus. 1584. P. Ciaconius. 1581. J. Fr. Commendon, cardinal. 1584. P. Danés, preceptor to Francis II. 1577. This was he, who, when bishop of Lavaur, declaiming ftrongly, at the council of Trent, againft the morals of the clergy, was interrupted by Sebaftian Vance, bifhop of Orvieto, who faid with a fneer, *Gallus cantat*; to which Danés made anfwer, *utinam ad Galli cantum Petrus refipifceret*. John Dorat. 1588. Arnauld du Ferrier. 1585. Lewis de Foix, engineer, living in 1585. Antony de Granvelle, cardinal. 1586. Lewis de Guife, cardinal. 1576. Paul de Foix. 1584. Philibert de Lorme, towards 1577. Charles, cardinal of Lorrain. 1574. John Maldonat. 1583. John de Montluc, bifhop of Valence. 1579. Antony Muret. 1585. Francis de Noailles. 1585. William Paradin, towards 1581. Ambrofe Paré, towards 1584. Paul Veronefe, painter. 1588. Guy du Faur de Pibrac. 1584.

Ff 2

REMARKABLE EVENTS under HENRY III.

near the person of the duke d'Alençon, over whom they had great influence. Henry duke of Guise is wounded with a pistol-shot in the face, in an engagement near Chateau-Thierry; and from thence he received the surname of *Balafré* *. Besme, the murderer of admiral de Coligny, is killed by the Huguenots. The king in vain endeavours to prevail with the Poles to continue their allegiance to him as their sovereign; they elect Stephen Battory, prince of Transylvania, and make him espouse the princess Anne, sister of their last king Sigismund. Henry was so fully convinced the Poles had no right to nominate a successor in his stead, that du Ferrier, his ambassador to the republic of Venice, had orders to complain to the senate, of their having appointed an ambassador to king Stephen, when they ought to have considered that prince as only his deputy. *(The history of Venice by Morosini.)* The post of grand master of the waters and forests, which till this reign had been exercised only by one officer, is suppressed in the person of Henry Clausse, lord of Fleury; and six masters general are created in his place. At present the jurisdiction of the waters and forests is divided into seventeen departments.

1576.

The king of Navarre, whom Henry III. at his return had set at liberty, escapes from court, and, joining the Huguenots, makes profession once more of the Protestant religion. The queen, according to her usual policy, finding this party too powerful, thinks seriously of peace. The duke d'Alençon, despised by the Huguenots, listens to his mother's proposals. A peace is concluded, the most advantageous the Protestants had hitherto obtained: in consequence hereof an edict of pacification is published at Paris in the month of May, and registered in parliament, (it was the fifth in favour of the Huguenots) by which they were allowed the public exercise of the *pretended reformed* religion, as it was called in the edict. Mention is made, that the priests or monks who had married, shall not be molested, and that their issue shall be deemed legitimate; yet in the king's library we meet with a great many legitimations at that time, which shews that they were looked upon as necessary, notwithstanding the edict. Bipartite

* *i. e.* Slashed or cut over the face.

The Third Race.

WARRIORS.	MAGISTRATES.	EMINENT and LEARNED MEN.
Marshals of France. James Goyon de Matignon. 1597. John d'Aumont. 1595. Will. de Joyeuse. 1592.	*King's advocates.* *thousand livres for it, the latter, who was advocate general, disposed of his place to James Faye for forty thousand livres.* James Mango. 1587. Antony Seguier. 1624. *He is the first that had the title of advocate general. Advocates general nominated in the month of January, 1589, by the officers of parliament, in the room of those who withdrew (James Faye, Seguier, &c.)* Peter de Beauvais. Felix le Vayer. John le Maitre. Lewis d'Orleans.	William Postel. 1581. Peter Ronsard. 1585. Lewis de St. Gelais. 1589. Carolus Sigonius. 1585. William Sirlet. 1585. St. Theresa. 1582. Titian, the painter. 1576. Peter Versoris. 1581. Simon Vigor. 1575. Peter Vittori. 1585.

chambers * are granted to the Reformed, in the eight parliaments of the kingdom; the arrets against the admiral, la Mole, and Coconnas, are reversed, their memory restored, and their heirs permitted to enter into possession of their estates. The dukedoms of Anjou, Maine, Touraine, and Berry, are added to the appanage of the duke d'Alençon.

Henry III. erected religious confraternities, and exposed himself in ridiculous processions, instead of promoting the cause of religion and his own, by banishing licentiousness and debauchery from court. Why should not we sometimes relate the failings of crowned heads? " We do not sufficiently love good sovereigns, " says M. de Tillemont, unless we hate the irregularities of bad " princes." The edict of pacification exasperates the Catholics, and occasions the famous confederacy, known by the name of the *Holy League.* Associations formed in different provinces of the kingdom. The Huguenots are insulted in several towns. The states held at Blois. A deputation from the states to the king of Navarre and to the prince of Condé, inviting them to repair to that assembly, and to give their consent to an article, which prohibited the exercise of any other than the Catholic religion. The duke of Anjou declares against the edict of pacification. After a great many consultations, the above edict is revoked, and the league is signed by the king, the duke d'Anjou, &c. Maimbourg, having recovered a copy of the instrument, signed by the nobility of Picardy and the magistrates of Peronne, has published it at the end of his history of the League: strictly speaking, this confederacy began in 1576, with the above cited treaty of Peronne. The cardinal of Lorrain formed the original plan of it at the council of Trent; but the death of his brother, Francis duke de Guise, interrupted the design for some time, till his nephew Henry was of age; then he resumed the enterprize, and his death did not prevent the duke de Guise from carrying it into execution.

A declaration published at Blois, reforming the ancient usage, and ordaining, that the princes of the blood shall precede all peers, whether those princes be peers or not, or whether their peerages are of a later date than others; it likewise regulates the precedency among the princes of the blood, according to their proximity to

* That is half Catholics, half Protestants.

REMARKABLE EVENTS under HENRY III.

the crown. After the regiſtering of this declaration, Chriſtopher de Thou, then firſt preſident, aſſured the king, that, ſince the reign of Philip de Valois, no ſtep whatever had been ſo conducive to the maintenance of the Salic law.

A great peſtilence at Milan, where St. Charles Borromeus ſet the ſtrongeſt example of paſtoral care: this we ſaw revived by the biſhop of Marſeilles at the time of the plague of Provence in 1720.

1577.

The duke of Anjou makes himſelf maſter of la Charité and Iſſoire.

The king, being afraid leſt the Proteſtants ſhould invite foreign troops into the kingdom, puts a ſtop to this war, in which he had too haſtily engaged; and, notwithſtanding his preſent ſucceſs, with the ſame levity he concludes a new peace with the Proteſtants, leſs favourable indeed than the former, and ſigns it at Poitiers. What is very extraordinary, in the edict of pacification, his majeſty declares, " that he publiſhes this law, in expectation that " God will grant him the grace of bringing back all his ſubjects " into the pale of the Catholic church, by means of a good, " free, and legitimate council." *Courayer, appendix to the hiſtory of the council of Trent.* What! was not the council of Trent held but fourteen years before? and was not that a good, free, and legitimate council? or was Henry III. afraid to irritate the Proteſtants? The king of Navarre came into this peace with greater readineſs than any of the whole party.

Henry III. grants a brief, on the 13th of December, to the duke de Montmorency, declaring, that he ſhall have the precedency of the chancellor in council: he likewiſe iſſues out letters patent, ordaining, that none of the new created peers ſhall take place of the crown officers, namely, the conſtable, the chancellor, the keeper of the ſeals, the lord ſteward of the king's houſhold, the lord chamberlain, the admiral, the marſhals of France, and the maſter of the horſe.

1578.

The diſturbances continue in Guienne. Don Sebaſtian III. of Portugal is killed in battle by the Moors: in this engagement fell

fell three kings; the king of Morocco; his nephew Mahomet, whom he had dethroned; and Don Sebaſtian. This was the firſt king of Portugal that took the title of majeſty, which was given him by Philip II. He was ſucceeded by cardinal Henry, his great uncle. Coneſtaggio ſays, "that, although this cardinal had more "virtues than vices, yet he was rather a vicious than virtuous cha- "racter; his virtues being private, his vices public." A combat between de Cailus, (Levis) de Maugiron, and de Livarot, on one ſide, and Balzac d'Antragues, d'Aidie de Riberac, and de Schomberg, on the other. Cailus and Maugiron loſt their lives: the king ordered a ſtatue of marble to be erected to each of them *, in the church of St. Paul; as alſo to St. Megrin, a gallant of the dutcheſs of Guiſe, whom Henry her huſband cauſed to be aſſaſſinated. Theſe monuments were pulled down by the Pariſians, after the death of the duke and cardinal of Guiſe.

The Netherlands at this time were in a ſtate of the utmoſt confuſion, the minds of the people being diſtracted by religion. The governors of that country for the king of Spain were ſucceſſively, the duke of Alva, recalled in 1573; Requeſens, deceaſed in 1576; and Don John of Auſtria, grown obnoxious to the Flemings, who, without conſulting Philip II, conferred the command on the archduke Matthias, the emperor's brother, with the advice of William prince of Orange. William reckoned he ſhould be able to govern Matthias; but, finding himſelf diſappointed, he perſuaded the Catholics of the Low Countries to call in the duke of Anjou, who had quitted the title of duke d'Alençon. This prince ſteals away from court, to put himſelf at the head of the Flemiſh malecontents. Henry IV, then only king of Navarre, had but a contemptible opinion of the duke of Anjou, as appears from theſe words: "he is ſo daſtardly, ſo deceitful, "and malicious, ſo deformed in body, &c." And queen Margaret, his ſiſter, uſed to ſay of this prince, though ſhe had a great affection for him, *"that, if all other inſincerity but his were ba-* *"niſhed from the face of the earth, he would be able to repleniſh it."* The bridge, called Pont-neuf, is begun to be built.

---

* They were the king's minions or favourites.

1579.

REMARKABLE EVENTS under HENRY III.

1579.

Henry III. inftitutes the order of the Holy Ghoft the 1ft of January, (the edict is dated the 1ft of the preceding December) in memory of his having been elected king of Poland, and fucceeded to the crown of France, on Whitfunday: but his real defign, as appears by the oath tendered to the new knights, was to detach the great lords from the Proteftant party; and at the fame time to oppofe the progrefs of the League, which feemed to be no longer under his control. The king of Navarre has recourfe again to arms, complaining of a total violation of the agreement at the conference of Nerac, which had been held the beginning of this year, with a view to interpret the laft edict of pacification. The conference proved favourable to the Huguenots, through Pibrac's weaknefs, who was fallen in love with queen Margaret.

The ordinance of Blois. As the council of Trent was not received by the French in matters of difcipline, we find here the true principles by which the Gallican church is directed. This ordinance, agreeable to the abovementioned council, has confirmed the chapter, which fixes the religious vows to the age of fixteen; though the ordinance of Orleans had forbid the males to make their profeffion of religion before twenty-five, and the females before twenty. The fame edict contains feveral other articles of importance, fuch as the 42d, which renders it capital to commit a rape; before this law the girl might fave the life of her ravifher, upon declaring her refolution to marry him: the 258th on nobility, ordains, that roturiers or plebeians, upon purchafing noble fiefs, fhall not be thereby ennobled, let the income and value of the fiefs be ever fo great. The cuftom of ennobling had introduced the fale of fiefs to the advantage of perfons ennobled, who became capable of poffeffing them; whereas they had not been allowed that privilege before. This innovation was owing to the nobles themfelves, exhaufted by their extravagance: defirous of reaping fome advantage from the ennobling of *roturiers*, who by their induftry or œconomy had got rich, they applied to the king, praying that he would permit thofe who were ennobled to purchafe fiefs: it is obvious, that this was a favour which the king would not refufe them. But it was enough to fee the nobility ftripped of their eftates, and grown

lefs

less considerable in the eye of the public; it would have been altogether indecent, that the common people, while they purchased those fiefs, should acquire the same honours and titles as were enjoyed by the former possessors. It was therefore determined they should have only the liberty of purchasing the land or estate, without purchasing the title along with it; at the same time this principle was established, that noble fiefs or lands do not ennoble their possessors; and that a marquisate and a county do not make a marquis or a count: in consequence hereof the ordinance was published, declaring, that nobility shall not be acquired without letters patent from the prince, or the possession of certain employments; this is the kind of nobility which we stile ennoblement, very different from that derived by birth. Though this ordinance was published at Paris, it is still called the *ordinance of Blois*, from its being issued out in consequence of the papers presented by the states, which were held at Blois in 1576.

An arret of parliament, ordaining, that the deeds or instruments before notaries shall be signed by the parties: this arret is agreeable to the 84th article of the ordinance of Orleans in 1560. Bussy d'Amboise is murdered in the castle of the lord de Montsoreau, who, being informed of the intrigue between that gentleman and his wife, obliges the lady to give an assignation to her gallant. Bussy had been also attached to queen Margaret; and, from the manner of her mentioning this in her memoirs, one would think she was willing the public should know it. An extraordinary sessions held at Poitiers. The king grants his protection to the city of Geneva against the duke of Savoy.

A duel between the viscount de Turenne, afterwards marshal de Bouillon, who had the baron de Salignac for his second; and the lord de Duras, whose second was James de Durfort, his younger brother.

1580.

The reformation of the custom of Paris. The revolution of Portugal, which, upon the decease of cardinal Henry, is seized by Philip II, in right of his wife Isabella, daughter of Emmanuel, King of Portugal. Don Antonio de Crato (grandson of Emmanuel, who was great grandfather to Don Sebastian) had been

proclaimed

REMARKABLE EVENTS under HENRY III.

proclaimed king, though his legitimacy was contested; but he was obliged to escape into France; and the duke of Braganza, who, in right of his wife, had the fairest pretension, was made constable of Portugal by Philip II. It was his grandson John that ascended the throne in 1640.

The duke of Anjou, upon his return from the Netherlands, concluded a peace between Henry III. and the Huguenots, in expectation that the king, his brother, would not only forward the match between him and queen Elizabeth, whom he had courted some time; but also promote his design of becoming sovereign of the Netherlands, where the king of Spain had lost all his authority. Notwithstanding the treaty, the war is carried on in Guienne. The king of Navarre makes himself master of the town of Cahors.

1581.

The states of Holland declare, that Philip II, king of Spain, has forfeited the sovereignty of the Netherlands, which they confer on the duke of Anjou, with the advice of William, prince of Orange. Queen Elizabeth and the duke of Anjou engage to assist each other in the defence of England and the Low Countries.

The duke of Anjou's first exploit was, that he obliged the duke of Parma to raise the siege of Cambray, which had been far advanced; he then went over to England, (he had been there before in 1579) to conclude his marriage with queen Elizabeth. This princess creates new delays, at the same time that she flatters the duke's expectations so far, as to give him a ring in plight of her faith, after signing the marriage contract. Henry was no more desirous the marriage should be accomplished than queen Elizabeth herself; for he was jealous of the duke of Anjou, as Charles IX. had been of him.

The king, upon erecting the county of Joyeuse and the barony of Epernon into dutchies and peerages, grants a precedency to those new dukes, next to the princes of the blood and the foreign princes, before all other dukes of more ancient creation. These distinctions were odious; but his majesty's prodigality was still more so: it is said that he spent twelve hundred thousand crowns at the nuptials of the duke de Joyeuse, without reckoning

four

REMARKABLE EVENTS under HENRY III.

four hundred thousand more, which he promised that nobleman: and indeed the *tailles* at that time were very near two and thirty millions, that is, they had been raised about three and twenty millions since the last reign.

The dutchy of Piney and Rameru erected into a peerage of France, in favour of Francis de Luxemburg, and his heirs, male and female. This dutchy passed successively, by means of Charlotte de Luxemburg, grand-daughter of Francis, to M. de Brantes, brother of the constable de Luines, whom she espoused; and afterwards to M. de Tonnere, her second husband: by the latter she had a daughter, who brought this dutchy to the marshal de Luxemburg. The marshal, having obtained letters patent of the king in 1661, pretended to take his seat from the day of erection in 1581; and the peers, on the other hand, insisted it should be only from the day of registering his new letters patent. However, these letters were verified in 1662, and he was admitted to his oath; but to take rank, till the contest was decided, only from the day of verification. The king having declared in 1676, that it was not his intention to create a new erection; and that his letters patent of 1661 had been only to approve of the marriage, and to consent to his being received as duke de Piney peer of France; the peers made a second opposition, affirming, that the letters of 1661 were not sufficient for that purpose: at length this dispute was determined by the famous edict of 1711, which ordains, that the duke of Luxemburg shall not take place, but from the day of registering the letters patent of the 20th of May, 1662.

1582.

An edict to receive the Gregorian reformation of the calendar. In France they cut off the ten days from the 15th to the 25th of December. This same calendar was adopted the year following in that part of Germany, which adhered to the Catholic religion. An attempt is made to assassinate the prince of Orange; and Philip II. is violently suspected of being the promoter of it. Renewal of the alliance with the Swiss. The defeat of Strozzi near the Azores: he had been sent thither by queen Catharine de Medicis, to support the rights of Don Antonio, prior of Crato, against Philip; and to obtain satisfaction for her own pretensions

REMARKABLE EVENTS under HENRY III.

to the crown of Portugal: in this expedition Strozzi loft his life. Solfede is quartered alive, for entering into a confpiracy againſt the king and the duke of Anjou: it is ſaid to have been at the inſtigation of the Guiſes.

1583.

The duke of Anjou, jealous of the prince of Orange, who had uſurped the whole authority, attempts to ſeize ſome of the principal towns in Flanders, and, among others, that of Antwerp, contrary to the remonſtrances of the duke de Montpenſier, and the marſhal de Biron. The burghers, animated by the prince of Orange, maſſacre the French; and the duke of Anjou, covered with the ſhame of his treachery and incapacity, returns to France, where he died the year following at thirty years of age. Bongars aſſures us, that he was taken off by poiſon; and it is mentioned in the memoirs of Nevers, that it was by a noſegay from one of his miſtreſſes, with whom he had retired to Chateau-Thierry.

1584.

The death of the duke of Anjou, having made the king of Navarre the next heir to Henry III, ſerves for a pretence to the duke de Guife to alarm the leaguers with the apprehenſions of a ſucceſſor to the crown, ſeparated from the communion of the church of Rome. The duke de Guife is at the head of the league. William, prince of Orange, is aſſaſſinated at Delft by Balthaſar Gerard, an emiſſary of the Spaniards. This prince of the houſe of Naſſau inherited the whole eſtate of the family of Orange and Chalon, and was prince of Orange by the teſtament of his uncle, René de Naſſau, ſon of Claude de Chalon: but the ſaid René, dying without iſſue, had no right to diſpoſe of the ſucceſſion of Chalon in favour of a ſtranger, contrary to the intail made by Mary de Baux, the ſtem of that family. William left three ſons, Philip William, Maurice, and Frederic Henry; the two latter ſucceeded him in their turn, in the abſence of Philip William, their elder brother, who, at the time of his father's deceaſe, was a priſoner in Spain, and did not recover his liberty till thirty years after, when he came to Bruſſels, where he died in 1618: he married the daughter of Henry I, prince of Condé. The United Provinces, thinking Maurice too young, for he was then only

only eighteen years of age, offered to put themselves under the dominion of king Henry III; but so advantageous a proposal, backed by the sage advice of Francis de Noailles, bishop of Acqs, was rejected by that weak prince. Maurice then stepped into the place of William, and shewed himself worthy of such a father: it was he that made the truce of 1609. Leaving no issue, he was succeeded by Frederic Henry, his brother, who obtained the title of Highness from Lewis XIII: this Frederic had a son, William, the same who attempted to surprize Amsterdam, and whose sudden death occasioned strong suspicions against the leading persons in the government; he was father to king William III.

Henry III. sends a deputation to the king of Navarre, to prevail with him to change his religion, that they might be able to act jointly in defence of the state. Catharine de Medicis, instead of endeavouring to stifle the league in the beginning, when the duke de Guise was but weak, is afraid of seeing her authority diminished by the king of Navarre; therefore she favours the house of Lorrain, with a view of placing the crown on the issue of her daughter, who was married to the duke of that name. But the duke de Guise, more attentive to his own interest than to that of the elder branch of his family, persuaded the old cardinal of Bourbon, uncle to the king of Navarre, that he (the cardinal) was presumptive heir to the crown; expecting, under the sanction of that name, to find an opportunity of doing something for himself.

The post of colonel-general of the French infantry erected into a crown-office, in favour of the duke d'Epernon; the letters patent were not registered till the year following.

The leaguers insert a prayer in the rituals of Vannes and Clermont, that it would please the Almighty to grant a son to Henry III; and another prayer for restoring the pragmatic sanction: they had not as yet felt the advantages of the concordate.

The Recollet friars established in France.

1585.

The king receives the order of the Garter.

A manifesto of the cardinal of Bourbon, dated the last of March, wherein he assumes the title of first prince of the blood, and exhorts

REMARKABLE EVENTS under HENRY III.

horts all Frenchmen to maintain the crown in the Catholic branch. This declaration, backed by most of the princes of Europe, with the pope at their head, was relative to a treaty concluded with the king of Spain, whose policy, cloked with the pretext of supporting the league, brought the kingdom to the brink of destruction. The dukes of Lorrain and Guise were stiled lieutenants-general of the confederacy. The king, instead of repelling this insult by force of arms, is content with publishing his apology.

The leaguers begin the war, and make themselves masters of several towns, among others, Toul and Verdun. A treaty of peace concluded at Nemours the 7th of July, by which Henry III. deprives the Protestants of their privileges, and grants new advantages to the league, subversive of his own authority.

Sixtus Quintus, the successor of Gregory XIII, without approving of this confederacy, which he looked upon as an insult to all sovereigns, yet foreseeing that it would lay Henry III. under a necessity of joining the king of Navarre, publishes a bull, in which he excommunicates the latter, together with the prince of Condé, and declares them unworthy of succeeding to the crown. The king of Navarre appeals from this bull to the parliament, and to a general council: some of the leaguers also are offended at the pope's encroachment, to which the parliament were far from giving their approbation. Henry IV. caused his appeal to be posted up at the gates of the Vatican: so bold a step made even Sixtus V. conceive a favourable opinion of this prince. The establishment of the council of *Sixteen*, a kind of association for Paris only, consisting of several persons, who were distributed in the sixteen wards of the town, and had engrossed the management of affairs, being entirely devoted to the duke de Guise, and sworn enemies of royalty.

The peace of Nemours suspended the hostilities of the leaguers, but induced the Protestants to have recourse to arms. The war is carried on by both parties with various success. The Guises acknowledge, that the male line of Charles duke of Lorrain, uncle of Lewis V, was extinct, in answer to those who said they pretended to be descended from that prince.

1586.

REMARKABLE EVENTS under HENRY III.

1586.

The war, known by the name of the three Henries, viz. Henry III, Henry king of Navarre, and Henry duke de Guife. The firſt was at the head of the Royaliſts, the ſecond headed the Huguenots, and the third was chief of the League. In the proſecution of the war, there happened no event of any conſequence; yet the kingdom was rent by this inteſtine diviſion.

The death of the baron des Adrets, a gentleman of Dauphiné, who, after making a great noiſe among the Huguenots, fell into oblivion, as ſoon as the duke de Nemours brought him back to the Catholic party. "The reaſon is, ſays le Laboureur, that "there is a wide difference between the manner of waging war "for one's ſovereign, and that of fighting on the ſide of rebellion: "on the latter occaſion, every extravagance is permitted, and a "commander ſhews himſelf in his natural colours; whereas, in "the ſervice of his prince, he appears as he ought, and is more "ſubject to military diſcipline." I ſhould add, that thoſe who have once tranſgreſſed the limits of their duty, imagine they can never go too far, nor make ſufficient efforts to compenſate, by their bravery, for the honour they have forfeited by their rebellion.

1587.

The execution of Mary queen of Scots, who was beheaded at Fotheringay-caſtle the 18th of February. During the whole courſe of this princeſs's reign, queen Elizabeth had fomented the rebellion of the Scotch againſt their lawful ſovereign, and introduced the new religion as the ſureſt way to break off the alliance between that nation and France, which had laſted eight hundred years: but ſhe did not ſtop there. The queen of Scots, having been married to Francis II. in 1558, took to her ſecond huſband, in 1565, Henry Stuart, earl of Darnley; and, after the death of this prince in 1567, ſhe eſpouſed that ſame year the earl of Bothwell, who was violently ſuſpected of the murder of her huſband. Some turbulent ſpirits, taking advantage of this conjuncture, had prejudiced a part of the nation againſt the queen, who was obliged, by the rebellion of her ſubjects in 1568, to fly to England, where, inſtead of protection, ſhe found a priſon,

REMARKABLE EVENTS under HENRY III.

a prison, to which she was confined the space of nineteen years, and was not released till led to the scaffold. Unfortunate princess; whose tragical exit her enemies would fain represent as unworthy of pity, by drawing every action of her life in the most odious colours!

Nicholas Poulain, deputy to the provost of the isle of France, discovers the confederacy of the *Sixteen* to the king, and the scheme they had formed to deprive him of his crown and liberty. But nothing could wake that prince out of his lethargy; lulled by Villequiers into a total oblivion of his glory, and of the welfare of his dominions, he neglected to make a right use of this intelligence; the duke d'Epernon, however, finding himself insulted, had the precaution to secure the Bastile and the arsenal, which the council of Sixteen wanted to get into their possession. The duke de Mayenne, afraid of his person, withdraws from Paris. The king of Navarre marches into Burgundy, to join the Germans, who were coming to reinforce his army. Anne, duke de Joyeuse, in order to prevent his junction with the Germans, resolves to give him battle. The battle of Coutras in Guienne, on the 20th of October, in which the king of Navarre obtains a complete victory, and the duke de Joyeuse loses his life: he was killed in cold blood, some say by la Mothe St. Heray, and others by two captains of foot, named Bordeaux and Descentiers. Such murders never happen but in religious wars: thus fell the duke de Guise before Orleans, the prince of Condé at Jarnac, the marshal de St. André at Dreux, and the constable de Montmorency at St. Denis. The king of Navarre does not make a right use of his victory; but returns to Bearne, to visit his mistress Corisande d'Andouins, countess de Guiche.

By the advantages which the duke de Guise obtained over the Germans at Vimory in Gatinois, and at Aulneau in the country of Chartres, that army was dispersed, and driven out of the kingdom. Strange decision of Sorbonne! *that it was equally lawful to take the government out of the hands of a prince who did not do his duty, as to deprive a suspected guardian of the administration of his pupil's estate.* (Daniel.)

The Feuillans, whose order had been founded the preceding year, are settled at Paris.

REMARKABLE EVENTS under HENRY III.

1588.

Henry I, prince of Condé, is poisoned at St. John de Angeli, at the age of thirty-five. His wife, Charlotte de la Trimouille, was tried by the magistrates of that place for the murder of her husband; but was declared innocent in the following reign, by an arret of parliament in 1596. The prince of Condé died the 5th of March, and the princess his wife, whom he left pregnant, was, on the 1st of September the same year, delivered of a prince, named Henry II, prince of Condé.

The county of Montbason erected into a dutchy and peerage in the month of May, 1588, in favour of Lewis de Rohan, count de Montbason. What is very remarkable, Lewis happening to die without issue, Henry IV. granted new letters patent to Hercules de Rohan, his brother, in 1594, to enjoy the said dutchy, *of the same date, and with the same rights and privileges as Lewis would have done, had he lived,* erecting that county again, so far as it was necessary, into a dutchy and peerage. The Rohan family is possessed of two peerages; that of *Montbason,* and that of *Rohan-Rohan,* otherwise *Soubise.* There had been a third, extinct by the death of the duke de Rohan in 1638: Margaret his daughter brought it into the family of Chabot, which took the name of Rohan by virtue of new letters of erection of this dutchy, registered in 1652.

The king, highly provoked at the council of Sixteen, drops some menaces, by which they are intimidated. They press the duke de Guise to return to Paris; but his majesty forbids him to set foot in this city: the duke comes, notwithstanding, well escorted, and waits on the king, who has neither the courage to put him to death, nor to secure his person. The day of the barricades, the 12th of May, when the king's troops are obliged to give way to the rebels. The duke de Guise appeases the insurrection. The queen presses him to withdraw from Paris; but he refuses to comply. Henry III. retires to Chartres, and leaves the duke de Guise sole master of the capital: this prince, after the king's departure, went to pay a visit to the first president, Achilles de Harlay, whom he found " walking in his garden, and so little " surprized at the duke's coming, that he did not so much as turn
" his

REMARKABLE EVENTS under HENRY III.

"his head about, or alter his pace; after he had got to the end of the avenue, he turned back, and saw the duke de Guise approaching towards him;" upon which this grave magistrate spoke these words aloud; *It is great pity the valet should drive his master out of his own house: however, I give my soul to God; my heart to my king; and my body is in the hands of wicked men, let them dispose of it as they will.* (Discourse on the life and death of the president de Harlay.) The duke de Guise seizes the Bastile and the arsenal, of which Buffi le Clerc, a proctor in parliament, and one of the Sixteen, is made governor. This duke was making large strides towards the regal dignity: but, as Montagne observes, "pretenders to the crown find every step, even to the footstool of the throne, of easy ascent; but the last is so high, they are never able to mount it."

Catharine de Medicis, having staid behind at Paris, continues to negotiate; and at length a peace is concluded by the edict of reunion, signed at Rouen: the king had been received in this city by Tanequi le Veneur, sieur de Carrouge, and by James, son of the count de Tillieres. M. de Thou, speaking of this Tanequi le Veneur, says, "he was of the first noblesse in that province, and a person of great lenity and moderation:" he took his name from the office of great huntsman, which his ancestors possessed in Normandy, at the time of William the Conqueror. This was a most scandalous treaty; it was even worse than that of Nemours: the chief design of it was to hinder the crown from devolving to a Protestant. It is thought that the king was determined to this peace from an apprehension of the Spanish *armada*, stiled the *Invincible*, then at sea, which equally alarmed the kingdoms of France and England; but it was dispersed, and almost intirely destroyed, by the English and by tempestuous weather. His majesty, perceiving, when it was too late, the precipice to which the queen his mother had hurried him, ceased to confide in that princess; but still dissembled his sentiments. Indeed all parties, whether Catholics or Protestants, had been ever the same to Catharine de Medicis, if she could but govern; and now, seeing her son without issue, she joined the duke de Guise, with a view of placing the crown on her grandson, the duke of Lorrain, in prejudice to the branch of Bourbon.

REMARKABLE EVENTS under HENRY III.

Bourbon. But as the duke de Guife was fcheming for himfelf, he made a proper ufe of this difpofition of the queen, without letting her fee into his defign: no body knew the real object of his ambition; he had a fecret to communicate to every one he treated with; the promifes he made to the pope, to the king of Spain, to the duke of Lorrain, and to the cardinal de Bourbon, were all different; and thofe princes, though promoting his private views, imagined they were purfuing their own interefts. The king affembles the ftates at Blois, and difcharges his minifters, meffieurs de Bellievre, de Cheverny, and de Villeroy. It is thought this ftep was in confequence of his having formed a defign of putting the Guifes to death: he apprehended his minifters would oppofe fuch a refolution, if he mentioned it to them; or, if he made a myftery of it, they might, by fome means or other, difcover his intention, and acquaint the queen mother. (*Mem. de Cheverny.*) Thofe minifters were replaced by Francis de Montholon, (who, as well as his father, was fit only to plead at the bar) by Martin Ruzé, Beaulieu, and Revol.

The duke of Savoy, taking advantage of thefe troubles, and holding a correfpondence, as it is faid, with the duke de Guife, feizes the marquifate of Saluzzo.

The infolent demands of the deputies at the ftates of Blois, and the intolerable audacioufnefs of the duke de Guife, at length obliged the king to get rid of this prince, who was become too powerful to be arraigned before a court of judicature. The fufpicion of that duke's ambitious defigns was well founded; and he feemed to be pretty much under the fame circumftances as thofe which Pepin converted to his advantage. Henry III. was not unlike the laft kings of the firft race; and the pretext of religion might have ftirred up fome pope or other of the fame difpofition as Zachary. "The only obftacle in the way, fays Laboureur, "was the right of fucceffion, more firmly eftablifhed in favour "of the collateral branches of the blood royal under the third race, "than under the two former: to which we may add the great "number of princes, the power of the king of Navarre, and the "valour of the prince of Condé his brother, of whom it may be "faid, that the war he maintained, ferved as a counterpoife to "the league; and the civil commotions of his time were a kind "of

REMARKABLE EVENTS under HENRY III.

"of cloud, under which he concealed the remains of the royal family." The duke de Guise is massacred on the 23d of December; and the cardinal de Guise, his brother, the day following. The season was excessive severe: and the king, says M. de Thou, was fretful, almost to a degree of madness, in frosty weather. The cardinal de Bourbon is arrested. The king's officers had like to have taken the duke de Mayenne at Lyons. Henry III. committed a very great mistake, in not marching directly to Paris, and in missing several of the chiefs of the league. Are we to believe what d'Aubigny says, that, when this execution was proposed in council, and they represented the danger to which his majesty exposed himself from the court of Rome, "the king took a letter out of his pocket, in "which Sixtus Quintus advised him to become absolute master "by any violence whatever." In the midst of these disturbances, Catharine de Medicis died at Blois, the 5th of January following, greatly encumbered with debt, and aged seventy-one years: she advised her son, in her last hours, to be reconciled to the king of Navarre. The death of this princess, who had made so much noise in her life-time, was almost unnoticed. Such was the end of Isabella of Bavaria; and such also that of the duchess of Angouleme, mother of Francis I; as if heaven were sometimes pleased to condemn ambitious persons to oblivion. Catharine de Medicis was, without doubt, a princess of great capacity; but having been corrupted by the Italian education of that time, she imagined, that, in public affairs, the ends were to be obtained by any means whatever. (*Mabli.*) Too regardless of prejudices, she found it a much shorter way to make use of violence for the removing of difficulties, which a person of her genius might have surmounted in a fair and lawful manner. Outrages committed by the Leaguers in Paris, upon hearing of the death of the duke de Guise.

The invention of bombs, by an inhabitant of Venlo; though perhaps they are of more ancient date, as appears from the manuscript accounts of the siege of Rhodes in 1522, where mention is made of their being used by the Turks.

The duke of Parma is obliged to raise the siege of Bergen-op-zoom, one of the strongest towns in the Netherlands: it stood an-

REMARKABLE EVENTS under HENRY III.

other siege in 1622, against Spinola, who was forced to desist from his attempt, with the loss of upwards of ten thousand men. This conquest was reserved for Lewis XV, who, having obtained a victory in person at Lawfeld, the 2d of July, 1747, over the allied army of the Austrians, English, and Dutch, commanded by the duke of Cumberland, caused the count de Lowendahl to lay siege to that place. Situated on a canal near the Scheld, and surrounded by morasses, there was no possibility of investing it: besides, it was covered by an army, from which the garrison received constant succours; and, since the siege under the duke of Parma, it had been fortified by the famous Coehorn, the greatest engineer the Dutch nation ever boasted of, who looked upon it as his master-piece: but French valour proved superior to the strength of the situation; the trenches were opened the 14th of July, and the town was carried by assault the 17th of September.

1589.

A decree of the Sorbonne, releasing the subjects from their oath of allegiance to the king.

Bussy le Clerc sends the parliament to the Bastile. The president Brisson exercises the office of first president; Molé, a counsellor, that of attorney-general; and the advocates, John le Maitre and Lewis d'Orleans, act as advocates-general. The duke de Mayenne, with reluctance, saw himself called upon to revenge the death of his brother, whom he did not love, and to whom he had formerly sent a challenge: besides, he was sensible, that, sooner or later, the rebellious party would be overpowered; yet he came to Paris, where he was declared *lieutenant-general of the kingdom of France, by the council of the Union.* This council of Union, originally composed of the *Sixteen*, was increased to the number of forty, to whom the duke de Mayenne added fourteen more. After the death of Henry III, the duke de Mayenne dissolved that assembly.

The duke d'Aumale is made governor of Paris. The king, by an edict published at Blois in the month of February, transfers the parliament of Paris to Tours; and another part of that body was removed to Chalons upon the Marne. In regard to this subject, we find the following passage in a manuscript of

Blan-

REMARKABLE EVENTS under HENRY III.

Blanchard: *Aug. de Thou,* in conjunction with *Nic. Poitier,* presided in the chamber at *Chalons,* when the parliament was transferred to *Tours* by the edict of the month of February, 1589. Henry III, being reconciled to the king of Navarre, has an interview with this prince at *Pont de la Mothe,* within four leagues of Tours, where great demonstrations of friendship pass between them. The king of Navarre, after accompanying Henry III. to Tours, where he lay one night, retires to his quarter, but returns very soon to the assistance of that monarch, whom the duke de Mayenne had surprized at Tours. So important a service banished all diffidence between the two princes, so that they advance with their army towards Paris, having under them the marshal de Biron and the duke d'Epernon: after some advantages obtained by their detached parties, they take the town of Pontoise, which was defended by d'Alincourt the governor. Sancy arrives with a reinforcement of ten thousand Swiss; and the royal army, consisting of more than thirty thousand men, lays siege to Paris, where the duke de Mayenne commanded. In return for so singular a piece of service to the government, Sancy was made colonel of the Swiss, whereas before he had been only a master of requests. Henry IV, to whom this reinforcement was of such consequence, raised him afterwards to the post of superintendant of the finances. But Gabrielle d'Etrées having quarrelled with this officer for speaking too freely about her children, got him turned out of the superintendancy; and it was given to the marquis de Rosny. The pope's monitorial letters against the king.

Henry III. is assassinated on the 1st of August, by James Clement, a Dominican friar: upon his death-bed, he declares the king of Navarre his successor. It is believed that madam de Montpensier, the duke de Guise's sister, had a great share in this murder. The queen Louisa also charged the duke de Mayenne with it.

The office of cabinet-secretary was not known till under this reign; it was enjoyed by M. de Renoise, who, before that time, had been clerk of the chamber. (*Fauvelet du Toc.*)

The League is perhaps the most extraordinary event in history; and Henry III. may be reckoned the weakest prince, in not foreseeing that he should render himself dependent on that party, by becoming their chief. The Protestants had made war against him as the enemy of their sect; and the Leaguers murdered him on account of his uniting with the king of Navarre, the chief of the Huguenots. Suspected both by Catholics and Protestants, from his levity, and grown contemptible to all parties by leading a life equally superstitious and criminal, he appeared worthy of empire till he possessed it; *a character incomprehensible*, says M. de Thou; *in some things superior to his dignity; in others, weaker than an infant.* Not one of the preceding reigns has furnished a greater number of volumes, anecdotes, prints, and fugitive pieces, &c. In such a multitude there must be many useless papers; but, as Henry III. lived in the midst of his people, not a single action of his life escaped their notice; and as Paris was the theatre of the principal transactions of the League, the burghers, who were the chief actors in that farce, carefully preserved the memory of every little fact that passed under their eye; the most minute transaction appeared important to them, because they were concerned in it; and from their representation we are curious, in regard to facts, most of which did not perhaps at that time make any great noise in the world. We may fix, with father Daniel, the intire decline of the French navy, to the time of the civil wars of the Huguenots.

With king Henry III. ended the line of Valois, which began to reign in 1328; and there remained no male issue except Charles, duke d'Angouleme, a natural son of Charles IX. We may take notice of a very extraordinary fact, viz. that Frances de Nargonne, that duke's wife, consequently daughter-in-law of Charles IX, did not depart this life till the year 1713, which is near a hundred and forty years after the death of her father-in-law. Henry III. was said to have been assassinated at St. Cloud in the hotel de Gondi, and in the same room where the massacre of St. Bartholomew's had been resolved upon; but this is known to be a fabulous account.

The End of the FIRST VOLUME.

www.ingramcontent.com/pod-product-compliance
Lightning Source LLC
Chambersburg PA
CBHW022102300426
44117CB00007B/550